The Making of
A MIDSUMMER NIGHT'S DREAM

The photo on the front cover shows David Waller as Bottom (aloft), Sara Kestelman as Titania and John York and Hugh Keays Byrne as Fairies (*Photo: Joe Cocks*). The back cover shows Terrence Hardiman as Starveling playing Moonshine and Barry Stanton as Snug playing Lion (*Photo: Donald Cooper*).

David Selbourne

The Making of
A MIDSUMMER NIGHT'S DREAM

An eye-witness account of Peter Brook's production
from first rehearsal to first night.

With an introductory essay by
Simon Trussler

Methuen · London

List of Illustrations

vi

Illustrations 1-6, 12, 18, 19 and 21-24 are reproduced by courtesy of Donald Cooper; 7-10, 13-17 and 20 by courtesy of Joe Cocks; and 11 by courtesy of the Governors of the Royal Shakespeare Theatre, Stratford-upon-Avon, on behalf of David Farrell.

Bottom: Masters, I am to discourse wonders: but ask me not what . . .

(Wm. Shakespeare, *A Midsummer Night's Dream*, IV.i.26)

Introduction

'Shakespeare and the Theatre of Peter Brook'
by Simon Trussler

'Shakespeare is a model of a theatre which contains Brecht and
Beckett, but goes beyond both. Our need in the post-Brecht
theatre is to find a way forwards, back to Shakespeare.'

Peter Brook, *The Empty Space*

Before directing *A Midsummer Night's Dream* for the Royal Shakespeare Company in the summer of 1970, Peter Brook was already making plans for his Centre International de Créations Théâtrales, which began its work during the following year in Paris and Shiraz. Since then, most of his time has been spent among the Centre's closely-knit 'community' of players, and when Brook did briefly return to Stratford in 1978, to direct Alan Howard and Glenda Jackson in *Antony and Cleopatra*, it seemed to some that his personal Shakespearian moment had passed. As moments go, it had been both protracted and elliptic: in a professional stage career spanning some thirty-five years, Brook has directed fewer than a dozen Shakespeare plays, of which a significant proportion might have been accounted minor works – had not Brook's own productions helped to bring them back to life for the contemporary theatre.

In retrospect, it is ironic that, though Brook first surfaced during the theatrically conservative years following the Second World War, he made little direct contribution to the theatrical revolution which erupted in 1956. Rather, he prepared the way for a younger generation, which drew its inspiration from the many 'events' of 1968 – only to depart for Paris just as his prophetic voice was receiving due honour in his own country. And so Brook joined Artaud and Grotowski in that triumviral pantheon which shaped, *in absentia*, the style and thinking of much of the experimental theatre of the early 'seventies – having himself sounded the resonances of Artaud in the *Theatre of Cruelty* season of 1964, and introduced Grotowski to British theatre during rehearsals for *US* in 1966. Four years later, with *A Midsummer Night's Dream*, Brook seemed to be making a less eclectic, more personal bequest to the nation from which he was about to go into exile. His written testament had been published, appropriately, in 1968, and was entitled, no less appropriately, *The Empty Space*.

*

Peter Brook's parents were Russian emigrés, who married just before the First World War. Fleeing as the Germans advanced into Belgium, they found themselves penniless in London in 1914: but both were able to offer a solid scientific training, and determinedly set out to build new lives – and then to start a family, of which the second son, Peter, was born on 21 March 1925. The young Peter Brook had early experience of surviving within the constraints of institutionalized English life – first at public school, then as a precocious undergraduate at Magdalen College, Oxford, from which he narrowly escaped being sent down for showing more interest in making films than in studying medieval French. His film treatment of *A Sentimental Journey*, seen fleetingly in London at the tiny Torch Theatre in 1943, had no dialogue, a voice-over commentary spoken as if by Sterne himself, and character actors recruited from the back streets and corner pubs of wartime Oxford.

Through directing an apparently straightforward version of Shaw's *Pygmalion* for a forces tour, Brook was invited by Barry Jackson to mount *Man and Superman* at the Birmingham Repertory Theatre in the summer of 1945 – and then to cut his teeth on Shakespeare with an evidently refreshing but little-noticed *King John*. J.C. Trewin (later to become both historian to Birmingham Rep and Brook's own biographer) was one of the few national critics present. This 'chronicle of pull-devil-push-baker contention, sharp dagger-stabbing verse', as Trewin described it, usually opened 'with a tableau in uneasy wax'. But

> Brook began it with what looked like a Court bacchanal, all a gimble and a gyre. Later, with the swiftest assurance . . . he crossed the Channel and back and brought the King to death at Swinstead. The rhetoric had its ring, the action its surge, and though intermittently baffled by the peripatetic trinity of Pembroke, Salisbury, and Bigot, he never let the piece drift into a monotony of booming barons. At the centre was Paul Scofield's Bastard, a creation of extraordinary personal magnetism.

The association which began in Birmingham between the unknown director Peter Brook and the unknown actor Paul Scofield was, of course, to survive many years of almost telepathic association. And it was quickly to be consolidated, when Barry Jackson took both Brook and Scofield with him to Stratford in the spring of 1946, for the first season of a valiant three-year attempt to revive the ailing artistic fortunes of the Memorial Theatre – then as newly nasty in its intractable auditorium as it was wearisomely traditional in its productions.

Jackson asked 'the youngest earthquake I've ever known' to direct *Love's Labour's Lost*, with Scofield as Armado. This was one of those seminal productions which acquire a sort of retrospective veneer, and in 1976 Kenneth Tynan recalled its 'incredible, leaping, visual imagination' and 'very precise sense of startling intonation'. Reviewing the season at the time, Philip Hope-Wallace welcomed the 'revivifying' effect of Brook's 'original and highly imaginative handling of that early but delightful play', which in his hands

> became not so much a masque as a sort of inspired Watteauesque *fête champêtre*, all atmospherics and attitudes: something to linger long in the mind's eye. This production, which used all the resources of the theatre, set the play for our eyes in the kind of climate which it must have had for its first audience . . . a deft fantastication of a highly artificial species. Conceived in this way it could make do

with acting that was highly un-Shakespearian in being apparently unconscious of its audience; the characters seemed to be all playing to amuse each other. . . . The evening was full of delightfully witty strokes of comedy or 'applied' fooling . . . and whimsicality suited to modern notions.

Such a welcome was general – and the label Watteauesque scarcely less so. Now, it offers early evidence of the visual strength and unity of Brook's work, as of his ability to mould an ensemble from a group of assorted players even during this, one of the most *ad hoc* periods of English acting. How far the critical welcome for his *Love's Labour's Lost* was one of sheer gratitude that a play traditionally considered verbose and unstageworthy could be made to bristle with life – and at its close speak momentously of death – is now impossible to judge. What is certain is that, ever since, the comedy has been regularly revived without apparent trepidation, and with more or less success. The 'enfant terrible' of British theatre, as Brook was predictably coming to be called, had achieved a lasting breakthrough on Shakespeare's behalf.

A reaction was inevitable, and set in with the notices for *Romeo and Juliet* the following Stratford season. But critical opinion was not undivided. Brook had somewhat lowered his guard by announcing that '*Romeo and Juliet* is not a play for ageing *prima donnas*'. He wanted *his* Juliet to look fourteen (she was actually nineteen, and fresh from RADA), and he was judged accordingly. The play had, claimed Philip Hope-Wallace, 'meant so much to him as a romance that he encouraged the lovers to run at their parts with the abandon of young co-eds'. Conversely, the play itself 'meant so little to him as a moral legend of two warring houses that he cut the final scene of reconciliation and stopped the play where Gounod stopped his opera'. Harold Hobson praised the verse-speaking, and found Paul Scofield 'richly rewarding' as a 'Mercutio who has really seen the fairies and wishes, perhaps, that he had not': but 'young' was the kindest epithet he could find for Laurence Payne's Romeo and Daphne Slater's Juliet – who, though she might be only fourteen, 'is not to be found in a child's garden of verses'.

Defiantly, Kenneth Tynan – now himself an undergraduate at Magdalen – railed against that 'elderly group of critics which insists that Mr. Brook is not nearly old enough to appreciate *Romeo*: to them I say (and I hope rudely) that they are not nearly young enough. *Romeo* is a youthful play about miserable young people who confuse catastrophe with tragedy.' Although he too had some doubts about the acting, he was fully persuaded by the atmosphere Brook had evoked, which was of a Verona 'intemperately dry, tawny, and madding'.

Peter Brook plays out this young tragedy under a throbbing vault of misty indigo: the streets crackle underfoot with aridity: it is very warm indeed. Canopies, loosely pendant from the flies, are a necessary shield against this daze of heat. Mr. Brook's colours are dusty whites, sun-bleached reds, and dull greys: and the brown, somnolent crowds in his market-place are all bemused and fly-blown. The sets, designed by Rolf Gérard, and poised, tenuously erect, on slim flimsy pillars, are thrown open to the bare sky: silhouettes balancing in the naked sun. Everyone sweats.

According to this fledgling (but already wondrously fluent) critic, Brook had now 'acquired a recognizable style', and to this the visual instinct was clearly no less essential than the 'novelty of inflexion' which Tynan detected in the 'pure drops of unexpected naturalism which Mr. Brook teaches his actors to wring out of Shakespeare's lines'.

Peter Ustinov also sprang, tongue-in-cheek, to Brook's defence, in the pages of *New Theatre*. To please the critics who claimed that this *Romeo* was 'not Shakespeare', Brook should, he cautioned, have relied for his music on the usual 'sainted battery of acidulated little trumpets'; for sets he should have employed 'innumerable tastefully cramping drop-cloths' and 'turrets galore'; in his characterization he should have utilized the 'beards and wimples' of 'experienced ladies and gentlemen'; and, instead of daring to treat the play as a 'complete adventure', he should have paid respectful homage to a 'sequence of literary gems'. To his greatest discredit was 'the lamentable fact that the play had no feeling at all of being a revival'. Spoiled as we now are at Stratford by a Royal Shakespeare Company which, if anything, goes to the opposite extreme of treating even the most familiar of Shakespeare's plays as if they regularly need to be rescued from total obscurity, Ustinov's is a pertinent reminder of 'respectable' post-war Shakespeare at its most memorialized. In the same magazine, Brook himself wrote of getting back in his production to 'the violence, the passion, and the excitement of the stinking crowds, the feuds, the intrigues'. He wanted, he said, 'to recapture the poetry and the beauty that arise from the Veronese sewer'.

Brook was not invited to direct at Stratford in 1948, and Barry Jackson's own contract was not renewed at the end of that season. Neither, a year later, was Brook's, after a frustrating experiment in dragging Covent Garden opera into at least a late-nineteenth-century acceptance of naturalism. Brook's verdict on the experience was straightforward: 'After two years' slogging I came to the conclusion that opera as an artistic form was dead'. He had, however, also been able to direct plays during this period, and, from all his early work on more modern writers, Tynan later singled out 'extraordinarily realistic productions' of Sartre's *Vicious Circle* (*Huis Clos*) and of Howard Richardson's *Dark of the Moon* – the latter at the Lyric Theatre, Hammersmith, with which Brook was developing something of a special relationship. The claustrophic four-walled microcosm of hell in Sartre's play, and the darkly-shadowed ritual quality he discovered in Richardson's study of superstition in rural America, were motifs which were to recur in Brook's later work.

Between 1950 and 1955 Peter Brook allowed his now eminently marketable talents to be applied to an assortment of West End whimsy, mostly associated with the then equally marketable talents of Jean Anouilh or Christopher Fry

(and sometimes, Fry being a regular translator for Anouilh, of both at once –
with the addition of Scofield, playing identical twins, to form an intriguing
juxtaposition of wits for *Ring Round the Moon*). Not that Brook's temperament was ill-adapted to this theatre of 'colour and movement, of fine fabrics,
of shadows, of eccentric, cascading words, of leaps of thought and of cunning
machines', as he later called it: and it is easy now to underestimate the
attraction of such gossamer attributes in that period of frantic (and often
frantically resisted) social adjustments, continuing material shortages, and
pervasive drabness. John Whiting's *A Penny for a Song*, which Brook
directed at the Haymarket in the Festival year of 1951, thus fought out its
mock-Napoleonic invasion against a sunlit Emmet landscape, and affirmed
both the eccentricity and the absolute propriety of being English come what
may. Whether or not Brook relished the romanticism behind these
sophisticated (or would-be sophisticated) comedies, he certainly seems to
have enjoyed the technical challenge of winning over Shaftesbury Avenue
audiences to their freewheeling visual and verbal invention.

Appropriately enough, Brook's two Shakespearian productions during this
period were both of plays which stretch our modern capacity for sexual
credulity, and seem discomfiting in their arrival at the reconciliations which
are compulsory to comedy and romance. His *Measure for Measure* was staged
during the Stratford season of 1950, and its Angelo, John Gielgud, rejoined
Brook in the role of Leontes for a commercial production of *The Winter's Tale*
at the Phoenix Theatre in the year following. (Tynan later saw these
productions as giving Gielgud's career 'a second lease of life' – his Angelo 'a
much more restrained, realistic, unromantic performance than he had ever
given before'.)

Designing *Measure for Measure* himself, Brook travelled from the sewers of
Verona to those of Vienna, so recently graven upon filmgoers' consciousness
in *The Third Man*. Here, it is true, the sewers came in the guise of
subterranean prison cells, through which George Rose's Pompey conducted a
grisly roll-call of creatures from the criminal underworld. In their wake came
'Wild Half-Can who stabb'd pots', described by Kenneth Tynan as 'a very
aged man, naked except for a rag coat, twitching his head from side to side,
and walking poker-stiff, bolt upright on his bare heels, with his toes turned
up' – an ancestor, clearly, of the maniacs of *The Marat-Sade*.

> Brook's triumph, however, is his fifth act: a scene of such coincidences and lengthy
> impossibilities, such forced reconciliations and incredible cruelties, that most
> producers flog it through at breakneck speed towards the welcome curtain. Fully
> aware of the tension his flawless timing has created, Brook here has the effrontery
> to sit down and let it ride: into this dreadful act he inserts half a dozen long pauses,
> working up a new miracle of tension which Shakespeare knew nothing about. The
> thirty-five seconds of dead silence which elapse before Isabella decides to make her
> plea for Angelo's life were a long, prickly moment of doubt which had every heart
> in the theatre thudding.

Whether knowledgeable critics' disbelief was so entirely in suspension that they indeed forgot what Isabella's decision was destined to be is beside the point: but Brook's tendency to assume that every night, even of a Shakespeare play, is a first night, and every audience always in thrall to *know what happens*, has on occasion become self-defeating – as when the press quickly stripped the gilt of surprise from the golden phallus at the end of Brook's *Oedipus*, and shock dwindled into schlock.

As if Brook were aware of the fine line which separates individual style from mere idiosyncrasy, his work has often alternated between the visually extravagant and the deceptively undecorated. According to T.C. Worsley, his *Winter's Tale* of 1951 not only confirmed Gielgud's liberation from his own romantic legend, but was 'in its first and last acts the quietest and most straightforward Shakespearian production we have seen for years'. There was 'no fussing, no dragged-in business, the minimum of movement. The voices are left to reign supreme'. And J.C. Trewin also looked back on 'a production of uncompromising austerity', in which Brook, 'still cheerfully out of character . . . let himself go only in the moan and surge of the wind across the desolate coast of Bohemia, and in the blizzard when Time turned his glass to direct us across sixteen years'.

Late in 1951, Brook was married to the twenty-one-year-old actress Natasha Parry, and has remained so. But his young bride was taken ill in the New Year, and Brook was consequently inactive in the theatre until he brought Gielgud and Scofield together at the Lyric, Hammersmith, for Thomas Otway's rarely-revived Restoration tragedy, *Venice Preserved*. Gielgud was Jaffeir, cast to now-discarded type as the romantic revolutionary who joins with the cynical and calculating Pierre, played by Scofield, to overthrow the government of Venice. Personal and political motives are inextricably confused, and Jaffeir eventually kills Pierre at his own pleading, before turning the sword upon himself. Highly regarded in its day, in Brook's production the play evidently realized its own erratic intensity beneath the brooding, painted arches of Leslie Hurry's set.

After two further years of commercial work in the West End and on Broadway – which included a light, leaden comedy about tax evasion called *Both Ends Meet*, and a musical about rivalry amongst brothel-keepers by Truman Capote – came Brook's year of triumph and tribulation with Shakespeare: success against all expectation with *Titus Andronicus*, and failure for the seemingly sure-fire combination of Brook and Scofield in *Hamlet*.

The Memorial Theatre at Stratford had done little more than strike intermittent sparks since Barry Jackson's brief management. Scarcely had the virtues of the permanent set been rediscovered than it began to be decked out with excrescences, and textual sanctity seemed now to go hand in buskin with a fear of boring audiences, who were duly distracted with interminable tricks of physical punctuation – a tendency that hardened into orthodoxy where Shakespeare's more intractably Elizabethan jokes were concerned. There was some surprise when *Titus Andronicus* was announced for the 1955 season, the first production of this bloodiest and muddiest of the tragedies in the history of the Memorial Theatre: but Brook, again at his best in tackling 'impossible' plays, struck a delicate balance between the horrific and the merely melodramatic in the play, cutting passages which have become irredeemably bathetic, and muting some of the gorier moments – notably, the armless and tongueless Lavinia holding a bowl between her stumps to catch the blood which will make the gravy for human pie, destined to be consumed by the mother of its contents. 'Why, there they are both – baked in that pie', Olivier's Titus ought to have said, had not Brook tactfully excised the last five words.

In addition to directing, Brook both designed the set of three ribbed pillars and wrote the music – 'quarter-ear' music, he called it, intended to be persistent but not insistent, and to emphasize 'texture, rhythm, and timbre' rather than melody and counterpoint. As J.C. Trewin described the opening:

> He began the night in a brooding Rome . . . where the music . . . wailed and thudded; processions coiled; and priests, green-habited, moved in hieratic solemnity. When Titus appeared . . . he was a veteran white-haired warrior, a man desperately tired. All the lines of the body drooped; his eyes, among the seamed crows-feet, were weary. Standing in mid-stage like some limestone crag, he greeted Rome because it was a thing of custom, but there was no spring in his voice, no light.

Brook got under the guard of the audience with such naturalistic characterization, allowing the note here struck of weary formality to transform itself into ritualistic acceptance of the inevitability of slaughter piled on slaughter. For Olivier's 'battered veteran' of a Titus, such desperate resignation became a human necessity: as Tynan put it, 'A hundred campaigns have tanned his heart to leather, and from the cracking of that heart there issues a terrible music, not untinged by madness'.

Much later, reassessing the first ten years of Brook's career, Tynan was to comment:

> Up to that time there was no doubt in anyone's mind that Peter Brook was the leading Shakespeare director of the post-war era. And he continued to go from strength to strength. There was a feeling at the back of one's mind that he was a reclaimer of the secondary plays rather than an interpreter of the major plays, that he was a great man for taking a neglected text and imposing on it his own image. He had done this with plays which were regarded as less than the top rank of Shakespeare – *Love's Labour's Lost*, *Measure for Measure*, and later *Titus Andronicus*. But when he took on *Hamlet*, with Paul Scofield, it was a great disappointment: he had nothing to bring to a masterpiece, as if the masterpiece were a self-sustaining monument, and Peter, instead of reconstructing it to fit his own vision, was rather dwarfed by it. He just chipped away at the edges.

This was to be Scofield's second Hamlet. He had previously alternated the role with Robert Helpmann at Stratford in 1948, and now few of the critics of Brook's West End production at the Phoenix were able to resist an unkind comparison between the tormented soul of the earlier production and the sulking yet cold-blooded adolescent of the new. Besides, Richard Burton's Hamlet at the Old Vic was barely two-years fresh in the memory, and Alec Guinness's eccentric version had come only a year earlier. So Brook conscientiously tried to clear away the undergrowth of received ideas, and evidently set a cracking pace – achieving, Tynan noted at the time, 'changes of scene which are both swift and stunning'.

> Yet, though movement is there, destination is lacking. In the crowd scenes – the play and the duel – he brings off grand slams, but elsewhere his direction is oddly tentative, with niggling cuts and ear-distressing transpositions, and when he seeks to play a trump – by giving the court musicians toy drums and trumpets – one is merely conscious that he has revoked.

Another contemporary critic, Caryl Brahms, attributed the speed of the production to the director's greater interest in 'the fell clutch of circumstances that impels people to behave according to its dictation' than in the hearts and feelings of the people themselves. With unwitting prescience, she described Brook as 'an inspired puppet-master' – for he was, indeed, on the verge of making the acquaintance of that puppet-master extraordinary of twentieth-century theatre, Gordon Craig, and Brook's admiration for the eighty-year-old exile was evidently reciprocated. Brook was more reconciled than Craig had ever been to the use of living actors rather than super-marionettes: whatever his own feelings were about the intrusive playwright – whose presence Craig felt so to disrupt the pure vision of the director – Brook certainly seemed to thrive best himself where his own creative contribution could be most substantial. Shakespeare needed no such collaborator in *Hamlet*.

Apparently ignoring the political turmoil and theatrical excitements of 1956, Brook spent the year directing a sort of anthology of just such plays as were about to be displaced from the British stage – an adaptation of Graham Greene's novel, *The Power and the Glory*; T.S. Eliot's tragedy of drawing-room furies, *The Family Reunion*; and a mildly scandalous American import, Arthur Miller's *A View from the Bridge*. He also travelled to Paris to stage Tennessee Williams's *Cat on a Hot Tin Roof*. In the following year he reproduced *Titus Andronicus* for a London run at the Stoll, after a European tour which included a triumphant visit to the Théâtre des Nations in Paris. The production also went to Warsaw, where it was seen by a university professor called Jan Kott, with whom Brook became serendipitously acquainted in a night club: but that friendship was to take a few years yet to bear theatrical fruit.

Later in 1957 Brook returned to Stratford, to make the first of his three attempts upon the 'unplayable' *Tempest* – Shakespeare's 'complete final statement', as he was to call it in *The Empty Space* ('usually', he observed, 'it only serves to put generations of schoolchildren off theatre for life'). Here, John Gielgud's Prospero turned out to be beautifully spoken but somehow peripheral. For the action had been taken out of Prospero's hands, and put into those of the clowns – and of Alec Clunes's hermaphroditic Caliban, who in taking possession of so much of the poetry was also repossessing his isle (itself full of Brook's inventive noises, a music more pebbledash than concrete). The sets – also Brook's – evoked an austere seashore, strewn with rocks and creepers, the characters merging with and emerging from their unlocalized surroundings.

If the masque – according to Trewin 'a reiterated, fertility-rite chanting of key phrases about barns, garners, vines, and plants' – was 'a sign of the Brook to come' so too was the setting. Its quality was not so much 'archetypal' – a characteristic of the now-commonplace permanent set even before John Bury's reign as the RSC's head of design – but, rather, quintessential, expressing not a 'representative' version of reality but the filtration of a dominant feeling. There was, too, an increasing sense of dissatisfaction with merely orchestrating a sweep of action, however vividly, and the complementary need to make a total statement – though the statement might be Brook's (or, in the case of the coming *King Lear*, Jan Kott's) as much as Shakespeare's. And, perhaps most crucially, Brook was beginning to absorb the new mood of the British theatre at large – not uncritically, but at least in a way which made connections with his own concerns.

Between 1958 and 1960, he staged his first musical, *Irma La Douce*, and directed the Lunts in Dürrenmatt's absurdist thriller, *The Visit*; but he was working in Paris and New York as well as in London, and also writing little discontented articles for *Encore* magazine about the state of the British theatre (of which *Encore* itself was generally rather proud). In one such piece in 1960, he asked:

> is there nothing in the revolution that took place in painting fifty years ago that applies to our own crisis today? Do we know where we stand in relation to the real and the unreal, the face of life and its hidden streams, the abstract and the concrete, the story and the ritual? What are 'facts' today? Are they *concrete*, like prices and hours of work – or *abstract* like violence and loneliness? And are we sure that in relation to twentieth-century living, the great abstractions – speed, strain, space, frenzy, energy, brutality – aren't more concrete, more immediately likely to affect our lives than the so-called concrete issues? Mustn't we relate this to the actor and the ritual of acting to find the pattern of the theatre we need?

Most of Brook's theoretical writings, it may as well be admitted, have never struck me as either original or very profound: he works through his work, not through the printed word. Yet before 1956 he had, after all, been the only British director capable of bridging the gap between the institutionalized theatre on Shaftesbury Avenue or in Stratford and the embryonic 'fringe' of little and club venues. Now, experimental theatre was flourishing, and he wasn't sure he liked the direction it was taking. Yet the work of a new generation of British dramatists could be more readily defined in terms of such abstractions as Brook lists than in 'concrete' terms of 'prices and hours of work' – issues which, if anything, were of more concern to the agitprop writers of the early 'seventies than to the likes of Osborne, Pinter, or Wesker. No: what mattered was the fact that there was now a theatrical climate in which such debate about the purpose of theatre could be engaged – and that there was some serious theatre for Brook to react *against*. He began, in that process, to define the pattern of his own future theatre.

Soon after Peter Hall formed the Royal Shakespeare Company in 1960 – dememorializing Stratford, as it were – and found for it a London home at the Aldwych Theatre, he invited Brook, together with the ageing Michel Saint-Denis, to join him in the artistic direction. Brook was then preoccupied with completing the film version of William Golding's novel *The Lord of the Flies*, a parable purporting to show human nature stripped of the trappings of civilization. The film's combination of Brook's apparent misanthropy with his sense of man's need for shaping even his worst instincts into patterns of ritual formed an apt prelude for the next phase of his theatre work. This began with Brook's first production for the new régime at Stratford – a *King Lear* played according to Jan Kott's rules as a Beckettian *Endgame* in which death rescued Scofield's Lear only from confrontation with an existential void.

In his biography of Brook, J.C. Trewin reminds us that Lilian Baylis at the Old Vic always insisted that the blinding of Gloucester in *Lear* should be played as the first scene after the interval, 'so that those playgoers who wished could remain in the coffee-bar until it was over: many did'. There was no such escape in Brook's production: not only did Cornwall commit the act with a pair of golden spurs in the same strong light as bathed the rest of the action, but the scene was played *before* the interval, and the house lights cruelly came up as Gloucester blunderingly tried to make his escape – here, roughly pushed aside by servants clearing the stage, instead of being assisted away by those who take pity on him, as in Shakespeare's text.

The world of the play was here 'in a constant state of decomposition', as Brook's collaborator, Charles Marowitz, put it – even the geometrical set, of metal thunder-sheets, was ginger with corrosion. But this 'abstracted' mood sat oddly at times with an element of domestic psychologizing, which had us seeing Regan and Goneril's view of Lear as a geriatric old nuisance, and in quest of motivations for Edgar's metamorphosis from vegetable to avenger. As Marowitz's published rehearsal log revealed, lengthy cerebral attention was indeed given to these matters – more so, apparently, than to Scofield's verse-speaking, which, in Marowitz's words, forced the verse to 'adjust to his patterns of delivery', and 'rattled together more than it . . . pieced out'. The production *was* revelatory in its applied rawness, but it was not ultimately satisfying – indeed, in the sense of achieving a catharsis, it was not intended to be. But Shakespeare had, simply, put more into the play than Brook wanted to bring out of it, and Brook's version was the lesser of the two. Instead of chipping away round the edges of a monument, as with *Hamlet*, he'd gouged out great chunks of the masonry. The rubble fell on a stricken landscape.

It was not as if Brook failed to recognize the achievement of his author: in an article contributed to *Crucial Years*, an RSC pamphlet published in 1963, he wrote of Shakespeare as having discovered, three centuries before Picasso, a 'realistic image of life' that had nothing to do with the conventions of consecutive time or of photographic realism, but with capturing a 'totality of information, visible and invisible, that corresponds to what we *instinctively* know as reality.' In the theatre, the problem was

> to bring the actor, slowly, step by step, towards an understanding of this remarkable invention, this curious structure of free verse and prose which a few hundred years ago was already the cubism of the theatre. We must wean the actor away from a false belief: that there is a heightened playing for the classics, a more real playing for the works of today. We must get him to see that the challenge of the verse play is that he must bring to it an even deeper search for truth, for truth of emotion, truth of ideas, and truth of character – all quite separate and yet all interwoven – and then as an artist find, with objectivity, the form that gives these meanings life.

The temptation, as ever, is to quibble with the substance here – to argue that Brook himself was, in full awareness, setting limits to the permissible 'truth' of *Lear*, or to suggest that English actors desperately *needed* the 'works of today' which, far more than drama schools or directors, had weaned them from the grosser artificialities of bourgeois drama, and left them responsive to just the kind of demand Brook was now making. More important to stress, however, is the spiritual need here being expressed for quite other 'works of today', which could find their way towards his own version of 'truth'. In an *Encore* article of 1961, Brook had, indeed, confessed that 'truth is a pretty relative, pretty meaningless thing', and called for a theatre of the future able to acknowledge that the implements of the past were outworn – rejecting 'a return to pageantry and verse', or even 'a new use of words'.

> I believe in the word in classical drama, because the word was their tool. I don't believe in the word much today because it has outlived its purpose. Words don't communicate, they don't express much, and most of the time they fail abysmally to define. There have been great theatres in the history of the world with a concrete language of their own that is not the language of the streets nor the language of books.

Beyond the modish McLuhanism of this passage lies, again, Brook's personal search for a *new* kind of 'language'. And, peppering his article, were quotations from someone who appeared to offer it – the French poet, mystic, and theoretician of theatre, Antonin Artaud. Brook even gave Artaud the last word in the article, though he reserved for himself the last but one:

> I want to see a flood of people and events that echo my inner battlefield. I want to see behind this desperate and ravishing confusion an order, a structure which will relate to my deepest and truest longing for structure and law. I want through this to find the new forms, and through the new forms the new architecture, and through the new architecture the new patterns and the new rituals of the age that is swirling around us.

One may or may not share Brook's vision, but here at last it is expressed as a personal quest for a personal truth. In its pursuit Brook was finally to cross the disputed frontier that separates interpretive from creative art.

In this restless spirit Brook must have found his productions of 1963 somewhat transitional experiences. Dürrenmatt's *The Physicists* at the Aldwych was a thoroughly professional job, its ever-lurking threat of violence meshing with a claustrophobic single-room setting reminiscent of *Vicious Circle* to produce a solid intellectual whodunit, with overtones of a Pirandellian question – who-was-it-anyway? In his second *Tempest*, directed in Stratford with Clifford Williams, a sense of dissatisfaction was clearer, and only Farrah's illuminated eggshell of a setting marked this out as more than a stepping stone between the seashore of 1957 and the fisherman's shed of 1968. At last, late in the year, Brook got what he had been asking for – a hand-picked troupe of a dozen actors able to work without the constraints of a set rehearsal period or, indeed, a predefined end-product. What the group eventually found its way towards was the *Marat-Sade*, a workshop version of Genet's *The Screens*, and the ambivalently-titled *US* – but first came the series of experiments which Brook, again with Marowitz as collaborator, now began to conduct in the little adaptable theatre belonging to the London Academy of Music and Dramatic Art (LAMDA). Its public manifestation was the five-week *Theatre of Cruelty* season which opened, somewhat tentatively, in January 1964.

This revue-like programme comprised an assortment of playlets and sketches which were intended to ring changes on the possibilities of Artaudian acting – employing gestures, non-verbal sound, surreal speech, and visual shock-horrors of various kinds, to produce, among other things, a one-acter by John Arden; a twenty-minute fold-in *Hamlet* (the first and briefest of Marowitz's series of collage versions of Shakespeare); Artaud's own three-minute *Spurt of Blood*, which was what it said it was, twice over; and a sketch by Brook called *The Public Bath*, with Glenda Jackson as a Christine Keeler ritually purified into a Jacqueline Kennedy. The evening was exploratory rather than revelatory, though its sampling of scenes from Genet's *The Screens* whetted one's appetite for a full-length version: but this, in the event, never got further than a workshop tryout in the Donmar rehearsal studio – the very space which, over ten years later, was to become the RSC's own Warehouse Theatre (and house just the sort of proletarian, socially-conscious drama from which Brook was supposed to be helping his company to escape).

It was ironic, too, that when the members of Brook's experimental group were duly injected like an anti-toxin into the parent Aldwych company, the full flowering of their work at LAMDA did not give us a production of Genet – arguably about the only truly Artaudian dramatist around – but a play by an earnest German Marxist called Peter Weiss. The full title of this wordy and somewhat worthy play, *The Persecution and Assassination of Marat as Performed by the Inmates of the Asylum of Charenton under the Direction of the Marquis de Sade*, also serves as a synopsis, and conveys something of the rather precise quality of the dialectically-balanced original. Brook seized on this raw material for the potential he saw in it of pitting intellectual arguments against instinct, Brechtian against Artaudian theatre. Although declaring that he wanted to preserve the balance between Marat's revolutionary rationalism and Sade's anarchic nihilism, and to find ways of synthesizing epic theatre with theatre of cruelty, Brook in the event tilted the balance away from derided words, and towards sheer theatricality – in the process achieving some spectacular effects in the bath-house which served as Sade's theatre. In such circumstances, Marat, Brecht, and allied angels of intelligence could only be swept away by the 'flood of people and events'.

In an ecstatic review in *The Guardian*, Gerard Fay remarked that the play was a 'bloodbath, violently attacking the emotions and sensibilities of any audience. . . . The story is acted out in a deadly, insane charade which as it approaches moments of meaninglessness becomes the more emphatically true and moving.' (So much for balance.) The actors, however, were matchless in their mimicry of lunatics, heeding Brook's instructions to 'dig out the madman' in themselves, though not without some trepidation. 'We were all convinced that we were going loony', declared Glenda Jackson, of their attempts to find ways of staying apparently insane for two and a half hours – a circumstance in which the assistance of Artaud and Brecht was probably negligible compared with the technical lifebelt offered by boring, old-fashioned Stanislavsky.

With that combination of phlegmatic cunning and sublime incongruity in which the English establishment delights, Brook was awarded the CBE in the New Year honours of 1965. He went on to deliver a series of Granada lectures, which were to form the basis for his book *The Empty Space*, to direct a play-reading of Weiss's gut-rending memorial for Auschwitz, *The Investigation*, and to reproduce *The Marat-Sade* for Broadway – where, incidentally, it initiated a far more searching debate about the relevance or otherwise of its author's intentions than the London critics had even attempted.

Brook himself was unimpressed by *The Investigation*. His biographer, who had been present at the midnight reading, could not recall 'a quieter audience, either in the theatre or as it came out into the hush of an early-morning

London'. Such a silent reception is usually a sign of a deeply attentive audience, but Brook told his collaborators on *US* that 'all the evening had achieved, in the end, was to demonstrate to the audience that they, too, could come to accept atrocity as boring'. For the first twenty minutes, he said, 'you were shocked; then you began to get bored; in the end you waited impatiently for the catalogue of horrors to end. We could never communicate to an Aldwych audience in this way.'

What Brook was now beginning to look for was a way of communicating horror of a more immediate kind – that of the war in Vietnam, and, more specifically 'what we, in London, could do about it'. Albert Hunt, who contributed a brief history of the project to the published text of *US*, recalls that Brook felt

> that the show would have to be made in a new way. Reading through the scripts that came into the Royal Shakespeare Company, he was brought up against the fact that no individual playwright, working alone, seemed able, at the moment, to handle a direct statement of this size.

I think that there was a curious mixture of truth and self-deception in this attitude. In spite of everything, we still talk of *The Marat-Sade* as Peter Weiss's play, but I doubt that many people who saw *US* when it opened at the Aldwych in October 1966, after four months' rehearsal, would now recollect that the writer who shaped the material was Dennis Cannan. The others credited were Brook himself, his collaborating directors Albert Hunt and Michael Kustow, the lyricist Adrian Mitchell, and the musician Richard Peaslee, together with the actors who were to 'improvise on material we would offer them'. Of course such a play was likely to get nearer to the truth if it utilized both original and imaginative sources: equally, that 'truth' was likely to be closer to the director's personal view of it if the presence of the writer was subsidiary to such a collaborative mishmash.

I was infuriated by *US*. When the actors came downstage to stare at the audience at the end, defying applause and with the apparent intention of staring us out of such countenance as we had left, I was second only to Ken Tynan in making a furious exit. Tynan is alleged to have cried, 'Are you waiting for us, or are we waiting for you?' before leaving. I didn't hear him, and the fact that theatre acoustics are not intended for audiences to communicate with the actors speaks, as it were, for itself. In the heat, I wrote in *Tribune*:

> Making us care, in Peter Brook's dramaturgy, seems inextricably bound up with making us embarrassed. And, contemporary audiences being fashionably maso-chistic, they *love* being embarrassed: so that the process shocks into narcissistic but not into objective awareness. . . .
>
> In part, the escapism consists in Peter Brook's favourite device of bringing up the house lights while the action on stage continues. . . . First time round, a lot of suffering wounded, wearing white paper bags – meant to indicate blindness, but

more reminiscent of the ku klux klan – invoke the audience's aid in stumbling along the aisles and out of the exits. The buck, as it were, is passed.

Well: so bloody what? So we feel good and committed if we lend an actor, revelling in every moment, a helping hand? What does this prove when, before the last thespian has wended his eyeless way, we're crashing purposefully to the bar, or making real, existential choices between neapolitan and tutti-frutti ice cream? . . . Here, as other parts of the evening warn, the gestures replace and reduce the reality.

Judged merely as theatrical gimmicks, these can only work, in any case, until the second night, or however long it takes for the word to get round. Next time the trick will have to be more brutal, the embarrassment more intense . . .

Next time, the trick was to be the ten-foot-tumescent golden phallus of Seneca's *Oedipus* – or, to be precise, of Brook's. He had rejected the original translation offered, preferring an entirely new version by Ted Hughes, which Kenneth Tynan, then literary manager at the National, described as 'virtually a new play . . . which echoed Hughes's view of life as expressed in his *Crow* poems,' and which 'came very close to Peter's brand of despondent nihilism'. Sophocles, of course, would have offered an even less malleable text – indeed, as Tynan put it, 'Seneca's *Oedipus* is Sophocles without the redeeming philosophical graces'. Or, as Ted Hughes wrote in the note to the published text: 'The radiant moral world of Sophocles is simply not present here'. Seneca's figures were 'by nature . . . more primitive than aboriginals' – much more suitable than the 'fully civilized' creatures of Sophocles for an exploration of 'ritual possibilities'.

And so, as we went into the Old Vic for the opening in March 1968, we found the whole auditorium already littered with the chorus, pendant from pillars and balconies, their response to the action resonating through every muscle of their bodies as well as their vocal chords. The stage itself was lined with glittering sheets of gold, variations of level being achieved by dropping the sides of a raised, revolving box to form multiple combinations of surfaces. A play by Seneca the stoic was transformed into a hedonistic happening, to which the sufferings of the human body were less important than their Freudian reflection of the desires of the loins. There were some wonderfully effective moments – the austere Creon spinning like a human top into a frenzy of revelation; the shepherd shuffling at agonizingly slow speed down the aisle to set his confirmatory seal on Oedipus's fate; and Jocasta's fully meditated, symbolic suicide, an ugly orgasm of death. Yet the play seemed to me to be too technically controlled ever to approach the ritualistic – a finely-honed exercise in sound and movement which put even the knife-edged responses of John Gielgud and Irene Worth to the test, and discovered from the lowlier members of the chorus depths of resource of which they were previously unaware. If this was a summation of Brook's recent work, it also revealed the contradictions behind it. Here was the very stuff of myth, taken from a play untrammelled with traditions of staging, yet which uniquely expressed both the classical and the Elizabethan world-view, and was now transformed to reflect its own director's moral philosophy – but it remained, in the end, a brilliant spectacle making a statement of mere 'despondent nihilism'.

However, from most critics and audiences the response to Brook's recent productions had been little short of adulatory. He stood at the pinnacle of his career – yet, for all the lesser collaborators on whom he was apt to depend, he stood alone. Invited to Paris by Jean-Louis Barrault in the spring of 1968 to open an international centre of theatre research, he went to work a third time on *The Tempest* – then, driven before political events back to England, turned it into a workshop project at the Roundhouse. But Brook's biographer makes no mention of any direct involvement on his part in the various 'events' of 1968, on either side of the Channel. Important though his ideas (notably, as expressed in *The Empty Space*, published that year) were to be for the new generation of theatre workers, he appears to have expressed little solidarity with the wave of student protest which swept the western world, and which, among many other things, was to change the direction of British theatre. Ironically, much of the protest was against the war in Vietnam. But Brook had seemingly worked that out of his system, and went off to Jutland to film *King Lear*.

He returned to Stratford in the summer of 1970 to direct *A Midsummer Night's Dream* – a play, unlike *Love's Labour's Lost* or *Titus Andronicus*, with a continuous history of often elaborate staging, barnacled about with tradition; a play, unlike *Measure for Measure* or *The Tempest*, without much apparent opacity of interpretation; a play, unlike *King Lear*, generally regarded as light relief even among the comedies. And here, coming to meet it in its author's birthplace, was a director now answering to a creative urge beyond the usual limits of his craft; who wished to work with a small and cohesive group of actors; and for whose next production rapt audiences and expectant critics could be guaranteed.

Eclectic as ever, Brook had drawn on Kott for *King Lear*, on Artaud for *The Marat-Sade*, on Grotowski in *US*. But in the programme for the *Dream* – freer than most of Stratford's glossy souvenirs from erudite background notes – only four quotations were included – two from the play itself, one from Meyerhold, and one from *The Empty Space*:

> Once, the theatre could begin as magic: magic at the sacred festival, or magic as the footlights came up. Today, it is the other way round. . . . We must open our empty hands and show that really there is nothing up our sleeves. Only then can we begin.

Such were the few clues scattered for the critics as they waited on the evening of 27 August for the performance to start. But as Peter Roberts, the editor of *Plays and Players* who had already seen an interview with Brook which was to appear in his October issue, pertinently noted, 'there is almost invariably a gulf between a director's intentions (stated or otherwise) and an audience's perception of them (particularly in the heightened tension of an especially edgy first night)'. The difficulties that this raised should not, Roberts felt, be ducked – especially, one might now add, in introducing a book such as this, which makes clear that among the 'director's intentions' was the belief that there should *be* no definitive moment of public realization – least of all the formal first night that the theatrical etiquette of the RSC required.

In the event, audiences were wildly enthusiastic, the reviewers almost unanimously so – though the few critics who did dislike the production disliked it intensely. They included, perhaps significantly, two writers in the weekly reviews who had had time to read and reflect upon their colleagues' raptures. According to Kenneth Hurren in *The Spectator*, it was 'a bleak comment on the wayward standards of contemporary Shakespearian criticism that this impertinent travesty has been received with tolerance and even fervour', while Benedict Nightingale in the *New Statesman* found the *Dream* Brook's 'most dispiriting production' to date. 'The mountain has laboured and brought forth, among other things, Mickey Mouse' – for what else, asked Nightingale, could Bottom's black bulb of a nose, small black ears, and huge black clogs be meant to evoke?

With such dissentients compare and contrast Clive Barnes, who had travelled back to his native England to report for the *New York Times* on one of those 'very rare' occasions destined to 'exert a major influence on the contemporary stage'.

> It is a magnificent production, the most important work yet of the world's most imaginative and inventive director. If Peter Brook had done nothing else but this *Dream*, he would have deserved a place in theatre history.
>
> Brook has approached the play with a radiant innocence. He has treated the script as if it had just been written and sent to him through the mail. He has staged it with no reference to the past, no reverence for tradition.
>
> He has stripped the play down, asked exactly what it is about. He has forgotten gossamer fairies, sequined eyelids, gauzy veils, and whole forests of Beerbohm-trees.
>
> He sees the play for what it is – an allegory of sensual love, and magic playground of lost innocence and hidden fears.

But while Barnes proceeded to deduce that 'sex and sexuality are vital in the play', Harold Hobson, reviewing the Aldwych transfer which opened in the same week as *No Sex Please – We're British*, observed that the title of that farce also encapsulated his 'overwhelming impression' of the *Dream*, with its 'Arctic setting, . . . the women's long concealing dresses, and cold, hard lighting plan'. (*No Sex Please* was still running ten years later, almost a case-study in what Brook would call 'deadly theatre'.)

According to Hobson, Brook had created a pagan world of 'calm passion and . . . attained peace', where 'the well-being of humanity' depended on the restoration of harmony between an omniscient Oberon and Titania. Roberts, on the other hand, saw the doubling of roles as suggesting 'a pre-marital dream on the part of Theseus' – while Irving Wardle, in *The Times*, found the doubling just one of several stylistic devices employed to express 'social harmony . . . by means of emphasizing the parallels between the three groups of characters'. Full of praise for the production's 'breathtaking' effects and circus skills, Wardle none the less felt that Brook had been 'at least as much concerned with the voice as . . . with the body' – while in the *Financial Times* B.A. Young was bemoaning a style of stage speech 'full of those wrong accents and misplaced caesuras that used to be the Royal Shakespeare Company's hallmark'. Alan Howard's Oberon was allegedly the worst offender: 'how he has the impertinence to mock at a man for "making periods in the middle of sentences" I don't know, for he makes them in the midst of almost every line'. Hobson, meanwhile, was commending the 'supreme gravity and beauty' of Howard's performance' . . .

In the light of David Selbourne's book, such disagreements about intentions and achievements appear understandable. At the time, I wrote in *Tribune* of having enjoyed the production – against expectations, after dissenting from the approving choruses for *The Marat-Sade* and *US*.

> Maybe this success is because Brook is not the supreme philosopher or politician who might have made those earlier productions more satisfying, but quite simply a supreme theatricalist. . . . As a total vision of the play, this *Dream* is riddled with contradictions or irrelevancies: but as a succession of brilliant theatrical conjuring tricks it is a delight to the ear and the eye – full of imaginative genius, but short, not that it matters in this case, on intellect.

Conjuring tricks, after all, have no moral. Juggling is not a philosophical art. Even the act of love makes no public statement – although it *had* seemed, certainly, that sexual consummation was devoutly being wished:

> If there is a unifying conception to the production, it must be that the whole affair is an elaborate, good-natured preliminary to love-play. The doubling of roles, made as self-conscious as the text can be stretched to suggest; the trapezes that make fairy footwork a matter of circus acrobatics; the sado-masochistic struggle over the Indian boy: all combine with an unusual degree of seeming calculation to suggest a plotted and preconceived game rather than a developing drama . . .

In such a sexual *schema*, it made perfect sense that Bottom's enchantment should be manifestly more phallic than facial. But neither the mechanicals *en masse* nor the unusually kind reception for their play seemed quite to fit: it was as though they had interrupted 'a private party'.

> I suppose that, in a way – dressed hopefully in their Sunday bests – that's just what they have done. But on their own – whether displaying the quiet, controlled camp of Philip Locke's Quince, or the roaring one-upmanship of David Waller's Bottom, a sort of factory-floor prima donna – they might be in another play. A good play, mind you, but another one.

The reader can best judge what sense these comments make in the light of the account of the rehearsal process that follows. What were necessarily concealed from us at the time – and with complete success, it seems – were the hidden tensions and worries which clearly continued until a very late stage indeed: for the play's celebratory note rang true, and the final joining-of-hands with the audience seemed a gesture of shared affirmation, not of tribulations triumphantly overcome. And few in the audience would even have known about the equivocal success of the workshop production a few days earlier at the Midland Arts Centre, with which David Selbourne ends his record – equivocal not in its reception, which could be measured clearly enough in the standing ovation it won, but in its unexpected distillation of shared response, method, and context, the play coming to life in a way that was neither more nor less 'successful' than the full-scale experience, but quite simply 'other'.

But this is to anticipate David Selbourne's story – as, indeed, it also anticipated the rediscovery of 'studio' Shakespeare in such productions as Buzz Goodbody's *Hamlet* and Trevor Nunn's *Macbeth*, when the RSC opened its Other Place later in the 'seventies. When Brook himself next visited Stratford, it was to direct that indifferent *Antony and Cleopatra* with Glenda Jackson and Alan Howard – predestined, perhaps, to be a 'star-vehicle', in spite of the fact that it was Brook who had helped to create its stars, in very different kinds of production. No less certainly was the *Dream* itself ordained to become a 'product' of multinational theatre. After playing 32 times during the remainder of the 1970 Stratford season – and visiting the Roundhouse with a 'rough' version played for two nights to packed and ecstatic houses without costumes or décor – the production toured the USA and Canada for fourteen weeks in the following spring, amassing no fewer than 112 performances in six cities, including an eight-week run on Broadway. The Aldwych transfer opened after a couple of previews on 10 June 1971, and stayed in the London repertoire to add over 90 performances to the tally by the end of March 1972 (not counting a week back in Stratford among the 'winter visitors' to the parent theatre). The *Dream* company packed its bags again in August, for a couple of dozen performances in three English towns *en route* for a tour of Europe and a further 74 performances, to which sixteen more were added in Liverpool and Cardiff in December. Back in the USA in January 1973, the production played 47 times in Los Angeles and 23 in San Francisco, travelling thence to Japan and Australia to notch up another 108 nights' *Dreams*. Inevitably, in playing a total of 535 performances in 36 cities and towns, the production accreted to itself the polished veneer that reveals and conceals a prestige 'event'. As Brook reflected, 'for better or worse it had to repeat itself. In the end for worse, because the actors had to do their duty rather than what came from life.'

Brook himself wanted to escape from a theatre which imposed such necessary but unhappy obligations. It is ironic that he felt his best chance of now obtaining the 'freedom' he needed lay in securing financial backing by courtesy of the Shah of Iran, then propping up waning popular support with the supposed international credibility of the festivals in Shiraz. There, in the summer of 1971, Brook invented *Orghast* – the 'language' in which Ted Hughes 'wrote' the 'play' that shared its name. A.C.H. Smith has given us a full account of the experiment in *Orghast in Persepolis*, as has John Heilpern of the trek across Africa which produced *Conference of the Birds* in the following year. The Centre International de Créations Théâtrales, under whose banner Brook had been assembling his itinerant company for these productions, returned to Paris in 1974. They settled in the Théâtre aux Bouffes du Nord, where they have remained, working on a relatively small number of productions which have ranged from *The Ik* to *Ubu* (both seen in London, in the relatively sympathetic environments of, respectively, the Roundhouse and the Young Vic), and from *Timon of Athens* to *The Cherry Orchard*.

It is difficult to comment on this work from a limited exposure: but *The Ik*, at least, suggested that Brook's *Dream* had been a brief one – a benign blink, as it were, in the narrowing focus of his misanthropic (and politically myopic) vision. Kenneth Tynan's reaction to *The Ik* was thus of 'great, baffled sorrow'. Brook had

> discarded all the immense technical skills that he had used previously to dazzle, startle, amaze, and stun audiences. . . . He had abandoned the strength of language, and he seemed to me to be doing a surprisingly conventional documentary dramatization of Colin Turnbull's book about an African tribe forcibly removed from its hunting grounds and declining into a state of brutalized amorality. . . . In other words, Peter was harking back to his earlier preoccupations – saying, if you remove the necessities of life, remove the social conventions, people will behave appallingly. Now you would have thought that this was something of a truism: but Peter was presenting it gravely, as a horrific revelation.

Moreover, Tynan noticed the curious detachment the production maintained from 'the present state of the Ik tribe':

> the book was written some years ago, and in the programme it just said, 'as far as anyone knows, the Ik still exist'. *As far as anyone knows?* Here we were, invited to feel compassion and horror at their plight, but nobody in the production had even bothered to find out whether they still existed!

If I have given apparently undue emphasis to such adverse views of Brook's 'political' theatre, this is in part because such were my own reactions – but it is also to suggest the quality of somewhat perverse innocence which blinds Brook to his own greatest strengths. In a continuing endeavour to break new ground, to prevent his own work from atrophying into 'deadly theatre', he has taken upon himself the mantle of philosopher and poetaster, but in so doing cast off the rougher, more practical garb of the rogue-and-vagabond professional. As such, he had scaled all but the Shakespearian heights, and for

Shakespeare he had performed the arguably more valuable work of illuminating the hidden depths of supposedly lesser works. The Brook of the newly-enchanted *Dream* was recognizably the Brook who had long before rediscovered *Love's Labour's Lost*: alas, the parlour-masochist of *US* was no less clearly the amoral misanthropist of *The Ik*, caring less for his apparent subjects than for the ways in which they demonstrated both his own bleak 'political' view, and the impotence of the 'liberal' western response.

David Selbourne's book touches on other kinds of relationship, to which those quotation marks around 'political' and 'liberal' – and, indeed, 'theatrical' – may or may not be appropriate. It is an important work, both in the critical portrait it offers of a leading director at work, and in its demonstration of the kinds of bluff, self-deception, and unhappy accident that can as much contribute to the making of a theatrical 'triumph' as our more orthodox expectations of creative struggle, fruitful improvisation, and dialectic discovery – present also in full measure though these undoubtedly were. *All* the ingredients are there in the seven-week mix of rehearsals of which the detailed record now follows. Whether we regard them as part of the price that genius must inevitably command, or as telling us something more generally revealing about the creative relationship between any director, author, and players, will depend on our individual attitudes towards the 'empty space' that is theatre, as towards Brook's brilliant and bloody-minded, creative and cussed approaches to filling it.

SIMON TRUSSLER

Preface

On 30 June 1970, at Peter Brook's invitation, I began to attend the rehearsals in Stratford of his production of *A Midsummer Night's Dream*. At the time, I wanted to be neither the public diarist nor the critic of the production. I saw myself then not as a writer *about* the theatre – least of all, about 'director's theatre' – but as a writer *for* it. But in fact, as the detailed notes I took of the rehearsals make plain, my own doubts as a playwright, as well as a process of self-questioning about the nature and purpose of the theatre, were beginning to develop in that period. And throughout the rehearsals, as the meaning of Shakespeare's text was explored day by day, so these questions multiplied.

I had met Brook for the first time some weeks before, in order to discuss my play *The Damned* with him. It was then that he invited me to Stratford; and living 25 miles away, I made the daily journey (on most days) to watch the making of *A Midsummer Night's Dream*. I wrote down during the rehearsals what I saw, heard and felt, transcribing and expanding my notes each evening; and I have been faithful here, in this further transcription, to those immediate responses.

But a decade has passed since then. My own practical involvement with the theatre has diminished, so that the personal travails of the aspiring playwright seem, and are, less important to me now than the wider artistic and social issues raised by what I witnessed. These issues are posed in the text as questions, not answers, just as they were posed in the original. For in this sequence of changing and deepening impressions, with their shifts of judgment, is a description of a long drawn-out and complex theatrical event, not a political or aesthetic analysis of it. Yet in the asides of a decade ago, a critical and sceptical position was being worked out, and justly so; moreover, I do not think now that the questions I asked then were the wrong ones.

In one respect, however, there is a difference. Hanging on to the hints my own notes gave me, I have been able – I hope – to make more use now of the immensely rich possibilities with which that theatrical encounter presented me, than I could have done then. I have also lost some of the arrogant political dogmatism which led me, in the weeks and months following the rehearsals, bitterly to reject their validity almost entirely: it was a privileged theatre for the privileged, the work of an autocrat with exploited actors, a pseudo-intellectual form of show-biz, and so on. Going back deeply into my own account of it, I came to see that this had been an unwarranted *volte-face*. The whole truth of the matter was different, and much more complicated. And it was my own written notes at the time which turned out, on re-examination, to contain a painstaking and elaborate response to my immediate experience; my retrospective recoil from it had been much less considered.

What follows, then, is not hindsight. It is, instead, an attempt to re-instate the true density of first impressions, and to rescue them from the structured simplicities of a shallow political and artistic judgment; as well as to recover fleeting moments in the posthumous life of Shakespeare's writing, in one of the very greatest of his plays. I must thank Marc Pellerin for his suggestion that this book should be written, Peter Brook for his invitation to rehearsals, Mary White of the Shakespeare Centre Library in Stratford for her assistance in obtaining the illustrations to this book, the Oxford University Press for permission to reprint the plot synopsis of *A Midsummer Night's Dream* which appears in their New Clarendon Shakespeare edition, first published in 1939, and Sybil Brooke for her swift and accurate typing from my manuscript.

In the numbering of acts, scenes and lines, I have followed Peter Alexander's authoritative edition of *The Complete Works of William Shakespeare* (Collins, London and Glasgow, 1951).

D.S.

The Plot of the Play

I.i. *A Midsummer Night's Dream* opens with a short dialogue between Theseus, Duke of Athens, and Hippolyta, his love, from which we learn that their marriage will take place on the night of the new moon, four days hence. Egeus, his daughter Hermia, and her two lovers, Lysander and Demetrius, enter, and Egeus asks for judgment on Hermia for her refusal to accept as husband his choice, Demetrius, because she loves Lysander. The Duke explains to her that if she does not obey her father she must either die or be condemned to perpetual chastity in a nunnery, and gives her until his wedding-eve to decide.

Left alone, Hermia and Lysander determine to meet in a wood outside the town the following night, and thence to make their escape from the law of Athens. They acquaint Helena, who is in love with Demetrius, and was formerly loved by him, with their decision, and she, in a soliloquy after they have gone, expresses her determination to win Demetrius's gratitude by warning him of their plan, and to follow him to the wood after them.

I.ii. The clownish characters of the play, Bottom, Quince, Flute, Snout, Starveling and Snug, meet to make their arrangements and allot the parts for a play they propose to give before Theseus on his wedding night. They decide to meet by moonlight on the following night in the wood outside the town, where they can hold their first rehearsal without fear of interruption.

II.i. The scene now shifts to the wood outside Athens, and we learn from a conversation between Puck and a fairy of Titania's train of the quarrel between the fairy king and queen, Oberon and Titania, over an attendant of Titania's whom Oberon covets as a page.

Oberon and Titania enter, and we find out that they are both in the neighbourhood of Athens for the purpose of honouring and blessing the wedding of Theseus and Hippolyta. Titania departs with the quarrel still unappeased, and Oberon then sends Puck for a flower whose juice has the magic property of causing those to whose eyes it is applied to love the next thing they see, whether animal or human. This he proposes to use on Titania, and to leave her thus charmed until she yields him the boy.

Demetrius, in search of Hermia and Lysander, enters pursued by the love-sick Helena, whom he angrily attempts to shake off. Oberon hears their conversation, and decides to use the magic to cause Demetrius to love Helena. He dispatches Puck with orders to anoint the eyes of a man whom he will know 'by the Athenian garments he hath on', and himself sets out to apply the love-juice to Titania's eyes.

II.ii. Oberon finds Titania asleep in her bower, and charms her eyes with the juice. He goes away, and Hermia and Lysander, who have lost their way in the wood, and are weary, come on the scene and lie down to sleep in different places. Puck enters, and seeing Lysander in Athenian garments, mistakes him for Demetrius, anoints his eyes with the love-juice, and goes away.

Demetrius, pursued by Helena, now arrives. He fails to observe Lysander and Hermia in the darkness, and runs out, but Helena, who is tired from her pursuit, finds Lysander on the bank as she prepares to rest. Lysander awakes, and, through the virtue of the charm, falls instantly and violently in love with her. Helena thinks him to be mocking her, and indignantly departs, followed by him.

Hermia wakes up, finds herself alone, and sets out in search of Lysander.

III.i. Puck stumbles upon the clowns' rehearsal in the wood, and, in pure mischief, transforms Bottom into an ass. His fellows run away, and the song he sings to show his indifference wakens Titania, who at once falls in love with him under the influence of the magic flower, and has him led to her bower.

III.ii. The crisis of the main plot and the first steps towards its solution both take place in this long scene.

Puck informs Oberon of the success of his trick on Titania, and tells him that the Athenian is duly anointed with the love-juice. Hermia enters at this point, rejects Demetrius' pleas for her love, and leaves him in her search for Lysander.

Demetrius lies down to sleep. Oberon recognizes Demetrius, sees that Puck has made a mistake, and commands him to find and bring Helena to the spot, while he himself charms the eyes of Demetrius in preparation for her appearance.

When she enters, Lysander is with her, offering her his love, which she rejects since she indignantly regards it as a mocking insult. Demetrius now wakes up, sees Helena first, at once falls in love with her, and expresses his passion in extravagant terms. Helena regards this as part of the plot to humiliate her, while the two men – bewitched into becoming her rivals – quarrel over her.

Hermia now comes on the scene. For a short time she also thinks that Lysander is mocking Helena, since she knows no reason why his love for her should have changed. Finally she discovers that she is now desired by neither of the men, and, thinking that Helena has robbed her of her love, turns on her in a rage.

Helena, in her turn, thinks her old school-friend is in the plot to make fun of her. A quarrel of cross-purposes now takes place between the two women on one side and the two men on the other. The men also heap insults on Hermia, and try to protect Helena from her, to each other's growing fury.

In the end, Lysander and Demetrius set off to find a place to fight in, and the timid Helena runs away from the vixenish Hermia. Oberon and Puck have been spectators of this scene. The former now bids Puck, whom the confusion has delighted, to 'overcast' the night, and lead the men separately astray until they are exhausted and sleep without doing each other any damage.

He is then to apply 'Dian's bud', the antidote to the love-juice, to the eyes of Lysander, so that he shall return to the love of Hermia. Puck does this. The scene closes with the two pairs of lovers sleeping unknowingly in close proximity to one another.

Oberon goes to beg the page from Titania, and to release her from the charm.

IV.i.   Oberon finds Titania and Bottom asleep in one another's arms. He uses the antidote to release her from the love-charm, after telling Puck that he had met her earlier, and had obtained the changeling child from her. Titania wakes, and now finds her former love, Bottom, loathsome. She is reconciled to Oberon, and they depart with Puck, after the latter has removed the ass's head from Bottom.

Theseus and his train enter on a hunting expedition. They see and wake the lovers, who remember the events of the night in a dazed way, as if they were happenings in a dream.

Lysander's love for Hermia has returned, and Demetrius, under the power of the charm, has recovered the love he had for Helena before the events of the play began. They go out; and Bottom, awaking with vague memories of greatness, goes home.

IV.ii.   Bottom meets the rest of his cast, and sends them to prepare for the Interlude before the Duke that night. For he has heard that their play is accepted for performance.

V.i and ii.   The last act is by way of an epilogue. Theseus and the rest of the courtly characters attend the performance of the clowns' Interlude. When it is over, and actors and spectators gone, the fairies enter. They bless the three marriages and the house. Puck speaks the last words, asking for indulgence for the play and the actors.

The Cast for Brook's Production

Theseus/Oberon	:	ALAN HOWARD
Hippolyta/Titania	:	SARA KESTELMAN
Philostrate/Puck	:	JOHN KANE
Egeus/Quince	:	PHILIP LOCKE
Bottom	:	DAVID WALLER
Flute	:	GLYNNE LEWIS
Starveling	:	TERRENCE HARDIMAN
Snout	:	NORMAN RODWAY
Snug	:	BARRY STANTON
Hermia	:	MARY RUTHERFORD
Lysander	:	CHRISTOPHER GABLE
Helena	:	FRANCES DE LA TOUR
Demetrius	:	BEN KINGSLEY
Fairies	:	HUGH KEAYS BYRNE
		RALPH COTTERILL
		CELIA QUICKE
		JOHN YORK

First week, first day

It seems a lonely life, setting off and driving through the lanes of the silent summer countryside. To a play? To play? There is a sunny wind on the river at Stratford; under the sun, the studio roof gives off a cracking and creaking sound, the sun-blind flapping at the window. There is stained canvas on the floor, and a litter of boxes, drums, barrels, lighting-equipment, scaffolding, a bicycle, a piano. I receive a warm welcome from Brook – or rather, a sudden brief geniality, as the *dramatis personae* gather. But what is a writer of other plays doing here, at this *fest* of action?

There is a pressure in Brook to begin, a pressure to such action. But there seems also to be a lack of bonhomie among those who are gathering here. Is it the casualness of the professional, or because they know each other? Brook kisses the designer on both cheeks when she enters. But it is not really a kiss. It is the shape on the lips of a kiss, angled into the air, only the sides of their faces touching. Are they bored, the actors, or interested? Awe-stricken, nervous?

On the sidelines, the spectator is already rendered null. And as the actors mills about, limbering and flexing, one of them strikes up on the drum. Brook, a small man, is suddenly militant, fists clenched, conducting the pugnacious rhythm. The actors themselves seem insignificant, all but one. He is fat and perspiring, balding; larger than life. Surely, he must be Bottom? No, he is – or will be – Snug the joiner, and Snug the lion. Bottom is polite, discreet, withdrawn. What transformations are possible in these people? Any?

These are the 'mechanicals', and this is *A Midsummer Night's Dream*'s first rehearsal. Large-striding, with the drum beating, the actors stalk the stained canvas; stretching and striding to the rhythm, Brook conducting the drumming, and shouting 'Find out the largest stride you can make', the movements growing larger. The drum beats faster and louder, Brook (with clenched fists) conducting the striding

1 Rehearsal discussion: (l. to r.) John Kane (Puck), Peter Brook, Ben Kingsley (Demetrius), David Waller (Bottom), and Hugh Keays Byrne (Cobweb).

and drumming. Only two of the actors have familiar faces: Norman Rodway and David Waller. Do they really look like this in civvies? In the hubbub (where shall I sit? what am I doing?) Brook says 'Tomorrow, let us have tools: a bale of cloth, a plane, a loom, something for beating metal, a hammer and a few bellows'.

The actors, some breathless, sit in a semi-circle around Brook, himself sitting on the canvas, self-conscious. (And if I creak my chair, or write in my notebook, or turn the pages of the text, will I disturb them?) One of them suggests 'research on Elizabethan implements'. Brook dismisses it. 'We must search,' he says, 'for the experienced physical gesture'; the 'gesture of physical experience in the craftsman', the 'immediately recognizable gesture of the experienced carpenter, joiner, weaver . . . Each of you,' he continues, 'must find a gesture, recognizably deep and true, in which the object you are using is an extension of the lines, and is felt to be part of the body'. He says nothing of the social elements of the mechanicals' world. Labour is the gesture of labour. 'And each of you must follow what the other does, and become absorbed in it, intensifying and enlarging the moment through collaboration'. The closed circle seems to draw closer, the roof creaking in the summer sun. 'You must do nothing actorish,' he says in the moment's silence; 'you must retain the integrity of your movements.'

His legs crossed beneath him in an uncomfortable squatting on the canvas, a thin white spindle-shank is visible. There is both delicacy and impatience in Brook; and some caprice in his manner. 'This is a mysterious play,' he says, 'and there is nothing in it by accident, nothing by chance. Other playwrights' meanings can be fully fathomed. But here the material is as if beyond Shakespeare altogether.' The fat actor is easily distracted; another, to be Quince, briefly looks at me. Or is he – he is – boss-eyed, and looking elsewhere? 'A microcosm of the play as a whole,' Brook continues, 'is to be found in the mechanicals' play-acting. It raises questions as to the nature of "reality", and the nature of "acting".' There is a fly buzzing. 'It asks, "What is a role?" and "What is the meaning of the actor's transformation?".'

The sun-blind flaps at the open window. The playwright sits on his metal chair in a limbo, role-less, a text on his knee before him. 'Does simplicity convince more than sophistication? Are the "rude mechanicals" nearer to the truth,' Brook asks, 'than the court and the courtiers? Moreover, they face "real" rehearsal problems during the

¹ *Qince:* But there is two hard things; that is, to bring the moonlight into a chamber; for, you know, Pyramus and Thisby meet by moonlight.

Snout: Doth the moon shine that night we play our play?

Bottom: A calendar, a calendar! Look in the almanac; find out moonshine, find out moonshine . . .

Quince: . . . Then, there is another thing: we must have a wall in the great chamber; for Pyramus and Thisby, says the story, did talk through the chink of a wall.

Snout: You can never bring in a wall. What say you, Bottom?

Bottom: Some man or other must present Wall.

(III.i.42–59)

² *Pyramus:* O grim-looked night! O night with hue so black!
O night, which ever art when day is not!
O night, O night! Alack, alack, alack,
I fear my Thisby's promise is forgot!
And thou, O wall, O sweet, O lovely wall,
That stand'st between her father's ground and mine!
Thou wall, O wall, O sweet and lovely wall,
Show me thy chink, to blink through with mine eyne!

(V.i.167–175)

³ *Titania:*   The spring, the summer,
The childing autumn, angry winter, change
Their wonted liveries; and the mazèd world,
By their increase, now knows not which is which.
And this same progeny of evils comes
From our debate, from our dissension;
We are their parents and original.

(II.i.111–117)

⁴ *Helena:* Things base and vile, holding no quantity,
Love can transpose to form and dignity.
Love looks not with the eyes, but with the mind,
And therefore is winged Cupid painted blind.

(I.i.232–235)

4

action[1]; a "more real" situation than in the rest of the play, particularly when their drama is played as if for the first time to a ducal audience, or for the first time in their roles as actors.' Eyes wander. (The observer already has his own questions.) 'Your task,' Brook tells them, 'is to bring *A Midsummer Night's Dream* to life through your rehearsal of *Pyramus and Thisby*. And the reappearance of Pyramus and Thisby at the end of the action[2] will shed light on the whole play's meaning and purpose. But what this is, must be found.' The fat actor, sweating, wipes his neck and head with a towel.

Yet, surely, what is real and what apparent needs no *play* to enact it? In any case, today in this place, even my own appearance – let alone that of Brook and the actors – puts me at a loss. And the distraction of figures passing and re-passing, of doors opening and closing, seems endless. Brook talks through it, sometimes reticent and hidden, sometimes fluent and clear in gesture and expression; at others subsiding into non-coherence, unintelligible and uneasy. There is a tea-break, in which he speaks of the ass as a 'copulatory emblem'; of the Golden Ass as a 'walking cock'; and thence, *de haut en bas* – to the sound of sipping and slurping – of the feigned buggery in the New York production of *Che*, which had become 'real erections'. The cast, he says, had been arrested. His theatrical vernacular suddenly seems patronizing, and is greeted in silence; as if the actors were awkward, and Brook, quick to sense it, uncertain.

The play is to be read for the first time, squatting. And since, today, only the 'mechanicals' are present, they will take all the parts between them. Brook tells them that 'the associations, the lines, the correspondences' must be 'searched out', in order to 'enlarge and intensify the text's meaning'. Flicking through his copy, he instances Titania's 'And this same progeny of evils comes/ From our debate, from our dissension'.[3] This, he says, anticipates both theme and mood of the play's *coda*. The actors are silent and burdened; their reading cautious. At Helena's 'Things base and vile holding no quantity,/Love can transpose to form and dignity'[4], he talks of the play's 'transformations' – including those of physical appearance – from dream-world to waking, and of transfigurations wrought by force of the imagination. There are transitions through 'different levels of the real', as from the quandaries of tormented and bewitched lovers to the mechanicals' rehearsal struggles. 'We are just beginning to take the characters as "real", in which speech can express "real hatred and loathing",' Brook says of the *contretemps* between Lysander and Hermia at the end of Act

5

⁵ *Hermia:* Alack, where are you? Speak, an if you hear;
  Speak, of all loves! I swoon almost with fear.
  No? Then I well perceive you are not nigh.
  Death or you I'll find immediately.   (*Exit*)

*ACT THREE. Scene One. The wood. TITANIA lying asleep. Enter
QUINCE, SNUG, BOTTOM, FLUTE, SNOUT and
STARVELING.*

Bottom: Are we all met?
Quince: Pat, pat; and here's a marvellous convenient place for our
  rehearsal.

  (*II.ii.153–156, III.i.1–3*)

⁶ *Bottom:* . . . You must name his name, and half his face must be seen
  through the lion's neck, and he himself must speak through, saying
  thus . . . 'If you think I come hither as a lion, it were pity of my
  life. No, I am no such thing. I am a man as other men are.'

  (*III.i.32–39*)

⁷ *Oberon:* And, gentle Puck, take this transformèd scalp
  From off the head of this Athenian swain,
  That, he awaking when the other do,
  May all to Athens back again repair,
  And think no more of this night's accidents,
  But as the fierce vexation of a dream.

  (*IV.i.61–66*)

⁸ *Theseus:* Come now, what masques, what dances shall we have,
  To wear away this long age of three hours
  Between our aftersupper and bedtime?
  Where is our usual manager of mirth?
  What revels are in hand? Is there no play,
  To ease the anguish of a torturing hour?

  (*V.i.32–37*)

⁹ *Theseus:* The poet's eye, in a fine frenzy rolling,
  Doth glance from heaven to earth, from earth to heaven;
  And as imagination bodies forth
  The form of things unknown, the poet's pen
  Turns them to shapes, and gives to airy nothing
  A local habitation and a name.

  (*V.i.12–17*)

Two[5], when 'we are suddenly back to acting as acting,' as the mechanicals enter for their Act Three rehearsal.

And yet Bottom, unable to anticipate his own imminent transformation into an ass, within seconds advises Snug to allay audience fears of *his* appearance as a Lion, with the words 'I am a man as other men are'[6]. It is already, and at first hearing, an admonition from deep within the world of the actor, and the truth of a drama within a drama. The rehearsal room seems to shrink in the heat before it. Some of the actors are attentive and eager (is their energy real or apparent? is it because they are actors that they can conceal their puzzlement and confusion?), others adrift and out of focus. (Who, if any, is falsifying his responses to gain in favour?) The moments of Bottom's physical transformation, Brook says, might be gradual in performance, but they will be moments of 'intensification and enlargement'; 'first an ear will appear, then another ear, then a snout and so on.'

Somewhere, the hard world outside roars on, beyond this play-acting. Is everyone in here, myself included, in flight from life and looking for arousal? Do we all hope to find *A Midsummer Night's Dream* within these walls, and under these studio skylights? (Or am I just a writer covertly seeking production, as actors seek attention?) Yet, as the afternoon wears on, I think I begin to hear in the play's cadences, carefully and inquiringly read, neither the easy tenor nor the even rhythm of a sleep which is untroubled, but the 'fierce vexation of a dream' which Oberon speaks of[7]. Am I imagining it, or dreaming? Will Brook and the actors hear it? Will they make of *A Midsummer Night's Dream*, as well as of *Pyramus and Thisby*, a 'play to ease the anguish of a torturing hour'?[8] They sit in front of me now on the stained canvas, reading; trying to get their bearings.

But how much of all this will be 'the poet's eye in a fine frenzy rolling'[9], and how much the director's drumming? Quince's 'O monstrous! O strange!'[10] and Puck's 'I'll follow you', at Bottom's apparition, will be a 'marvellous opportunity', Brook says, 'for a lunatic, moving, farcical chase, and for miming'. Speech, in the lyrical love-passages of the play, may 'broaden into intoning, and then into singing'. Will this be Brook's Dream, or Shakespeare's? Why are Oberon, Titania and Puck to be doubled with Theseus, Hippolyta and Philostrate? Ill-at-ease in this company, I watch the actors trudging away at the day's end: an ensemble walking singly into the late afternoon sunlight.

(*Re-enter PUCK, and BOTTOM with an ass's head*)

Pyramus: If I were fair, Thisby, I were only thine.

Quince: O montrous! O strange! We are haunted. Pray, masters! Fly, masters! Help!

(*Exeunt all but BOTTOM*)

Puck: I'll follow you, I'll lead you about around,
Through bog, through bush, through brake, through brier.

(*III.i.93–97*)

11 *Hippolyta:* But all the story of the night told over,
And all their minds transfigured so together,
More witnesseth than fancy's images.
And grows to something of great constancy;
But, howsoever, strange and admirable.

(*V.i.23–27*)

12 *Bottom:* I have had a most rare vision. I have had a dream, past the wit of man to say what dream it was. Man is but an ass, if he go about to expound this dream. Methought I was – there is no man can tell what methought I was – and methought I had – but man is but a patched fool if he will offer to say what methought I had.

(*IV.ii.200–207*)

Today, puzzlingly, Brook greets me before the rehearsal begins with great warmth and effusion, claiming that yesterday he had 'no idea' who I was. It had only occurred to him, he says, after I had left. Until then, he was unsure whether I was 'publicity', a carpenter, an unknown extra. Can this possibly be true, after our lengthy conversation at his house only a few weeks before? And if it isn't true, for what truth is he searching in *A Midsummer Night's Dream*?

Then, in intimacy (is it feigned? is it real?) – with his hand on my shoulder – he spoke of how he had chosen the actors for their parts six months ago. They had had a 'long time to get used to the idea of ultimately working together', but he had not told them 'what the play was about'. He complained, *sotto voce*, that the actors 'believed it was sufficient to know each other', and relied on a general 'benevolence' as a 'source, or base, for working'. He also talked of his own fears of first rehearsals; of how it had been necessary, yesterday, to 'go into it gently', and to 'give reassurance to the actors'.

When they have gathered, there is a preliminary discussion. Brook declares to them that 'naturalistic questions', such as "Why does the mechanicals' play take place at all?" 'can't be asked'. 'It is a given,' he says, dictated by the 'logic of a morality play.' It is also 'a mystery', even a 'mystery play', whose meanings have been diminished by the Victorian fairy-tale tradition. And 'seeking out this mystery' is the object of their working together. He warns them, too, that all conclusions about it arrived at now will be inadequate and 'premature', since its meanings reside in the process of their discovery, layer by layer.

An actor asks, 'Is the whole play a dream?' And Brook replies: 'Don't impose a theory on it. Don't take it literally either. Discover the truth of it.' Moreover, the truth which they are seeking, he says, 'has to be found by each actor. It cannot be described.' There is in the play a 'reality beyond description', just as Hippolyta herself finds something unspecifically 'strange and admirable' in 'all the story of the night told over'[11]. In addition, Brook says, the play will 'yield its secrets, if each individual relates himself to the whole', to what he calls the 'total ceremony' of its enactment. And he quotes with approval Bottom's 'Man is but an ass, if he go about to expound his dream'[12]; it is 'the right attitude to something mysterious'.

Brook goes further. 'The rhythms of the play,' he asserts, 'are

¹³ *Egeus:* Full of vexation come I, with complaint
Against my child, my daughter Hermia.
Stand forth, Demetrius. My noble lord,
This man hath my consent to marry her.
Stand forth, Lysander. And, my gracious Duke,
This man hath bewitched the bosom of my child.

(I.i.22–27)

deeper than the words Shakespeare is able to use'; perhaps linguistic structuralism, also, has a tree growing in this Arcadia. And since this is so, listening to the rhythms of the words, rather than attending to their literal meaning, will take one towards a deeper understanding. 'Hearing the rhythm of each other's words,' Brook also tells the actors, will 'set up a preparedness for response', will 'draw one on to the next stage of understanding meaning.' 'Everything,' he says for good measure, 'has to be summoned up by the actor's imagination.' (Will the movements of Shakespeare's mind, as it stirred in the writing, also be discovered here, in this creaking studio?)

To begin to achieve these purposes, Brook declares, the actor must exercise himself to communicate by sounds which are not verbal. This is to be done, here and now, by throwing a sound, as if it were a stick or a hoop or a spinning plate, from person to person, catching it, using it and passing it on to another. Or, aided by the rhythms of drums and cymbals, a harmony of sounds can be found, together. 'Everyone recoils,' says Brook, 'at the dropping of the baton.' And so it must be with sounds, and the passage of sounds from one voice to another.

The two actors who are to play Hermia and Lysander are asked to kneel on the floor near one another, eyes closed. With sounds 'unrelated to verbal equivalents', they are to communicate with, and explore, each other. There is a long moment of silence, in which to see two sightless human creatures crouching before you. Into the silence comes a murmur of male searching, and a hesitant female answer. From this invitation and withdrawal, a long succession of gestures in sound slowly brings the actors to mutual arousal and acceptance; to a coupling not of bodies, but of voices. When they have done, does anything stir in the silence? What did it signify, this gamut of responses in two anxious actors? Were they the banal and culturally well-rehearsed reflexes – not less banal because 'pre-verbal' – of male and female? And is this to be the way to the rebirth of Shakespeare's creative moment, before the word was written?

The exercise is now transposed to the circumstances of the play's opening scene. Hermia's father, Egeus, has expressed his displeasure at his daughter's love for Lysander and is about to leave them together[13]. Brook asks Egeus to make a sound of rejection and dismissal and for Hermia and Lysander to respond to it. They do so, with what is intended to stand in sound for the innermost pulse of grief and longing. The reading of their words begins immediately after it. They are to speak them, Brook says, 'remembering the sounds which

(*Exeunt all but LYSANDER and HERMIA*)
Lysander: How now, my love! Why is your cheek so pale?
How chance the roses there do fade so fast?

(*I.i.127–129*)

Lysander: 'Tis no jest
That I do hate thee, and love Helena.
Hermia: O me! You juggler! You canker blossom!
You thief of love! What, have you come by night
And stol'n my love's heart from him?
Helena: Fine, i' faith!
Have you no modesty, no maiden shame,
No touch of bashfulness?

(*III.ii.280–286*)

16

Helena: Ay, do! Persever, counterfeit sad looks,
Make mouths upon me when I turn my back;
Wink each at other; hold the sweet jest up.

(*III.ii.236–239*)

came upon the deepest impulse'. And by these means, Lysander's 'How now, my love! Why is your cheek so pale?'[14] can, at the outset of rehearsal, be freed from what Brook calls the 'generalized sentiment' which has come to afflict the speaking of it.

Furthermore, 'each person has a rhythm,' Brook adds, again interrupting the reading, which has 'nothing to do with behaviour.' Thus, the same words can evoke 'different rhythms in different people'. A few moments later, however, he declares that 'the mere fact that words have a certain sound and rhythm, whatever their meaning, communicates something of the impulse and intention behind them'. The actors' brows lighten with inklings of knowledge, and darken with doubt, in alternation. Does he mean that there is an objective rhythm in the words, and a subjective rhythm in the speaker, rhythm upon rhythm? Must they be brought into consonance, or should one give way to the other? Or do the actors, who must survive in a cruel profession, perhaps think that it makes no difference?

There is also further reinterpretation from Brook, as the preliminary reading continues. In the lovers' quarrels and mistakings of Act Three[15], 'there is nothing to suggest comedy,' he tells the actors. It is 'black farce', 'a nightmare', with 'true nightmare emotions.' 'Standard productions,' he declares, 'fall into mannerism, dullness and "business"' with the fancy-sick lovers; it can produce only boredom. Instead, the actors should 'look for the dark qualities in the writing'. This sounds nearer to instruction than an invitation to seek out an inner rhythm. But Helena's cross exchanges with Hermia – 'Ay, do! Persever . . . make mouths upon me when I turn my back,' Helena says to her[16] – are taking on life, even in this uncertain reading. The syllables upon the inert page seem already to be moving, and in read insult and accusation it is as if the Chinese box of theatrical truth within truth, or falsehood within falsehood, might already be beginning to open.

In these exchanges, says Brook, sitting in the quiet circle, the actors must become victims of their own 'suggestive craft'. The trading of insult should hurt; the 'absolute truth,' he says, is what the lovers cannot take. But what Brook does not, and cannot, say is that the truth of the theatre can never be absolute. And, in any case, it is the playwright's truth in the last instance, and not that of the actors. A moment later he contradicts himself, in this early effort (a monologue and a struggle) for clarification. The 'central issue' of the play, he says, is the difference between 'good untruth', or the acting of the lovers,

17 *Helena:* O weary night, O long and tedious night,
 Abate thy hours! Shine comforts from the east,
 That I may back to Athens by daylight,
 From these that my poor company detest:
 And sleep, that sometimes shuts up sorrow's eye,
 Steal me awhile from mine own company.

(Sleeps)
(III.ii.431–436)

18 *Hippolyta:* I was with Hercules and Cadmus once,
 When in a wood of Crete they bayed the bear
 With hounds of Sparta. Never did I hear
 Such gallant chiding; for, besides the groves,
 The skies, the fountains, every region near
 Seemed all one mutual cry. I never heard
 So musical a discord, such sweet thunder.

(IV.i.109–115)

19 *Snout:* Will not the ladies be afeared of the lion?
 Starveling: I fear it, I promise you.
 Bottom: Masters, you ought to consider with yourselves. To bring in –
 God shield us! – a lion among ladies is a most dreadful thing . . .
 Snout: . . . Therefore another prologue must tell he is not a lion.

(III.i.25–31)

and 'bad untruth', or the acting of the mechanicals. In the puzzled silence, I would like to ask a not wholly relevant question: are 'bad untruth', and bad acting, less of a risk – in the political, as well as in the theatrical arena – to our capacity for judgment and to our freedom, because not believed in, and therefore not entrapping?

But here it is the way to 'good untruth' at its most beguiling which Brook, the actors, and the theatre in general are bent on finding. As Helena lies down to sleep, sitting bolt upright, exhausted by love's contentions, Brook asks her to sing 'O weary night, O long and tedious night'[17]. And having sung her lines, in her own plainchant, Brook says: 'Now speak them.' (This must be what he meant yesterday by 'broadening' the lyrical into singing.) To the silent spectator on his metal chair, her speech sounds for a fleeting moment like song. Yet within minutes – spent wondering what it was I heard – Shakespeare's own verse outsings it, spoken thoughtfully and without such prompting-to-music. 'I was with Hercules and Cadmus once,'[18] says Hippolyta, sitting on stained canvas, 'When in a wood of Crete they bayed the bear/ with hounds of Sparta. Never did I hear/ such gallant chiding . . .'; and, read steadily, the words seem to soar beyond the range of any possible voice which might speak them, as well as every device of the director. (Is this poetry in the spoken, or in the unspoken? In the verbal, or the pre-verbal?)

There are also longueurs in this patient reading, and distractions. Thighs and buttocks stir uncomfortably on the canvas. With the tea-mugs, a hesitant and unequal discourse begins between Brook and the actors. Flute the bellows-mender, stretched out in jeans, remarks that the mechanicals are 'very pure characters'. He tells Brook that he thinks they are 'not the usual rude yokels'; and they have 'respect for ladies'[19]. Brook does not take, or does not hear, the point. 'They have their own secure world,' he answers briefly. But this, too, is (characteristically?) an a-social reference, and without context. For the seeming truth about them, as Shakespeare delineates it and as Flute has discovered, is that they are also self-respecting craftsmen, with their own recognizable values. Is this vein of class one that Brook is not interested in exploring? Why not?

'Will there be fairies?' someone asks idly, sipping tea. There is laughter. 'There will be no fairies,' Brook says dismissively; 'only sound and choral voices.' 'Will there be a set?' someone else asks. 'Why should there be a set?' Brook answers. (Is this the tip of a caprice showing?) 'In a dream,' he says, 'places displace each other, contrary

²⁰ *Bottom:* All that I will tell you is, that the Duke hath dined. Get your apparel together, good strings to your beards, new ribbons to your pumps; meet presently at the palace; every man look o'er his part; for the short and the long is, our play is preferred. In any case, let Thisby have clean linen; and let not him that plays the lion pare his nails, for they shall hang out for the lion's claws. And, most dear actors, eat no onions nor garlic, for we are to utter sweet breath.

(*IV.ii.30–40*)

²¹ *Theseus:* This fellow doth not stand upon points.
Lysander: He hath rid his prologue like a rough colt; he knows not the stop. A good moral, my lord: it is not enough to speak, but to speak true.
Hippolyta: Indeed he hath played on this prologue like a child on a recorder; a sound, but not in government.
Theseus: His speech was like a tangled chain; nothing impaired, but all disordered. Who is next?

(*V.i.118–125*)

²² (*Enter LYSANDER, DEMETRIUS, HERMIA and HELENA*)
Theseus: Here come the lovers, full of joy and mirth.
Joy, gentle friends! Joy and fresh days of love
Accompany your hearts!

(*V.i.28–30*)

²³ *Hippolyta:* This is the silliest stuff that ever I heard.
Theseus: The best in this kind are but shadows; and the worst are no worse, if imagination amend them.
Hippolyta: It must be your imagination then, and not theirs.
Theseus: If we imagine no worse of them than they of themselves, they may pass for excellent men.

(*V.i.208–214*)

to all logic.' This is a conversation-stopper; the actors loll about in the silence. And when the reading resumes, it is again the theme of reality and illusion which regularly draws Brook's comments.

Thus Bottom's abrupt Fourth Act announcement to the mechanicals, when he has been restored to them from his enchantment, that 'our play is preferred'[20], is 'the actors' nightmare' played out in full view of an audience. Moreoever, Shakespeare's text has created the illusion, illusion within illusion, that the mechanicals have merely so far been rehearsing, and that the 'greater reality' of a first-night performance before the Court of Athens is now approaching. (That this is also a rehearsal within a rehearsal for a September opening on the banks of the Avon, no one cares to mention.)

The opening scene of the Fifth Act, for Brook, is even more deeply entangled in the coils of illusion. On the one hand, Theseus, Hippolyta and the courtiers – or, rather, the actors who play them – are acting out their court roles[21] ('behaving like shits', as Brook puts it), and at the same time celebrating a wedding, while several of them are also 'supposedly' in love[22]. On the other hand, the mechanicals are 'ostentatiously acting as actors', but wanting to be believed, while at the same time trying to enact a love, that between Pyramus and Thisby, which they do not feel. Moreover, though none of the mechanicals' court-audience will 'use its imagination' – instead, audibly mocking the players throughout – yet still their play of *Pyramus and Thisby* 'works in its ludicrous fashion' because 'we, the audience, use our imagination against the Court's'.

Indeed we could add that it is Theseus and Hippolyta (alias Shakespeare) who give us the advice to 'amend' the result of the players' poor efforts[23], though they do not appear to take the advice to heart themselves. 'Since the one thing which acting can't be is real,' Brook says at this point in the reading, 'it again raises the question: what is the difference between the worst and best acting, and whose imagination is it which will change the one into the other?' Or, as Theseus puts it, 'The best in this kind are but shadows; and the worst are no worse, if imagination amend them'[23]. But to the fact that behind these shadows stood Shakespeare, who conceived the whole in *his* imagination, and placed every word of their discourse into their mouths – in a writing which is as 'real' as pen-and-ink, or the text in our hands, can make it – no one refers for a moment.

And at the close of the text, and the day's rehearsal, with Puck's 'If we shadows have offended,/ Think but this, and all is mended:/ That

[24] *Puck:* If we shadows have offended,
Think but this, and all is mended:
That you have but slumb'red here,
While these visions did appear.
And this weak and idle theme,
No more yielding but a dream,
Gentles, do not reprehend:
If you pardon, we will mend.
And, as I am an honest Puck,
If we have unearnèd luck,
Now to scape the serpent's tongue,
We will make amends 'ere long.

(V.i.412–423)

you have but slumb'red here,/ While these visions did appear[24], which sustains a central theme of the play to its very last stanzas, Brook says that this is 'the most inner portion of the whole drama'. The end of it, he adds, is 'tantalizingly close to something secret and mysterious. We approach here whatever is behind the whole play.' That it is Shakespeare, no one is saying.

First week, third day

So far, and these are early days, the largest emphasis has been placed by Brook upon the actors' skills and imaginations. Might it be that the term 'director's theatre' (like the 'Theatre of Cruelty') is a distracting nonsense? Since Brook can plainly be moved only by his own impulse, what does it mean to say that he is a 'Grotowskian'? At least, if the actors are capable of it – which is by no means certain – the possibility seems to exist of a far-reaching exploration of *A Midsummer Night's Dream*, and even of its author's intentions.

And if fidelity to the text-as-written is the test of how far Brook's regard for himself – which is plainly considerable – overshadows his regard for Shakespeare, the value Brook ascribes to the search for the lines' 'inner rhythm' seems to point to an unexpected answer. Certainly there appears to be little likelihood, in this production at least, of gratuitous 'improvements' to 'the script'. Yet, metal plates and rods have made an appearance this morning, and are being falteringly spun, clangingly dropped and spun again, by way of exercise. A technique is being learned at a director's behest, for a purpose which does not appear to be clear to the actors, and is not the subject of discussion.

During the exercise, Brook comes up to me suddenly and talks about the production, while the plates spin, drop and are re-mounted in the background. He says that direction is a solitary task, and that response and suggestion are welcome. (Does he mean it? I am awkward, because as unsure whether I am being patronized, as the actors seem to be.) I ask him, *à propos* of his search begun yesterday with the company, whether he believes there is an 'objective rhythm' in the lines, a something certain to be uncovered, or a 'rhythm' in each actor which each actor must discover. He says, first, that 'of course there is no objective rhythm'. That there is, he adds, is an idea still vigorously peddled, both in the academic notion of the 'sub-text' and

[25] *Lysander:* How now, my love! Why is your cheek so pale?
How chance the roses there do fade so fast?
Hermia: Belike for want of rain, which I could well
Beteem them from the tempest of my eyes.
Lysander: Ay me! . . .
The course of true love never did run smooth.

(I.i.128–134)

in the Royal Shakespeare Company's own practice. Within the Company, it is still believed (by some) that there are 'correct and incorrect ways of speaking Shakespeare'; in our period, he says, it reveals itself in the emphasis on a 'realistic stress' to communicate a practical and prosaic meaning to today's audiences.

This is 'wrong', says Brook. Why? 'Because you cannot decide until the actor faces the words for the first time.' But then Brook qualifies his earlier answer (as he often does with the actors), though it does not become clearer. There is 'both a rhythm to be found and a particular actor to find it.' That is, 'what one actor finds will not be what another actor finds.' It will be his or her rhythm, married to the words' rhythm as he or she finds it. Yet, I say to him, this leaves a large number of problems unsolved, and (feebly) 'even beyond description.' Yes, Brook replies; you need 'an almost metaphysical explanation' of the process of 'finding the rhythm'. But, he adds, there are also moments when it emerges clearly in speech and action, and is 'felt to be right' by everyone, though 'rarely at this stage in the process of rehearsal.'

I referred to yesterday's sung speech. Would he keep it in performance? Did I mean good singing, or bad singing? Good singing. Possibly. But this 'word-singing', as he called it, was principally a means to rediscover lyrical impulse. Without it, the 'life of the line' is lost in 'the habit of concentration on the meaning of the individual word.' He mocks the actor who turns into a 'student of Eng.lit., with his pencil out, underlining the words'. But, as he returns to the actors, a shadow deepens.

What if the 'truth' which must be found, this 'rhythm beyond meaning' which must be revealed by the actors, is beyond their (or anyone's) reach? Or, what if this last recess of 'truth' was contained only in the mind of Shakespeare? Does not the ultimate unattainability of Brook's demands make the actors vulnerable to him? Why has the word 'exploitation' come into my mind, for the first time, this morning? If the actors must move beyond, or below, the threshold of rational understanding of meaning, does it not disable them, by plunging them into a world of mystification, whose key is for ever in the hands of the director, or the mind of Shakespeare? An image of the actor's isolation – as deep as my own – stands before me, like the ghost of Banquo, or Hamlet's father.

The reading resumes, once more from Act One, Scene One and the exchanges between Hermia and Lysander[25]. 'It is not necessary,' Brook tells the two actors, 'to follow the lines intellectually.'

26 *Hermia:* My good Lysander!
   I swear to thee, by Cupid's strongest bow,
   By his best arrow with the golden head,
   By the simplicity of Venus' doves,
   By that which knitteth souls and prospers loves,
   And by that fire which burned the Carthage queen,
   When the false Troyan under sail was seen,
   By all the vows that ever men have broke,
   In number more than ever woman spoke,
   In that same place thou has appointed me,
   Tomorrow truly will I meet with thee.
Lysander: Keep promise, love.

(I.i.168–179)

27 *Hermia:* I frown upon him, yet he loves me still.
Helena: O that your frowns would teach my smiles such skill!
Hermia: I give him curses, yet he gives me love.
Helena: O that my prayers could such affection move!
Hermia: The more I hate, the more he follows me.
Helena: The more I love, the more he hateth me.
Hermia: His folly, Helena, is no fault of mine.
Helena: None, but your beauty: would that fault were mine!

(I.i.194–201)

28 *Helena:* How happy some o'er other some can be!
   Through Athens I am thought as fair as she.
   But what of that? Demetrius thinks not so;
   He will not know what all but he do know.
   And as he errs, doting on Hermia's eyes,
   So I, admiring of his qualities.
   Things base and vile, holding no quantity,
   Love can transpose to form and dignity.
   Love looks not with the eyes, but with the mind,
   And therefore is winged Cupid painted blind.

(I.i.226–235)

Describing what he means with sinuous gestures, he says: 'One must feel the passage of the words slipping in and out of plot, and in and out of action, feel the deep impulse in Lysander to comfort and reassure her.' In the speaking and re-speaking which follow, under this guidance, the actors try to fulfil Brook's purpose. 'What kind of moment is she unfolding?', Brook asks of Hermia's speech 'My good Lysander! I swear to thee . . .'[26] This speech, he says, is 'like movement'. 'Find the movement,' he tells the actress. 'Find the shape and rhythm of the lines. Speak them with the lightest physical touch, so that you can't tell whether you are doing it to the words, or the words to you.'

Brook is attempting to get behind those responses to the language of their lines, in this case love's language, which have been prescribed, or imposed, by convention. It is as if he is trying to reach a state of pre-conventional innocence which, he says, attaches to the 'non-verbal'; and as if he is, at the same time, striving for a heightened sensitivity both to the text's language and (even) to the impulses which led Shakespeare to their particular selection. 'See,' Brook says of Hermia's 'By all the vows that ever men have broke'[26], how 'it moves by itself.' 'Allow yourself to swing in its direction,' he says to her; 'let each line be a separate trip, and you will see how each line in the speech is quite different from another.'

What is unremarked upon, however – and is today increasingly audible – is not the words' 'hidden rhythm', but the extent of the simple rhyming which Shakespeare employs in these lyrical exchanges[27]. Sometimes they continue for pages at a time. Moreover, these are (unsurprisingly) the same passages in which Brook's impulse to come as close as possible to song has been most insistent. And it is, above all, in rhyme that Shakespeare, this time unexpectedly, expresses the deepest anguish of his lovers; an anguish which also seems from today's reading to be both theme and mood of the whole drama.

Today, a sharper light shines too on the complexity of Shakespeare's concern with the nature of truth and illusion. It is Helena who, in the reading, suddenly seems to have some of the profoundest and most philosophically taxing lines on the subject. 'Love,' she says, 'looks not with the eyes, but with the mind,/ And therefore is winged Cupid painted blind.'[28] Is she, and Shakespeare, also saying that the deepest truth resides in the mind of the creator and not in the sight of the spectator? In the idea (or dream), and not in the

²⁹ *Helena:* O weary night, O long and tedious night,
    Abate thy hours! Shine comforts from the east,
    That I may back to Athens by daylight,
    From these that my poor company detest:
    And sleep, that sometimes shuts up sorrow's eye,
    Steal me awhile from mine own company.

                         (Sleeps)
                     (III.ii.431–436)

³⁰ *Fairy:* Over hill, over dale,
    Thorough bush, thorough brier,
    Over park, over pale,
    Thorough flood, thorough fire,
    I do wander everywhere,
    Swifter than the moon's sphere;
    And I serve the Fairy Queen,
    To dew her orbs upon the green.
    The cowslips tall her pensioners be:
    In their gold coats spots you see;
    Those be rubies, fairy favours,
    In those freckles live their savours.

                         (II.i.2–13)

³¹ *Hermia:* But, gentle friend, for love and courtesy
    Lie further off, in human modesty.
    Such separation as may well be said
    Becomes a virtuous bachelor and a maid,
    So far be distant; and, good night, sweet friend.
    Thy love ne'er alter till thy sweet life end!
Lysander: Amen, amen, to that fair prayer, say I,
    And then end life when I end loyalty!
    Here is my bed. Sleep give thee all his rest!
Hermia: With half that wish the wisher's eyes be pressed! *(They sleep)*

                         (II.ii.56–65)

visible elements of its portrayal, whether enacted in life or through a staged drama? But if we are deceived by appearance – as are Shakespeare's bewitched lovers – we can also be oppressed by the truth, and seek to flee it, as Helena does. For when she calls on sleep to 'shut up sorrow's eye' and 'steal me awhile from mine own company'[29], she is seeking escape into her own midsummer night's dreaming, and access to an inward world of wishful thinking. There is truth in thought, but there is illusion also.

The session ends with further tentative exploration. Its first subject is the speech 'Over hill, over dale'[30], which begins the Second Act. As an initial step, Brook asks that its lines be spoken in alternation by two actors; then that each *line* be divided in half between two actors; then that each *word* of each line be spoken in alternation by two actors. The same exercise is repeated, using four actors, the allocation of lines and parts of lines being made by the actors themselves on quick impulse. In a second step, the reading of the lines consists of alternation between one actor speaking his line, part–line or word alone – and two or three of the other actors speaking their allotted line, part–line or word simultaneously, in chorus. (In the initial stage, this was regarded as a mishap.)

For the third step, Brook says: 'Now bring something extra to the pattern. Listen to the rhythm of whoever is speaking. Complement it by echo and repetition of word or line. Take over one from the other. Take it like a jazz improvisation.' The effect of the swift susurration (in the creaking studio) is immediate and electric. But the tremor of excitement is cut off quickly by the experiment's final motion. 'Be freer still,' says Brook. 'Repeat words and lines freely, speaking simultaneously, adding free sounds to words in improvisation.' It is a counterpoint of the verbal and the non–verbal, in which the ear strains to catch at meaning, while the eye catches sight of the first stress in the actors.

Then, when the resumed reading reaches the Second Act exchanges between Lysander and Hermia, as they prepare to sleep[31], Brook says 'See, from the profusion and brightness of the words, how bright and alert they are.' Yet the reading itself is flagging. He asks that the closing lines of this passage be sung. Energies are waning. 'So far be distant; and, good night, sweet friend'[31], sung, is merely winsome. Lysander's 'Amen, amen, to that fair prayer'[31] proves unsingable. Brook, tauter, says 'Quietly find the sound, the rhythm. Then see how free you are to swing from line to line of it.' But there seems to have

2   The first rehearsal of *Pyramus and Thisby*, overseen by the court and fairies (Act One, Scene Two); (l. to r.) Barry Stanton (Snug), Glynne Lewis (Flute), Terrence Hardiman (Starveling), David Waller (Bottom), Philip Locke (Quince) and Norman Rodway (Snout).

been a deadly *volte-face* in the rehearsal. Under pressure, there is less – not more – freedom in song, or sing-song. And the two pages of lovers' rhyme which follow, spoken with relief and tired exhilaration, are Shakespeare's own requital of the urge to sing.

First week, fourth day

Amid all the exploration, the compulsion in some directors to dominate the actors emotionally goes unexplored. A submerged struggle of wills is going on here, but whether it will break out into the open is another matter. The moulding of words and bodies on the potter's wheel of theatrical direction is a cruel process. After all, the shaping of one's own interior impulse at the behest of another, who is invested with the task of command over the enterprise of theatrical manufacture, is a question of the subordination of one set of emotions to another. Is there yet another play in rehearsal here, in which Brook is not the director, but the chief actor?

Yesterday also seemed to reveal how taxing in its subconscious effects upon the actors – however well-trained to abnegation – is the pressure for a surrender of will, and the unequal alliance based upon it. Thus there are other truths and other illusions beyond those posed by Shakespeare's text; while the invitation to a baring of emotions, or to a search (in public) for the inner springs of the actor's own promptings, has also got to be 'good theatre'. Or could it be, instead, that the actor or actress who is experienced and knowing will simply find out what is wanted, and discover the means to provide it? Could the deepest truth (one free of directorial illusion) be that the best way to withhold, and protect, the self is to attend carefully to the director's directions? Is all this the building of castles in the air, illusion upon illusion?

Certainly, this complex relationship between actors and director, precisely because it is based on so many suppressed factors which few of the actual participants would want to acknowledge, seems to be at odds with the innocent quest for truth. This is particularly so when such a theatre's demand for integrity of response is also one which must be tailored to the needs of the box-office. At any rate, I try to explain to myself why my own uneasy feelings here (did I really bring them all with me?) have so far been shadowed by a sense that there is a lack of artistic and personal candour – even artistic deceit – in these relationships, for all the daily talk of truth in rehearsal. The actors, too,

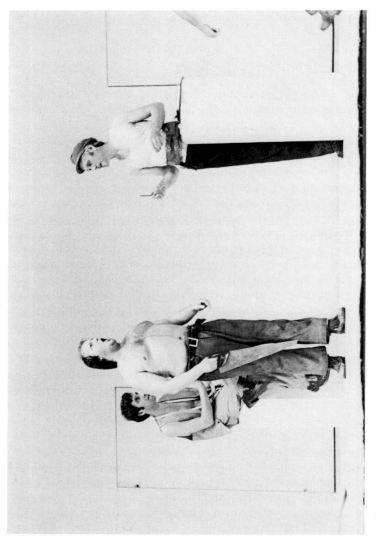

3 Quince: 'You may do it extempore, for it is nothing but roaring.' (Act One, Scene Two); (l. to r.) Terrence Hardiman (Starveling), Barry Stanton (Snug) and Philip Locke (Quince).

seem isolated from one another and from the director; and vice-versa. They seem to bring this isolation, and their insecurities personal and professional, to rehearsal with them. And yet, despite it, they must forge out of it a sense of ensemble, of artistic collaboration, and find 'the truth' together.

Another early source of puzzlement is this: Brook is an innovator. He is constantly in search of a new approach to Shakespeare. What is the nature of this newness, this innovation? To what species of politics, if any, is it attached? Is he a radical of the right, as I suspect, or of the left? Is this question in any case relevant? So far, his perception of the mechanicals has seemed to me a-social. And the word 'class', for good or ill, has not been mentioned. Yet even a casual reading of *A Midsummer Night's Dream*, let alone watching it in rehearsal, suggests it as a factor in Shakespeare's own perception of the relation between mechanicals and courtiers.

Brook's concerns are different. Two lines of inquiry have evidently been started. One is into the rhythmic properties of Shakespeare's speech, the other into the nature of truth and illusion as Shakespeare presents it in *A Midsummer Night's Dream*. As to the first: the beginnings of exploration into song-speech, a variety of *sprecht-stimme*, in order to find a way to the heart of Shakespeare's lyrical inspiration, seems to be coming up against both incapacity and incomprehension in the actors. For one thing (again, for good or ill) they lack an understanding of Brook's ceremonial intention. The gap between their artistic formation and his is a large, and perhaps unbridgeable, one. A priestly or hieratic theatre of ultimate truths is, in any case, alien to the English mode. Brook in accent, manner, bearing, appearance and intellectual-artistic preoccupation is palpably 'un-English'. Another puzzle: who and what is he? He seems to have more in common with Peter Ustinov than Peter Hall, but I cannot place it.

But Brook is much more right than wrong in searching for new ways of verse-speaking in general, and Shakespeare-speaking in particular. After all, theatrical sound in the classical or national theatres of Europe – whatever the fringe may have achieved – is not much developed beyond, say, the modernist equivalent of the Debussian in music. What the mainstream theatre needs, just to start with, is a first performance of Stravinsky's *Rite of Spring* in theatrical terms, with or without its accompanying riot. And that was nearly 60 years ago. The standard amalgam of nineteenth-century declamation, Victorian and

[32] *Demetrius:* Relent, sweet Hermia: and, Lysander, yield
    Thy crazed title to my certain right.
Lysander: You have her father's love, Demetrius;
    Let me have Hermia's: do you marry him.
Egeus: Scornful Lysander! True, he hath my love,
    And what is mine my love shall render him.
    And she is mine, and all my right of her
    I do estate unto Demetrius.

(I.i.91–98)

Edwardian kitsch, the prosaic realism of the 20th century and a space-age set is mere fustian. As for the curly-headed swains of Shakespeare's Arcadia, tremulous in voice and lithe in body, they have made of *A Midsummer Night's Dream* a world as frozen as that of *Swan Lake*, its nearest artistic compeer in our culture.

These actors, this morning, are swinging on gymnasium ropes, and spinning metal discs. No Arcadia threatens here, at least for the time being. Moreover, one of Brook's pre-verbal exercises followed. The whole company sat in a circle. Brook asked them to close their eyes, sitting close but not touching, and to communicate with each other by sound. They (the young, the older, the less staid and the staider) were to 'wait in total silence', until they could 'produce a deep inner sound, a vibration, in the solar plexus'. This sound was heard, just, after about half-a-minute, though it was impossible to say who was doing it, whether it was done in calculation or from a deeper impulse, and for whose satisfaction. Then, in what appeared to be – among some of the cast – a rapidly induced state of trance, others began to 'answer'. The sound was a low one, borborygmic, more like a movement of the bowels than a Socratic discourse.

Eventually, Brook stopped it. (Half of the cast remained in what appeared to be, or was simulated to appear to be, an hypnotized condition of suspended animation.) He told them 'not to control the sound intellectually, by mind', but to 'let it govern them'. 'There is also a kind of listening,' Brook continued (as some of the cast, with ostentatious subtlety, stirred from its slumbers) 'which releases something in everybody.' But at the proposition that one can both speak and listen with one's solar plexus, there was also a faint flicker of suppressed incredulity – suppressed by awe, or suppressed by profession. Only barely discernible, it was betrayed by the most covert and expressionless of exchanged glances; the briefest of spasms, passing like a (surprisingly small) cloud on a distant horizon.

Yet in these first three days, the ears are being pricked by Brook to many other sounds than either the pre-verbal or the sylvan. Thus, when the reading commences (once more from Act One, Scene One), Egeus seems to command Hermia in soul and body. 'She is mine,' he says, 'and all my right of her I do bequeath unto Demetrius'[32]; he as much the proprietor of her freedom of will and the play of her motions, as Brook has appeared in relation to all the actors. Her own isolation as an actress even seems to deepen; as if she were entirely confined within the play's matrix.

^{33} *Lysander:* Or, if there were a sympathy in choice,
War, death, or sickness did lay siege to it,
Making it momentany as a sound,
Swift as a shadow, short as any dream,
Brief as the lightning in the collied night,
That, in a spleen, unfolds both heaven and earth,
And ere a man hath power to say 'Behold!'
The jaws of darkness do devour it up:
So quick bright things come to confusion.

$(I.i.141–149)$

^{34} *Puck:* I am that merry wanderer of the night.
I jest to Oberon, and make him smile . . .
The wisest aunt, telling the saddest tale,
Sometime for three-foot stool mistaketh me;
Then slip I from her bum, down topples she,
And 'tailor' cries, and falls into a cough;
And then the whole quire hold their hips and laugh,
And waxen in their mirth, and neeze, and swear
A merrier hour was never wasted there.
But, room fairy! Here comes Oberon.
Fairy: And here my mistress. Would that he were gone!
                    (*Enter OBERON at one door with his train;
                    and TITANIA at another, with hers*)
Oberon: Ill met by moonlight, proud Titania.

$(II.i.43–60)$

^{35} *Oberon:*   Thou rememb'rest
Since once I sat upon a promontory,
And heard a mermaid, on a dolphin's back,
Uttering such dulcet and harmonious breath,
That the rude sea grew civil at her song . . .
Puck: I remember.

$(II.i.148–154)$

^{36} *Demetrius:* Tempt not too much the hatred of my spirit,
For I am sick when I do look on thee.
Helena: And I am sick when I look not on you.
Demetrius: You do impeach your modesty too much,
To leave the city, and commit yourself
Into the hands of one that loves you not.

$(II.i.211–216)$

And in Lysander's speech, 'Or, if there was a sympathy in choice'[33], already several times repeated but as if unheard until this reading, is more new light in darkness. Indeed, lightning is one of its subjects. ''Ere a man hath power to say "Behold!"'', Lysander tells Hermia, 'the jaws of darkness do devour it up:/ So quick bright things come to confusion'[33]. Love's course, thwarted by 'war, death or sickness', can also be 'swift as a shadow, short as any dream'[33], its truth – such as it is – glimpsed only for a moment. But so it is here too, in this rehearsal struggle for illumination and in the search for the 'moment of truth' for actor and audience.

Today, Brook also expects the actors to find their way to their own choice of vowels, syllables, words or lines to heighten and intone amid the spoken cadences. Thus Puck, swinging rhythmically back and forth above the rest of the cast, sings as he speaks 'I am that merry wanderer of the night'[34]. Below, the others – whispering, coughing, laughing, sneezing – echo, repeat, illustrate and counterpoint his singing, until he leaps down among them at 'Here comes Oberon'[34]. Oberon's voice is cold and proud against it; his 'Ill met by moonlight'[34] cuts into and extinguishes the rustle of still echoing sound. And within minutes, comes the first moment of raptness in rehearsal, close to thinking aloud. 'Thou rememb'rest,' Oberon whispers to Puck in a sharing as near to silence as words can come, 'Since once I sat upon a promontory,/ And heard a mermaid, on a dolphin's back'[35] . . . 'I remember,' says Puck, and there is in all the cast a held inhalation, a first sense of achievement. 'Now mystery is breaking through,' says Brook. 'Oberon is opening up in the right direction for you all. Borrow from each other. Listen.'

Demetrius and Helena promptly did so[36], but too literally, whispering 'inwardly' to each other, precisely as Oberon and Puck had just done. It immediately appeared contrived and monotonous, both unfelt and in every respect unfounded: a theatrical alchemy in which base metal can be made from gold, with a speed which is dumbfounding, 'so quick bright things come to confusion'. And yet also within seconds, an inwardness close to day-dreaming was again momentarily found, with what appeared to be the same devices of feelings, and once more by Puck and Oberon. 'I know a bank where the wild thyme blows'[37] seemed to be whispered thought made palpable for an instant, a dream-world conjured up by voice and presence out of a field of stained canvas. (Was the effort of it disciplined by the solar plexus, by reason, by feeling, by experience, or by all of them together? Is it in the words, or in the actors?)

33

³⁷ *Oberon:* I know a bank where the wild thyme blows,
Where oxlips and the nodding violet grows,
Quite overcanopied with luscious woodbine,
With sweet musk roses, and with eglantine.
There sleeps Titania sometime of the night,
Lulled in these flowers with dances and delight.

(II.i.249–254)

³⁸   *(The Fairies sing)*
1st Fairy: You spotted snakes with double tongue,
Thorny hedgehogs, be not seen;
Newts and blindworms, do no wrong,
Come not near our Fairy Queen.
Chorus: Philomele, with melody
Sing in our sweet lullaby;
Lulla, lulla, lullaby, lulla, lulla, lullaby.

(II.ii.9–15)

³⁹   *(Enter LYSANDER and HERMIA)*
Lysander: Fair love, you faint with wand'ring in the wood;
And to speak troth, I have forgot our way.
We'll rest us, Hermia, if you think it good,
And tarry for the comfort of the day.
Hermia: Be't so, Lysander.

(II.ii.35–39)

⁴⁰ *Hermia: (Awaking)* Help me, Lysander, help me! Do thy best
To pluck this crawling serpent from my breast!
Ay me, for pity! What a dream was here!
Lysander, look how I do quake with fear!

(II.ii.145–148)

⁴¹ *Hermia:* Hate me! Wherefore? O me! What news, my love!
Am not I Hermia? Are not you Lysander?
I am as fair now as I was erewhile.
Since night you loved me; yet since night you left me.
Why, then you left me – O, the gods forbid! –
In earnest, shall I say?

(III.ii.272–277)

'You spotted snakes with double tongue'[38] was in its turn counterpointed, at Brook's prompting, with echoes and *ritornellos*; and on this rare occasion, the text itself goes a long way to invite them. Moreover, the rehearsal suddenly seems, for the first time, to be taking fire. But Brook instructs Hermia and Lysander, 'faint with wand'ring'[39] in the magical forest, that they should 'draw their emotions' not out of a dream, but 'from nightmare'. Arms akimbo, it is he who seems now to be standing over the actors, his own mood bearing down hard upon them. And Hermia's 'Help me, Lysander, help me!'[40] now seems both a lost lover's cry, and panic under pressure; more a reaction to Brook, than to Shakespeare.

There is weariness in it, too – as if from nowhere – and a mood of isolation which is oppressive (is this volatility in me, or in the actors?). Those with least resilience and experience, such as Hermia, seem to exhaust their capacity to respond almost as soon as they have found it. Nervous and ill-at-ease, it is as if she has doused the rehearsal fire single-handed. A pall descends on the whole reading, during which Brook himself is thrown off-balance. For the first time without vivid or useful guidance to offer, he appears unable to interest the actors, who look as if they have stopped taking in what he is saying. The 'inner stillness' and the 'nightmare emotion' which, with such delicacy of voice and such ponderous insistence, he is demanding of them they seem quite unable to deliver.

It is a stalemate. Moreover, Brook lacks precisely the wit, brio and emotional virtuosity (or human warmth) which could have reanimated the actors' spirits. Instead, he persisted; not diminishing but increasing the pressure. Hermia is taken to task for being 'uncertain' and 'wounded' in her Third Act altercation with Helena[41], yet many of the lines which Shakespeare gives her are themselves questioning and uncertain in impulse, difficult to shape, and often serve as no more than a foil to the other actors. At the end of the Act, Brook, in a mood of thwarted endeavour close to anger, was doggedly instructing Helena, the dispirited Hermia ('I can no further crawl, no further go')[42] and Puck to sing their closing speeches[42]. He seemed to stand over them once more, as they now sang against the grain of their own feeling: an image which, with others from the first week's struggles, I took away with me into the streets of Shakespeare's Stratford.

⁴² *Hermia:* Never so weary, never so in woe;
    Bedabbled with the dew and torn with briers,
    I can no further crawl, no further go;
    My legs can keep no pace with my desires.
    Here will I rest me till the break of day.
    Heavens shield Lysander, if they mean a fray!   (*Lies down and*
      sleeps)
  Puck: On the ground
    Sleep sound:
    I'll apply
    To your eye,
    Gentle lover, remedy.

                (*Squeezing the juice on Lysander's eye*)

    When thou wak'st,
    Thou tak'st
    True delight
    In the sight
    Of thy former lady's eye.

                      (*III.ii.442–457*)

Second week, first day

It has taken me until now to realize that Brook does not himself speak any line as he wishes it to be spoken. Instead, he uses other words and sometimes complicated circumlocutions to indicate what he wants. Nor does he follow the text, in rehearsal. He appears to expect the actors to provide him with his bearings, as they do, without himself scrutinizing in detail, or even at all, what they are saying. He doesn't have an accurate memory of the lines either, but only an approximate one, and seldom refers to them by specific quotation.

And as with speech, so with gesture; which so far he has rarely himself demonstrated. Part of the reason must be his own physical awkwardness and inhibition. Indeed, he often seems embarrassed with himself and his appearance, which is perhaps merely the obverse of self-regard. I had always assumed that the theatre director was likely to be a playwright *manqué*. Could he also be the *manqué* actor?

Now, as the actors re-assemble, it is plain that after only one week of rehearsal they could not yet be in any sense the characters of *A Midsummer Night's Dream*. What they have said and done, for the most part, seems so far to have issued neither from thought nor feeling. They also seem characterless in themselves, as if they were lost in a limbo; as if they have not yet found a role in their lines, and as if their words and gestures are still without meaning. But how much of this characterlessness is in the text, or in the embryo form of this production? Is it a measure of success or failure, in terms of Brook's aspiration?

It is interesting that Hazlitt wrote of the play that 'when acted, [it] is converted from a delightful fiction into a dull pantomime. All that is finest in the play is lost in the representation . . . the spirit evaporated, the genius fled . . . that which was merely an airy shape, a dream, a passing thought, immediately becomes an unmanageable reality'. Brook is clearly trying, *inter alia*, to avoid and overcome this – not by a

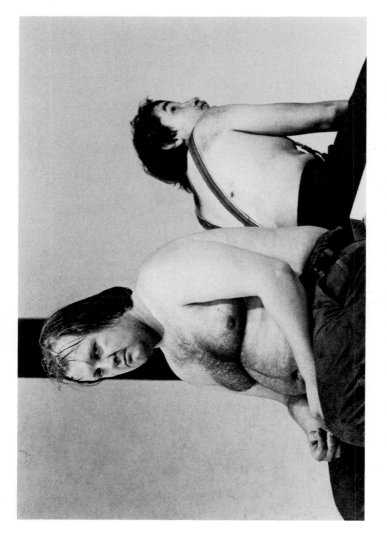

4 Two disconsolate mechanicals, after Bottom's claim on their roles (Act One, Scene Two); Barry Stanton (Snug), and Glynne Lewis (Flute).

technical mastery of the business of simulating the 'magic' of the play, but (hopefully) by recreating the processes and rhythms of thought which underlie its lines, the impulses which lie behind the notation of sounds inscribed on the page. But quite apart from other problems, including the portentousness of such an enterprise, the actors look and sound as if they are finding it difficult to share Brook's sense of purpose. Early days though these are, they also appear to lack any developing desire to enter the world of pre-verbal vibrations to which Brook is referring them.

Is this a lack of creative imagination? Does their training and upbringing in the English theatre extinguish the possibility of it? Or is it a case of the horse-sense of the mechanicals preserving them from the airy-fairy? Later today, I had a talk with Brook on this, and other subjects; and, in addition, he several times asked me for my reactions during rehearsal. Among the things I discussed with him were the images of isolation, anguish and confinement being suggested to me by the rehearsals. 'It is good to be so provoked by what you are seeing as to feel frustration,' he said quickly, a response as two-edged as my own. He acknowledged that there were such images which could be educed from the text of *A Midsummer Night's Dream*, but that 'whatever there is in Shakespeare of this, will also present its opposite.' I did not know exactly what he meant, but I took it to be a disclaimer of any one-sided interpretation of the play, in favour of a wider and more various reading of it. I did not tell him that his own view of it would (necessarily) be as particular as anyone else's.

We also spoke of the nature of the 'creative moments' in rehearsal, when a so-far fleeting sense of discovery and illumination suddenly raises the spirits, and – however briefly – suggests the ultimate possibility of exhilaration in performance. Was everyone aware simultaneously of such moments? He thought they were. For these moments, when feelings, words and movements came together and fused into new life, depended on 'the running of a current', an opening to which all present contribute. I asked him whether he thought that these and other experiences of rehearsal could be described, captured, in words. Were words adequate? 'Not at all. Of course not,' he replied with some asperity. 'And only if I can see what is written,' he added, in what I thought – with equal exasperation – was a gratuitous premonition.

I then put to him my view that theatrical innovation in general had not yet reached the iconoclastic point Stravinsky had reached in 1913.

5 Titania: 'The spring, the summer,/The childing autumn, angry winter, change/Their wonted liveries; and the mazèd world,/By their increase, now knows not which is which./And this same progeny of evils comes/From our debate, from our dissension;/We are their parents and original' (Act Two, Scene One); Sara Kestelman (Titania) and Alan Howard (Oberon).

Could he, and would he want to, contrive the *éclat* of that creation, and induce a frightened and angry audience to break up the theatre? He replied that if in this production he succeeded in 'forcing on the audience a realization that the present set-up of the theatre [with its formal institutional apparatus] provided the wrong arena for communication, ceremony and involvement,' then he would have achieved what he wanted. But in order really to succeed in this, he said he would have to 'leave this theatre altogether'; and he added that this was what he was shortly proposing to do.

I then raised the question with him of whether the present actors in *A Midsummer Night's Dream* could really share in, and sympathize with, what he was attempting in the present production. He singled out 'emotional inhibition' – a paradox, given his own acute form of it – 'training', and 'cultural factors' as the main obstacles to such an understanding. I asked him whether he thought that a 'sense of craftsmanship and its traditions' in the Shakespearian theatre in England had created a 'certain style of speaking and acting'. He thought it was more a matter of 'emotional security', which depended on 'not letting go of particular forms of acting'.

I then said (dishonestly) that I felt 'guilty' about my 'irresponsibility'. He swiftly inserted his own puzzlement at this. As often with the actors, it was closer to irritation than interlocution. While everyone else in the rehearsal – I was then driven to explain – was 'borne down with anxiety and labour on the play', I was 'sitting idle'. 'I suppose,' he replied without a pause, 'you are identifying with the author.' I was not sure whether to claim it, or deny it. 'As a writer,' he said, 'you would be beginning to identify with the play as if it were your own work.' This was certainly untrue; and I think could not be true in these banal terms, of any playwright. Indeed the remark itself, as well as being inconsequential, is an oddly maladroit one for a man of the theatre such as he. Perhaps it marks the distance and mutual incomprehension which has now been established between writer and director. But the exchange also has, for me, its own bitter undercurrent, of which – I think, or imagine – he is fully aware and on which (cat-and-mouse) he plays. There is a goad, perhaps pre-verbal in its impulses, in such a remark to a neglected writer; though only a neglected writer could be hurt by it, and only another neglected writer even understand it.

Rubbing salt in the self-made wound, with some delicacy and unerring aim, Brook shortly afterwards – *à propos* of a discussion of

41

6 Oberon: 'Fetch me that flow'r; the herb I showed thee once' (Act Two, Scene One); (l. to r.) John Kane (Puck) and Alan Howard (Oberon).

English playwrights whom I admired – declared that he kept none of the letters sent to him by playwrights. Can it be true? If it is, why? If it is not true, why does he say it? Thus he 'resented' the 'arrogance' (why 'arrogance'?) of a biographer of John Whiting, who inquired of his – Brook's – memories of the playwright. The biographer 'pursued' him; and eventually, Brook said, he had decided against 'any calculatedly evasive or unpleasant response', and had reluctantly decided to see him.

I changed the subject to Whiting's virtues, and declared my admiration for all those British playwrights who had written 'in a lyrical tradition', as they understood it: including John Arden and Brendan Behan. I asserted, though with little inner conviction, that the British theatre in a period of prosaic realism needed new forms of the lyric mode, needed a poetic drama. It needed to prize once more, as much as he did in *A Midsummer Night's Dream*, exploration of language, metaphor and rhythm against false and philistine criticisms of its improbability or irrelevance to the moment. (I was speaking for my own work also.) He made no comment. The living writer is an inconvenience; Shakespeare is three hundred yards down the road from here, but conveniently dead and buried.

Brook was not much kinder to fellow-directors. For when the conversation passed to the subject of Craig, and he had told me that he had made a film about him which had never been shown, he spoke of the 'deep roots' of Craig's life in the French *pension* where he spent his later years. I put to Brook, in reubttal, my sense of Craig's solitude and neglect. 'Ah yes,' said Brook, 'but it was a voluntary exile.' Our conversation ended, as it began, with *A Midsummer Night's Dream*. I told him that I thought Shakespeare's play, whatever else it was, was literally two hours of time filled and beguiled by poetic arabesque, sound and movement. Yes it was, he said; and this view of it he would like to bring the cast to, though it would have to be done gradually, or they would 'lose their sense of direction'.

The form of the set was now revealed to the actors. A model of it was carried in by the designer. It had been discussed, she said to me later, as early as January. The idea, for what looks like a white squash-court or gymnasium, had come to Brook and her together. Neither of them alone was its originator. To the actors, Brook says that the set 'will emphasize every sound, reveal every movement and give every freedom'. Brightly-lit, it 'will provide a white daylight magic'. In it, he warns, 'we must make an effort to avoid every suggestion of the strain

7   Oberon: 'Hast thou the flower there?' Puck: 'Ay, there it is. Oberon:' I pray thee, give it me' (Act Two, Scene One); (l. to r.) Alan Howard (Oberon) and John Kane (Puck).

of a muscular circus. The aim will be to reveal the moment of coolness'. He adds: 'Everyone will be taking part all the time, without the usual exits and entrances. There will be a continuous round of movement and stillness. All will be present, each taking up the baton from the other.'

'The costumes,' he continues, 'will say nothing.' Only the mechanicals' appearance will emphasize their 'fixed occupation' and its nature, in juxtaposition with that of the court and the courtiers. 'With a white background and a few objects,' Brook tells the actors, 'all the richness will have to come from the performing group.' It will have to 'paint the picture as it goes.' Moreover, 'literally illustrating the action is out.' If Puck 'says he is going', then 'it is sufficient that he says it, and stands still.' And 'when he says he is back, he is back.' Once more, the exploration of the nature of theatrical illusion, and of the role of the imagination, including the audience's, beckons.

Now, as if to compensate for the humourlessly (and dangerously) leaden ending to the first week's rehearsals, Brook says, surprisingly: 'We are not going to get bogged down into doing anything too seriously. It's all a game anyway.' He lightly suggests – but does it lighten or increase the load on the actors? – that the rehearsals should begin to explore a 'range of acting-styles', in order to achieve 'different kinds of illusion and presentation', and to discover 'which illusion is the most effective'. Into the white engine-room set, which will have high walls, gangways, rails, cradles, swings and ladders, Brook even threatens to introduce a live rabbit, as Reinhardt did, to create a 'reality' which would outface all the actors' struggles to defy gravity with Shakespeare's words and their bodies.

The actors, who have been gathered around the model of the set – and with which they seem taken – now disperse, energies apparently aroused by the new mood to a new beginning. Brook catches the moment swiftly. A circle forms, to drumming, a baton passing from hand to hand as the circle turns, dancing. Each member of the group takes it in turns to go to the centre, as the circle speeds into a frenzied gyration and a manic exchange of sounds in rhythm. The physical energy seems to express both frustration and hoped-for exhilaration; of a longing for action and for even intenser expression. Then Brook, anxious not to lose the electrical charge which has accumulated, says: 'Form as tight a circle, sitting on the floor, as we can get.' He is sitting among them. A complete and uninterrupted re-reading of the play is beginning. 'Read the entire play, touching,' he tells them. 'Bring it to

1 *Hermia:* I do entreat your Grace to pardon me.
  I know not by what power I am made bold,
  Nor how it may concern my modesty,
  In such a presence here to plead my thoughts;
  But I beseech your Grace that I may know
  The worst that may befall me in this case,
  If I refuse to wed Demetrius.
Theseus: Either to die the death, or to abjure
  For ever the society of men.

(*I.i.58–66*)

2 *Helena:* Sickness is catching. O, were favour so,
  Yours would I catch, fair Hermia, ere I go;
  My ear should catch your voice, my eye your eye,
  My tongue should catch your tongue's sweet melody.
  Were the world mine, Demetrius being bated,
  The rest I'd give to be to you translated.
  O, teach me how you look, and with what art
  You sway the motion of Demetrius' heart.

(*I.i.186–193*)

3   (*Enter THESEUS, HIPPOLYTA, PHILOSTRATE*
                                    and Attendants)

Theseus: Now, fair Hippolyta, our nuptial hour
  Draws on apace. Four happy days bring in
  Another moon; but, O, methinks, how slow
  This old moon wanes! She lingers my desires,
  Like to a stepdame, or a dowager,
  Long withering out a young man's revenue.
Hippolyta: Four days will quickly steep themselves in nights,
  Four nights will quickly dream away the time;
  And then the moon, like to a silver bow
  New-bent in heaven, shall behold the night
  Of our solemnities.

(*I.i.1–10*)

46

life just for us here. See if we can get an experience, now, of bringing the play alive together.' He tells them, too, that they also have a 'simple freedom' to add and improvise.

The experiment is, in fact, sustained for only twenty minutes. But in this time there seems to be established such a closeness of relation and interrelation, commitment and participation, that for the first time an ensemble sense of intimate collaboration is achieved among the actors. During these twenty minutes, it is as if reservations and hesitations, strengths and weaknesses are at last coming to be shared between them. Thus, Hermia's 'I know not . . . how it may concern my modesty,/ In such a presence here to plead my thoughts'[1] becomes an intimate question, between friends. Yet, like a circus ringmaster, Brook suddenly changes direction, whip cracking, throwing the actors (pleasurably?) off-balance. There is now to be an opening-out of movement, from enforced confinement into the whole area of the studio.

And the new sense of space immediately freed the actors for a wider and spreading invention. Taken back once again to the play's beginning, the actors are physically uncaged, now roaming the acting arena and moving freely in its new-found expanses, the canvas become dangerously boundless. To free rhythms of their own – but under the ringmaster's watchful eye – feelings, voices and gestures seem to have been liberated together. At the same time, voice is hollowed out by the new distance, facial expression and body's detail diminished, gesture expanded (into disorder) and the words' cadences roughened. Now Lysander, in the first scene, paced in time with his words. Helena entered swinging; while, strangely, the new physical intimacy between Hermia and Helena seemed even closer for the distance which separated them, and which they now had to traverse in order to touch each other.

Moreover, in Helena's 'My ear should catch your voice, my eye your eye'[2] – with speech and gesture communicated clearly across space – Brook's exercises in the exchange between the actors of sound and movement, were for the first time vindicated, ear catching voice, and eye eye, as Brook had ordered. Even Shakespeare's line itself appeared as if written to command also. The opening speeches of Theseus and Hippolyta[3] were spoken against a background of the rest of the cast's free movement, idling, calling out, moving, swinging. And when not speaking, Theseus and Hippolyta had merged back into this movement, taking part in it, just as Demetrius and Lysander are called

⁴ (*ACT ONE. Scene Two. Quince's house. Enter QUINCE, SNUG, BOTTOM, FLUTE, SNOUT and STARVELING*)
Quince: Is all our company here?

(*I.ii.1*)

⁵ *Bottom:* Let me play the lion too. I will roar that I will do any man's heart good to hear me. I will roar, that I will make the Duke say, 'let him roar again, let him roar again.'

(*I.ii.62–65*)

⁶ *Quince:* But, masters, here are your parts; and I am to entreat you, request you, and desire you, to con them by tomorrow night; and meet me in the palace wood, a mile without the town, by moonlight. There will we rehearse, for if we meet in the city, we shall be dogged with company, and our devices known.

(*I.ii.87–93*)

⁷ (*ACT TWO. Scene One. A wood near Athens. Enter a Fairy at one door, and PUCK at another*)

Puck: How now, spirit! Whither wander you?
Fairy: Over hill, over dale,
    Thorough bush, thorough brier,
    Over park, over pale,
    Thorough flood, thorough fire.

(*II.i.1–5*)

⁸ *Titania:* These are the forgeries of jealousy;
    And never, since the middle summer's spring,
    Met we on hill, in dale, forest, or mead
    By pavèd fountain or by rushy brook,
    Or in the beached margent of the sea,
    To dance our ringlets to the whistling wind,
    But with thy brawls thou hast disturbed our sport.

(*II.i.81–87*)

48

from it to address each other. These are the first clear signs of the 'free form' which Brook had earlier suggested would characterize the final stage version.

As the moment of the mechanicals' First Act entrance approaches[4], Brook says to the cast: 'All of you make the noise of working. Make it difficult for them to get themselves heard. Make noise with the props as well as with voices.' The mechanicals, exploring the possibilities of the putative set, are to enter from a height on a painters' cradle. Bedlam greets them. But it is composed of the sounds of their own work-process: hammering, sawing, floor-sweeping, taken over and shared among all the actors. The noise and distraction heighten the mechanicals' difficulties and anxieties in preparing their theatrical illusion for the court's entertainment. Against the noise, now rising to nightmare proportion, their actorish activity evokes pity (and irritation). All are taking part in the scene, interrupting Bottom's patient and earnest instructions to his fellow-actors; and as the cacophany brings the scene itself to the verge of raucous breakdown, the strange words of the mechanicals, set in noise, seem those of hallucination.

In the uproar, Bottom roars. 'I will roar that I will do any man's heart good to hear me. I will roar,' he roars, 'that I will make the Duke say, "Let him roar again",' and is greeted by an answering roaring chorus, 'Let him roar again!!'[5] Today's rehearsal is now fully and for the first time launched, the tide of energy running in full spate with it. 'Meet me,' says Quince against the clamour, 'in the palace wood, a mile without the town, by moonlight. There will we rehearse, for if we meet in the city, we shall be dogged with company . . .'[6]; and the laughter, itself quickly swept away by the momentum of the acting, is of complicity in new-found meaning.

The speed of movement now carries the rehearsal headlong over the barrier between Acts One and Two, bringing the actors in a pack to hound Puck also. Mocking and circling the speakers[7], sounds and voices are exchanged in fierce crescendo, and speeches riven by obstruction, as the first misshapen rehearsal climax approaches. It comes at Oberon's 'Ill met by moonlight', which cuts acridly and fiercely into the moment, snapping at the heels of the anarchy which dogs him. (Of this vocal astringency, Brook was later to say to me that it was merely 'actorish'.) But the hoodlum swarming of the actors is unabated, while Titania's homerically taxing speech, 'These are the forgeries of jealousy'[8] is also worried and harried. 'With thy brawls,' Titania says, rounding on her assailants, 'thou hast disturbed our

⁹ *Oberon:* How long within this wood intend you stay?
Titania: Perchance till after Theseus' wedding day.
   If you will patiently dance in our round,
   And see our moonlight revels, go with us.
   If not, shun me, and I will spare your haunts.
Oberon: Give me that boy, and I will go with thee.
Titania: Not for thy fairy kingdom. Fairies, away!

                                                    (*II.i.138–144*)

¹⁰ *Demetrius:* I love thee not, therefore pursue me not . . .
   Get thee gone, and follow me no more!
Helena: You draw me, you hard-hearted adamant;
   But yet you draw not iron, for my heart
   Is as true as steel. Leave you your power to draw,
   And I shall have no power to follow you.

                                                    (*II.i.188–198*)

¹¹ *Hermia:* (*Awaking*) Help me, Lysander, help me! Do thy best
   To pluck this crawling serpent from my breast!
   Ay me, for pity! What a dream was here!
   Lysander, look how I do quake with fear.

                                                    (*II.ii.145–148*)

¹² *Bottom:* I see their knavery. This is to make an ass of me; to fright
   me if they could. But I will not stir from this place, do what they
   can. I will walk up and down here, and will sing, that they shall
   hear I am not afraid.   (*Sings*)
                   The woosel cock so black of hue,
                   With orange-tawny bill,
                   The throstle with his note so true,
                   The wren with little quill.

                                                    (*III.i.110–117*)

sport'[8]. It is as if the line had been written for this very moment; but the glorious succession of rural metaphors which follows is drowned in merciless disorder.

And by the time the hampered Titania, appearing at the limit of her vocal resources, has reached 'Perchance till after Theseus' wedding day'[9], she seems unwell; to be swaying. It is either a shrewdly-calculated effect, much to be desired at this juncture, or the genuine response of an actress at the end of her tether. (Who can say?) Held up by the others who spot her seeming distress, she speaks on, fainthearted – and is carried off, ballet-like, by Lysander, springing from the ruck, over his right shoulder. These devices, though already driven to excess, are persisted in by Brook without remission. So, Demetrius and Helena likewise, while speaking[10], chase each other back and forth across the acting-area, up into the sound-box, and up and down the wooden steps at the rear of the studio, eluding the rest of the cast, which swarms after them.

Indeed both noise and harassment are intensified to, and beyond, breaking-point. The cast, become a brawling mob, steps up its actions. It is foolery, become tormenting. And, suddenly, this is the goad which at last drives Hermia, in her desperation to survive vocally, to a 'genuinely' despairing impulse. 'Help me, Lysander'[11], as Brook had originally wanted, is audibly drawn from panic feeling rather than from girlish coyness; and now not out of fear of the director, but of the other actors. She sees, or seems to see – and the watcher for a moment seems to see with her – in a coiled and suddenly whipping rope a 'real' serpent, and in tennis balls (absurdly) rolling across her line of vision a maddening distraction.

The second climax of the day's rehearsal was also the product of this brawling. The pedestrian but stalwart mechanicals had come through the din unscathed, their brawny characters reinforced by their determined resistance to all such tomfoolery and provocation. 'I see their knavery'[12], said Bottom, workmanlike and squaring his shoulders. 'This is to make an ass of me; to fright me, if they could.' The arena, still resonating, fell quiet before him, the mob with its catcalls and baiting quelled into a hangdog silence. His chest rose in stolid pride. 'But I will not stir from this place, do what they can. I will walk up and down here'[12], said Bottom, his voice growing out of its tremors and expanding into the stillness; 'I will walk up and down here, and I will sing,' he said, pitting his *gravitas* against his terrors, 'that they shall hear I am not afraid.'

13 *Bottom:* (*Sings*) The finch, the sparrow, and the lark,
          The plain-song cuckoo gray,
          Whose note full many a man doth mark,
          And dares not answer nay –
       for, indeed, who would set his wit to so foolish a bird? Who
       would give a bird the lie, though he cry 'cuckoo' never so?
                                                   (*III.i.119–124*)

14   (*Re-enter PUCK, and BOTTOM with an ass's head*)
    Pyramus: If I were fair, Thisby, if I were only thine.
    Quince: O monstrous! O strange! We are haunted. Pray, masters! Fly,
       masters! Help!
                                          (*Exeunt all but BOTTOM*)
    Bottom: . . . Why do they run away? This is a knavery of them to
       make me afeard.
                                               (*Enter SNOUT*)
    Snout: O Bottom, thou art changed! What do I see on thee?
    Bottom: What do you see? You see an ass head of your own, do you?
                                               (*Exit SNOUT*)
                                               (*Enter QUINCE*)
    Quince: Bless thee, Bottom! Bless thee! Thou art translated.
                                                   (*III.i.93–109*)

And then he sang[12], bestraddling the stage, legs apart, to struck-up drumming, in a deeply reverberant proletarian *basso*. Now, of his own accord entering an area of the playing surface not yet entered into, he came close to the watchers and spoke[13] with a grotesque flat-vowelled power against the frivolously fluting cuckoo-sounds of the chorus, in an improvised and inspired incantation. Energy had been aroused, to shake the studio rafters.

Brook, taken by the storm and buoyant, gives new instructions. 'Everyone, from today,' he says, 'must come off the book. Anyone using a book from now on is undercutting the work that can be done in rehearsals. There is also no need for notes. Anything forgotten is not worth remembering.' The day is drawing to an end, as the actors slowly come down from their exhilaration. Brook – as if he thought a triumph were already distantly in sight – tells them that 'old traditions of *A Midsummer Night's Dream* set up echoes which prevented anyone doing it directly'; that is, facing the text afresh. He adds, unexpectedly, that 'new styles of writing' in the modern theatre have 'enabled us to see, and grasp, the significance of the surreal in the play', as in Bottom's transformation and the succession of responses to it[14].

'When the play is flowing rightly,' he concludes, 'an added power arises, and there is a new resonance in its language.' He describes this as 'one of the strangenesses of *A Midsummer Night's Dream*'. The actors listen in silence, exhausted.

Second week, second day

What species of vanity and frustrated self-regard is it that today brought a deep wave of despair and preoccupation upon me, sitting silent on my metal chair? Is it that to be now vicariously caught up in this intense process of exploration, while at the same time remaining a passive spectator of the activity of others, deepens the sense of isolation and estrangement which I brought with me? Is it that these rehearsals have begun to generate such communicable feelings of elation and depression in the actors that the bystander is swept up in it? Am I, against my own interests and intentions, helplessly representing the 'superfluous' figure of the writer, in a theatre of directors? Did Brook intend me to sit here in order to crush or raise my hopes and spirits? And if neither, why did he invite me? Is he an innocent, without ulterior purpose?

[15] (*ACT ONE. Scene Two. Quince's house. Enter QUINCE, SNUG, BOTTOM, FLUTE, SNOUT and STARVELING*)

Quince: Is all our company here?

Bottom: You were best to call them, generally, man by man, according to the scrip.

(*I.ii.1*)

Or am I subconsciously acting too, brilliantly playing the almost silent role of the unwelcome guest, a part self-written? Am I merely an inert seated object, indistinguishable from the chair I am sitting on, impersonal and even invisible to the others? Or have I unwittingly become, even for them, part of the rehearsal? Has the shared experience, in this confined space, of their emotions and the unavoidable exchange of glances which pass back and forth across the acting area like beams of light, brought my thoughts and feelings into the common current?

I feel recoil also, assailed by a sense of guilt which is entirely my own, at passing the time – summertime – in this Plato's cave, with its flickering shadows. *A Midsummer Night's Dream* in 1970? For whom? *Cui bono?* The actors gather for another day of effort; but from my metal chair I suddenly see, as to a jaundiced man the whole world may appear yellow, not a court masque to celebrate a wedding, nor a sylvan comedy of Shakespeare's 'middle period', but a modern actor's tragedy of sacrifice and surrender to a new form of artistic coercion. I think I see, though the sight is quickly clouded, truth pursued at the expense of self, in a theatre-world laid waste by illusion.

'What can we use,' asks Brook, 'from yesterday's surrealistic marvels?' An actor ventures: 'The moment of Bottom's "Let him roar again".' Another: 'The interruptions of the mechanicals' rehearsal.' There is a listlessness or a wary caution, as the actors prepare themselves, perhaps presaging another day of alternating boredom and deepening invention. 'I don't know what I'm aiming at,' an actor playing a Fairy suddenly announces, with club-footed (or suicidal) asperity, pulling off his tracksuit top. 'As long as that's true, you'll be all right,' is Brook's comment. The actor begins to move away, downhearted, his love for the theatre inadequately requited. Calling after him, Brook adds 'Try endless tiny improvisations'; his Fairy part is appropriately tiny. 'Don't attempt a fixed and stylized "spirit" performance. It just becomes,' Brook says with scorn in his voice, 'semi-balletic. Bounce off the others,' he tells the sullen Fairy, who seems unreassured and not much wiser. 'Take your lead and ideas from them.'

The moment passes. Brook, beginning from the mechanicals' First Act entrance[15], strikes up the actors' movements, as though a *chef d'orchestre* – but these players have today been asked to enter stripped to the waist, barefoot and each from a different direction: from the painters' cradle, through doors, down ladders. Half-naked and solitary,

¹⁶ *Bottom:* In any case, let Thisby have clean linen; and let not him that plays the lion pare his nails, for they shall hang out for the lion's claws. And, most dear actors, eat no onions nor garlic, for we are to utter sweet breath.

(IV.ii.35–40)

¹⁷ *Bottom:* Yet my chief humour is for a tyrant. I could play Ercles rarely, or a part to tear a cat in, to make all split.

> The raging rocks
> And shivering shocks
> Shall break the locks
> Of prison gates;
> And Phibbus' car
> Shall shine from far,
> And make and mar
> The foolish Fates.

(I.ii.22–32)

¹⁸ *Puck:* I am that merry wanderer of the night
I jest to Oberon, and make him smile,
When I a fat and bean-fed horse beguile,
Neighing in likeness of a filly foal:
And sometime lurk I in a gossip's bowl,
In very likeness of a roasted crab.

(II.i.43–48)

they immediately appeared less as characters than as bodies, and – given their roles and *personae* – cruelly vulnerable to mockery at the hands of their social betters. They are 'rude mechanicals' venturing to act at court, who will be anxious (later in the play)[16] as to their breath, their language and the cleanliness of their linen. A conversation with Brook about this, afterwards, was revealing. He asked me if I had noticed 'how different they had appeared physically'. Being stripped, he said, 'emphasized the physical differences among them', and fixed attention on the variety of their appearances, while 'changing their responses to each other'. I put it to Brook that, at least equally important, was the heightened compassion their presence evoked in the spectator, and the greater the fear for their humiliation. I also put it to him that Shakespeare had discreetly observed something both of the dignities and unease of their class. The urbane bull sidestepped the red flag. To Brook, their 'worry' was 'not a class thing'; they were merely 'men going into the unknown'. It was a matter of 'daring, cash, excitement and danger'.

Carrying yesterday's work forward, the mechanicals and the idling throng of watching actors now began to improvise mocking exchanges of jibes and insults, the latter laughing at the mechanicals' efforts to act[17]. Brook stopped the rehearsal. He recalled, as a corrective, a 'village play in Persia' in which there was 'no self-consciousness, no mockery, no guying'. There was, instead, what he described as a 'simple, natural acceptance' of the 'known personalities of the actors', and of the 'seriousness of impersonation and acting'. (I suppose this will stand both for a theatrical credo, and a further illumination of the relation between dramatic reality and dramatic illusion.)

Puck, too, was curtly halted in mid-stride by Brook in his 'I am that merry wanderer of the night'[18]. Startling the actor, Brook accused him of 'acting "foal"' and 'acting "crab".' 'Everything is permissible,' said Brook sharply, 'except suiting action to the words.' The line, for Brook, between seeking out and sounding the words' impulses, and merely illustrating their meaning from the stock of conventional gesture, is an elementary one. However hard to explain – and, characteristically, he does not even attempt it – it is for Brook a fundamental issue of technique. The charge is one of banality; and Brook, severe, assumes that the actor understands him, even if he does not.

Thrown off balance by the irruption, by the problems of authenticity (arguably insoluble) which it poses, and under the new pressures

[19] *Oberon:* Tarry, rash wanton; am not I thy lord?
   Titania: Then I must be thy lady: but I know
      When thou hast stolen away from fairyland,
      And in the shape of Corin sat all day,
      Playing on pipes of corn, and versing love
      To amorous Phillida.

(II.i.63–68)

[20] *(Enter BOTTOM)*

Bottom: Where are these lads? Where are these hearts?
Quince: Bottom! O most courageous day! O most happy hour!
Bottom: Masters, I am to discourse wonders: but ask me not what; for
   if I tell you, I am not true Athenian. I will tell you everything,
   right as it fell out.
Quince: Let us hear, sweet Bottom.
Bottom: Not a word of me. All that I will tell you is, that the Duke
   hath dined. Get your apparel together, good strings to your beards,
   new ribbons to your pumps; meet presently at the palace.

(IV.ii.23–33)

58

of working 'off the book', Titania forgets her lines[19]. Suddenly isolated by the lapse and watched impassively by Brook in a stony silence, waiting for her to get it right, she struggles to remember. Again Brook intervenes. 'This isolation, apart from the others, struggling,' he says to her, 'is true to the part.' But, from my metal chair, I see that the rehearsal is again coming under pressure. There are the first (now familiar) signs that emotions will begin to be driven. Moreover, equally familiar, a tension between dissatisfaction and desire, together with a fear of unilluminating repetition, begins to work itself out in the voices and expressions of the actors.

Its effects are apparent in new signs of uncertainty and stress: in a taut tempo which has lost its rhythm, and in the cramped cadences of a lost conviction. The mind's ear, alerted, in turn becomes irritated and impatient. But the group, sweating in the heat, can only work uphill through four forced acts, as if looking for the opening which will release them into invention. Surprisingly, it is not the poetics of a dream, nor the unearthliness of hallucination, which frees them for creation. Instead, it is the bluff and genial reappearance of Bottom at the end of the Fourth Act[20], restored to his four-square self as well as to his leading role in *Pyramus and Thisby*. In one moment of conjuncture, it relieves both the accumulated tensions of today's frustrated acting and the text's anxieties for his safety. There was a shout of exhilaration at his beaming entrance; and a near-to-weeping relief, both for him and the play's rediscovered motion.

Intervening, Brook says: 'It is a moment of truth . . . None of the mechanicals believed any longer that their play was going to happen.' In fact, it signifies the development, within only ten days, of an already intensely-shared perception and apprehension, however fitful; and something not confined to the actors. Possibility has again been rescued, and as a result there is a new tremor of anticipation.

The play – exhaustingly – is to be run-through again. And, as the heat increased in the studio, came moment after moment of illumination. I could see and hear that this new fruition of the work of rehearsal, and the revival of energy which was built upon it, did not come from any abstract 'sense of ensemble'. Instead, it seemed to derive from individual practical effort. That is, the renewed hope of achievement itself arose from the putting of individual mind and action to work; each reciprocally drawing from the other both sound and movement, in an extending interchange of objects and rhythms, and of gestures both physical and vocal, precisely as Brook had demanded.

59

21 *Titania:* What, jealous Oberon! Fairy, skip hence.
I have forsworn his bed and company.
Oberon: Tarry, rash wanton; am not I thy lord?
Titania: Then I must be thy lady . . .
. . . Why art thou here,
Come from the farthest steep of India?
But that, forsooth, the bouncing Amazon,
Your buskined mistress and your warrior love,
To Theseus must be wedded.

(II.i.59–72)

22 *Oberon:* Why should Titania cross her Oberon?
I do but beg a little changeling boy,
To be my henchman.
Titania: Set your heart at rest.
The fairy land buys not the child of me.
. . . I will not part with him.

(II.i.119–137)

23 *Helena:* I am your spaniel; and, Demetrius,
The more you beat me, I will fawn on you.
Use me but as your spaniel, spurn me, strike me,
Neglect me, lose me; only give me leave
Unworthy as I am, to follow you.

(II.i.203–207)

24 *Helena:* Stay, though thou kill me, sweet Demetrius.
Demetrius: I charge thee, hence, and do not haunt me thus.
Helena: O, wilt thou darkling leave me? Do not so.

(II.ii.84–86)

25 *Chorus:* Never harm,
Nor spell nor charm,
Come our lovely lady nigh;
So, good night, with lullaby.
2nd Fairy: Hence, away! Now all is well.
One aloof stand sentinel.
(Exeunt FAIRIES. TITANIA sleeps)
(Enter OBERON, and squeezes the flower on TITANIA's eyelids)
Oberon: What thou seest when thou dost wake,
Do it for thy true love take;
Love and languish for his sake.

(II.ii.16–29)

The rehearsal, minutes ago run aground, suddenly seemed to become buoyant. There could be heard, for the first time in combination and sustained succession, the stillness of thinking aloud, the echoes of word-singing and softly drum-supported vocal rhythms, as the play, raised to a truer pitch, became once more vibrant to the senses. By the time the Second Act had been reached again, it was as if there was a newly-charged sexuality in the acting also. From where had this sexuality arisen? Not from Brook's suggestion or direction. Or is it merely the corollary of all creative effort, and even a synonym for it?

It was in the entrance of proud Titania[21], resting on the arms and backs of her attendants; at a sudden (sexual) impulse making a throne of their minds and bodies for her, like a *howdah*. It was in her inward smile, lewd as *La Gioconda*, as she slid, lissom, from them. Before our eyes, she had suddenly become the 'rash wanton'[21] whom the stern Oberon then addresses. And almost at her first spoken line[21], Titania began to discover, and then provoke in Oberon, not a magical but a sexual rhythm. Her words, at once beckoning and forbidding, became for a while all fire; her quarrel with Oberon, over the 'little changeling boy'[22], filled now with an idle menace, and an ambiguous sexual passion.

This transient feeling was passed to Demetrius and Helena, as well as to me on my metal chair. Her 'The more you beat me, I will fawn on you./ Use me . . . spurn me, strike me'[23], and 'Stay, though you kill me, sweet Demetrius'[24] are now the language of purest desire. Both in stillness and in movement – and especially as Titania slept[25] – the sexual charge was held erect and pulsing. It seemed to keep time with Titania's breathing, while Oberon, as he approached her, sleeping, moved to its rhythm. He held a stick in his hands; his 'squeezing' of the flower on her eyelids, as the text's stage-direction puts it[25], was its climax; her scream, one of seeming ecstasy, or orgasm.

It followed Hermia and Lysander also, and had now become that 'richness which must come from the performing group itself', as Brook had earlier called it. Lysander, enchanted by Puck's 'charm'[26], sank back among the enmeshing bodies of the chorus. Encompassed in arms which felt for, touched and cradled them, it was as if Hermia and Lysander were not sleeping, but swooning for pleasure. And in the still sexually-alive tumult of her fears on waking[27], with the 'serpent' at her breast and hedged around by predatory tormentors, Hermia was driven by the charge of her own excitement to a new opening of herself

61

²⁶ *Puck:*   Who is here?
Weeds of Athens he doth wear:
This is he, my master said.
Despised the Athenian maid;
And here the maiden, sleeping sound,
On the dank and dirty ground . . .
Churl, upon thy eyes I throw
All the power this charm doth owe.

(*II.ii.70–79*)

²⁷ *Hermia:* (*Awaking*) Help me, Lysander, help me! Do thy best
To pluck this crawling serpent from my breast!
Ay me, for pity! What a dream was here!
Lysander, look how I do quake with fear!

(*II.ii.145–148*)

to expression. It is in her eye and mouth, voice and gesture, and in the movement of her body, brought in near-breathless moments to new levels of arousal. In me, there was in turn aroused a curiosity and longing at the sight and sound of it; and a desire, one day, to order in words the bewildering and complex experience of it.

Second week, third day

I did not attend the rehearsal, but remained in my own world of weariness and depression.

Second week, fourth day

The cast is once more taking part in exercises, but today under the supervision of a 'movement coach', John Broome. In one exercise all eyes are closed, each actor standing alone, isolation visibly deepened. With eyes still closed, but moving towards and finding one another, touch brings solace. Bodies are consoling.

A group, with all eyes shut, is enclosed in a cluster of touching. The coach asks them slowly to withdraw from each other, but keeping in touch as long as possible, until only finger-tips are touching. Severance brings the deepest darkness – a sightless isolation, which can be seen by the sighted, watching, as a visible distress in a wilderness of blindness.

Each of the four actors at a time is asked to go to the room's four corners. Each sets out, eyes closed, to the centre: a blind approach, slowly, halting. There is not only solitude, but also fear, a sense of danger. Meeting, as it draws closer, promises, step-by-step, a bliss unknown to the sighted: the breathtaking relief of physical reassurance, not the idle untouched greeting of a passing moment. To meet is to touch, to touch is to feel human, to feel human is to be human. The lesson is simple, and moving. Moreover, Brook's rehearsals have this week already begun to embody such rapt moments of discovery; that is, of the finding and holding of mind by mind, and body by body.

Another exercise commences. Eyes closed, only hands touch each other. Each must recognize the other by the touch and shape of the hands alone. (Some touching is more knowing than others.) Hands are being read, not by the palmist, but by other hands. Fingers mistake or

63

8   Hermia: 'What, out of hearing? Gone? No sound, no word?/Alack, where are you? Speak, an if you hear;/Speak, of all loves!' (Act Two, Scene Two); Mary Rutherford (Hermia).

recognize fingers; and finders are, for the happy instant of correct recognition, smiling keepers. These are the same moments as in a Shakespearian round-dance, when a play's comic or tragic resolution is celebrated: with a blissful ring o' roses for a comedy's betrothed or blessèd, or with a gaunt wake, hand-held, such as staunches the flowing blood in a tragedy's survivors.

Now Brook's already partly-developed musical exercises are carried forward. There are four instruments used: two recognizable, two improvised. There is a guitar, and a small *tabla*-like drum; a stick with bells attached, and a chain rattling in a tin plate. The rhythm is given by the instructor, and – instrument in response to instrument – the actors must improvise within the rhythm as it changes. This is a musical metaphor for the words' impulses, and for the search to sustain response as a verbal rhythm varies. Movement is added to music. The actors must play and move together. And so they dance, while wooing with sound; wordlessly threaten and attack each other to a rhythm of their own making; a drum speaks to the stick-and-bells.

Is this any place for the wordsmith to be? Or is it *the* place? Is this racket to be found behind, and beyond, the words of Shakespeare, or would it – if he rose from his tomb down the lane – be beneath his notice? Outside the studio, Brook is talking in the sunlight to a group of *aficionados*, suitors for the director's attention. The tomb of the playwright, onlie begetter of this attention, is dead silent. Shakespeare is lying in shadow, beyond reach of all these words, spoken and unspoken, and all these touching moments.

Second week, fifth day

There is a startling paradox in all this 'work', and it has important consequences. The director-as-iconoclast and inventor is here treating the text as inviolable; Brook, a man of seeming whims and caprices in his relations, would not bend this play to suit them. There is daily and strenuous innovation, but there appears to be no question (so far) of additions or subtractions, cuts or alterations to the writ of Shakespeare. Ironically, it is the text not the theatre, which is holy. Indeed, I can see today more clearly that it is precisely the inordinate respect for the written words of *A Midsummer Night's Dream* which, day after day, invests them with their almost mystical significance. Rightly or wrongly, there is attributed to them near-unfathomable depths,

[28] (*ACT THREE. Scene One. The wood. TITANIA lying asleep. Enter QUINCE, SNUG, BOTTOM, FLUTE, SNOUT and STARVELING*)

Bottom: Are we all met?

Quince: Pat, pat; and here's a marvellous convenient place for our rehearsal. This green plot shall be our stage, this hawthorn brake our tiring house.

(*III.i.1–3*)

capable of being plumbed only through this sacral *Sturm und Drang* of the rehearsal process. Every day there is called forth, from the actors, exploration and exposure in service of a privileged truth, held to be hidden in every particle and syllable of the printed word. The 'empty space' is in fact pre-filled with words.

There is as much fear as celebration in it – and there is a great deal of celebration. The idle and momentarily gratifying thought crossed my mind, waiting for event on my chair, that this fear is also the director's fear of the playwright. Within this fear is a deep unfamiliarity with the *process of writing*, a chasm which such a director seeks to cross on a rope-bridge plaited out of actors' minds and bodies. Both Brook and Craig suffer from similarly bleak forms of unexpressiveness, as their own writings testify. And one of the dire results of this, in Brook's case, is now less paradoxical than at first sight it seemed: a reverence, often covert, for the written, coupled with a rejection – which is often open – of the writer. Usually, the writer can earn a partial forgiveness by dying; but alive, he is an archetypally scorned and ignored figure. (Whiting's death, however, was insufficient to earn him such remission.) Moreover, when it is the director and not the writer, nor the actor for that matter, who commands the costly resources of production, and thus presides over the whole theatrical production system, the balance of power and influence between them is very much in favour of the former.

The whole company gathers. Their voices are expectant and enthusiastic. Metal plates are again spinning, and the actors' skills increasing. Now there have been added finger-bells, hoops, trapezes and streaming black-and-white pennants for jugglery and acrobatics. Does this mean that there will be juggling and the suggestion of orientalism (why?) in the final version? Or is this merely actors' exercise, the development of a metaphorical balance and sleight-of-hand in which to poise the finished action?

The mechanicals' props, however, have become heavy and literal against this aerial whimsy. They have partly-worked beams, oak to lug, the parts of a real bellows. They will climb ladders, they will be 'real' workmen. Today's work-play will be re-enacted in a Forest of Arden. 'Let us go straight to the Act Three arrival of the mechanicals in the wood'[28], says Brook, 'and make the wood deceptively benign, absolutely harmless.' All the actors take part, sitting as spectators on the sidelines of the action, whistling and chirping the bird-calls of a peaceful sylvan setting. The innocent mechanicals struggle, as if

²⁹ *Quince:* But there is two hard things: that is, to bring the moonlight
into a chamber; for, you know, Pyramus and Thisby meet by
moonlight.
Snout: Doth the moon shine that night we play our play?
Bottom: A calendar, a calendar! Look in the almanac; find out
moonshine, find out moonshine.
Quince: Yes, it doth shine that night.

(*III.i.41–48*)

³⁰ *Quince:* Then, there is another thing: we must have a wall in the great
chamber; for Pyramus and Thisby, says the story, did talk through
the chink of a wall.
Snout: You can never bring in a wall. What say you, Bottom?
Bottom: Some man or other must present Wall: and let him have
some plaster, or some loam, or some roughcast about him, to
signify Wall; and let him hold his fingers thus, and through that
cranny shall Pyramus and Thisby whisper.

(*III.i.55–63*)

³¹ *Quince:* Come, sit down, every mother's son, and rehearse your parts.
Pyramus, you begin. When you have spoken your speech, enter into
that brake; and so everyone according to his cue.

(*Enter PUCK*)

Puck: What hempen homespuns have we swagg'ring here,
So near the cradle of the Fairy Queen? . . .
Quince: Speak, Pyramus. Thisby, stand forth.
Pyramus: Thisby, the flowers of odious savours sweet –
Quince: Odours, odours.

(*III.i.64–74*)

³² *Thisby:* I'll meet thee, Pyramus, at Ninny's tomb.
Quince: 'Ninus' tomb', man. Why, you must not speak that yet. That
you answer to Pyramus. You speak all your part at once, cues and
all. Pyramus enter. Your cue is past; it is 'never tire'.
Thisby: O – as true as truest horse, that yet would never tire.

(*Re-enter PUCK, and BOTTOM with an ass's head*)

Pyramus: If I were fair, Thisby, I were only thine.
Quince: O monstrous! O strange! We are haunted. Pray, masters!

(*III.i.87–94*)

oblivious of what watches and awaits them, with the problems of their rehearsal. They are so rapt that when a spirit, or Fairy, prods the hide of the witless Snout with a long stick, he brushes the object away with a vacant reflex, deep-sunk in his own absorption. And when Snout asks, 'Doth the moon shine that night we play our play?'[29] — Bottom calling for 'A calendar, a calendar!' – it is a Fairy who presents it, his physical presence become invisible to their preoccupations. So blind and guileless are they, that with it comes the first menacing hint of danger in their blindness.

Moreover, the sense of danger (and delight) seemed to deepen with the innocent relief which the mechanicals, ensnared in the woods, find in solving their problem of how 'to bring the moonlight into a chamber'[29]. It gave an impulse to the fear which we feel for them, because they – in their innocence – do not feel it for themselves. And as the ponderous Quince, anxious for his play and labouring minutely over the problems of production ('Then, there is another thing')[30], spoke his way slowly into an even deeper unawareness of the watching and waiting spirits, a blissful tension mounted. (That Shakespeare makes the carpenter Quince both playwright and director, no one, least of all Brook, is saying!)

The mood of fear, deliberately prolonged to bursting by the slow motion, did not conceal Shakespeare's deepening concern in this scene with the question of reality and illusion: in this case, of how to signify one thing by another. 'Some man or other must present Wall'[30], says Bottom at this ludicrous and fearful juncture. 'And let him have some plaster . . . to signify Wall; and let him hold his fingers thus, and through that cranny shall Pyramus and Thisby whisper'. Ten pairs of hands, some of them those of the spirits, then made a 'cranny' – a 'wall of hands', as Brook put it. Meanwhile, Puck's entrance[31], unremarked by the mechanicals, does not interrupt the search for technical solutions, nor abate the menace which threatens. The mechanicals are drifting unawares into enchantment. Earthbound, they are preparing one illusion while another, of which they know nothing, is about to claim them.

Quince, his lonely voice now itself transformed by what Brook calls an 'endless slow take' and an unease which is mounting to its climax, corrects Thisby's pronunciation[31]. He gives instructions as to cues, and now, at the apogee of the fearful crescendo, calls upon Pyramus (*alias* Bottom) to re-enter[32]. Bottom (*alias* David Waller) stands close to me, bare to the waist, his body out of shape and ageing. Can such as

³³ *Bottom:* I see their knavery. This is to make an ass of me; to fright me, if they could. But I will not stir from this place, do what they can. I will walk up and down here, and will sing, that they shall hear I am not afraid. (*Sings*)

> The woosel cock so black of hue,
> With orange-tawny bill,
> The throstle with his note so true,
> The wren with little quill –

Titania: (*Awaking*) What angel wakes me from my flow'ry bed?

(*III.i.110–118*)

³⁴ *Titania:* I pray thee, gentle mortal, sing again:
> Mine ear is much enamoured of thy note;
> So is mine eye enthrallèd to thy shape;
> And thy fair virtue's force perforce doth move me
> On the first view to say, to swear, I love thee.

(*III.i.125–129*)

³⁵ *Titania:* Out of this wood do not desire to go . . .
> . . . I'll give thee fairies to attend on thee,
> And they shall fetch thee jewels from the deep,
> And sing, while thou on pressèd flowers dost sleep:
> And I will purge thy mortal grossness so,
> That thou shalt like an airy spirit go.

(*III.i.138–147*)

³⁶ *Titania:* Be kind and courteous to this gentleman;
> Hop in his walks, and gambol in his eyes;
> Feed him with apricocks and dewberries,
> With purple grapes, green figs, and mulberries;
> The honey bags steal from the humblebees,
> And for night tapers crop their waxen thighs,
> And light them at the fiery glowworm's eyes,
> To have my love to bed and to arise;
> And pluck the wings from painted butterflies,
> To fan the moonbeams from his sleeping eyes.

(*III.i.150–159*)

³⁷ *Titania:* Come, wait upon him, lead him to my bower.
> The moon methinks looks with a wat'ry eye;
> And when she weeps, weeps every little flower,
> Lamenting some enforced chastity.
> Tie up my lover's tongue, bring him silently.

(*III.i.182–186*)

he be transfigured? Then, like forked lightning before thunder, 'The wood comes alive!!', shouts Brook over an explosion of joyful fright and clamour, as Quince's 'O monstrous! O strange! We are haunted. Pray, masters!'[32] become words of awesome terror. Brook's voice in the din demands 'distempo' and 'cross-rhythms of speech and movement', as Bottom enters to the fiercely counterpointed sound of rattling metal, rung bells and beaten drums, and cartwheel acrobatics. 'O Bottom,' says Snout, the trembling tinker, 'thou art changed!' 'Bless thee, Bottom! Bless thee!' says Quince, the stricken carpenter-playwright, 'thou art translated.'

They flee, and Bottom (in an ass's head which we must, and now do, imagine) is alone. The pulse of the play races, in silence. 'Paint, in sound', Brook tells the actors, 'that the moon has gone in.' The eye and ear of the mind narrow to Bottom's tremors. Gone now is the steadfastness and courage of a previous run-through. Bottom is dwarfed by his own dread, and roars in the dark against it[33]. He is clumsy, roistering, frightened; his bird-speech[33] sung more in anger than in sorrow. And now Titania awakens, sinuous and stretching, to the already tangled knot of Bottom's flustered emotions. 'I pray thee, gentle mortal,' she says, softly beckoning him to a dreamy solace for his fevers, 'sing again'[34]. Bottom, the beast, gazes upon beauty; and, for us, he is joyfully vulnerable to the comfort she offers.

Titania, her voice heavy with a seeming desire, speaks swooningly to him[35]. Her 'I will purge thy mortal grossness so'[35] becomes a promise of bliss in a houri's heaven. Surrounded by Fairies, she offers him the fruits of Eden; she Eve, he a donkey-Adam. 'Be kind and courteous to this gentleman'[36], she tells them. ('Sing,' Brook tells her.) Her voice, already close to crooning, woos him with sung 'glowworms . . . butterflies . . . and moonbeams'[36]. Bottom, asinine, in a hoofed swaying and jigging, is near to dancing. Brook interrupts, and warns him: 'It must be in your own rhythm, or in no rhythm at all.' And, resuming, Titania sings Bottom into his own beastly enchantment, slowly leaving mankind's world behind him. Gently braying into a cloud of blown bubbles as the song enfolds him, he tries to snap at them with a snout which we must and do imagine; entranced ourselves, we are unaware of the workings of our own imagination.

In this dream-world, there was not only the translated Bottom (perceived moments before as merely an out-of-shape and ageing body), but also a new music and a new horror. 'Come, wait upon him,'[37] says Titania to her Fairy attendants, while Brook – wolfish

³⁸ *Oberon:* Thou see'st these lovers seek a place to fight.
Hie therefore, Robin, overcast the night.
The starry welkin cover thou anon
With drooping fog, as black as Acheron.

(*III.ii.354–357*)

³⁹ *Lysander:* Where are thou, proud Demetrius? Speak thou now.
Puck: Here, villain; drawn and ready. Where art thou?
Lysander: I will be with thee straight.

(*III.ii.401–403*)

⁴⁰ *Puck:* Thou coward, art thou bragging to the stars,
Telling the bushes that thou look'st for wars,
And wilt not come? Come, recreant! Come thou child!
I'll whip thee with a rod. He is defiled
That draws a sword on thee.
Demetrius: Yea, art thou there?
Puck: Follow my voice. We'll try no manhood here.
(*Exeunt. Enter LYSANDER*)
Lysander: He goes before me and still dares me on:
When I come where he calls, then he is gone.
The villain is much lighter-heeled than I.
I followed fast, but faster he did fly,
That fallen am I in dark uneven way,
And here will rest me. (*Lies down*) Come, thou gentle day!

(*III.ii.407–418*)

with excitement – signals for soft drumming, saying 'I think the moon comes out for the first time at this moment.' And neighing brutishly as if in rut, Bottom is lifted up, a four-legged carcase for the shambles, but borne into the air by love and made light of. Titania and Bottom, swathed in an unrolled bale of mechanicals' cloth in which to couple, are carried away to their own transports.

But if to have muscular fairies, biceps a-ripple, subverts the fay of the Victorian tradition, a stylish acrobatics, the artifice of trapezes and pennants, and the finger-cymbals of an oriental drama begin in turn to threaten an eclecticism which is even more spurious, and just as mannered. 'Thou see'st these lovers seek a place to fight'[38], says Oberon, later in the Third Act, 'hie therefore, Robin, overcast the night.' So saying, a silken Chinese gonfalon is swirled, literally matching word and gesture in a black flourish. 'Where art thou, proud Demetrius?'[39], Lysander asks. Riding on Puck's shoulders is the visual answer, a courtly lover and an Arden Spirit become Japanese wrestlers, or Kathakali figures. And grimacing together like *Samurai* warriors, Demetrius and Puck respond together: 'Here, villain; drawn and ready.' Puck speaks, and on his back, in exaggerated synchrony, Demetrius gestures; his suddenly-fanged persona both stylized and adventitious.

Will these elements become fixed and settled in the production? And how do they consort with the search for the play's innermost rhythm? Or is Puck's 'I'll whip thee with a rod. He is defiled/ That draws a sword on thee'[40], suffocated as it is by an alternate tradition, in fact a good deal closer to a *samurai*'s brutal courage than to the footstamping of a Peter Pan in Kensington Gardens? Yet, as has already happened in these rehearsals, reservation is itself quickly overridden. For there is a bare and plangent tone, unheard before, in Lysander's 'Come, thou gentle day,'[40] and the sound of an odd melancholy reaching to the crux of the play, at 'fallen am I in dark uneven way.'[40] At this deeply resonating echo of an Anglo-Saxon (not Japanese) saga, or of a cadence from Gawain, Brook himself haltingly describes the moment of Lysander's thraldom as 'the bedrock', as 'the nightmare coming home to him', as 'almost going into tragedy'.

Indeed an abyss seems to open as the actors begin to bear the dark weight of the play downwards, on their shoulders. Each of the four lovers in the enchanted wood seems to speak with the exhausted despair of the old Christian hero lost in a medieval world of wonders, and assailed by temptation. Brook says of their speeches, as they lie

⁴¹ *Puck:* Come hither. I am here.
   Demetrius: Nay, then, thou mock'st me. Thou shalt buy this dear,
      If ever I thy face by daylight see.
      Now, go thy way. Faintness constraineth me
      To measure out my length on this cold bed.
      By day's approach look to be visited.

                                           (*Lies down and sleeps*)
                                              (*Enter HELENA*)

   Helena: O weary night, O long and tedious night,
      Abate thy hours! Shine comforts from the east,
      That I may back to Athens by daylight,
      From these that my poor company detest:
      And sleep, that sometimes shuts up sorrow's eye,
      Steal me awhile from mine own company.

                                                      (*Sleeps*)
                                              (*III.ii.425–436*)

⁴² (*ACT FOUR. Scene One. The wood. LYSANDER, DEMETRIUS,*
   HELENA and HERMIA, lying asleep. Enter TITANIA,
   BOTTOM, FAIRIES and OBERON, behind, unseen)
   Titania: Come, sit thee down upon this flow'ry bed,
      While I thy amiable cheeks do coy,
      And stick musk roses in thy sleek smooth head,
      And kiss thy fair large ears, my gentle joy.
   Bottom: Where's Peaseblossom?
   Peaseblossom: Ready.
   Bottom: Scratch my head, Peaseblossom.

                                                      (*IV.i.1–8*)

⁴³ *Titania:* What, wilt thou hear some music, my sweet love? . . .
      . . . Or say, sweet love, what thou desirest to eat.

                                                      (*IV.i.25–26*)

⁴⁴ *Titania:* Sleep thou, and I will wind thee in my arms.
      Fairies, be gone, and be all ways away.

                                              (*Exeunt FAIRIES*)

      So doth the woodbine the sweet honeysuckle
      Gently entwist; the female ivy so
      Enrings the barky fingers of the elm.
      O, how I love thee! How I dote on thee!

                                                   (*They sleep*)
                                              (*IV.i.37–42*)

themselves down to sleep[41], that 'there are deep inner movements here.' They are 'movements more serious than a common-or-garden dropping to the ground'; they 'trust in sleep because there is nothing else to trust to'. But, for once, Brook is unequal to what the actors are themselves revealing of this descent into the underworld of the imagination: a return by Shakespeare to an ancient idiom, which reaches deep into the rhythm and language of the progress of the pilgrim through a vale of terrors, deep-shadowed. 'All four characters,' he says cryptically, 'will end up hanging or swinging like butterflies on a beam.' Will they hang by their hands from the parallel bar, at this point, when the production opens?

'O weary night, O long and tedious night'[41] says Helena, like Eurydice descending now to Pluto's kingdom, her own tense weariness (of rehearsal) taking her far into the darkness. 'Sing it,' says Brook; 'sing it to the darkest, deepest, black chords that can be found.' And so she does. It is a singing melancholy, and a dark radiance, far beyond what has been achieved before in these rehearsals. Hermia is (today) as transfigured in darkness as Bottom; finding her own deeply resigned and languid rhythm, her body a dark flower, her voice the palest blossom.

Now Act Four becomes a rude awakening into daylight[42]. It is the dazed morning after, too bright and glaring. For Titania and Bottom, it is post-coital, he muted or melancholy and she 'pleased to have contented him', as Brook puts it. There will be a 'precious moment of return to reality,' says Brook, when Bottom, vine-draped and trailing clouds of glory, 'rediscovers his trousers'. As to Titania, Brook tells her that in her 'Come, sit thee down upon this flow'ry bed'[42] there is no longer sensuality – against which he warns her – but an 'impulse to organize Bottom's comforts'[43]. It expresses the passing of desire into contentment. She falls asleep with Bottom in her arms[44]; it is the sleep of the sated, freed of sexual anguish and as if basking in a midsummer sunlight.

At the end of the rehearsal, Brook asks all the actors to assemble. He tells them that 'the work which has been done up to now, after less than two weeks, is of remarkable quality', and that the rehearsals have been 'interesting'. 'This is good,' he says, because 'it is what we are living through.' (The comment is also too oblique to be immediately understood.) He then points out that 'all the marvellous possibilities' for each actor to explore his or her part would 'go by the board', were there not so much time available to them for rehearsal. This is

9   Bottom: '. . . and let him hold his fingers thus, and through that cranny shall Pyramus and Thisby whisper.' (Act Three, Scene One); (l. to r.) Barry Stanton (Snug), Celia Quicke (Fairy), David Waller (Bottom), and Norman Rodway (Snout).

particularly so where the 'power and strength of the play in performance' will rest upon the 'overall experience' which each has of 'the play as a whole'.

He tells them that in three weeks' time he plans to have an audience of children to watch their performance, 'to see if we can learn anything from their responses'. There will also be two 'working rehearsals', done in public and away from Stratford, in which they will use 'whatever props and costumes we have arrived at'. This will be 'to get added life and light', as well as 'freedom from the burden of the idea of a first definitive performance at an opening night'. And, finally, he tells the actors that 'ultimately the purpose of all the preparatory work' is 'to get to the point where things work almost by themselves'.

It is not clear what this means. (The actors have listened with respect, but in their own silence.) Certainly what it seems to mean, from the vantage-point of my chair, bids fair to deny much of what Brook has so far been seeking: the personal and painstaking search for impulse, rhythm and deepest levels of meaning; an ensemble exchange of every kind of awareness, among a cast alive to the whole play's range and radiance; and a re-creation of *A Midsummer Night's Dream* in a new and fresh reading. But if it means little or nothing, no one is saying, and it may not matter. For the art, or technique, of the director – like that of his orchestral twin, the conductor – clearly demands greater mastery of the sub- and pre-verbal, than of the verbal. And today, the spirits of *A Midsummer Night's Dream* have been rising.

Second week, sixth day

It occurred to me today that Brook's rehearsals are performances. That is, they are less rehearsals towards a future performance – though they are necessarily that too – than performances themselves. It is perhaps for this reason that he makes no conscious attempt to recapture and repeat earlier creative moments. As a result, the focus of creative discovery has shifted, from one rehearsal to another; resting now on one illumination (which may not recur), and now on another. However, today, Brook said to me that he regretted that there had been no tape-recording made of yesterday's rehearsal, when the lovers, one by one, found a dark music in their lines not found by them before, and which may even not be repeated.

Before the rehearsal began, Brook – standing among a group of actors – casually referred to yesterday's achievement. Helena, who had

(*Enter LYSANDER and HELENA*)

Lysander: Why should you think that I should woo in scorn?
Scorn and derision never come in tears:
Look, when I vow, I weep; and vows so born,
In their nativity all truth appears.
How can these things in me seem scorn to you,
Bearing the badge of faith, to prove them true?

(*III.ii.122–129*)

46 *Helena:* O spite! O hell! I see you all are bent
To set against me for your merriment:
If you were civil and knew courtesy,
You would not do me thus much injury.
Can you not hate me, as I know you do,
But you must join in souls to mock me too?

(*III.ii.145–150*)

47 *Hermia:* Why, get you gone. Who is't that hinders you?
Helena: A foolish heart, that I leave here behind.
Hermia: What, with Lysander?
Helena: With Demetrius.
Lysander: Be not afraid. She shall not harm thee, Helena.
Demetrius: No, sir, she shall not, though you take her part.
Helena: O when she's angry, she is keen and shrewd!
She was a vixen when she went to school;
And though she be but little, she is fierce.
Hermia: 'Little' again! Nothing but 'low' and 'little'!
Why will you suffer her to flout me thus?
Let me come to her.
Lysander: Get you gone, you dwarf;
You minimus, of hind'ring knotgrass made;
You bead, you acorn!

(*III.ii.318–330*)

herself helped to find and lead the way for the others, was listening. With round-eyed insouciance and a hint of pouting, she denied (as did Hermia) all awareness of it and moved away to prepare for the rehearsal. I assumed it to be merely a form of coquetry, by which to attract attention to her (as if) interestingly naive talent; while Brook remarked caustically to me: 'If yesterday was a moment of truth, then here is another one!' I reminded him of an earlier conversation in which he had said that he thought actors were conscious of the heightened moments of creativity in which they had participated. He shrugged his shoulders. Two of the cast's principals had apparently been unaware of the effect they had created. What, then, is the nature of such inspiration? How far, and in what ways, can it be willed by the actor, or be evoked by the director?

It was as if such unanswered (and perhaps unanswerable) questions, and the irritation quickly evoked in the irritable Brook by the two actresses' blank – and bland – incomprehension, then helped to provoke a succession of angry responses from him to the rehearsal. The scene of the conflict was Act Three, Scene Two[45]; in which, in addition, Shakespeare expends on the quartet of misled lovers a tangled, and even tedious, poetry of repetitive amazement and muddled impulses, hard to animate and harder to follow.

Helena was the first to flounder. Her 'O spite! O hell!'[46] was described by an exasperated Brook as 'mere elocution'. 'All that you are doing,' he said to her fiercely, 'is getting the words out well. This is precisely what blocks all your responses.' Thereafter, the other lovers too, pushing for a resonant meaning, could produce from the words only the stress of a false self-pity and an unfelt pathos: their gestures and movements caught up in clutches of despair, and the writhings of a synthetic anguish.

Brook shouted across them. 'The moment you go into pathos, you are playing the wrong line completely. If you cultivate emotional states,' he threatened them, 'you cannot find anything. When your emotions swamp your sense of what is happening second-by-second, you are wrong!' There was a dispirited silence. 'It is the difference between a generalized emotion and being with the intimate course of the unfolding words. In it, every word is an action.' But in these very words which Shakespeare has given the lovers, as the four actors know better than the director, is no sacred text, but blank – and even very blank – verse.

They resumed, and again the scene foundered in a wasteland of Shakespeare's dull speech[47] and their washed-out feeling, not made

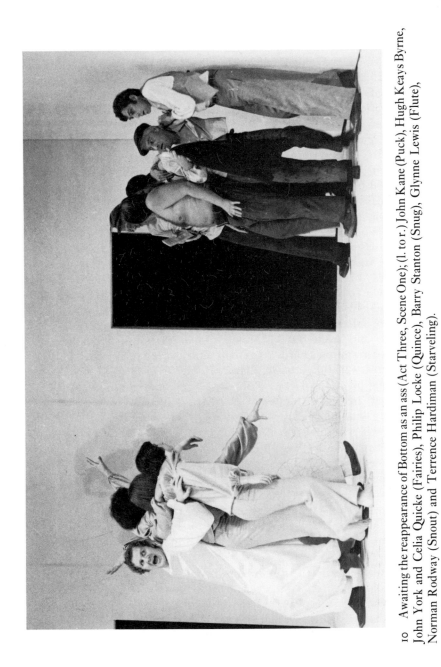

10 Awaiting the reappearance of Bottom as an ass (Act Three, Scene One); (l. to r.) John Kane (Puck), Hugh Keays Byrne, John York and Celia Quicke (Fairies), Philip Locke (Quince), Barry Stanton (Snug), Glynne Lewis (Flute), Norman Rodway (Snout) and Terrence Hardiman (Starveling).

good by over-acting. Brook halts them. This time, they are 'simply taking hold of one another for no purpose', and 'matching words with action in the crudest cliche sense'. The whole, he says angrily, is an 'unfelt reaction'. Brook is particularly severe with Hermia, as he has been before. She is 'hiding behind a sentimental mannerism', failing to open out beyond fixed and pathetic gestures, or to come out from behind a mask of acting. The actors' bewilderment deepened. And the text was unyielding.

Later, Brook said to me that the four lovers had been 'out of harmony with each other'. One, Lysander, had 'never been trained as an actor'; Hermia was 'just too emotional'; Demetrius was 'too rigid and unexploring'; and Helena – the best of them in his judgment, and an 'inventive' actress – was being defeated by the others. I told him that I thought the scene in which they had failed was the most difficult of *A Midsummer Night's Dream*. He agreed that it was. I said that in it Shakespeare had set himself a hard task: to write, with equal imaginative energy and sustained engagement in each case, for four largely unexplored and equi-valent characters simultaneously, all intimately involved with one another. The result, I told him, was an 'artificial *tour-de-force*', and what I called 'a four-part invention', in a near madrigal form.

In such writing, I thought there was (and could be) little concern with 'real' feeling or characterization. Instead, it was a 'sequence of stand-up exchanges', and that was how it should be played. Brook said that 'it could not be done'. Why not, I asked him. Because 'it would take a Gielgud, or a Renaud.' Why? 'To play everything with rightness and speed. To play even the full stops and the commas'. I told him that I did not agree; and that 'if you are exploring different kinds of acting style and "reality", then I do not see why this form should not also be present, or at least attempted'.

The rehearsal, after yesterday's successes, was difficult and exhaust-ing. The causes of such debacle are as complex as they are impalpable. Destructive, like creative, mood is a communicable infection, swiftly caught and swiftly transmitted. Brook, any actor (even a spectator?) can be as much a bearer of the one as of the other. Involuted, as he was at times today, Brook is at his worst. He then becomes the very embodiment of the unease and inauthenticity from which he seeks to extricate the actor. You can see and hear his geniality fading before your eyes, sometimes into an awkward withdrawal, miscalled shyness, and sometimes into a hiding as coy as Hermia's.

If there is a play within a play before us, this is yet another.

[1] *Theseus:* Now, fair Hippolyta, our nuptial hour
   Draws on apace. Four happy days bring in
   Another moon; but O, methinks, how slow
   This old moon wanes! She lingers my desires,
   Like to a stepdame, or a dowager,
   Long withering out a young man's revenue.
Hippolyta: Four days will quickly steep themselves in night,
   Four nights will quickly dream away the time.

                                          (*I.i.1–8*)

Third week, first day

Against the rhythm of previous rehearsals – signifying some continuing stress, carried over the weekend, in Brook himself – he
unexpectedly and peremptorily ordered the actors, as exercises began
the day, to 'walk like water'. The actors were thrown. I had a sense,
from his gait and posture and the sound of his voice, that it was his
tension not theirs which he was subconsciously trying to resolve. And
in the impossible struggles to undulate which followed, I had a
premonition of disaster. Some light-footed it trippingly, others waded;
some, Christ-like, walked on water; some swayed, others rippled.
Above all, a purposeless chinoiserie seemed once more to be stalking
the rehearsal. 'Show me a waterfall,' Brook commanded. They could
not; they were treading water.

   Irritation now expressed in the exaggerated calm of his demeanour,
and speaking in a pent-up *sotto voce*, Brook pushed his own mood of
abrupt demand further. The exercises were brusquely swept aside.
The play was to be run through again from the beginning, but now the
actors were to 'come on with full power'. They were being asked to
pass from 'walking on water' to a world of heroic gesture. My earlier
suppositions that Brook was working, *inter alia*, to some inexplicit
notions drawn from the 'oriental' theatre was now vindicated. 'As in
Japanese theatre,' he instructed the actors, 'the characters must arrive
with a primitive urge and pressure. Find it in the rhythm'[1]. They did
not. It is not in the rhythm. It is, instead, a stylistic – or stylish –
quirk, imported by the director into the production. Theseus and
Hippolyta tried the opening lines again, and again failed to find a
Japanese pressure.

   Then, with the strange desperation which he had brought with him
to the rehearsal, Brook began to betray much of the refinement of his
previous insights. 'The whole play,' he said to the floundering
Hippolyta, 'is about sex.' It is not. Theseus began the first lines again:

83

2 *Theseus:* Go, Philostrate,
   Stir up the Athenian youth to merriments,
   Awake the pert and nimble spirit of mirth,
   Turn melancholy forth to funerals;
   The pale companion is not for our pomp.

                                                    (*Exit PHILOSTRATE*)

   Hippolyta, I wooed thee with my sword,
   And won thy love, doing thee injuries;
   But I will wed thee in another key,
   With pomp, with triumph, and with revelling.

                                                    (*I.ii.11–19*)

3   (*Enter LYSANDER and HERMIA*)
   Lysander: Fair love, you faint with wand'ring in the wood;
   And to speak troth, I have forgot our way.
   We'll rest us, Hermia, if you think it good,
   And tarry for the comfort of the day.
   Hermia: Be't so, Lysander. Find you out a bed;
   For I upon this bank will rest my head.
   Lysander: One turf shall serve as pillow for us both,
   One heart, one bed, two bosoms, and one troth.
   Hermia: Nay, good Lysander. For my sake, my dear,
   Lie further off yet, do not lie so near.

                                                    (*II.ii.35–44*)

4 *Hermia:* But, gentle friend, for love and courtesy
   Lie further off, in human modesty.
   Such separation as may well be said
   Becomes a virtuous bachelor and a maid,
   So far be distant; and, good night, sweet friend.
   Thy love ne'er alter till thy sweet life end!

                                                    (*II.ii.56–61*)

'Now, fair Hippolyta, our nuptial hour/ Draws on apace. Four happy days bring in/ Another moon . . .' Brook again interrupted. 'You were not listening,' he told Hippolyta; 'get the sex from Theseus's rhythms.' There is not much sex in Theseus's rhythms. 'Don't use logic,' he said to her, as the rehearsal's logic foundered. 'Don't give explanations.' Brook gave none either.

Within a few lines[2], the Japanese in Brook re-surfaced. 'Hippolyta,' says Theseus, 'I wooed thee with my sword,/ And won thy love, doing thee injuries.' Brook interrupted: 'Here Theseus will produce a blood-stained sword. It will be a reminder of the play's dark background, remote from all dreams and revels.' The action will be simply (and literally) suited to the word. The supposedly essential search by each actor for the play's deep impulses is thus being displaced, without more ado, by a briskly dictated rhythm – without possibility, given Brook's mood, of the actor's objection.

And as Theseus's brief introductory speech ended, there again came the whirling-metal discs-on-sticks of previous rehearsals, now being handed on, spinning, from one to the other with a skill which is increasing. The actors, breaking off from speech and speech's propulsions, are now turning into acrobatic figures who seem to have stepped out of a tableau from the Chinese circus. We will see this orientalizing business, I fear, in the final version. Then, what appears to have begun as a directorial device to enhance ensemble skills and rhythms will have become a mere decoration. Or was this always its purpose? Is it nothing more than the whim of a director intent above all on putting a new gloss, a new sheen, on an old play tired out by reiteration?

This dire question became more insistent as the actors, their performance dulled, struggled on against Brook's irritation, expressed even in his silence. But the fuse of criticism of the actors seemed gradually to be growing shorter, while my own boredom and preoccupation began to deepen. The lovers' exchanges of Act Two, Scene Two[3], its problems unsolved, again provoked Brook to protest. Something of Hermia's now customary inhibition and physical maladroitness has today affected Lysander. Brook criticizes the acting of both as 'suburban'. But, then, even in the text, Hermia's reiterated 'lie further off yet, do not lie so near'[3], and 'lie further off, in human modesty'[4], seem coy or prudish. 'Why don't they have it off together?' Brook asks them, impatience become jocular.

The simplest answer that this is a play, that they are characters in it

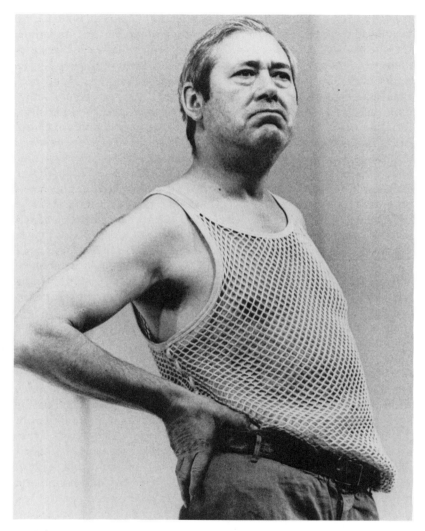

11   Bottom: 'I see their knavery. This is to make an ass of me; to fright me, if they could. But I will not stir from this place, do what they can. I will walk up and down here, and will sing, that they shall hear I am not afraid.' (Act Three, Scene One); David Waller (Bottom).

created by Shakespeare, and that they have no life nor will of their own beyond the lines they have been given, would be an intolerable blasphemy, and end the very illusion upon which all theatre is founded. Lysander, abashed, answers: 'Because it would not be respectable'; Hermia, meekly, 'because it would not be right'. Brook is aghast, and their discomfort is deepened. At a loss, they stand before him, wanting in their responses, both in their roles and outside them. In fact, Hermia is a decorous creature, who seems to find it difficult – though there have been exceptional moments, which she has not repeated – to reveal her own sexual impulses. There survives in her instead a rare quality: that of the seeming virgin.

Later on, I put this to Brook, who by the end of the day seems to have his back to the wall, a condition he has himself done much to provoke. 'No,' he said fiercely (and crudely), 'she is frigid.' Caged and cornered by his own doubts and exasperations, as now, his unease can also make him gnomic and incomprehensible to others (not least to the actors). Tired, he speaks in a syncopated fashion, in this mood of withdrawal, conveying little of what he intends, and (wilfully?) making it difficult to follow. He suggests to me, or seems to be suggesting, that another play is needed. It would explore the enforcement of a 'pure and modest' morality in the lovers on the one hand, and the court's 'double-standards' on the other, while 'making both comprehensible to a modern audience'. Or, perhaps, this is not what he meant at all.

Certainly, a significance and value are attached, in this as in other of Shakespeare's plays, to virgin purity, a value which was translated with an ease of moral recognition into the Victorian tradition. But it is hard in 1970, even if we wanted, to reanimate such a morality with fervour, or re-invest it with cultural significance and meaning. Does the play then lose, for today's audience, a large part of the sexual charge in its virginal impulse? I think that this is what he was getting at, though he was unable to put it clearly. He said that he wanted to do a film on the subject: one which would 'go against the tide' by recognizing (I think) virginity's range of meanings, while re-exploring its force and value. I engaged him on this topic without being much interested in it, though as if I were; his own convoluted manner of discourse shamingly driving me, in turn, to display my own capacity for intellectual make-believe and deception. Or is this provoked masquerade merely something which happens in rehearsal – and which he must make happen – and which was carried over from it into the motion of our conversation?

⁵ *Lysander:* Stay, gentle Helena; hear my excuse:
   My love, my life, my soul, fair Helena!
   Helena: O excellent!
   Hermia: Sweet, do not scorn her so.
   Demetrius: If she cannot entreat, I can compel.
   Lysander: Thou canst compel no more than she entreat.
      Thy threats have no more strength than her weak prayers.
      Helen, I love thee; by my life, I do!
      I swear by that which I will lose for thee,
      To prove him false that says I love thee not.
   Demetrius: I say I love thee more than he can do.
   Lysander: If thou say so, withdraw and prove it too.

                                                    (*III.ii.245–255*)

⁶ *Puck:* What, a play toward! I'll be an auditor;
   An actor too perhaps, if I see cause.
   Quince: Speak, Pyramus. Thisby, stand forth . . .
   Pyramus: . . . But hark, a voice! Stay thou but here awhile,
      And by and by I will to thee appear.

                                                    (*Exit*)

   Puck: A stranger Pyramus than e'er played here!

                                                    (*Exit*)

   Thisby: Must I speak now?
   Quince: Ay, marry, must you. For you must understand he goes but
      to see a noise that he heard, and is to come again.

                                                    (*III.i.70–82*)

88

In the rehearsal itself Brook had again sought unavailingly to escape the impasse of the lovers' quartet in Act Three, Scene Two[5]. He had even called for music, in order to invoke tender feelings where neither the words, nor the circumstances, not the actors' skills could themselves evoke them. But this had merely succeeded in suggesting the kind of generalized emotion, in this case a tawdrily sentimental one, for which elsewhere he had expressed abhorrence. Moreover, today, I could see how directorial devices might be used – however rarely in Brook's case – not to express invention, but to hide the lack of it.

Thus, during the passages in Act Three, Scene One[6], of the Spirits' terrorization of the mechanicals, Brook seemed to me to seek refuge from the day's earlier failures, by arbitrarily widening his search for effects without sufficient causes. (This is perhaps as good a definition as any for a *bad* theatre of directors.) Each mechanical was tormented in turn; and a gymnast's mat became the focus of the acrobatic tumblings which, at Brook's still orientalizing direction, expressed the actor's response to such torments. He also asked the actor-mechanicals, himself toying all the while with the techniques of provocation, to make the widest and most distant ring permitted by the studio's acting area. With long sticks and remote gestures, the spirits thus made their slow-witted victims, writhing on and over the mat, dance to their bidding.

It was a strange dalliance, itself tormented, which seemed to express less the moods of the play or of the actors, than of the director.

Third week, second day

I did not attend today's rehearsal. From conversation, I gathered that it had centred around improvisations by the quartet of lovers. This work had obviously itself flowed from the previous day's alarms and inhibitions.

Third week, third day

From the doorway, I saw Brook approaching the studio. And I again saw, in his taut gait and cold expression, something which boded ill for the actors: tension, frustration, suspicion. In fact, it turned out to be a

7   (*Enter DEMETRIUS, HELENA following him*)

Demetrius: I love thee not, therefore pursue me not.
    Where is Lysander and fair Hermia?
    The one I'll slay, the other slayeth me . . .
Helena: . . . You draw me, you hard-hearted adamant;
    But yet you draw not iron, for my heart
    Is true as steel. Leave your power to draw
    And I shall have no power to follow you.
Demetrius: Do I entice you? Do I speak you fair?
    Or, rather, do I not in plainest truth
    Tell you, I do not nor I cannot love you?

                                 (*II.i.188–201*)

8   (*Exit DEMETRIUS*)

Helena: I'll follow thee, and make a heaven of hell,
    To die upon the hand I love so well.
                                   (*Exit*)

Oberon: Fare thee well, nymph: ere he do leave this grove,
    Thou shalt fly him, and he shall seek thy love.
                            (*Enter PUCK*)

    Hast thou the flower there? Welcome, wanderer.
Puck: Ay, there it is.
Oberon: I pray thee, give it me.

                                 (*II.i.243–248*)

9   (*Enter LYSANDER and HERMIA*)

Lysander: Fair love, you faint with wand'ring in the wood;
    And to speak troth, I have forgot our way.
    We'll rest us, Hermia, if you think it good,
    And tarry for the comfort of the day.
Hermia: Be't so, Lysander. Find you out a bed;
    For I upon this bank will rest my head.
Lysander: One turf shall serve as pillow for us both,
    One heart, one bed, two bosoms, and one troth.

                                 (*II.ii.35–42*)

day of climactic hostilities which ended in weeping. Exhaustion and a suffocating sense of claustrophobia and futility in me were compounded in my own reactions; while Brook's contradictory explanations and incoherently suppressed feelings imposed new burdens on the actors. Moreover, my own prejudice led me, blindly or with clairvoyance, to perceive the actors as men and women struggling to serve not their own, but primarily Brook's, emotional and artistic needs and expectations.

I thus thought I had at last been given a full and privileged glimpse of 'director's theatre' at its worst and barest, a conception which today seemed both real and absurd together – as absurd, say, as the cognate notion of conductor's music. Or was it that I had merely heard the sounds, at high volume, of that battle of the egos which the theatre in general could be said both to serve and embody, and which my own bruised sense of the playwright's primacy in turn expresses?

The day began calmly with the actors' increasingly deft juggling: with plates, with flags, and now with yo-yos. (Whither?) Behind them, stood a dance band's full drum-set. Bodies, sounds, movements, devices are spread before the director. Add a text of whatever provenance, and the whole must be articulated. Is this the director's role? And what does it amount to? Is it all, or nothing? Is it much or little? (And, wearily, do the questions matter?)

The run-through begins, at the point where the present problems lie: with the lovers, Helena and Demetrius to start with, in Act Two, Scene One[7]. 'I love thee not,' says Demetrius, a negation, succeeded by negation upon negation, which itself contains the heart of the problem of enactment. Brook is visibly in a dangerous mood. He taps softly on a drum, drawing to himself all attention and distraction. At the same time, he is marking out the punctuations of their speech with a drummed insistence, while heightening the actors' exposure. He has told them that they may stop where they wish, recapitulate, continue. He does not interfere; yet the actors themselves sink slowly into limbo, since each foot is being dogged by drumming. There is rescue only in Oberon's and Puck's arrival. 'Hast thou the flower there?' asks Oberon; 'Ay, there it is,' Puck answers[8]. It is a spinning plate, not a summer flower, which passes between them.

It is the entrance of Lysander and Hermia[9] which now arouses the whole studio's foreboding. 'One turf shall serve as pillow for us both[9], sings Lysander, immediately struggling against some of Shakespeare's most limp but least yielding couplets; and whose

¹⁰ *Hermia:* But, gentle friend, for love and courtesy
       Lie further off, in human modesty.
       Such separation as may well be said
       Becomes a virtuous bachelor and a maid,
       So far be distant; and, good night, sweet friend.
       Thy love ne'er alter till thy sweet life end!
Lysander: Amen, amen, to that fair prayer, say I,
       And then end life when I end loyalty!
       Here is my bed. Sleep give thee all his rest!
Hermia: With half that wish the wisher's eyes be pressed!

                                    (*They sleep*)
                                    (*II.ii.56–65*)

emotion seems here as generalized as the actors' acting is – rightly – commanded not to be. Both sense and sound ring false and hollow, while my own feeling of the pointlessness of it all is redoubled. Awkward and sentimental, Hermia goes under[10]. By the time she has reached the thankless 'with half that wish the wisher's eyes be pressed!'[10], all life is extinct.

Brook now explodes with the anger and anxiety he had brought with him. 'This is a descent into suburbia,' Brook says to her coldly; 'a T.V. play of mumbled intimacy, a Stratford bus-stop meeting.' The actress is mute, one hand tugging at the other. 'Where is the emotional life of it? Where is the vibration of the words? Where is your line through it?' There is not much of a life or vibration in the text, but who dare say it? 'This is written in a special form called Shakespeare,' Brook insultingly tells her. She is being stripped naked. And it is not true; there is no such 'special form'. (But that Brook thinks there is, is more revealing than the actress's failure.) She looks down, wilted. 'What you are doing is no longer a true expression of feeling,' he announces. She is isolated by the tirade, and seems also to have been abandoned by the other actors. 'You can't play a sub-text in Shakespeare at the wrong moment,' he tells her fiercely, 'as you can in any fucking ordinary naturalistic drama. At this stage of rehearsal, you are wasting your time and our time also.'

It is the *coup-de-grace*. She is lost, humiliated. Brook, not without reason (and an increase in his own tension) is trying to get back to the impulses which, in last week's rehearsals, had driven the lovers, including Hermia, to sing. But he and they cannot. And against his stated principles, he is now using an intimidating mood to induce responses which the text does not yield, and the actors cannot deliver. I hear Lysander, first into the lifeboat, say, 'I know what he wants me to do,' but with the lack of conviction of a man – and not just an actor – who is losing his sense of direction. And as the rehearsal breaks for the morning, Hermia is called over by Brook and stands in front of him (seated), while he, now avuncular, pats her hand consolingly. For a moment, I think I see the archetypal figures of the unequal: the user and the used, the exploiter and the exploited, of the theatre's production system. He tells her, quietly, what he wants her to do, out of earshot of the others; she is anxious and attentive. When she withdraws, meek and frightened, Brook lights up a small cigar, as the whirligig of emotions continues.

It reached its climax in the afternoon, coming in Act Four as the

(*Exeunt THESEUS, HIPPOLYTA, EGEUS and train*)

Demetrius: These things seem small and undistinguishable,
　Like far-off mountains turned into clouds.
Hermia: Methinks I see these things with parted eye,
　When everything seems double.
Helena: So methinks:
　And I have found Demetrius like a jewel,
　Mine own, and not mine own.
Demetrius: Are you sure
　That we are awake? It seems to me
　That yet we sleep, we dream. Do not you think
　The Duke was here, and bid us follow him?
Hermia: Yea, and my father.
Helena: And Hippolyta.
Lysander: And he bid us follow to the temple.
Demetrius: Why, then, we are awake. Let's follow him,
　And by the way let us recount our dreams.

(*Exeunt*)
(*IV.i.184–196*)

lovers awakened from their experience of the enchanted wood. From Demetrius's 'These things seem small and undistinguishable'[11] to his 'Why, then, we are awake. Let's follow him'[11], the exchanges with Helena, Hermia and Lysander were soft and bated; delicate, muted, inward. Brook, face pale and cold eye shining, was provoked into insensate but controlled outrage. What had just been said had been spoken 'without any sense of what had passed in rehearsal'; it was 'unrelated to the rehearsal experience'. The room froze. Brook's jowls quivered; he again seemed – from where I was sitting – blenched and wolfish.

'We can't go on,' he declared, 'unless we know what it is about.' Three weeks ago, at this point, he had said, 'What happens in this wood must be found.' They (but he too) had evidently not yet found it. 'Have any of you thought about it?' he said with ill-disguised contempt, but also with his lip trembling. There was a silence. 'This is calamitous and disturbing incoherence,' he said. And then, revealingly: 'Only if I create the circumstances, can you do interesting work.' He is pronouncing them puppets of the theatre of directors, and blaming them for it. 'You are developing techniques, but no shared understanding of the play's meaning.' There is an even deeper and stonier silence. This theatre does not encourage boldness of spirit.

'You must be constantly questioning yourselves, others, and me as to what it is about. Without an understanding of the whole play, we cannot go on any longer,' he says flatly. In the silence, his body is tense, his face shiny. But he has himself got his own variable sense of the play, much of which has remained unexpressed, and some of which may be inexpressible. He seems once more to be transferring to them his own difficulties and burdens. 'You must *see* what the function of each scene is in relation to the whole,' he says, with a leaden and weary emphasis, 'otherwise we cannot go on any longer.'

There is no comment. The actors stand both motionless and speechless, in an unrehearsed moment of perfect stasis. They form a hieratic tableau of acolytes, at a standstill before the altar. 'This isn't commonplace theatre,' Brook says in token of dismissal, now speaking less to them than to himself. 'Call it poetic, mystical, religious, ceremonial, holy, metaphysical, whatever you like' – a range of choice which seems confined to Brook's own predilections – 'but it isn't *commonplace*.' The last word has contempt's inflexion about it. 'Commonplace' is an insult, and with such an intonation signifies not 'ordinary' or 'everyday' but 'common', in its various meanings.

12 *Hermia:* Methinks I see these things with parted eye,
   When everything seems double.
Helena: So methinks:
   And I have found Demetrius like a jewel,
   Mine own, and not mine own.
Demetrius: Are you sure
   That we are awake? It seems to me
   That yet we sleep, we dream.

(IV.i.186–191)

This is a monologue drama. And then the phone rings, a *deus ex machina*. Brook is called away to answer it. As the door bangs behind him, the freeze dissolves and the actors instantly find their voices. There is confusion, spoken and unspoken doubt, deference, unconcern and resentment in the day's first free moments of expression – though muted, and even whispered. I hear: 'Yes, but what's his view of it?'; 'you can't say what it means'; 'it's outside the normal kind of play'; 'it's spiritual, a dream'; ' he said you can't impose a theory on it'; and, shrugging, 'does he really know any better?' Theseus/Oberon – that is, Alan Howard – alone speaks with conviction, but in the voice of his master. The play is all spirit, says the King of the Fairies, who is also the Duke of Athens. (He has donned the purple of the Prince Regent, in Brook's absence.) Beyond this, explanation is halting; and has halted, before Brook's re-entry.

He has returned to a now deeper but covert scepticism, which does not express itself. These actors are professionals, not rebels – and Brook is Brook. They have jobs to do, with a succession of master-directors, each in turn wanting something different from them. It is their task to provide it; and whatever Brook's intention for them, less to reason why than to do, and not to die. 'Ask yourselves,' Brook resumes, still tight-lipped but apparently retreating, 'what is sleeping, and what is waking.' A discussion followed, often confused, and from the actors' side professional, rather than honest. Sceptics when his back was turned, they became necessarily convinced in his presence. The actors said what he hoped they would say, needed them to say, and prompted them to say. The play was about certainty, discovery, clarification; Shakespeare's characters passed by way of revelation to 'completion' by experience. So that the actors, at this point in the Fourth Act, are 'awaking to a new truth', in which everything seems transformed by renewal.

But Brook was himself now struggling through a new bout of involution and withdrawal. Its results were familiar. A particular kind of uncertainty and obfuscation began to deepen. Of the awakened Hermia's 'Methinks I see these things with parted eye,/ When everything seems double'[12], Brook said: 'Being awake is more like a dream than sleeping.' And when puzzlement was registered on the anxious faces around him, 'Shakespeare is trying to explain something beyond words.' Then, 'My own words are just approximations. I know you hear them differently.'

At this, I could see that many of the actors, bewildered, and irritated

13 *Helena:* O weary night, O long and tedious night,
Abate thy hours! Shine comforts from the east,
That I may back to Athens by daylight,
From these that my poor company detest:
And sleep, that sometimes shuts up sorrow's eye,
Steal me awhile from mine own company.

(*Sleep*) . . .

. . . *Hermia:* Never so weary, never so in woe;
Bedabbled with the dew and torn with briers,
I can no further crawl, no further go;
My legs can keep no pace with my desires.
Here will I rest me till the break of day.
Heavens shield Lysander, if they mean a fray.

(*Lies down and sleeps*)
(*III.ii.431–447*)

to be bewildered, had lost their bearings, while the frailer and less secure had begun to feel 'intellectually' inferior because they could not make head or tail of what Brook was now saying. But Brook, as if in order to start anew, suddenly asks instead, 'Do you think that Shakespeare was writing from experience?' There is no answer. Discourse has broken down, and Brook for the moment does not pursue the question. Yet it is plain that he is trying to arouse a deeper and more considered response in the actors to what they are doing. But abused a few moments before, they have no taste – if they ever had it – for such a cerebral disquisition, or for such an effort.

'See the small numbers of sounds and rhythms Shakespeare uses here,' said Brook, persisting. He was referring to, but without himself speaking, such lines as Demetrius's, 'Are you sure/ That we are awake? It seems to me/ That yet we sleep, we dream'[12]. But again getting no response, Brook again changed direction, once more only to create confusion. 'You must have respect for words as magical elements,' he said, seeming to shift or even to abandon his view, advanced in the first rehearsal period, that 'words interfere with feeling' and that, hence, the actors must seek out the pre-verbal impulse.

'Work can only be done,' he continued, 'with a sense of the magical word. Then a whole world opens.' His tone and manner now conciliatory, but no less confusing, Brook asks the actors to 'listen to what the movement of the words is telling you'; while at the same time telling them both that the words are 'magical elements' and that 'Shakespeare is trying to explain something beyond words' altogether. But facing the immediately *practical* problem of finding their way to an articulable meaning by a choice of three routes which appear to travel in different directions, the actors are stranded.

Yet it is Brook who presents himself as hurt and disappointed. He recurs to the singing of Helena and Hermia[13] in last week's revelatory run-through of Act Three, Scene Two, which he describes now as 'one of the most magical moments I've known in rehearsal'. Then, using the same words he had used to me, he tells Helena bitterly that 'it was also a moment of truth for me, that you said you actually weren't aware when the magic moment happened.' Taken aback, but easily resisting the emotional pressure (with or without new falsification of her responses), she says firmly: 'I don't admit it to anyone, when I know something magical has happened. It would destroy it.'

There seems to have been some subtle reversal in the emotional balance. Brook, beneath the now unruffled surface, appears to be

(*Enter LYSANDER and HELENA*)

Lysander: Why should you think that I should woo in scorn?
　Scorn and derision never come in tears:
　Look, when I vow, I weep; and vows so born,
　In their nativity all truth appears.
　How can these things in me seem scorn to you,
　Bearing the badge of faith, to prove them true?

(*III.ii.122–127*)

15 *Lysander:* You are unkind, Demetrius. Be not so;
　For you love Hermia; this you know I know.
　And here, with all good will, with all my heart,
　In Hermia's love I yield you up my part;
　And yours of Helena to me bequeath,
　Whom I do love, and will do till my death.
Helena: Never did mockers waste more idle breath.
Demetrius: Lysander, keep thy Hermia; I will none.
　If e'er I loved her, all that love is gone.
　My heart to her but as guestwise sojourned,
　And now to Helen is it home returned,
　There to remain.
Lysander: Helen, it is not so.
Demetrius: Disparage not the faith thou dost not know,
　Lest, to thy peril, thou aby it dear.
　Look, where thy love comes; yonder is thy dear.

(*III.ii.162–176*)

16 *Puck:* Captain of our fairy band,
　Helena is here at hand;
　And the youth, mistook by me,
　Pleading for a lover's fee.
　Shall we their fond pageant see?
　Lord, what fools these mortals be!

(*III.ii.110–115*)

pleading with the actors; while they seem to be listening to him with no more than tolerant attention. Is this itself feigned, a mock-show? Or is it, rather, that on both sides there is a resumed recognition of the obvious – that it is the actors, not Brook, who must act the play for the audience, that it is their task and a daunting one, not his? 'I can help you,' says Brook, apparently reduced by the confusions he has himself created. 'I can help you by eliminating the false experiences you are using. You can only understand, if you use the right experience of your own to draw from. I can know whether it is not right, but I cannot discover the experience for you. This is what Shakespeare is saying too', he tells them, speaking for the playwright. 'He is saying, "my words are only an approximation to my experience, so you must bring your own experience to them".'

The silence is stunning. Then Brook asks them: 'When have you felt most complete, most in stability with the rest of the world? Don't tell me. Think about it.' For the first time, there is a reply. It is Lysander, surrendering. 'I am not practised enough,' he tells Brook, 'to find the rightness you want. I want you to tell me.' He has delivered himself (on behalf of the other actors also?) to Brook. Brook, gaining reassurance and again confident enough to be capricious, says simply, 'It can't be pinned down.' The answer is astonishingly flat and dismissive. There has been no reversal at all in the balance of forces between them.

'There is something consistent,' Brook (once more in his stride) continues, 'which happens when the play bursts into life. Watch for this,' he tells them. 'After such a moment has passed, it can't be switched on again, or mechanically pieced together. What has to be recalled are the meanings which come out of a burst of life. This becomes the starting point for new invention. Ultimately we build up a variety of different experiences of the same area of the play, by trying it from new angles. A free intuition,' he says, 'comes from a group sharing the same direction.' (But whether its provenance is his or theirs, is not a question which will be asked, let alone answered.) And as the actors, after one hour of this discussion, prepare to resume the run-through, a wary peace seems to have been made. 'Rehearsing a play is like going into the woods,' Brook tells them, his voice once more on an even keel; 'sense the life of the words as you speak them.'

Now, from the entrance in Act Three, Scene Two of Lysander and Helena[14], the quartet of lovers once more did battle with Shakespeare's often stilted invention[15]. With Puck[16] told by Brook to

12 Titania: 'I pray thee, gentle mortal, sing again.' (Act Three, Scene One); Sara Kestelman (Titania) and David Waller (Bottom).

act as if he were a puppeteer and to prod them into motion, there was in the actors a renewed vigour, though it seemed to owe more to their frustration than to the director's complex instructions. Yet, by the scene's end, its longueurs, misunderstandings and repeated expostulations had not been successfully managed. Brook asked each of them for his or her reactions.

There was an anxiously hopeful consensus. It had been, they felt, a 'leap forward'. Brook weighed his response coldly. 'It went well for all of you, except Hermia,' he said. It had in fact gone equally well, or badly, for each of them. None had shown more, or less, insight into the scene's awkward impulse than another; only more or less physical and emotional energy, which is another matter. Hermia, again singled out and isolated by the criticism (and with Brook impassive), wept bitterly. None of the other actors stirred. They had again frozen. In distressed misery, and unable to stop weeping – is this the irruption of the real upon hours of illusion? – she broke a spell. For she had, she said, 'no idea of what was going on.'

Brook patted her hand, as he had done in the morning. But when she continued to weep, he grew unsympathetic. He talked against her tears. 'This is work,' he said sharply. 'There is no time for tears.' As I left with head splitting, Hermia, her shoulders heaving, was being comforted in a corner. Brook was standing on his own, in the centre of the studio.

Third week, fourth day

I came to the rehearsal *expecting* a lifting of yesterday's emotional pressures. This is not merely the product of my now sharing the volatile succession of moods in the actor and director, which I do despite my own feeling of isolation and physical containment. It is also because yesterday's gloom and intimidation, surliness and weeping, could not have been allowed to continue. After all, the seeds of disaster as well as of success have now been planted. They are in any case twins, and there is as fine a line between them as there is between a good rehearsal day and a bad one. Physical self-command and the collapse of physical precisions are also theatrical consorts; so are mastery by the actors of technique, and technique's mastery of the actors; obscurities and clarities of purpose; integrity of meaning and the irrelevant gimmick. (These rehearsals and this production now seem to promise both the one and the other.)

103

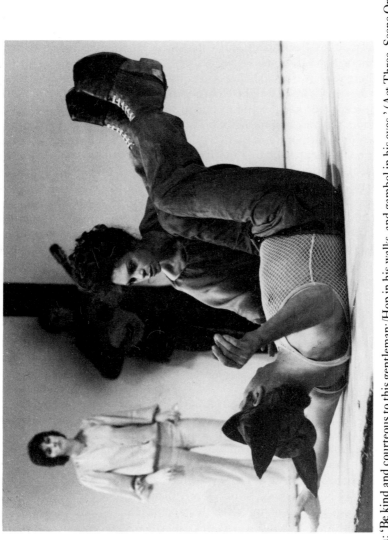

13 Titania: 'Be kind and courteous to this gentleman;/Hop in his walks, and gambol in his eyes.' (Act Three, Scene One); (l. to r.) Celia Quicke (Fairy), David Waller (Bottom) and Sara Kestelman (Titania).

There is an uncomplicated greeting from Brook. It is his own token of a release from yesterday's tensions. It is also in the actors' faces and movements, and in my own feelings. How is this? What, as Brook might ask (but doesn't), can be learned from it? Certainly, that we bear our own dualities about with us, and reflect them – or impose them – upon others, as they upon us, is obvious. But so, too, is the fact that in a collective artistic endeavour, working upon the inscribed dualities of a text, of its characters and of its long-lost author, further duality, mutual incomprehension and contradiction are more likely to arise than a single-minded and linear sense of purpose.

Perhaps the director's practical function is merely, in the interests of order, to impose his own individual set of (contradictory) impulses upon those of others and upon the text, as Brook often appears to be doing; in the hope, often borne out in Brook's case, that his tensions and insights will be more fertile than those of others, and thus deserve their emotional primacy. If so, then this primacy – challenged yesterday by failure, and momentarily lost but quickly regained in a storm of weeping – has been restored this morning in a new equilibrium. But it is one which will be based less on concessions by Brook than by the actors. Yet the paradox is that this restoration, or defeat, and on these terms, seems to be willed and wanted by them. It is in the actors' victorious smiles, to greet the morning.

Sounds are to be exchanged once more. The actors, in a circle, are first to sing a single note, together. (Is this the best metaphor of a harmony achieved by artifice? Is it, even, a form of artistic coercion?) Brook tells them that 'this note is to be felt from head to toe'. It is 'to be used as a mode of communication with one another'. The actors are to speak to each other in sound. Brook, swiftly oblique and obscure once more, says: 'The sound takes you into something different. A different way even of holding yourself, of standing'. It is not clear what he means. And, observing it, it does not appear to be clear to the actors either, even if – prompted by Brook's suggestion – they now hold themselves and stand in awakened and reassembled poses.

In fact, I think Brook is in search of inducements to 'inspiration' in all the word's senses, though he does not say it. The sounds the actors make are now multiplied; become choral and contrapuntal. But at a pause in the sung sound, the spell is once more broken. An actor suggests that 'a guitarist should be used'. A celebrant has broken wind at Holy Communion. Brook is appalled. 'The music must be provided by the cast,' he says testily. 'It is a completely different thing if

(*Enter LYSANDER and HELENA*)

Lysander: Why should you think that I should woo in scorn?
   Scorn and derision never come in tears:
   Look, when I vow, I weep; and vows so born,
   In their nativity all truth appears.

                                        (*III.ii.122–125*)

¹⁸ *Hermia:* Lysander, whereto tends all this?
Lysander: Away, you Ethiope!
Demetrius: No, no; he'll
   Seem to break loose; take on as you would follow,
   But yet come not; you are a tame man, go!
Lysander: Hang off, thou cat, thou burr! Vile thing, let loose,
   Or I will shake thee from me like a serpent!
Hermia: Why are you grown so rude! What change is this,
   Sweet love?
Lysander: Thy love! Out, tawny Tartar, out!
   Out, loathed med'cine! O hated potion, hence!
Hermia: Do you not jest?
Helena: Yes, sooth; and so do you.

                                        (*III.ii.256–265*)

¹⁹ *Demetrius:* These things seem small and undistinguishable,
   Like far-off mountains turned into cloud.
Hermia: Methinks I see these things with parted eye,
   When everything seems double.
Helena: So methinks:
   And I have found Demetrius like a jewel,
   Mine own, and not mine own.

                                        (*IV.i.184–190*)

someone is imported to do it.' (But will this really be the noise of the production? It is hard to believe it.) Sound resumes, in crescendo. The studio vibrates to it.

Once more, work is to resume on Act Three, Scene Two[17]. It is both literally and metaphorically a neck of the wood, from which all escape is proving impossible. In an attempt to reduce the pressure and break the deadlock, Brook quotes Brecht in paraphrase. 'The best rehearsals of his work,' Brecht had said, 'were done in the boredom of understudy rehearsals.' That is, when quickly and perfunctorily running through the text, the salient physical and verbal emphases had been established, and in an understated shorthand – barely audible, and with a minimum of movement. It is this which Brook now asks of the actors.

They stand close together, as if for a reading rather than an enactment. The results are swift in coming. There is a drive towards intimacy and proximity, and away from hostility and estrangement. And as the actors pass quickly and quietly through the words and the action, they bring the lovers' quartet precisely to the mood and style of that 'four-part invention' which Brook had earlier told me it was not possible to achieve, without a Renaud or a Gielgud. Speed, virtuoso artifice, lack of strain, subtlety, poise and private feeling were brought to, and discovered in, what had seemed to be leaden in Shakespeare's invention. In a sudden reversal of expectation, a *tour-de-force*, barely within earshot, was being constructed out of this renewal of the actors' spirits, and out of Shakespeare's writing.

As the lovers' quarrels deepened[18] (and acting began to displace reading under an irresistible impulse), full mobility and volume were restored also. Now, character blossomed where previously there had been only pasteboard and tedium. Hermia is now a vixen, Helena manipulative, a schemer; Demetrius is smug and Lysander aggressive. Moreover, there is a new and rich duality in it. For it is as if the *worst* of their characters is now being disclosed in their enchantment. Their awakening[19], therefore, will now contain suppressed within it – for us, and for them – an embarrassed recollection, more embarrassing for being beyond precise recall, of how they had behaved when unrestrained and unanchored. That is, they are being revealed by the dream itself, or nightmare. And are we not also being told now that there is no 'true' self, no 'real' person, but, instead, Manichaean dualities of daylight and darkness, of sleep and waking, of love and hatred, which alone can give life to the characters before us?

20 *Hermia:* O me! You juggler! You canker blossom!
      You thief of love! What, have you come by night
      And stol'n my love's heart from him?
   Helena: Fine, i' faith!
      Have you no modesty, no maiden shame,
      No touch of bashfulness? What, will you tear
      Impatient answers from my gentle tongue?
      Fie, fie! You counterfeit, you puppet, you!

                                                    (*III.ii.282–288*)

21 *Helena:* O, when she's angry, she is keen and shrewd!
      She was a vixen when she went to school.
      And though she be but little, she is fierce.
   Hermia: 'Little' again! Nothing but 'low' and 'little'!
      Why will you suffer her to flout me thus?
      Let me come to her.
   Lysander: Get you gone, you dwarf.

                                                    (*III.ii.323–328*)

22 *Hermia:* You, mistress, all this coil is 'long of you:
      Nay, go not back.
   Helena: I will not trust you, I,
      Nor longer stay in your curst company.
      Your hands than mine are quicker for a fray,
      My legs are longer though, to run away.
   Hermia: I am amazed, and know not what to say.
                                    (*Exeunt HELENA and HERMIA*)
                                                    (*III.ii.339–346*)

23 *Oberon:* Thou see'st these lovers seek a place to fight.
      Hie therefore, Robin, overcast the night.
      The starry welkin cover thou anon
      With drooping fog, as black as Acheron;
      And lead these testy rivals so astray,
      As one come not within another's way.

                                                    (*III.ii.354–359*)

Here Brook is vindicated too. At an earlier rehearsal, I recall him drawing attention to Helena's abuse of Hermia as a 'puppet', and to Hermia's equally abusive responses[20]. He had felt this to be 'a turning-point', tipping them all into extremes of language, and into self-betrayal or revelation. What he had said at the time had fallen, as interpretation, on stony ground. But here (and now) Hermia's exchanges with Helena[21], driven by the actresses' own energies, became the crux of the scene, the core of its reverberant conflict. A sufficient and right pressure had at last charged the actors, and found the lines' meaning. And once found, but only then, this meaning had become obvious. Their lines, delivered at speed and with matched impulses, were a counterpoint of wit and gaiety which drew in the listener's understanding, dulled before by the actors' own dullness. At Hermia's 'You, mistress, all this coil is 'long of you'[22], the women, briefly left alone for a final spitting encounter, were near to physical combat, egged on (at Brook's new suggestion) by Puck. They were now circling the stage like caged tigresses, or prize-fighters. Only the orientalizing addition of grunts – immediately proposed by Brook – was needed to turn them into Japanese wrestlers.

It was as if an obstacle to the whole company's creation was now being cleared by the solution of the quartet's problems. With the pace maintained, and confidence, energy and invention growing, the voice of Oberon (up a ladder and high above the rest of the cast, on what will be a catwalk in the final production) was rhythmically sprung and racing[23]. 'Hie therefore, Robin,' he says, now in fuller command of his regal resources than ever, 'overcast the night./ The starry welkin cover thou anon/ With drooping fog, as black as Acheron . . .' 'You can blow smoke from your mouth here,' says Brook, aside, to Puck. And in the high tension of Puck's voice is a new premonition of creation. It bursts surging into the small studio, striding in on Puck's new stilts, energy ten feet high above the other actors[24]. Unleashed and grotesque, it dwarfs Demetrius and Lysander. 'Up and down, up and down' it passes, as if invisible, over them, Puck's voice growing with a wooden stride which rhythmically pounds the ground, terror stalking.

Brook can be heard telling Puck consciously to tap out a measured rhythm in his giant striding. Lysander, finding his own impulse as Brook has for long been demanding, is moved to a contrariwise and (again) counter-pointing motion, propelled by fears drawn not from dream but nightmare. Puck, gigantic, is now an awesome sound and fearful presence, his voice at 'Here, villain; drawn and ready', and

24 *Puck:* Up and down, up and down,
   I will lead them up and down:
   I am feared in field and town:
   Goblin, lead them up and down.
   Here comes one.

(Enter LYSANDER)

Lysander: Where art thou, proud Demetrius? Speak thou now.
Puck: Here, villain; drawn and ready. Where art thou?
Lysander: I will be with thee straight.
Puck: Follow me, then,
   To plainer ground.   (*Exit LYSANDER*)

(Enter DEMETRIUS)

Demetrius: Lysander! Speak again!
   Thou runaway, thou coward, art thou fled?
   Speak! In some bush? Where dost thou hide thy head?

(III.ii.396–406)

25 *Demetrius:*   Faintness constraineth me
   To measure out my length on this cold bed.
   By day's approach look to be visited . . .
Helena: O weary night, O long and tedious night,
   Abate thy hours! Shine comforts from the east . . .
Hermia: Never so weary, never so in woe;
   Bedabbled with the dew and torn with briers,
   I can no further crawl, no further go.

(III.ii.428–444)

'Follow me, then, to plainer ground'[24], bellying and lurching among Lysander's terrors. As he backs away and Demetrius enters shouting[24], Brook shouts out against him that Lysander must be 'literally driven to the wall' by Puck's sound and striding; where he will be 'hoisted into position' and, like a stuck and painted butterfly, sleep out his nightmare, elevated.

At the end of the rehearsal, Brook is telling the actors that 'the rhythmic and resonant sound is heightening the whole thing', and that it is 'moving us towards the sung words which will follow'.[25] The actors' spirits are on stilts also, awaiting tomorrow.

Third week, fifth day

There was a collective predisposition and a pressure of expectancy in the air, as the actors gathered. It had survived the night, and imparted a sense of urgency to their gesture and movement as they prepared themselves for rehearsal. I saw that Brook had noticed this instantly on his arrival. Yet he kept the actors waiting, breaking away from them for an half-hour conversation, as they chafed for action. It seemed as if he wanted to speak to me, or perhaps to anyone, of the tensions of the preceding days, their failures and their achievements, while the actors themselves champed at the bit. They could see but not hear us, while he spoke about them. Momentum temporarily expired, they stood like idle chess-pieces waiting for their prime mover.

He referred, with an easy animation, to the 'drama' and emotional strain of the rehearsal process. I told him that 'working for profundity required hard effort'; and that, despite myself, I now felt governed, even overwhelmed, by the changing moods of the actors. I had even begun to feel (ego temporarily in the ascendant) that my own facial expression and physical comportment, in turn, was now a part of the circumstances which confronted the actors, and thus helped to determine – by whatever filiations of feeling – their own responses in rehearsal. He agreed, with unwonted enthusiasm, or so I felt. He said that he himself came to rehearsals thinking he 'could do something to relieve tension' by what he said and did, only to find that he was himself being 'drawn into the prevailing mood', and its stresses. He thus sidestepped the issue of the transmission to the actors of his own tensions, and the manipulation of emotion which lies deep at the root of his kind of theatrical 'direction'; while I, now more convoluted than he, lacked the will to pursue it. He said only that a sociologist, or social

14 Titania: 'Come, wait upon him; lead him to my bower.' (Act Three, Scene One); (l. to r.) Sara Kestelman (Titania), David Waller (Bottom), John York and Hugh Keays Byrne (Fairies).

psychologist, would find it difficult – if not impossible – to detect and analyze the 'currents and cross-currents in such a working group'.

My main interest was to raise with him what I called the 'simulation of awe', which I believed was possible, in particular, for the 'more cynical, more experienced and more talented actor'. He was quickly on his guard. For I too have a view on the question of 'reality' and 'illusion', and one which includes a deep scepticism about the authenticity of the search for the primordial – whether it be the primal scream, or an impulse which is 'pre-verbal'. And just as the 'spiritual' can be raptly spoken of (and enacted) by the most glib and this-worldly of an ostensibly other-worldly priesthood, why cannot the theatrical 'search for truth' be faked by the skilful actor? Isn't there, I asked him, also a 'vocabulary of dramatic awe', as there is a vocabulary of prayer and intercession, which once mastered admits to a priesthood not of truth, but of professional masquerade and illusion?

Brook gave as little hint as I – because neither of us could afford it – that the cap might fit. Indeed, talking to him as I had done before in a closely guarded fashion, for my own complex reasons, I did not allow myself even to think that the cap fitted; not even in passing. The point was made as if in the abstract, and deftly taken so. He said that there was an 'awful awesome' at large in the theatre, about which he would like at some time to talk further. It stemmed, this hieratic theatre of falsehood, from what he called 'naivete and childishness'. Yet even if this description (I conceded by implication) did not fit his theatrical work, I nevertheless persisted; the actors waited in a visibly growing impatience, but he made no effort to terminate the conversation. How can an actor, I asked him, 'working with a succession of directors, or even on two plays simultaneously with two different directors', as in this company, aspire towards and achieve the deepest and most inward self-searching with one, and the most callow – or callous – display of box-office style with another, without *faking his responses?*' And, though I did not feel able to say it directly, without faking his responses in this very production?

The question was short-circuited, rather than fielded; earthed, or by-passed, not answered. He said only, 'It wouldn't be fair, however, to tell the actors to burn down the theatre,' as if I had confronted him with a dilemma of which he too was the victim. This was false ingenuousness, but by now we had created between us a new maze, by each using the same methods of oblique indirection and subterfuge. There was no way out of it except to change the subject or end the

15　Puck: 'Up and down, up and down,/I will lead them up and down:/I am feared in field and town:/Goblin, lead them up and down'. (Act Three, Scene Two); John Kane (Puck) and Ben Kingsley (Demetrius).

conversation. He did neither. Instead, he said that 'communication with the actor' was 'extremely difficult', and that 'the danger with the vocabulary of awe' was that it made the task more difficult still. 'It comes to stand for the real,' he said. 'It would be better to speak in the simplest terms.' (What an irony!) But, I said to him, 'the more simple and less explicit you become, the less the actors are able to follow'. He didn't answer. I had now become, by choice as well as by necessity, the stranger at this midsummer wedding.

The actors sat once more in a circle. They held hands, while sounds were exchanged between them. Brook, moments after our conversation, asks them to evoke 'the noises of night'. These noises, he says, 'should arise spontaneously from silence' and 'be communicated around the circle'. Irritably, he demanded that the silence be 'absolute'. And then, with all eyes closed in a deepening semi-trance (or the simulation of it), the first stirrings of sound began to arise from the actors, and gradually grew to a raucous and caterwauling climax. Once more the whole room – and my metal chair – vibrated. Now, Brook asked the actors to form two seated circles. To one group, he gave the word 'moon', and to the other 'sun'. Neither of the words was to be spoken, nor sung, nor 'illustrated'. Instead, each actor or actress was to emit the sound which the word assigned to the group evoked in him, or her. And each group, while making its own sound in chorus, was to listen to the sound made by the other – not to echo it, nor to answer, but 'for mutual awareness'. But this sun shed no warmth, and this moon no light. For they were metaphors of pure sound; and beyond reason.

Sounds are then 'thrown across the room' from one group to the other, as if they were juggling objects, flung arrowing through air. At Brook's instruction, the noise of the builders' yard follows, in a generalized mouth-made chorus. Finally, Brook orders each actor to communicate with a selected partner at long distance, using a chosen sound from the repertoire of the builder, in a mounting discord of shouted brick and metal. And when this is over, the texture of the stage floor for the finished production is announced by the designer. There is talk of hessian, to give the actor-turned-acrobat a good foothold and purchase, while Brook gives his new orders of the day, as well as the further perspective. Those actors who, at any moment, are not taking part in the 'actual spoken story' will drop out of the acting but 'comment on it by their presence'. The next rehearsal stage is to 'make sure the story-line is clear'; while at the end of the rehearsal period as a

²⁶ *Oberon:* Why should Titania cross her Oberon?
   I do but beg a little changeling boy,
   To be my henchman.
   Titania: Set your heart at rest.
   The fairy land buys not the child of me.
   His mother was a vot'ress of my order,
   And, in the spicèd Indian air, by night,
   Full often hath she gossiped by my side,
   And sat with me on Neptune's yellow sands,
   Marking th' embarked traders on the flood;
   When we have laughed to see the sails conceive
   And grow big-bellied with the wanton wind;
   Which she, with pretty and with swimming gait
   Following – her womb then rich with my young squire –
   Would imitate, and sail upon the land,
   To fetch me trifles, and return again,
   As from a voyage, rich with merchandise.
   But she, being mortal, of that boy did die;
   And for her sake do I rear up her boy,
   And for her sake I will not part with him.

                                    (*II.i.119–137*)

²⁷ *Demetrius:* Do I entice you? Do I speak you fair?
   Or, rather, do I not in plainest truth
   Tell you, I do not nor I cannot love you?
   Helena: And even for that do I love you the more.
   I am your spaniel; and, Demetrius,
   The more you beat me, I will fawn on you . . .
   Demetrius: Tempt not too much the hatred of my spirit,
   For I am sick when I do look on thee.
   Helena: And I am sick when I look not on you.
   Demetrius: You do impeach your modesty too much,
   . . . To trust the opportunity of night
   And the ill counsel of a desert place
   With the rich worth of your virginity.

                                    (*II.i.199–219*)

whole, Brook warns the actors, 'there must be a discipline as tight as a drum'. This discipline, he tells them, 'will not be an external one'. It will have been 'derived from their work' and, as he puts it, be 'self-imposed'; an assertion, such is Brook's authority, which is (paradoxically) beyond challenge.

And then a new run-through began. It straightaway reached new levels of clarity and illumination. In turn, the spectator-and-listener was swiftly brought to a new acuity of response, senses suddenly alerted to the actors' insights. Moreover this time, and for the first time since the rehearsal began, there was a pitch of sustained revelation of the hitherto unheard and unseen which lasted throughout much of the rehearsal. Indeed the lines' pulse and impulse in the creaking studio, and on stained canvas, seemed to become irresistible, against whatever resistance. It was as if the actors, fleeting and impetuous shadows, were being borne along in this Plato's-cave by the momentum of their own energies and by the play's rhythms together.

The characters, with or without benefit of transformation by plot, appeared one by one transfigured. And, outside any formal rule of epistemology, the eye of the beholder – even if refusing surrender – for long periods became wholly lost in its object. Titania, for example, when she refuses Oberon his 'little changeling boy' in Act Two, Scene One[26], brought to 'Set your heart at rest' a changing swiftness of cadence such as seemed to dissolve the written word into the spoken moods which charged them. It was almost as if word and thought had been brought into a unison beyond the reach of either. Her speech had become flamboyant, tense and breathless. At its climax, 'I will not part with him'[26], with her hair wildly tossing, seemed to be spoken from within a female tension close to hysteria. Pitted in unstable dissonance against Oberon's toying laughter and deep anger, it drove her last lines to the very edge of screaming.

As *A Midsummer Night's Dream* again took fire, Brook kept silent but was visibly astounded. For Titania has, until this moment, shown little of this. But what is 'this'? A mood, a passing fancy, 'inspiration', feigning? And how much of 'this' is in the mind's eye of the spectator? But Demetrius seemed caught up in it also[27]. By an impulse of the moment (is it?), he appeared to have found his way to a new reading which seems no longer acted – quarrelling with Helena as if bound by mood and nature, rather than by the text, to do so. Moreover, he was now teasing her with love[27]; against the tense words of rejection, inviting; now finding within himself, while quarrelling, the means for

²⁸ *Demetrius:* I will not stay thy questions. Let me go!
  Or, if thou follow me, do not believe
  But I shall do thee mischief in the wood.
 Helena: Ay, in the temple, in the town, the field,
  You do me mischief. Fie, Demetrius!
  Your wrongs do set a scandal on my sex.
  We cannot fight for love, as men may do;
  We should be wooed, and were not made to woo.

(*II.i.235–242*)

²⁹ *Oberon:* What thou seest when thou dost wake,
  Do it for thy truelove take;
  Love and languish for his sake.
  Be it ounce, or cat, or bear,
  Pard, or boar with bristled hair,
  In thy eye that shall appear
  When thou wak'st, it is thy dear.
  Wake when some vile thing is near. (*Exit*)
      (*Enter LYSANDER and HERMIA*)
 Lysander: Fair love, you faint with wand'ring in the wood;
  And to speak troth, I have forgot our way.

(*II.ii.27–36*)

³⁰ *Oberon:* Now, my Titania, wake you, my sweet Queen.
 Titania: My Oberon, what visions have I seen!
  Methought I was enamoured of an ass.
 Oberon: There lies your love.
 Titania: How came these things to pass?
  O, how mine eyes do loathe his visage now!
 Oberon: Silence awhile. Robin, take off his head.
  Titania, music call . . .
 Titania: Music, ho, music!

(*IV.i.72–80*)

³¹ *Hippolyta:* I was with Hercules and Cadmus once,
  When in a wood of Crete they bayed the bear
  With hounds of Sparta. Never did I hear
  Such gallant chiding; for, besides the groves,
  The skies, the fountains, every region near
  Seemed all one mutual cry. I never heard
  So musical a discord, such sweet thunder.

(*IV.i.109–115*)

an ambiguous duality of emotion and gesture not found before. 'We cannot fight for love,' says Helena, her coquetry matching his, 'as men may do;/ We should be wooed, and were not made to woo'[28]. And now, his kiss in flight and her laughter at refusal seemed, as with Titania, poised at that very pitch of sexual feeling beyond which verbal expression can, and need, go no further.

But as Oberon and Titania, and Demetrius and Helena, found new means for themselves, the strain on Hermia and Lysander began to grow with the others' exhilaration. They seemed to become apprehensive for their entrances[29] into such a siege of the emotions. Yet they need not have done. For, on this occasion, they were borne along by the current. Moreover, the play's shape and figure, now becoming sharply delineated in the lucidities of the rehearsal, today began to provide a more definite and secure context for performance. That is, the actors seemed to begin to know their places more exactly within the whole play's movement, however swift and electric its passage now, from enchantment to disillusion, from safety to danger.

Thus, sleeping and waking are today clearly seen to frame a large part of the action, and to give form to its transitions. Now, as Titania is 'sung asleep' to Oberon's 'Wake when some vile thing is near'[29], the fierce scream of horror which accompanied her fall into slumber, seems to mark a vividly grasped sense of structure. Her awaking, two acts later[30], to 'My Oberon, what visions I have seen' and 'O, how mine eyes do loathe his visage now!' brought not only a feeling of recovery but also of formal balance, absent before. It gave her responses[30] of wonder and fearful recollection, found and expressed in the fewest words, a sense of completed understanding on the one hand, and of a discovered harmony on the other.

Now, too, Act Four was scaled in all its poetic heights. Hippolyta – doubling with Titania, a matter not discussed (at least within my earshot) since the rehearsals began – found in her '. . . all one mutual cry . . . so musical a discord, such sweet thunder'[31] sounds which opened the inward eye, and set it rolling. With its bated sense of wonders beheld in far-off regions inaccessible to mind, it surpassed all previously heard resonance of voice and feeling. And when Bottom awoke[32], minutes later, it was not merely to slough off sleep with jovial interrogation, but as if he were re-born; while beneath the asked, the listener strained to catch the unasked questions, and the ungiven answers. 'I have had a most rare vision', he says; 'past the wit

32 *Bottom:* (*Awaking*) When my cue comes, call me and I will answer . . .
I have had a most rare vision. I have had a dream, past the wit
of man to say what dream it was. Man is but an ass, if he go
about to expound this dream. Methought I was – there is no man
can tell what methought I was – and methought I had – but man
is but a patched fool if he will offer to say what methought I had.

(*IV.i.197–207*)

33 *Pyramus:* Come, tears, confound;
  Out, sword, and wound,
  The pap of Pyramus;
  Ay, that left pap,
  Where heart doth hop. (*Stabs himself*)
  Thus die I, thus, thus, thus.
  Now am I dead,
  Now am I fled;
  My soul is in the sky.
  Tongue, lose thy light;
  Moon, take thy flight. (*Exit MOONSHINE*)
  Now die, die, die, die, die. (*Dies*)
Thisby: O Sisters Three,
  Come, come to me,
  With hands as pale as milk;
  Lay them in gore,
  Since you have shore
  With shears his thread of silk.
  Tongue, not a word.
  Come, trusty sword,
  Come, blade, my breast imbrue! (*Stabs herself*)
  And, farewell, friends.
  Thus Thisby ends.
  Adieu, adieu, adieu. (*Dies*)

(*V.i.287–338*)

34 *Theseus:* This palpable-gross play hath well beguiled
  The heavy gait of night. Sweet friends to bed.
  A fortnight hold we this solemnity,
  In nightly revels and new jollity.

(*Exeunt*)
(*Enter PUCK, with a broom*)
(*V.i.356–359*)

of man to say what dream it was'[32]. (And as we grasped clearly for the first time today, so has Titania.) Rubicund, awkward, coarse-voiced, he searches his vocabulary to speak what he has seen; shakes his head, ransacking his mind to catch at the memory of it as it passes, and conducts us to a tragic moment of recognition, or shared knowledge, of the evanescence of *A Midsummer Night's Dream*.

For Act Five, Brook asked that the studio blinds be drawn, and the lights switched on. A new departure was near. There were twenty or thirty candles standing on a table. The actors are asked to sit in a circle, for a simple reading of the last act in the changed conditions. As they prepared themselves, it was as if the room itself, and everyone in it, was for the first time ready for a crowning of effort. And in new light, there could be heard in this simple reading – how? why? am I imagining it? – a new solemnity and pattern in Pyramus's and Thisby's dying speeches[33], albeit spoken with minimum gesture and with no attempt at enactment.

'This palpable-gross play', says Theseus, of the mechanicals' seated performance in the blacked-out studio, 'hath well beguiled/The heavy gait of night'[34]; and two lines later, at Puck's entrance, Brook stops the reading. He then came over to me, unexpectedly. I told him that Thisby's speech, with its triplicated 'adieu, adieu, adieu' and Pyramus's 'die, die, die, die, die'[35] had seemed almost Lear-like in this reading. 'Yes,' he said, 'and you won't hear them like that again for six weeks, if at all.' He then added, as if rehearsing a thought or thinking aloud, 'What we have experienced is that the discoverer of truth at first sight, is the self-conscious bungler at the second.' I took it, with some difficulty, that he feared that the 'innocent' reading which the actors had just given in the changed physical setting, would lose by repetition. (But when he repeated it to the actors later, I had the impression that they could not follow his meaning.) He also said to me that *A Midsummer Night's Dream* itself was 'about man as innovator' and 'discoverer of truth upon a first experience', and 'fucker-up of the truth' upon a second. This I could not follow.

Brook now tells the actors to change. That is, the actors of the court are directed by Brook to put on court costumes 'as for a party', and the mechanicals to don their proletarian 'Sunday best'. In an adjoining room, there is a tumbled wardrobe of cast-off clothes prepared for them, and they spend some minutes choosing from it and dressing, as the candles are lit and the lights extinguished. (When had this been planned? Did the actors know in advance about it?) Brook says that when they are ready, Act Five is to be 'walked through in candlelight'.

³⁵ (*ACT FIVE. Scene One. Athens. The palace of Theseus. Enter
      THESEUS, HIPPOLYTA, PHILOSTRATE, Lords and
      Attendants*)
   Hippolyta: 'Tis strange, my Theseus, that these lovers speak of.
   Theseus: More strange than true. I never may believe
      These antique fables, nor these fairy toys.
      Lovers and madmen have such seething brains,
      Such shaping fantasies, that apprehend
      More than cool reason ever comprehends.
      The lunatic, the lover and the poet
      Are of imagination all compact.
      One sees more devils than vast hell can hold,
      That is the madman. The lover, all as frantic,
      Sees Helen's beauty in a brow of Egypt.
      The poet's eye, in a fine frenzy rolling,
      Doth glance from heaven to earth, from earth to heaven;
      And as imagination bodies forth
      The forms of things unknown, the poet's pen
      Turns them to shapes, and gives to airy nothing
      A local habitation and a name.
      Such tricks hath strong imagination,
      That, if it would but apprehend some joy,
      It comprehends some bringer of that joy;
      Or in the night, imagining some fear,
      How easy is a bush supposed a bear!
   Hippolyta: But all the story of the night told over,
      And all their minds transfigured so together,
      More witnesseth than fancy's images,
      And grows to something of great constancy;
      But, howsoever, strange and admirable.
      (*Enter LYSANDER, DEMETRIUS, HERMIA and HELENA*)
                                                      (*V.i.1–27*)

³⁶ *Theseus:* Come now, what masques, what dances shall we have,
      To wear away this long age of three hours
      Between our aftersupper and bedtime.
      Where is our usual manager of mirth?
      What revels are in hand? Is there no play,
    . To ease the anguish of a torturing hour?
      Call Philostrate.

                                                      (*V.i.32–38*)

And, one-by-one, in the half-dark, they begin to reappear, the men and women of the court first. Transformed and elevated, they try out the look and feel of their improvised costumes. For the first time jeans and sweat-shirts, pullovers and track-suits, are translated into plumed hats and thigh-boots, ruffs and long dresses, and billowing cloaks of gold and russet. Their shapes and shadows, which a moment ago were familiar faces and homely bodies, seem to be passing out of this world before my eyes, into a candle-lit and flickering darkness.

The mechanicals, with hair slicked – and two of them in spectacles – can be seen waiting in ties and jackets. They look as nervous as a wedding-party waiting for a funereal and white-ribboned taxi; while the court now reclines, as if post-prandially, on soiled cushions made (in the mind) of satin and velvet. They talk among themselves with ease and condescension, masters of the situation, their faces blackened or flaring, the stained canvas hidden in pools of darkness beneath them. Flame makes them appear princes in shot-silk, and sovereign in bearing; but in its penumbra they are hollow-eyed and spectral, ghosts in purple. Or are they merely men and women restored now to the condition of Shakespearian actors, and at last dressed in finery for the dumbshow? And if they are insubstantial before the corporeal spectator, who remains all the while comfortably *in propria persona*, is he not nevertheless as much a moth at the flame as they are?

In this darkness, Act Five was now taken from the beginning: Hippolyta's 'story of the night'[35] was truly to be 'told over'. And as Theseus (lately Oberon) discoursed[35] of the tricks that imagination can play, and of how in the night, 'imagining some fear', a bush may be turned into a bear, the shadows of his gestures reared and yawned behind him. Previous rehearsal perception of the scene was now changing before me; while even Pity-and-Fear seemed ready to enter this Athenian palace, if anyone should bid it. Instead, it was the lovers who entered[35]. Gaunt in the darkness, and holding sparklers which hissed their little festive light around the actors' shoulders, they brought with them a cold and spitting image of tinsel gaiety, pale and wafer-thin. But there was no Victorian silver in it; nor was it drawn from any twinkling fairy-tradition.

Theseus's face, more deeply blackened by the fitful and sparkling light, is now an inquiring voice only, darkly-edged and anxious. 'Is there no play,' he asks, 'to ease the anguish of a torturing hour?'[36] This is suddenly no orgulous or arrogant prince, but a fearful ghost seeking his quietus. 'The battle with the Centaurs' and the Bacchanals'

37 *Theseus:* 'The battle with the Centaurs, to be sung
   By an Athenian eunuch to the harp.'
   We'll none of that. That have I told my love,
   In glory of my kinsman Hercules.
   'The riot of the tipsy Bacchanals,
   Tearing the Thracian singer in their rage.'
   That is an old device; and it was played
   When I from Thebes came last a conqueror.
   'The thrice three Muses mourning for the death
   Of Learning, late deceased in beggary.'
   That is some satire, keen and critical,
   Not sorting with a nuptial ceremony.
   'A tedious brief scene of young Pyramus
   And his love Thisby; very tragical mirth.'
   Merry and tragical? Tedious and brief?
   That is, hot ice and wondrous strange snow.
   How shall we find the concord of this discord?

                                                    (*V.i.44–60*)

38 *Theseus:* What are they that do play it?
   Philostrate: Hard-handed men, that work in Athens here,
   Which never laboured in their minds till now;
   And now have toiled their unbreathed memories
   With this same play, against your nuptial.
   Theseus: And we will hear it.

                                                    (*V.i.71–76*)

39 *Theseus:*   I will hear that play;
   For never anything can be amiss,
   When simpleness and duty tender it.
   Go, bring them in: and take your places, ladies.
                                          (*Exit PHILOSTRATE*)
                                                    (*V.i.81–84*)

124

'tearing' of 'the Thracian singer in their rage'[37] are no longer contemptuously read items of the players' repertoire. Instead, in this dark intonation, they are strange and distant echoes of an imaginative world become tragic and abyssal. Now there can be heard in Theseus' reminiscence of the time 'When I from Thebes came last a conqueror'[37], sounds which are as grave as those of a Dead March, solemn and sepulchral. What he speaks of seems an impossible hallucination, his expression hollowed out and lost in darkness. Now, his weary dismissal of the satire of the Muses, 'mourning for the death of learning'[37], is itself deathly in its resignation. And 'merry and tragical', 'tedious and brief', 'hot ice' and 'wondrous strange snow'[37] speak no longer of witty contradiction or of a paradox of nature, but of a nightmare emotion.

And all the while, 'the cast' is struggling in near-darkness to choose the right play and the right actors to suit the moment. It is more than ever a Chinese box of a problem, at this very moment (here and now in rehearsal) within the moment of *A Midsummer Night's Dream*, and with other moments receding within and radiating beyond it. It turns us all into the heirs and assigns of the deceased playwright, while dissolving in a dazzling *trompe l'oeuil* the distinction between actors and spectators, off-stage and on it. What now is 'real', and what 'illusion'? Who is the actor and who the acted, when they are thus inextricably interwoven?

And as to *Pyramus and Thisby*, 'What are they that do play it?' asks our Theseus of our Philostrate here before us[38]. 'Hard-handed men, that work in Athens here' (where?), he (who?) answers. Reclining (as if) at ease, these actors who both are and are not actors, now choose others – the mechanicals – who also both are and are not actors. Indeed, they are actors pretending to be mechanicals who are pretending to be actors. And they will be mocked for their pains by actors pretending to be princes and courtiers – and all this itself in rehearsal, with isolated spectators as willing or unwilling accomplices.

But paradox of paradoxes, it was precisely this sense of reality's recession into a deepening and inaccessible distance which now drew the mechanicals' performance towards a grotesquely immediate impact. Unreality made a spectacle of them; but gross enactment at close quarters demolished distance. In addition, the artifice of a courtly theatre (not unlike this one in Stratford-on-Avon) was now thrown into sharpened relief by the summoning of groundlings to 'act' for their betters[39]. This also might be Brook's 'total ceremonial', but it

40 *Prologue:* Consider, then, we come but in despite.
We do not come, as minding to content you,
Our true intent is. All for your delight,
We are not here. That you should here repent you,
The actors are at hand; and, by their show,
You shall know all, that you are like to know.
Theseus: This fellow doth not stand upon points.
Lysander: He hath rid his prologue like a rough colt; he knows not
the stop. A good moral, my lord: it is not enough to speak, but to
speak true.
Hippolyta: Indeed he hath played on this prologue like a child on a
recorder; a sound, but not in government.
Theseus: His speech was like a tangled chain; nothing impaired, but
all disordered. Who is next?
(*Enter PYRAMUS and THISBY and WALL and MOONSHINE
and LION
(as in dumbshow)*)
Prologue: Gentles, perchance you wonder at this show;
But wonder on, till truth make all things plain.
This man is Pyramus, if you would know;
This beauteous lady Thisby is certain.
This man, with lime and roughcast, doth present
Wall, that vile Wall which did these lovers sunder.

(*V.i.112–131*)

was to be presented by gawky, proud and graceless characters in humdrum clothing. Solidly mundane and physical, this had become a fantasy in three dimensions and not any longer a figment of the imagination.

Here was the fruition of effort, and at its heart the question 'What is theatre?' burned furiously in the near-darkness. How is it that these characters, known to us from daily meeting, undifferentiated in dress from us and of 'ordinary' appearance, deliberately working against those theatrical conventions which seek an elevated sense of presence, and in the face of stubborn resistance, should now seem figures of greatest portent? Looming, they stood beside me on the dark threshold of the action. Heavy-handed and doom-laden heralds in ties and collars, they were coming with bad jokes and worse tidings; angels of death, in comic black suits, spectacles glinting, their shadows thrown before them.

Poor 'Quince', the 'carpenter-playwright', tense and earnest – hands twisting, hands hanging, hands folded – has brought his workaday world with him, and stands before 'the court', to read 'his' Prologue[40]. The 'courtiers' sit in their circle, torches flaring in darkness. It is a scene which hints at splendour, but is deep in the uncertainties of shadow. His speech, mis-spoken and halting in its broken rhythms, is a thing of pity and folly. Yet the more he is mocked[40], the prouder; the more refined the worldly sallies, the more he is pig-headed. 'Gentles,' he says to their laughter, 'perchance you wonder at this show;/ But wonder on, till truth make all things plain'[40]. And suddenly in the court's giggles, there is only vanity, in darkness; and in Quince, anxious master of these cod-revels, brow furrowed with effort, a dignity to match their own, and an equal length of shadow.

'This man,' says Quince, his voice relentless, 'with lime and roughcast, doth present Wall'[40]. It is none other than 'Tom Snout, the tinker', who is greeted with ironic applause and laughter: a bird-slight and ugly figure, with uptufted sprouts of hair. He mops and mows before them, trying to go beyond himself to please his audience. But he has suddenly become, too, a thing of danger and terror in these uncertain shadows. As he crouches and grins at their feet, mirth is paling. In the candlelight, open eyes and mouths seem black-filled, or blood-filled, with horror, while Brook, beside himself with exhilaration, can be seen moving quickly around the circle of actors.

Fear and restless unease as well as mockery, hollow as an eyesocket,

⁴¹ *Pyramus:* O grim-looked night! O night with hue so black!
O night, which ever art when day is not!
O night, O night! Alack, alack, alack,
I fear my Thisby's promise is forgot!

(*V.i.168–171*)

⁴² *Lysander:* Proceed, Moon.
Moonshine: All that I have to say is to tell you that the lanthorn is the
moon; I, the man i' th' moon; this thorn bush, my thorn bush; and
this dog, my dog.
Demetrius: Why, all these should be in the lanthorn; for all these are
in the moon.

(*V.i.249–254*)

⁴³ *Pyramus:* Approach, ye Furies fell!
O Fates, come, come,
Cut thread and thrum;
Quail, crush, conclude, and quell!
Theseus: This passion, and the death of a dear friend, would go near
to make a man look sad.
Hippolyta: Beshrew my heart, but I pity the man.

(*V.i.276–282*)

⁴⁴ *Pyramus:* Come, tears, confound;
Out, sword, and wound
The pap of Pyramus;
Ay, that left pap,
Where heart doth hop. (*Stabs himself*)
Thus die I, thus, thus, thus.

(*V.i.287–291*)

⁴⁵ *Thisby:* Asleep, my love?
What, dead, my dove?
O Pyramus, arise!
Speak, speak. Quite dumb?
Dead, dead? A tomb
Must cover thy sweet eyes.
These lily lips,
This cherry nose,
These yellow cowslip cheeks,
Are gone, are gone.
Lovers, make moan.

(*V.i.315–325*)

128

now kept company with Pyramus and Thisby, as their truth gained ground in darkness[41]. But there was stress in it, and distress also. Moonshine is wan and despondent, his voice catching, when he tells the jesting court:[42] 'All that I have to say is to tell you that the lanthorn [holding it aloft] is the moon'; is saddened and disheartened at having to explain that he is himself 'the man i' th' moon'; despairing of his poor props at 'this thorn bush, my thorn bush'; and close to tears at 'and this dog, my dog'[42]. This last was almost a question, and spoken out of a newly discovered dejection at the court's mockery of his and his fellow-actors' efforts. It is this moonshine which the courtiers (unlike us) have found wanting, and it is Moonshine who suffers. These were new notes, unheard before, of pity and self-pity at the unrewarded toils and trials of the actor. Hippolyta's 'Beshrew my heart, but I pity the man'[43] is for the first time its fitting coda.

Today, Pyramus' 'Thus die I, thus, thus, thus'[44], in such a dark and plangent mood, was in Shakespeare's major key as tragedian, not the comic minor. In turn, Thisby, played by a male actor in an aching and desperate falsetto, reached (despite it) deep into the black silence which now fell upon the courtiers. 'Asleep, my love?' he asked, 'what, dead, my dove?'[45] But there was only an eerie spitting and sparkling in the enclosing darkness for answer. Laughter and levity had seemingly, once and for all, been silenced. 'These yellow cowslip cheeks, are gone, are gone'[45], he keened, the hair rising, 'lovers, make moan'. His eyes were black-ringed, his body in shadow, as he stabbed himself and cried, like any Lear, 'adieu, adieu, adieu'.

Now Theseus' 'Lovers, to bed . . . I fear we shall outsleep the coming morn'[46] spoke for recovery and relief; spoke too for the felt desire to be spared access to further torments. But today Theseus is no majestic Duke of Athens. He is a cardboard figure, gilded over and back-lit, who has called a halt to an action of such force and power that it has dwarfed him. Indeed, it is as if the rude mechanicals have committed *lèse-majesté* by usurping the court's pretended monopoly of truth-telling; or as if a crude dumbshow has turned the tables upon a court masque, under cover of darkness.

There was a rich satisfaction in this for the spectator, silent on his chair; and it is beyond the critic's cavil. The actors stand in a circle, holding candles, as Brook asks for the lights to be switched back on. 'Hold the mood,' he tells them. 'Take your costumes off as you stand, and then read to the end without moving.' In the cold light, breaths

⁴⁶ *Theseus:* Lovers, to bed; 'tis almost fairy time.
I fear we shall outsleep the coming morn,
As much as we this night have overwatched.
This palpable-gross play hath well beguiled
The heavy gait of night. Sweet friends, to bed.

(V.i.353–357)

⁴⁷   *(Enter PUCK, with a broom)*

Puck: Now the hungry lion roars,
And the wolf behowls the moon;
Whilst the heavy plowman snores,
All with weary task fordone. . . .
And we fairies, that do run
By the triple Hecate's team,
From the presence of the sun,
Following darkness like a dream,
Now are frolic. Not a mouse
Shall disturb this hallowed house:
I am sent, with broom, before
To sweep the dust behind the door.

(V.i.360–379)

⁴⁸ *Oberon:* With this field-dew consecrate,
Every fairy take his gait,
And each several chamber bless,
Through this palace, with sweet peace,
And the owner of it blest
Ever shall in safety rest.
Trip away; make no stay;
Meet me all by break of day.

(Exeunt, all but PUCK)

Puck: If we shadows have offended,
Think but this, and all is mended:
That you have but slumb'red here,
While these visions did appear.
And this weak and idle theme,
No more yielding but a dream,
Gentles, do not reprehend:
If you pardon, we will mend.

(V.i.404–419)

130

bated, Puck speaks[47] as if time has been suspended. All action is hushed and at a standstill; 'not a mouse,' he says, 'shall disturb this hallowed house'[47]. And Oberon's 'Trip away, make no stay'[48] now has the cadence of a tragic parting; of loss, the words receding.

'If we shadows have offended,' says Puck[48] . . . but the instinct in the spectator, now, is for denial and protest. 'Gentles, do not reprehend,' he pleads, but who, at this level of performance, would think to? It is instead a poignant valediction. It is also the end of the third week's rehearsals. Brook tells the actors: 'This rehearsal was three quarters of what it should be. It had complexity with simplicity. It cannot however be set, technically, to recur. We will have to find our own way back to it. But the way is now open.'

¹ *Egeus:* Full of vexation come I, with complaint
     Against my child, my daughter Hermia.
     Stand forth, Demetrius. My noble lord,
     This man hath my consent to marry her.
     Stand forth, Lysander. And, my gracious Duke,
     This man hath bewitched the bosom of my child.
     Thou, thou, Lysander, thou hast given her rhymes,
     And interchanged love tokens with my child.

                                                    (*I.i.22–29*)

² *Theseus:* Hippolyta, I wooed thee with my sword,
     And won thy love, doing thee injuries;
     But I will wed thee in another key,
     With pomp, with triumph, and with revelling.

                                                    (*I.i.16–19*)

³ *Demetrius:* Relent, sweet Hermia: and, Lysander, yield
     Thy crazèd title to my certain right.
   Lysander: You have her father's love, Demetrius;
     Let me have Hermia's: do you marry him.
   Egeus: Scornful Lysander! True, he hath my love,
     And what is mine my love shall render him.
     And she is mine, and all my right of her
     I do estate unto Demetrius.

                                                    (*I.i.91–98*)

⁴ *Hermia:* But I beseech your Grace that I may know,
     The worst that may befall me in this case,
     If I refuse to wed Demetrius.
   Theseus: Either to die the death, or to abjure
     Forever the society of men.
     Therefore, fair Hermia, question your desires.

                                                    (*I.i.62–67*)

132

Fourth week, first day

The production, with its heights and depths, is seemingly fixed in outline, the space and volume of the play's structures determined. Brook has now begun to concentrate on narrative meanings. In such a procedure as his, these become (relatively) matters of detail. They pose literal not metaphorical problems, questions not of metaphysics but of communication, of giving the plot to a still imagined – but determinate – audience, whose time is approaching.

Thus in Act One, Scene One of a new run-through, Brook stopped Egeus' 'Full of vexation come I, with complaint against my child'[1] when he had barely started. His speech had been clamant, a rhetoric of tumbling words, signifying little or nothing. Brook insisted upon clarity of intention and meaning, on his 'taking time' with his narration. This Egeus now did, but without losing 'discovered rhythm', as Brook put it. Instead there was added to it, as there was throughout the day, point and purpose: explanation. More unexpectedly, Brook is now also plotting movement in detail, and according to a conventional method. He is placing characters, or steering them into his (not their) chosen positions. It is 'blocking' at its most literally pedestrian. Is this not strangely at odds with the preceding search for impulse and rhythm? Or is it a final gloss upon inwardly discovered movement?

Busy with details, while the actors are coasting, Brook himself marks – on clashed cymbals – Theseus' 'with pomp, with triumph, and with revelling'[2], which he describes as 'in effect the end of a scene'; as he plots their positions, calls for 'sustained tension as in the Japanese theatre' between Theseus, Egeus, Demetrius and Lysander in the male encounters of the play's earliest stages[3]; and hurriedly tells Theseus, at 'Either to die like death, or to abjure/ Forever the society of man'[4], to 'avoid incantation'. Yet, little by little, Brook is drawn deeper into the action, with varying effect on the actors. For

5 *Lysander:* How now, my love! Why is your cheek so pale?
　　How chance the roses there do fade so fast?
　Hermia: Belike for want of rain, which I could well
　　Beteem them from the tempest of my eyes.
　Lysander: Ay me! For aught that I could ever read,
　　Could ever hear by tale or history,
　　The course of true love never did run smooth.

(I.i.128–134)

6 *Hermia:* God speed fair Helena! Whither away?
　Helena: Call you me fair? That fair again unsay,
　　Demetrius loves your fair. O happy fair!
　　Your eyes are lodestars, and your tongue's sweet air,
　　More tunable than lark to shepherd's ear,
　　When wheat is green, when hawthorn buds appear.
　　Sickness is catching. O, were favour so,
　　Yours would I catch, fair Hermia, ere I go;
　　My ear should catch your voice, my eye your eye,
　　My tongue should catch your tongue's sweet melody.
　　. . . O, teach me how you look, and with what art
　　You sway the motion of Demetrius' heart!

(I.i.180–193)

7 *Hermia:* And in the wood, where often you and I
　　Upon faint primrose beds were wont to lie,
　　Emptying our bosoms of their counsel sweet,
　　There my Lysander and myself shall meet.

(I.i.214–217)

8 *ACT ONE, Scene Two. Quince's house. Enter QUINCE, SNUG,
　BOTTOM, FLUTE, SNOUT and STARVELING.*
　Quince: Is all our company here?
　Bottom: You were best to call them generally, man by man, according to
　　the scrip.
　Quince: Here is the scroll of every man's name, which is thought fit,
　　through all Athens, to play in our interlude before the Duke and the
　　Duchess, on his wedding day at night.
　Bottom: First, good Peter Quince, say what the play treats on; then read
　　the names of the actors; and so grow to a point.

(I.ii.1–9)

Demetrius' 'Relent, sweet Hermia'[3], spoken with a sinuous or unctuous menace (and found at some pains), Brook suddenly expresses distaste. 'Where a line gets stretched beyond its natural life,' he astringently tells him, 'the life goes out of it.' Once more, confusion raises its head. It is in Demetrius' surreptitious frowning. What is a line's 'natural' life? And who can tell him? Hermia's and Lysander's following exchanges[5] are also once more stilted. 'Turn away into your own thoughts,' Brook tells them. And so they do, embracing, on this occasion momentarily entering deeper into their parts, and (as if) into each other.

Brook tells Helena, too, at 'Call you me fair? That fair again unsay'[6], to 'turn away' also – and suddenly she finds, in inward preoccupation, means which were lacking or blunted in extroversion. Solitary and downcast, she is now unable to look at Hermia as she sings the latter's praises[6]. I can see in her hands the faintest tremor (is it 'real'? is it feigned?), as she becomes dumbfounded in speech at the other's beauty. 'O teach me how you look, and with what art/ You sway the motion of Demetrius' heart!'[6] is as if spoken wordlessly to her mirror, sighing. She then had her photograph taken with Brook, for the archive or a poster, lips moving as if in conversation.

Within moments, the 'blocking' of movement and the search for narrative clarity brought further details of illumination, which in turn began to dominate the technical proceedings. In Helena's love-lorn presence, Hermia makes her assignation with Lysander;[7] seeming to go out of her way to tell Helena that she and Lysander are to meet in the wood 'where often you and I/ Upon faint primrose beds were wont to lie'. Brook describes this as 'tasteless, considering Helena's state', adding that she is 'hurt by the lovers' rapture', which in turn helps to clarify for the audience the 'meaning of her character'. Likewise, at what is now to be a rhythmic entrance of the mechanicals, in procession, for the rehearsal scene which follows[8], Brook – ostensibly merely judging the appearance of their movement – stops the action. He tells Bottom, giving him his marching orders, that he must enter 'in counterpoint with the rest'. He must 'pace on stage first'; he must 'use the idea of the long-striding walk as a structure', passing the oncoming mechanicals, himself absorbed (in gesture and expression) with anticipation of his role in the drama of *Pyramus and Thisby*. But, says Brook, now dictating not inviting impulse, 'the scene has at its centre Bottom's social and psychological assurance'. This is an insight, or an instruction, new to the rehearsals, undiscussed and more than a

9 *Snug:* Have you the lion's part written? Pray you, if it be, give it me, for I am slow of study.

Quince: You may do it extempore, for it is nothing but roaring.

Bottom: Let me play the lion too. I will roar that I will do any man's heart good to hear me. I will roar, that I will make the Duke say, 'Let him roar again, let him roar again.'

Quince: An you should do it too terribly, you would fright the Duchess and the ladies, that they would shriek; and that were enough to hang us all.

All: That would hang us, every mother's son.

(*I.ii.58–69*)

10 *Bottom:* Some man or other must present Wall: and let him have some plaster, or some loam, or some roughcast about him, to signify Wall; and let him hold his fingers thus, and through that cranny shall Pyramus and Thisby whisper.

Quince: If that may be, then all is well. Come, sit down, every mother's son, and rehearse your parts. Pyramus, you begin.

(*III.i.59–65*)

136

technical detail. 'There must be no unease in you,' Brook tells Bottom.

He also stops the actors when Quince, resisting Bottom's gluttonous claim to the part of Lion and his roaring, tells him 'An you should do it too terribly . . . that were enough to hang us all'[9]. Brook speaks, unexpectedly in Hebraic terms, of a darkened moment, newly found. 'The angel of death,' he says, 'should at this point pass over you all,' and 'That would hang us, every mother's son' be 'hushed' and 'fearful'. (But there is no angel of death in Shakespeare's text here, either on the lines or between them.) Now directly giving notes, rather than even indirectly looking to the mood of the actors, Brook also tells them that upon the expression of these fears of Quince's, 'there will be a silence and then a murmur of two voices.' Shakespeare's text is to be minutely amended. 'That would hang us, every mother's son' is now to be divided between two frightened voices.

The mechanicals break for a while at the scene's end. And for the first time I hear directly – because they are addressed to me, in lieu of any other audience, though I am non-committal and unwilling – of their discontents. Quince and Snug evidently think, and say, that the mechanicals' stage labours with wood and metal are contrived and 'phoney'. There is 'no necessity for them', one of them tells me. Indeed Snug says as much to Brook later, and suggests to him that instead of this artisan 'business', the mechanicals should have a canteen trestle-table, over which they can discuss the play they are rehearsing. Brook at once becomes characteristically cold and uneasy; this is one discovered impulse which he has no desire to encourage. It goes flatly against his sense of the play and its meanings, even if not against theirs. Snug is shrugged off, and the carpenter-playwright with him.

Moreover, later, during the mechanicals' second rehearsal in Act Three, Scene One[10], Brook reinforces this dismissal, and suffocates their near-mute rebellion. (But how many similarly deep undercurrents of actors' unease and disagreement are secretly flowing? Is the truth below this surface and illusion upon it, or vice-versa?) 'Everything,' Brook now declares, 'must be taken at a completely naturalistic level.' That is, he says of the mechanicals, 'we do not want to suggest that they are actors.' Some evidently do, or did, want to suggest it, but their voices are silenced. 'Your only needs,' he tells them, 'are the needs of craftsmen.' This is palpably not so, either in the text or in Brook's direction of it – until this moment.

It is therefore perverse, too, as well as deeply confusing to the

16 Puck: 'Come, recreant! Come, thou child!/I'll whip thee with a rod. He is defiled/That draws a sword on thee.' Demetrius: 'Yea, art thou there?' (Act Three, Scene Two); (l. to r.) John Kane (Puck), Ben Kingsley (Demetrius) and Christopher Gable (Lysander).

actors. It is also the familiar price which they must pay, on the nail, for Brook's unease, though on this occasion it swiftly passes. Nevertheless, much more important – as I have come to see during these unguarded, but carefully observed, weeks of rehearsal – is the overall consistency of Brook's pronouncements. (Even the contradictions and obscurities are consistent.) His intention, as well as his principles of interpretation and guidance, have held steady, and without undue repetition, from the outset. Their internal coherence has now survived many days of intense rehearsal. Whether he is as open to the actors' impulse as he professes, and how far they have had to subordinate themselves to his *idées fixes* and pre-made choices, is another matter.

But since truth and illusion, actors' fact and director's fancy, are inseparable elements of the stock-in-trade of drama, it might be better not to press the questions; particularly if the answers are slowly becoming obvious. And, in any case, isn't this the moonshine which lends enchantment, inside the theatre and outside it?

Fourth week, second day

Brook declares, this morning, that the actors representing 'spirits' (the word 'fairies', I notice, is sedulously avoided) will carry perspex batons. These objects, he declares, will be the 'focus of spirit'; or, rather, 'the objects will represent the spirits'. He says: 'The main spirit is the object. The man [sc. actor] is not usually the spirit, for it weighs the idea down.' He also indicates that 'at times' the eye and the hand of the actor-playing-spirit would 'come near to being manifestations of spirit'. What the actors make of this latter-day Shamanism I cannot tell. They are impassive. In the face of it, they betray not the barest flicker of judgment in their expressions. It passes on the nod, or over them. They have, after all, now successfully adapted themselves to the juggling mode of Chinese acrobatics, and the heroic mannerisms of Japanese tension. A few anthropologically inspired gestures drawn from Pacific island ritual, and expressed in perspex, are unlikely to throw them; or Shakespeare.

Today, in addition to the clarification of narrative line already embarked on, Brook also demands that the actors 'move towards greater intensity' in rehearsal. Indeed, at the outset of the day's exercises, the juggling itself seemed more intensely assiduous and expert. (I learned later that some of the actors have attended a special

¹¹ *Puck:* How now, spirit! Whither wander you?
   Fairy: Over hill, over dale,
      Thorough bush, thorough brier,
      Over park, over pale,
      Thorough flood, thorough fire.

$$(II.i.1-5)$$

¹² *Puck:* The King doth keep his revels here tonight.
   Take heed the Queen come not within his sight.
   For Oberon is passing fell and wrath,
   Because that she as her attendant hath
   A lovely boy, stolen from an Indian king.

$$(II.i.18-22)$$

¹³ *Oberon:* Ill met by moonlight, proud Titania.
   Titania: What, jealous Oberon! Fairy, skip hence.
   I have forsworn his bed and company.
   Oberon: Tarry, rash wanton; am not I thy lord?
   Titania: Then I must be thy lady.

$$(II.i.60-64)$$

¹⁴ *Titania:* . . . The moon, the governess of floods,
      Pale in her anger, washes all the air,
      That rheumatic diseases do abound.
      And thorough this distemperature we see
      The seasons alter: hoary-headed frosts
      Fall in the fresh lap of the crimson rose,
      And on old Hiems' thin and icy crown
      An odourous chaplet of sweet summer buds
      Is, as in mockery, set. The spring, the summer,
      The childing autumn, angry winter, change
      Their wonted liveries; and the mazèd world,
      By their increase, now knows not which is which.

$$(II.i.103-114)$$

¹⁵ *Oberon:* Give me that boy, and I will go with thee.
   Titania: Not for thy fairy kingdom. Fairies, away!
      We shall chide downright, if I longer stay.
                    (*Exeunt TITANIA with her train*)
   Oberon: Well, go thy way. Thou shalt not from this grove
      Till I torment thee for this injury.

$$(II.i.143-147)$$

demonstration of juggling – by a Japanese juggling instructor – which had been specially organized by Brook for them.) Batons and skills are pressed quickly into service. Today's run-through is to begin with the Act Two, Scene One entrance of the spirits[11]. 'Let the sticks vibrate in your hands as each of you speaks,' Brook says to the fairies who are to divide 'over hill, over dale', between them; 'throw the sticks as you throw the words,' he instructs them. And at Puck's 'The King doth keep his revels here tonight'[12], Brook tells them to 'move their sticks in relation to Puck's staff in geometrical rhythm'.

Scepticism, tempted, was held at bay by the outcome. The hieratic, and hierarchical, juxtaposition of the symbols of status of the princely Puck and the commonalty of the spirits, might not summon up the sense of a magical encounter in Arcadia. (It had about it, instead, something of a tribal meeting of Polynesians, or the schoolboy anthropology of a William Golding.) Yet, within the pulse of speech and the passage of the moments there now seemed to grow precisely the 'stillness, tremors and flourishes' for which Brook is here striving. Under this impulse, Oberon's 'Ill met by moonlight'[13] – earlier in rehearsal an icy and acrid intrusion into wanton disorder, which Brook had once thought 'merely actorish' – and his following exchanges with Titania[13], now have the 'speed and bite of electricity, as well as a pace which is slow and gliding', as Brook describes it. 'Put them together,' Brook tells the actors; 'the electrical charge is under the lines.' Do we really have to believe that it is also in the tips of these perspex batons?

Moreover Titania, as if propelled by a new motion in her quarrel with Oberon, is carried (or pushes) towards a whispered fear and anger which is intenser than ever. There is a current of such vibrant energy in 'the spring, the summer, the childing autumn' and 'angry winter'[14] that it seems to irradiate the whole studio. 'You want to go into a vision of the end of the world here,' Brook tells her – without asking – as her fear of the 'progeny of evils', which 'comes from our dissension', fills her voice with deepest foreboding. Oberon now finds a fiery anger with her in his lines[15], and Titania a freezing disdain for him in hers[15]. Yet through this fierce counterpoint, they had come to the very pitch and balance of perfect expression. This was 'wondrous hot ice', discovered between them. (In the last act, Theseus will ask, 'How shall we find the concord of this discord?'[16] Here, Oberon and Titania seemed for a moment to have already found it.) At the scene's end, Brook told all the actors to 'capture and hold the whole movement of it', while the spirits – whose perspex batons, Brook said,

[16] *Theseus:* 'A tedious brief scene of young Pyramus
And his love Thisby; very tragical mirth.'
Merry and tragical? Tedious and brief?
That is, hot ice and wondrous strange snow.
How shall we find the concord of this discord?

(*V.i.56–60*)

[17] *Quince:* Francis Flute, the bellows mender.
Flute: Here, Peter Quince.
Quince: Flute, you must take Thisby on you.
Flute: What is Thisby? A wand'ring knight?
Quince: It is the lady that Pyramus must love.
Flute: Nay, faith, let not me play a woman. I have a beard coming.
Quince: That's all one. You shall play it in a mask, and you may
speak as small as you will.

(*I.ii.35–43*)

had 'principally to do with rhythms' – had the task of 'supporting the words and movements of others'.

In delayed reaction to yesterday's muted revolt by dissidents among the workforce of mechanicals, led by Snug the joiner, Brook now paid new attention to their First Act rehearsal. He says today that he wants to 'search for its most naked possibilities'. This is evidently his reconsidered reply to the desire among them to withdraw the enactment of their labour. 'Can the scene,' he asks, 'be got off the ground without any sense of place? Can sufficient energy be produced without realistic supports?' In order to find out, he tells the mechanicals to enter at a distance from one another, and to encircle the acting area. But this, in fact, ensures precisely what follows. Their speech is merely declamatory, energyless and statuesque. They are also too remote from each other, physically, to find in Shakespeare's words the intimacy of exchange and effort which might establish their identities, make sense of their relations and abolish the redundant device of symbolic labour. The 'experiment' has been rigged to provide the desired result. (Is this the case with all theatre of the laboratory and the workshop?)

Brook stops them. He says, first, that there is 'a certain kind of realistic energy in Shakespeare's prose' in this scene of rehearsal[17]. In order to achieve a similar energy in their acting, he tells them, 'a continuous stripping away is needed'. Is this a theatrical cliché, a profound truth, a meaningless conundrum? What they do must be, he says, 'realistic and non-theatrical' on the one hand, and on the other strive for 'roundness and richness' by providing 'the sense of a real and active working area'. The actors, not surprisingly, do not seem to understand the distinction. But there is a counter-suggestion, as plain as a pikestaff. 'Their accents,' one of the mechanicals tells Brook, 'should all be the same', instead of being as unspecifically or randomly rustic as they are now. 'They are obviously all from the same town and district,' he says, speaking from within his own knowledge of the text, and his own experience of rehearsal. To this Brook says quickly and without proofs that the 'thought-rhythm' of the characters' words will 'give the various accents'. They will be seen, he concludes *ex cathedra*, to be 'different from each other.' But the 'thought-rhythms' are not so easily seen to be different from one another, nor do they sound so in the speaking. And there the matter of their accents rests.

Nevertheless, as if provoked by this level of renewed attention, the mechanicals' rehearsal immediately begins to deliver new insight into

¹⁸ *Bottom:* Let me play the lion too. I will roar that I will do any man's heart good to hear me. I will roar, that I will make the Duke say, 'Let him roar again, let him roar again.' I will aggravate my voice so that I will roar you as gently as any sucking dove; I will roar you an 'twere any nightingale.

Quince: You can play no part but Pyramus: for Pyramus is a sweet-faced man; a proper man as one shall see in a summer's day; a most lovely, gentleman-like man: therefore you must needs play Pyramus.

(I.ii.62–79)

¹⁹ *Bottom:* An I may hide my face, let me play Thisby too, I'll speak in a monstrous little voice, 'Thisne, Thisne!' 'Ah Pyramus, my lover dear! Thy Thisby dear, and lady dear!'

Quince: No, no; you must play Pyramus: and, Flute, you Thisby.

(I.ii.44–47)

²⁰ *Quince:* Is all our company here?

Bottom: You were best to call them generally man by man, according to the scrip . . . First, good Peter Quince, say what the play treats on; then read the names of the actors; and so grow to a point.

Quince: Marry, our play is, 'The most lamentable comedy, and most cruel death of Pyramus and Thisby.'

Bottom: A very good piece of work, I assure you, and a merry.

(I.ii.1–12)

²¹ *Bottom:* What is Pyramus? A lover, or a tyrant?

Quince: A lover that kills himself, most gallant, for love.

Bottom: That will ask some tears in the true performing of it: if I do it, let the audience look to their eyes. I will move storms, I will condole in some measure. To the rest: yet my chief humour is for a tyrant. I could play Ercles rarely, or a part to tear a cat in, to make all split.

> The raging rocks
> And shivering shocks,
> Shall break the locks
> Of prison gates . . .

This was lofty! Now name the rest of the players. This is Ercles' vein, a tyrant's vein. A lover is more condoling.

(I.ii.18–34)

character. Bottom now sees himself as a wayward genius with a 'professional' temperament, condescending, hypersensitive and moody. Denied the Lion's part by Quince[18], he is ready to go off in the high dudgeon of the *prima donna*. Quince himself is the fussily vain creator; but is also concerned and kindly from long-suffering, and able to deal with Bottom's artistic tantrums[19]. Snug the joiner is as thick as two planks, and a butt for the others, yet wounded now by the presumption of Bottom's efforts to steal his Lion's part, and abashed by the swagger of Bottom's roaring[18]. And Bottom, greedily laying claim to Flute's role as Thisby also[19], makes such skilful and affecting trial of it now, that Quince hesitates for a moment over his casting.

It is Bottom's character, above all, which is deepened by the quality of this invention. 'A very good piece of work, I assure you'[20], he tells the playwright of his play, and with a knowing confidence which Brook describes as 'sailing along happily towards the dream of every actoR'. That he is a *buffo* character in the text is obvious. So is the fact that he sees himself as legitimately chief among the *dramatis personae*[20]. That he is a man of truculent moods, as he is today, is however much less apparent. And with all his art (of the artiste rather than the artist) he is more artless than ever. 'This is Ercles' vein, a tyrant's vein'[21], he declares roundly, of his own acting. His aside – 'A lover is more condoling'[21] – for the first time evokes laughter, but both his confidential manner and his wordly knowledge are innocent and unself-knowing. A polymath and man of parts in his own estimation, he claims to be capable, too, of roaring 'as gently as any sucking dove'[18]. Indeed, so taken with his role and himself is he that, as Brook puts it, 'he is losing himself, eyes closed, in the part', promising Quince that he will even roar like a nightingale if the Lion's part were his.

But it is his pretension to a knowledge which is expert that sets Bottom apart. And it is this which today's rehearsal has uncovered. On his every subsequent appearance, Bottom brings this sense of election with him. At its shallowest, it exasperates the friction of his encounters, as a journeyman actor, with Quince the proud playwright. At its profoundest, it suggests there is a nemesis in his enchantment, gives edge to his visions, and promises riches in his 'discourse'[22] upon them – if he were willing to speak – which would have been beyond the reach of his fellows. It is a productive tension which the actor himself has found in the part of Bottom, and today he opened up the text with it. The other mechanicals, and the haunting spirits too, were revived

²² *Bottom:* Masters, I am to discourse wonders: but ask me not what; for if I tell you, I am not true Athenian. I will tell you everything, right as it fell out.

Quince: Let us hear, sweet Bottom.

Bottom: Not a word of me. All I will tell you is, that the Duke hath dined.

(IV.ii.26–30)

²³ *Bottom:* Why do they run away? This is a knavery of them to make me afeard.

(Enter SNOUT)

Snout: O Bottom, thou art changed! What do I see on thee?

Bottom: What do you see? You see an ass head of your own, do you?   *(Exit SNOUT)*

(Enter QUINCE)

Quince: Bless thee, Bottom! Bless thee! Thou art translated.   *(Exit)*

Bottom: I see their knavery. This is to make an ass of me; to fright me, if they could. But I will not stir from this place, do what they can. I will walk up and down here, and will sing, that they shall hear I am not afraid.

(III.i.102–113)

themselves by the new strength of character in their friend and victim. Rising above them, he was now terrorized and transformed at a pitch which in turn rose to reach him. 'O Bottom, thou art changed!'[23], says the quivering Snout the tinker, backing away (dwarfed) from this new colossus. And Bottom's 'What do you see?' is now an anguished and angered bellow. Transfigured, he is both fearful and fearsome, terror-struck and striking terror[23]. But to be in fear while unwittingly frightening others, in turns confounds and terrifies him; and in the confusion and disorder, of which our fears are also a part, the frisson of fear was redoubled, and became for a moment the purest horror.

Soon afterwards, exhausted by the acting pressures and plagued by his entourage of spirits (whose trembling perspex batons are now impediments in the way of his feeling) the actor playing Bottom, David Waller, lost his temper. Pushing the spirits aside, he broke out of his role and began shouting that he did not know what he was doing. It was as if, in his shouts of anger, all the fears and hopes and confusions of the actors were confounded, while his voice seemed still to speak from deep within the disordered world of terrifying enchantment which, moments before, he had himself created. 'This is to make an ass of me, to fright me if they could'[23], he had said, frightened, looking to the spectators for reassurance. 'But I will not stir from this place, do what they can. I will walk up and down here, and will sing, that they shall hear I am not afraid.'

These words had already seemed to me to contain Shakespeare's own articles of faith, or an Hippocratic code for actors. And never more so than today, in the echo of Bottom's unanswered shouting.

Fourth week, third day

Brook's rehearsing of the mechanicals' rehearsals continues. But this is a day of dulled effort in the wake of crisis and climax, as has happened before. The actors also appear newly preoccupied and anxious, for no evident reason. Brook himself is almost incommunicado. Even time stirs fitfully, or hangs heavy, and the spirits of the actors seem weighed down and lowered. Yet much of the day was given over by Brook, against the tide of the actors' almost palpable feelings, to the search for a wider range of comic business in the scenes of rehearsal. But at the level of a simple naturalistic invention, Brook seems gauche and limited in the range of his ideas. He lacks wit,

[24] *Bottom:* There are things in this comedy of Pyramus and Thisby that
will never please. First, Pyramus must draw a sword to kill himself;
which the ladies cannot abide. How answer you that?

Snout: By'r lakin, a parlous fear.

Starveling: I believe we must leave the killing out, when all is done.

Bottom: Not a whit. I have a device to make all well. Write me a
prologue, and let the prologue seem to say, we will do no harm
with our swords, and that Pyramus is not killed indeed.

(III.i.8–17)

and often, too, all sense of humour. Today's mood of humourlessness, however, is general and, for a long time, irresistible. Nevertheless, Brook persists in his expectation of the comic. In addition, the tension between the 'free intuition' which Brook strives to stimulate in the actors, and the imposition upon them of his own contrivance, becomes more acute when natural invention (stifled by circumstances, whether of weariness, boredom, unspoken reservation or this morning's preoccupation) fails. For the surly to evoke laughter from the sullen, is beyond today's rehearsal.

But Brook intends, come what may, that a vein of naturalistic comedy or 'comic business', will course through this production, as it must. Certainly, the eclectic and abstract expressionism which he has found as a governing style – at worst, a 'cool' freight of Orientalism, acrobatics and the tricks of the Western *shaman*, at best a delicately poised geometry of exposed feeling and movement – seems to require relief by humour. And, preferably, humour at its most homely. Of course, there can be no argument that the romantic and the sexual, the frightening and the philosophical are all present in Shakespeare's text, and are being skilfully drawn from it in this production. Indeed, with his additional devices, Brook may well have found the ingredients, however egregious some of them seem (and are), of a *succès d'estime*, which will bring the boulevard of the rich theatre and the cloister of the poor one together, and join the box-office to the ivory-tower. However, if the production fails, as on some days like today seemed possible, and on other days is out of the question, it will be because 'the centre does not hold' the various parts together. But whether the prices of a 'success' will be that the problems of the relation between reality and illusion, contrivance and invention are lost from sight in a *beau monde* spectacular, and that the sounds of the play's despairs are drowned in cheering, is another matter.

Now, at the same time as plotting and blocking with close attention to the appearance and configuration of bodies, Brook is one more pushing the actors on to new details of movement and intonation. And out of it, illumination of meaning, however fitful, continues. Technique and creation, inseparable in any art, are inseparable here also. It is no accident that the mechanicals' rehearsal within a rehearsal reveals it; or, rather, that first Shakespeare, and then the actors, reveal it between them. 'There are things in this comedy of Pyramus and Thisby that will never please,' says Bottom[24]. Among them is Pyramus' suicide. 'I believe we must leave the killing out,' says the

149

25 *Bottom:* To bring in – God shield us! – a lion among ladies, is a most
dreadful thing. For there is not a more fearful wild fowl than your
lion living; and we ought to look to it.

Snout: Therefore another prologue must tell he is not a lion.

Bottom: Nay, you must name his name, and half his face must be
seen through the lion's neck and he himself must speak through . . .
and tell them plainly, he is Snug the joiner.

Quince: Well, it shall be so. But there is two hard things; that is, to
bring the moonlight into a chamber . . .

Bottom: Why, then may you leave a casement of the great chamber
window, where we play, open, and the moon may shine in at the
casement.

Quince: Ay, or else one must come in with a bush of thorns and
a lantern and say he comes to disfigure, or to present, the
person of Moonshine. Then there is another thing: we must
have a wall in the great chamber.

(*III.i.27–55*)

26 *Bottom:* Heigh-ho! Peter Quince? Flute, the bellows mender? Snout,
the tinker? Starveling? God's my life, stol'n hence, and left me
asleep? I have had a most rare vision. I have had a dream, past the
wit of man to say what dream it was. Man is but an ass, if he go
about to expound this dream . . . I will get Peter Quince to write a
ballet of this dream. It shall be called 'Bottom's Dream', because it
hath no bottom; and I will sing it in the latter end of the play,
before the Duke. Peradventure to make it the more gracious, I shall
sing it at her death.

(*IV.i.198–215*)

27 *Flute:* O sweet bully Bottom! Thus hath he lost sixpence a day
during his life. He could not have scaped sixpence a day. An
the Duke had not given him sixpence a day for playing Pyramus,
I'll be hanged. He would have deserved it. Sixpence a day in
Pyramus, or nothing.

(*Enter BOTTOM*)

Bottom: Where are these lads? Where are these hearts?

Quince: Bottom! O most courageous day! O most happy hour!

(*IV.ii.18–25*)

actor-tailor Starveling. And so they discuss how their script and the story might be amended, how to overcome the technical difficulties of lighting by moonshine, and how a lion might be acted[25] – just as the rehearsal which encompasses their efforts has considered how to animate the lines of the lovers, impersonate spirits, and solve the mechanicals' own rehearsal problems for them. 'We see in their struggles,' says Brook, 'the progress of the theatre through invention. They are trying to work towards a better play than they had at the beginning of their rehearsals.' Both Brook and Quince are carpenters of their productions.

Today, Bottom's energies, drained yesterday, were at a low ebb. As a result, both Brook's and Quince's rehearsals ran aground, or floundered. His speech on waking (in Act Four, Scene One)[26] from the first play into the second, had lost its sense of wonder. This is now no 'rare vision' that he has had, but a prosaic nap which has left him thick-headed. Brook, characteristically wary of him after yesterday's outburst, in turn leaves him to his own shrunken and lustreless devices. It is merely the rough and ill-humoured awakening of a man who has got out of the wrong side of the bed, both in his role and out of it. All that Brook will say, as Bottom's once resonant and leaping lines petered out at 'Peradventure . . . I shall sing it at her death'[26] into flatness and silence, is 'We'll have to think more about this later'. Bottom is being left to his distemper, or theatrical hangover. Thus, when Flute sang 'O sweet bully Bottom!'[27], it had now become a cajoling appeal to him to return to the life of *this* rehearsal, as well as a sad premonition of his absence from the cast of *Pyramus and Thisby*. It was even as if a shared fear of theatrical failure had dissolved one rehearsal into the other.

Perhaps it was this which paved the way for the briefly rapturous return of Bottom a moment later[27]. Unexpectedly restored to the mechanicals and to the two rehearsals, he seemed momentarily restored to himself also. There was an involuntary sigh of joy and relief at his genial reappearance. His 'Where are these lads?' and, especially, 'Where are these hearts?'[27], with its sense of bluff good humour and a loving fraternity among them, for a while cancelled his low and mean-spirited condition. Here were familiars, now familiar to me also, restored to one another, and, at these close quarters, men as well as actors. If this is what Brook had earlier intended when he spoke of 'things happening by themselves', then this seemed to be such a moment. That is, it was as-if-not-acted, neither rehearsal nor rehearsal

28 *Bottom:* Get your apparel together, good strings to your beards, new ribbons to your pumps; meet presently at the palace; every man look o'er his part; for the short and long is, our play is preferred. In any case, let Thisby have clean linen; and let not him that plays the lion pare his nails, for they shall hang out for the lion's claws. And, most dear actors, eat no onions nor garlic, for we are to utter sweet breath, and I do not doubt but to hear them say it is a sweet comedy. No more words. Away! Go, away!

(*IV.ii.31–43*)

within rehearsal, but an extempore human greeting beyond script or programmed gesture. Yet actors' tragedy of tragedies, it was not and could not be. For it remained theatre (did it not?), and with its deeper truth came merely a deeper illusion also.

Moreover, Bottom's own release from personal embarrassment and inhibition now took him, in turn, into a relaxed bluster and banter[28]. 'Get your apparel together,' he tells his friends; 'good strings to your beards', 'new ribbons to your pumps', and 'meet presently at the palace'. He speaks with the easy jocularity of manner of the 'not-acted'. But, in consequence, what we see and hear is neither art unmasked nor art and life united. Instead, paradoxically, neither art nor life survive this realistic mummery, which seeks to outwit both the text and the spectator. So that to bring him back to his (actor's) senses, and from as-if-not-acting consciously to acting, Brook has to tell him: 'This is deadly serious. This is the serious moment of truth, when comic invention must fall away entirely.'

The wheel of today's arduous rehearsal had come full circle; but without moving forward.

Fourth week, fourth day

I stayed at home, as sated with rehearsals as some of the actors seemed to be. And several perfectly-shaped but unanswered questions formed in my mind during the day. One was: Is this a theatre of forms, or of substance? (And what, if any, is the difference?) The other was of old plays, and new playwrights: Why gild the old lily, when you might bring a new lily to flower? Beneath the second question a bitter and self-preoccupied truth was rooted. To be wilfully denied life is death's own anticipation, sitting on my metal chair.

Fourth week, fifth day

Two days ago, to enter the rehearsal was as if to intrude on some private grief, whose sources were hidden. I had fleetingly gathered only a sense of pained preoccupation in Brook, and a strange distraction – or resentment – in the actors. That neither was derived directly from these rehearsals themselves but was focused elsewhere, I had no means, until today, of knowing. Two days ago I had noticed

17 Oberon: 'There lies your love.' Titania: 'How came these things to pass?' (Act Four, Scene One); (l. to r. below) David Waller (Bottom), Alan Howard (Oberon), Sara Kestelman (Titania); (l. to r. above) Mary Rutherford (Hermia), Christopher Gable (Lysander), Frances de la Tour (Helena) and Ben Kingsley (Demetrius).

intent discussions, out of earshot of Brook himself, going on among small groups of actors; there had been a lack of concentration on the rehearsal; and an unexpressed unease which they had appeared to share between them. Only today, as the actors gathered, did I hear animated mention of the current production, by Robin Phillips, of *The Two Gentlemen of Verona*. It had been in its last stages of dress rehearsal, and is preceding *A Midsummer Night's Dream* into the Stratford auditorium. From exclamations and whispers, and snatches of conversation, I at first gained only a disjointed impression of conflicts, jealousies, last-minute changes in the production and even of interventions by Phillips' fellow-directors, Brook included.

Now, however, there is an hour-long and excitable discussion, steeped in pent-up and bitter feeling, between Brook and the actors, on last night's first performance of the Phillips' production. The discussion, which raged unchecked, ate deep into the time of the morning rehearsal, took emotional and artistic precedence over it, and bitterly divided the actors. Spite, Envy, Vanity and Malice took the places of Mustardseed, Moonshine and Peaseblossom. If there is a rival search under way – and suddenly I gather that there must be – for the deepest truths hidden in the texts of Shakespeare, and the finest or most luminous gloss which can be put upon them by one director and one set of actors or another, then last night's outcome of it seems to have set these actors deeply at odds with each other.

For a while Brook himself took no part. Barbed and even fiercely hostile criticism, counter-criticism and defence of Phillips flew back and forth across an arena hitherto reserved for the flight of Shakespeare's words, metal plates, and perspex batons. Brook listened intently. Phillips' production was 'cheap', 'clever without point', 'a private spectacle'. 'Words and meanings had been lost', and 'the romantic element excluded'. It was 'indulgent', 'camp' and 'vulgar' (there is a swimming pool in it); as well as so despoiled and ravaged, one actor exclaimed, his spleen boiling into Anger, that he 'did not know what it was about, from the first to the last moment'. From those of his party there was instant agreement. From those opposed to him – 'even the foreigners in the audience understood it', said one – there was an equal shock and anger, as the actors were sundered.

At loggerheads, Oberon and Titania, Demetrius and Helena, Quince and Bottom all forgot themselves and were forgotten. *A Midsummer Night's Dream* was turned into a cats' chorus. Those who fought back for Phillips hotly claimed that his production had been

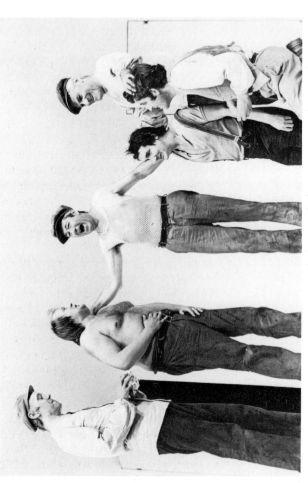

18 Bottom: 'For the short and the long is, our play is preferred' (Act Four, Scene Two); (l. to r.) Philip Locke (Quince), Barry Stanton (Snug), David Waller (Bottom), Glynne Lewis (Flute), Norman Rodway (Wall) and Terrence Hardiman (Starveling).

maliciously interfered with by other directors; that Phillips' cast, unlike other casts in the current season (to which cast are they referring?) was 'happy and committed'; that the hostilities and backbiting which marred other productions were entirely absent.

Brook did not bat an eyelid even when being glanced at, and had listened without expression to the partisan praise and blame of Phillips, as if deaf to the cymbal-like clashing of egos. Now he suddenly broke into the discussion. The 'agreed reading of the play' – which he made sound like a treaty – to which the cast of *The Two Gentlemen of Verona* had arrived 'by their work', their commitment to this reading, and the audience's patent enjoyment of the performance were all 'substantial achievements'. It had been, he said, 'the right production for the audience at the time'; it was 'a success'; and 'more could not be asked for'. There was a silence. The faintness of his praise was not in the words, but in his manner. He corrected himself. 'More can be asked for,' he added, adding also to the resentment of Phillips' supporters. 'But in its own terms,' he said softly, again damning Phillips by the reduction, 'it was successful.' Later, Brook told me that Phillips was 'limited', that his production 'stopped short', and was 'essentially unsatisfying'.

His own court, the mechanicals and the spirits, were all divided. There was as little harmony among the quartet of lovers as ever. But Brook was now directly challenged about the changes imposed on Phillips' production. These changes, though the actors did not say it, were also in flat contradiction of that rapt and private search for a text's inner truths insisted upon by Brook himself, in his own production. Breaths were drawn, and fairy lips curled, at his bland claim that these changes – which he agreed had been made, though not by him but by others – were 'all in accord with the director's wishes'. Some of the actors, visibly dismayed by this apologia and the absence of any criticism from Brook of the interference, withdrew into silence. After all, they are being called upon by Brook during these very days to open themselves, without reserve, to the search for the truth within them. (Is this dispute, instead, the truth which the theatre offers? Might not *A Midsummer Night's Dream*, as well as *The Two Gentlemen of Verona*, be merely superficial scintillation? And if there is no more and no less truth in one than in the other, why all this cerebral hard labour?)

But when an actor protested that Phillips' production of *The Two Gentlemen of Verona* had been 'the most enjoyable of any production for several seasons,' and the best of that particular play that anyone

[29] *Bottom:* (*Awaking*) When my cue comes, call me and I will answer. My next is 'Most fair Pyramus'. Heigh-ho! Peter Quince? Flute, the bellows mender? Snout, the tinker? Starveling? God's my life, stol'n hence, and left me asleep? I have had a most rare vision. I have had a dream, past the wit of man to say what dream it was . . . Peradventure to make it the more gracious, I will sing it at her death.

(*Exit*)
(*IV.i.197–215*)

[30] *ACT FIVE. Scene One. Athens. The palace of Theseus, Enter*
THESEUS, HIPPOLYTA, PHILOSTRATE, Lords and
Attendants.
Hippolyta: 'Tis strange, my Theseus, that these lovers speak of.
Theseus: More strange than true. I never may believe
These antique fables, nor these fairy toys.
Lovers and madmen have such seething brains,
Such shaping fantasies.

(*V.i.1–5*)

could remember, Brook, both provoked and wearied by the discussion, said flatly: 'I don't know the play, have never seen it before, and have nothing to compare it with.' A fierce hour had passed. 'Even if I had seen the play before,' he added, pugnaciously, 'I wouldn't have remembered it. I can never remember Shakespeare, not even when I'm watching it.' The actors were silent and listless. They themselves knew (I supposed) that to have continued would have raised too many questions of motive, of honesty of purpose, even of purpose itself. 'What does the press say?' someone asked. 'Who cares?' someone else answered. The discussion was over.

Brook, fists clenched, now ordered a massive barrage of drum-beats in crescendo, the sound not of music, but of a depressed anger. Yet not even this pounding could obliterate new questions which began to shape themselves in the bedlam. Is one man's form another man's substance, as one man's meat is another man's poison? Is the distinction between them merely a matter of taste and predilection? Is a 'successful' production dependent as much upon chance and circumstance, as upon insight and intention? Without striving for significant meaning, may not significant meaning be created?

But the striving, and the deep inner stress of it, now continue. Bottom is once more on.the point of waking[29], or under pressure to wake, with the rarest of visions. Today, however, it is as if Bottom's only visions are of last night's rival triumph. Their dark wings flapping, they seem to cast a shadow across his dreaming. Brook himself, his brow clouded, is now at his seeming lowest, and palest; while Bottom's own tension is in the leaden gait of his bottled speaking. He seems to be quelling his feelings, lest they leap out and betray him. At a second attempt 'Peradventure to make it the more gracious, I shall sing it at her death'[29] is gravidly spoken, pregnant with meaning, but stillborn. Worse, Flute has overslept after last night's junkets and celebrations, and has not yet appeared for rehearsal. Mischievously looking to Brook for signs of increasing impatience, the actors find only placidity at the rehearsal's broken rhythms. Brook is, or pretends to be, unconcerned, casual. The forms of this unspoken struggle, their impulses often as inaudible as Shakespeare's, may shift from tit to tat and from moment to moment; but their substance, like Shakespeare's text itself, does not alter.

The rehearsal must jump a scene (Act 4, Scene 2) in Flute's absence, and go straight to the 'Athens' of Act Five and the Palace of Theseus[30], last seen and heard by candlelight. Brook's instructions to

31 (*Enter LYSANDER, DEMETRIUS, HERMIA and HELENA*)
Theseus: Here come the lovers, full of joy and mirth.
   Joy, gentle friends! Joy and fresh days of love
   Accompany your hearts!

(*V.i.28–30*)

32 *Prologue:* If we offend, it is with our good will.
   That you should think, we come not to offend,
   But with good will. To show our simple skill,
   That is the true beginning of our end.
   Consider, then, we come but in despite.
   We do not come, as minding to content you,
   Our true intent is. All for your delight,
   We are not here. That you should here repent you,
   The actors are at hand; and, by their show,
   You shall know all, that you are like to know.

(*V.i.108–117*)

33 (*Enter PYRAMUS, THISBY, WALL, MOONSHINE and LION,
            as in dumbshow*)
Prologue: Gentles, perchance you wonder at this show;
   But wonder on, till truth make all things plain.
   This man is Pyramus, if you would know;
   This beauteous lady Thisby is certain.
   This man, with lime and roughcast, doth present
   Wall, that vile Wall which did these lovers sunder.

(*V.i.126–131*)

34 *Wall:* This loam, this roughcast, and this stone, doth show
   That I am that same wall; the truth is so;
   And this cranny is, right and sinister,
   Through which the fearful lovers are to whisper.
Theseus: Would you desire lime and hair to speak better?
Demetrius: It is the wittiest partition that ever I heard discourse, my
   lord.

(*V.i.160–166*)

the actors, in accents which have become familiar, express his mood more clearly than any overt statement would. 'You want to reconstruct cold-bloodedly what was achieved last time,' he tells them. Equally cold-blooded, his voice is dry as a bone, as a fundamental principle is silently discarded. 'You must show,' he says to the lolling courtiers, 'a complete lack of concern for the mechanicals' real feelings. You must show instead an absolute security with one another.' And again: 'a high and relaxed attitude towards them, as if they were performing animals.'

Question crowds on question as the scene gets under way, and the lovers enter[31]. For Brook has demanded that the actors try to 'reconstruct' the effects of the last run-through; effects, not causes. What were those effects in the first instance? Were they the unexpected result, in manipulated conditions, of the creativity of the actors? Were they the set-up product of the director's artifice and refinement? Is experience and technique now seeking, with sweat on its brow, to recapture innocent impulse? And if so, what is the point of juggling with the pre-verbal?

The effort to find the effects of a few days ago was unavailing. Even the words on Shakespeare's page seemed cold and unyielding in the banal light of day (or the morning after the night before), as if nothing could be done with them. What had flickered and flamed brightly in that darkness was now entirely extinguished. The poignancy of the mechanicals' Prologue[32], which had then been spoken out of a brave struggle with the court's pitiless disdain for the actor, dissolved into nothing. 'Treat him as an animal,' Brook – fanning the ashes – bitingly told the courtiers. 'Ask yourselves what animal he looks like.' Stubbornly, he looked like an actor, forlorn at failure. 'All for your delight, we are not here,' spoke Prologue[32], mangling his punctuation to the court's callous and forced laughter, in turn forcing his delivery into declamation. 'The play of *Pyramus and Thisby*,' Brook told him, 'has no such meaning. It must be spoken simply.'

But today neither simplicity nor innocence nor energy, toiling uphill where joys had been unconfined a few short days ago, are going to be recovered. Brook's remarks, still game but wearied, are themselves flagging. When Pyramus and Thisby, Wall, Lion and Moonshine enter[33], Brook can only tell them that 'they have come into the presence of privilege'. And when Theseus and Demetrius begin the exchange of their mannerly (and mannered) series of aristocratic jibes[34] at the expense of the helpless plebeians, 'they assume,' Brook

(*Enter THISBY*)

Thisby: O wall, full often hast thou heard my moans,
For parting my fair Pyramus and me!
My cherry lips have often kissed thy stones,
The stones with lime and hair knit up in thee.
Pyramus: I see a voice: now will I to the chink,
To spy an I can hear my Thisby's face.
Thisby!
Thisby: My love thou art, my love I think.
Pyramus: Think what thou wilt, I am thy lover's grace;
And, like Limander, am I trusty still.
Thisby: And I like Helen, till the Fates me kill.

(*V.i.186–196*)

36 *Theseus:* Here come two noble beasts in, a man and a lion.
(*Enter LION and MOONSHINE*)
Lion: You, ladies, you, whose gentle hearts do fear
The smallest monstrous mouse that creeps on floor,
May now perchance both quake and tremble here,
When lion rough in wildest rage doth roar.
Then know that I, as Snug the joiner, am
A lion fell, nor else no lion's dam;
For, if I should as lion come in strife
Into this place, 'twere pity on my life.
Theseus: A very gentle beast, and of a good conscience.

(*V.i.215–224*)

37 *Lysander:* This lion is a very fox for his valour.
Theseus: True; and a goose for his discretion.
Demetrius: Not so, my lord; for his valour cannot carry his discretion, and the fox carries the goose.
Theseus: His discretion, I am sure, cannot carry his valour; for the goose carries not the fox. It is well. Leave it to his discretion, and let us listen to the moon.
Moonshine: This lanthorn doth the hornèd moon present –
Demetrius: He should have worn the horns on his head.
Theseus: He is no crescent, and his horns are invisible within the circumference.
Moonshine: This lanthorn doth the hornèd moon present;
Myself the man i' th' moon do seem to be.
Theseus: This is the greatest error of all the rest.

(*V.i.226–239*)

flatly tells them, 'that either the mechanicals are stone-deaf, or that it does not matter whether they are or not.' Now what had once created fear and suggested the 'unearthly' in Thisby's male falsetto[35], merely becomes – under failure's cold and close scrutiny – an embarrassingly high-pitched guying of the voice of a female. Brook is angry. 'This is a love scene like the others,' he tells him. 'Thisby must not be played as a joke old woman, but simply and for truth.'

There is an honour in this doggedness, and a reassertion of basic skills in what follows[36]. But there is little in it of the simplicity and innocence, the fear and the pity, of the occasion which Brook had sought to rediscover. And yet this very persistence brought its own reward, as has previously happened. The disdainful and haughty banter between Theseus, Demetrius and Lysander on the subject of foxes, geese and valour[37], previously heard – but not registered – as the dullest of Elizabethan repartee, courtly logic-chopping in an intellectual mode long consigned to dusty oblivion, is at last given a point. It is the humour of the actors, Brook's swift instinct, the oafish presence of the weary mechanicals and even the very failure of the rehearsal which, between them, find it and prick the passage into life.

For these (incomprehensibly) witty exchanges are being loudly and crushingly spoken not to, but at, Lion and Moonshine. The two of them have been halted in their tracks by Shakespeare's text[37], and by their own depression – and suddenly it is the meaningless wit itself which is heard, to an outburst of laughter, to have cowed them into their awe-stricken silence. Brook seizes the moment and, at his best, instantly sees beyond it. 'It is word-play,' he says, 'to defeat their play of words.' And marrying a creative insight to a practical suggestion in the twinkling of an eyelid, he adds: 'They are playing Shakespeare to the mechanicals. They have turned the mechanicals, *in the middle of their own play*, into an audience. They are forcing the mechanicals to admire their courtly acting.'

Playwright's truth or director's illusion, Brook's consistent concern with the deep themes of the text was again being revealed, and at a point where it could have been least expected. Momentarily *A Midsummer Night's Dream* was drawn by it from depression, and seemed to step out from *The Two Gentlemen of Verona*'s shadows. But in this brief light of the day's last moments, I saw no more than a search for the real in the vanities of a dream, and for living truths in a deadly fiction. As for the actors, I saw them striving for inner impulse at another's direction, and seeking the spontaneous with sweating effort. On this metal chair, it is hard going.

Fifth week, first and second days

I stayed at home for two days, during which I ordered my notes and wrote of the production. The pleasures of the writing were greater than, and different from, those of attending the rehearsals. To be pen in hand was as if, at last, to master the experience; as if, too, to articulate what at many moments had seemed to be beyond both Brook and the actors. (If these are my own self-serving illusions, if I know that they are, and if I nevertheless continue to believe in them, then they become – for me – self-serving truths also; akin to those of the actors, and akin to those to which the audience is being invited.)

Yet in the effort to find what Brook, a few days ago, had called a style which is 'not-acting', where 'things happen as if by themselves', was there not a tacit admission of the primacy of the written? Is he not saying to the actors that, with sufficient sensitivity, a form can be found where the written word, in its simplest and truest evocation, will arouse and sustain all meaning?

Fifth week, third day

The cast has moved to a new place of rehearsal – the Conference Hall – a newly-constructed rehearsal set, a new space, new sounds, new feelings. There is a first shock to be undergone in getting my bearings. Familiar figures, preparing for the morning's rehearsal, seem transmuted in this new setting. There is a revised sense of self and a changed perception of others, together. It is as if the new environment, no longer improvised, provides for both a new physicality and a renewal of emotions: there is a subtly shown-off élan in the one, and a charged energy in the other. Does this signify, as I asked myself earlier, that 'accident' – here, the accident of place – counts for as much as, or more than, strenuous effort and invention? How far and in

165

19   Theseus: 'Or in the night imagining some fear,/How easy is a bush supposed a bear!' (Act Five, Scene One); Alan Howard (Theseus).

what ways does the setting, or the set (to put it at its most banal), determine our very sense of seeing and hearing, and our deepest feeling?

Even before the figures appear upon or against it, the new narrowed verticals of the space – grey flats, high scaffolding and gangplanks, hung with a cat's-cradle of ropes, catwalks and ladders – have begun to shape our responses. When the actors, when Brook, when the stage hands, (when I) step within its confines, it is place, in its new scale and proportion, which seems to govern. If the pre-verbal comes before the verbal, does place come before both of them? Or is it we who read meaning into space, faster than it could ever suggest it? Can persons become bodies, merely by force of their setting, and humans objects? Here, even before anyone sets to work on them, there are fore-shortened figures on the high scaffold at its topmost level, twenty feet up, who appear to hang in elevation above us. On the ground are dwarfed bodies, now overhung and caught within a new confinement. But at eye-level and from another angle, the latter stare at us and outstare us, larger than life at such close quarters.

For in this space there will not merely be close-ups, but frontal exposures; not merely production and presentation, but confrontation. Is it the courage of Brook's convictions which will be thrust before us? Or is it that the most skilled magician, with the most cunning sleight-of-hand, seeks to come closest to his audience before rolling up his sleeves and casually plucking the rabbit out of air, bare-faced and (as if) bare-handed? Clothes like *kimonos* also drape the scaffolding, awaiting the actors. Or is it Japan which is awaiting this production?

The day begins with an answer. Richard Peaselee, house-composer and armed with music-paper, is being briefed by the director. That is, Brook is placing a musical order with him, and he is writing it down as if he were a grocer. Brook is asking Demetrius and Helena to sing to Peaselee a song that Demetrius has arrived at, by improvisation at rehearsal. Voice and guitar, amid the din of the day's preparation, are dictated to the composer; who, a few moments later, sings it back, reordered, to Demetrius. And during the next five minutes Peaselee, on his knees at a small table, writes quickly to the noise of thudding exercise – reverberant in the new setting – and a babel of shouted instructions. The actors are also now armed with long and shining coils of fine steel wire, and Brook begins the proceedings by shouting 'Let's look to the wires! Make them into a forest!' Wires are strewn and

167

¹ *Lysander:* How now, my love! Why is your cheek so pale?
  How chance the roses there do fade so fast?
  Hermia: Belike for want of rain, which I could well
  Beteem them from the tempest of my eyes
  Lysander: Ay me! For aught that I could ever read,
    Could ever hear by tale or history,
    The course of true love never did run smooth;
    But, either it was different in blood –
  Hermia: O cross! Too high to be enthralled to low!
  Lysander: Or else misgraffèd in respect of years –
  Hermia: O spite! Too old to be engaged to young!
  Lysander: Or else it stood upon the choice of friends –
  Hermia: O hell! To choose love by another's eyes!

  (I.i.128–140)

² *Hermia:* My good Lysander!
  I swear to thee, by Cupid's strongest bow,
  By his best arrow with the golden head,
  By the simplicity of Venus' doves,
  By that which knitteth souls and prospers loves,
  And by that fire which burned the Carthage queen,
  When the false Troyan under sail was seen,
  By all the vows that ever men have broke,
  In number more than ever women spoke,
  In that same place thou hast appointed me,
  Tomorrow truly will I meet with thee.

  (I.i.168–178)

³   *(Enter DEMETRIUS, HELENA following him)*
  Demetrius: I love thee not, therefore pursue me not.
    Where is Lysander and fair Hermia?
    The one I'll slay, the other slayeth me.
    Thou told'st me they were stol'n into this wood;
    And here am I, and wood within this wood,
    Because I cannot meet my Hermia.
    Hence, get thee gone, and follow me no more!
  Helena: You draw me, you hard-hearted adamant:
    But yet you draw not iron, for my heart
    Is true as steel. Leave you your power to draw
    And I shall have no power to follow you.

  (II.i.188–198)

168

snaked, tinkling and writhing, over the playing-area. They are draped, coiling and bouncing, from the scaffolds. But there is no forest. There are only the actors' caught-up feet and bodies, and the steel coils of a new, cold – or cool – Arden.

The impedimenta now cleared for the play's beginning, the actors swiftly find and hold the note of simplicity and passion. Is the lyric discovered by the place and the actor in it? If not, why should suffocated thought and feeling revive in a new setting? Is there not more space and light and air here, than there? Here, for example, Lysander makes light of 'How now, my love! Why is your cheek so pale?'[1] And, Samurai-like, carrying a short staff which emphasizes his tread and presence, he arrests and keeps attention where previously the eye and mind had wandered. (When an actor ceases to be a mere figure of speech, even his most fleeting comment can seem a portent.) Hermia, too, is no longer a speaking cipher. Her 'My good Lysander!/ I swear to thee by Cupid's strongest bow'[2] has throughout been an awkward text, awkwardly spoken. Now, for breathless moments, it sounds to be the voice of her own innermost thought and feeling. And in the heard – almost felt – flurry of her clothes and physical movement, the air seemed to shake with a fresh assault on the alerted senses.

The Second Act appears all new effect and new motion. In its first scene, Demetrius and Helena must now enter[3] through a thin filigree of strewn wire. Ensnared in filaments which might have been spun and hung by Puck, who stands on the topmost catwalk high above them, they are oblivious of his presence. 'My heart is as true as steel'[3], Helena – enmeshed in steel – tells Demetrius. There is a split second of choice before us. Should we laugh at the correspondence, and by making it absurd destroy the moment? Or, eye and ear awakened, catch and keep this concurrence (is it by accident or design?) of word and image? Is this an appeal to our imagination which we should welcome, or the conceit, in both senses, of the director? Is the audience mocked, or its power strengthened? For Demetrius must now step through these trembling coils to reach Helena. Moreover, to make of this *matériel* the snares of a dream-forest depends as much on us, as on the actors; perhaps more so. 'I will not stay thy questions'[4], Demetrius now says, as if to me as much as to Helena; and shouts 'Let me go!', trapped in bouncing wire.

But this is becoming as dangerous as it is literal, and I can see that Brook is made uneasy by it. Demetrius' 'I shall do thee mischief in the

⁴ *Demetrius:* I will not stay thy questions. Let me go!
  Or, if thou follow me, do not believe
  But I shall do thee mischief in the wood.
Helena: Ay, in the temple, in the town, the field,
  You do me mischief. Fie, Demetrius!
  Your wrongs do set a scandal on my sex.
  We cannot fight for love, as men may do;
  We should be wooed, and were not made to woo.
                                          (*Exit DEMETRIUS*)
                                          (*II.i.235–242*)

⁵   (*Enter LYSANDER and HERMIA*)
Lysander: Fair love, you faint with wand'ring in the wood;
  And to speak troth, I have forgot our way.
  We'll rest us, Hermia, if you think it good,
  And tarry for the comfort of the day.
Hermia: Be't so, Lysander. Find you out a bed;
  For I upon this bank will rest my head.
                                          (*II.ii.35–40*)

⁶ *Hermia:* Nay, good Lysander. For my sake, my dear,
  Lie further off yet, do not lie so near.
Lysander: O, take the sense, sweet, of my innocence!
  Love takes the meaning in love's conference.
  I mean, that my heart unto yours is knit,
  So that but one heart we can make of it:
  Two bosoms interchainèd with an oath;
  So then two bosoms and a single troth.
  Then by your side no bed-room me deny,
  For lying so, Hermia, I do not lie.
Hermia: Lysander riddles very prettily.
  Now much beshrew my manners and my pride,
  If Hermia meant to say Lysander lied.
  But, gentle friend, for love and courtesy
  Lie further off, in human modesty.
                                          (*II.ii.43–57*)

wood'[4], feet entangled in these steel briars, leads him only to a hard and aggressive kissing of Helena, as if they were both caught in a vicious circle. And Helena's 'Ay, in the temple, in the town, the field,/ You do me mischief'[4], once both mischievous and erotic, now has wire braces fixed upon it. This is wooing amid metal, and beyond the skills of either. Helena is brought to a standstill by it. 'I should not mind being entangled at this point,' she says, threshing in the wire but apologetic, 'nor even notice'. But in this setting, where only a moment before every sense was expectant, joy has abruptly vanished. Demetrius himself flees[4] straight up a ladder.

It is a maypole climbed by a monkey, arse in air, and not the headlong flight of a lover. His improvised motion has fitted action not to meaning or to rhythm, but to the ladder. It is an expedient and ingenious gesture. But it is also one imposed upon the actor by the need to find uses for a stage-machine which has been invented, for him, by the director. For the briefest moment, the entry of Hermia and Lysander[5], lost in the wood and now snared in whorls of wire, seemed helped not hindered by such devices. But as soon as the spectator refused complicity and belief was suspended, the spectre of Farce reared up, roof-high, over the actors. 'Fair love, you faint with wand'ring in the wood'[5], sang Lysander, feet in wire and stalked by Folly. Nevertheless, Brook – as if not hearing any suppressed laughter – tells him to 'take this singing as a ballad, with an easy tiredness, without strain and without despair'.

Has Lysander, without knowing it, fallen off the theatre's tightrope, held at one end in the hands of the actors, and at the other by the spectator? I, at any rate, have dropped it among the coils of wire. 'Keep the character and his thoughts in your singing,' Brook continues. 'Think of what you're trying to say with the music.' As Lysander stands here in front of me, is it I alone who refuse him his identity and his meaning? He is not Lysander, not a love-sick swain consoling his frail and tired Hermia, nor even a Shakespearian actor. Suddenly, to me, he is merely a paid and patched dupe in a theatrical charade, dumb but vocal. I can hear only Brook's distant voice saying that 'the scene has enormous range, if you don't get locked into one line in it'. Am I alone locked out of it entirely? If not, why is everyone else so attentive? Is it deference, stupidity or politeness? 'O take the sense, sweet, of my innocence!/ Love takes the meaning in love's conference'[6], he (?Lysander) says to the young girl (?Hermia) beside him. Does it matter?

(*Enter PUCK*)

Puck: Through the forest have I gone,
But Athenian found I none,
On whose eyes I might approve
This flower's force in stirring love.
Night and silence. – Who is here?
Weeds of Athens he doth wear:
This is he, my master said,
Despisèd the Athenian maid;
And here the maiden, sleeping sound,
On the dank and dirty ground.
Pretty soul! She durst not lie
Near this lack-love, this kill-courtesy,
Churl, upon thy eyes I throw
All the power this charm doth owe.
When thou wak'st, let love forbid
Sleep his seat on thy eyelid.
So awake when I am gone,
For I must now to Oberon.

(*Enter DEMETRIUS and HELENA, running*)

Helena: Stay, though thou kill me, sweet Demetrius.
Demetrius: I charge thee, hence, and do not haunt me thus.
Helena: O, wilt thou darkling, leave me? Do not so.
Demetrius: Stay, on thy peril! I alone will go.   (*Exit*)
Helena: O, I am out of breath in this fond chase!
The more my prayer, the lesser is my grace.
Happy is Hermia, wheresoe'er she lies,
For she hath blessèd and attractive eyes.
How came her eyes so bright? Not with salt tears.
If so, my eyes are oft'ner washed than hers.
No, no, I am as ugly as a bear,
For beasts that meet me run away for fear.
Therefore no marvel though Demetrius
Do, as a monster, fly my presence thus.

(*II.ii.66–97*)

It is as if this uncertain mood in me, closer to anger than irritation, has itself been provoked by the relentlessness, now weeks long, of the actors' appeal to my imagination. Yet, the scene and the sound slowly swim back into focus. They are speaking to each other[6], within my earshot. I have no option but to listen. I see them exchanging glances and touching, stretched out on the ground before me. He seems earnest, and she playful. They seem even to be thinking aloud of making love to each other. As she speaks, telling him to 'lie further off'[6], she seems to struggle inwardly with her feelings, and he with his conscience. They would, but they cannot; and not here, watched over by sprites and a handful of spectators. Drawn back again, against my will, into the life before me – they feeling for the pulse of Shakespeare's rhythm and each other's, and I feeling for theirs – there is, in these moments of sentience, once more a sense of sharing also.

His metal plate softly whirring, Puck now enters[7] 'stirring love'. But its correspondence is not jarring. He bends over Hermia, 'sleeping sound', and you can see her breathing, her bodice rising and falling. In close-up, 'Pretty soul!'[7] escapes him, inviting the spectator's confidence, and himself confiding. And into this moment Demetrius and Helena come running[7], as into an embrace, its arms extended to catch them. 'Stay, though thou kill me, sweet Demetrius,' she tells him breathlessly, pausing in a chase so real that it must end not in the mind, but in the body. All is as clear as daylight . . . and is suddenly interrupted. 'This is night,' says Brook. 'Remember the darkness.' (And adds: 'Play a Chinese theatre darkness,' though how and why they should play for further chinoiserie, in looped coils of steel, he does not explain to the actors.)

It is in the night-words of both the lovers, but not in their voices. 'Do not haunt me thus'[7] he says lightly to her, while her 'O, wilt thou darkling leave me?'[7], is wide-awake and pleading, not sombre or nocturnal. Their exchanges are as bright as high-noon, and still bounding from the chase of bodies. But now Demetrius leaves Helena. She is alone. And against all the odds, the streaming sunlight among them, darkness fell upon her[7]. It was a darkness of mind, jealous and self-hating. Melancholy, and gazing inwards into the eye of night – 'no longer fighting,' Brook says, 'with the outer darkness' – her brow seemed to lour darkly, without technical benefit of a spotlit stage-darkness. She sees herself to be 'as ugly as a bear'[7]; while the sleeping Hermia, (as if) unseen and her own eyes sealed in darkness, 'hath blessèd and attractive eyes'. There are many eyes, 'eyes so bright', in

⁸ *Lysander:* Not Hermia but Helena I love:
      Who will not change a raven for a dove?
      The will of man is by his reason swayed,
      And reason says you are the worthier maid.
      Things growing are not ripe until their season:
      So I, being young, till now ripe not to reason.

                                                    (*II.ii.113–118*)

⁹ *Hermia:* (*Awaking*) Help me, Lysander, help me! Do thy best
      To pluck this crawling serpent from my breast!
      Ay me, for pity! What a dream was here!
      Lysander, look how I do quake with fear.

                                                    (*II.ii.145–148*)

174

this make-believe and watching darkness: Helena's, the spirits on their scaffold, the small knot of spectators, and the waking Lysander's.

'The will of man is by his reason swayed'[8], the bewitched Lysander now says, fully risen from his slumbers. His voice and gesture – and his body also – seem to grow into a (Japanese) moment of gross enlargement and hieratic declaration. Brook was standing near me, jingling the money in his trouser-pocket. 'And reason says,' says Lysander to Helena, pausing, his delivery stunned, his eyes rolling, 'you are the worthier maid./ Things growing are not ripe until their season.'[8] The moment has been inflated to bursting, and his voice is like thunder. 'The words are so extreme,' says Brook, 'that the delivery can be colossal. It is a species of ultimate revelation.' It is nothing of the sort; flickering night-thought is being fanned into a raging inferno. Lysander's vocal heroics have become merely histrionic, and he has turned himself into a Grand Guignol or Kurosawa presence. Brook deftly blows the fuse and blames the actor. 'You are forgetting the sense,' he tells him. 'You are making an exterior comment on it. Follow what is unfolding in him. Discover, do not comment.'

These are the first familiar symptoms in Brook – the jingling of money included – of a renewed dissatisfaction. The lovers' relations, whether played from a courtly distance or in the immediately erotic, are as intractable as ever. The coils of meandering and snaking steel which link them one to the other, the sleeping to the waking and the silent to the speaking bodies, cannot bring them to a close harmony of impulse and a shapely rhythm. As Hermia awakens in turn[9], to find Lysander vanished, Brook stops the action, sits on the tinkling floor, and draws the quartet about him. 'This scene,' he says, his voice forced into its coldest calm under pressure, 'opens up a world of relationships. You must explore all its shades of meaning, from Victorian sentiment to sexual attack. The whole mood of the Sonnets is in it, all the stages between Will and Reason. Above all, you must be open to the totally genuine sensitivities of the other person, capable of following the other's wishes. Demetrius and Lysander,' he adds, 'must be able to go beyond the impulse merely to grab a woman.'

Gimlet-eyed and pushing his pressure upon them, Brook urges them to be 'open to the kind of circumstances in which one word of rejection by the person you love is as hurtful to the senses as a blow to the body. Lock on to the purely physical, and your behaviour becomes pure "West Side Story". In playing this truly,' he says in a dead silence, 'you should be able to improve the quality of your own, real,

¹⁰ *ACT THREE. Scene Two. Another part of the wood. Enter OBERON.*
  Oberon: I wonder if Titania be awaked:
    Then, what it was that next came in her eye,
    Which she must dote on in extremity.

                                                    (III.ii.1–3)

¹¹ *Oberon:*   How now, mad spirit?
    What night-rule now about this haunted grove?
  Puck: My mistress with a monster is in love.
    Near to her close and consecrated bower,
    While she was in her dull and sleeping hour,
    A crew of patches, rude mechanicals,
    That work for bread upon Athenian stalls,
    Were met together to rehearse a play,
    Intended for great Theseus' nuptial day.
    The shallowest thickskin of that barren sort,
    Who Pyramus presented in their sport,
    Forsook his scene, and entered in a brake.
    When I did him at this vantage take,
    An ass's nole I fixèd on his head.
    Anon his Thisby must be answerèd,
    And forth my mimic comes. When they him spy,
    As wild geese that the creeping fowler eye,
    Or russet-pated choughs, many in sort,
    Rising and cawing at the gun's report,
    Sever themselves and madly sweep the sky,
    So, at his sight, away his fellows fly.

                                                    (III.ii.4–24)

¹² *Hermia:* What's this to my Lysander? Where is he?
    Ah, good Demetrius, wilt thou give him me?
  Demetrius: I had rather give his carcass to my hounds.
  Hermia: Out, dog! Out, cur! Thou driv'st me past the bounds
    Of maiden's patience.

                                                    (III.ii.62–66)

¹³ *Lysander:* Why should you think that I should woo in scorn?
    Scorn and derision never come in tears:
    Look, when I vow, I weep; and vows so born,
    In their nativity all truth appears.

                                                    (III.ii.122–125)

relationships with others.' But intimacy of this kind seems only to widen the distance between them. 'What is the difference,' he asks Christopher Gable, 'between you and Lysander?' There is no answer. 'Christopher Gable as Lysander,' Brook answers, 'must be totally alive and therefore totally free.' The *non-sequiturs* are daunting. 'Your personal jadedness, cynicism, anger, self-pity take energy out of you as an actor. Live-ness and open-ness bring energy in. As long as you are alive in the part, the combination of you and the part can never cease from endless creation.' Brook stands up. He has put his finger on Lysander, as in earlier rehearsals on Hermia. 'Don't comment on the part in your acting,' he tells him.

The rehearsals now moves on, jumping the mechanicals' second rehearsal and Bottom's transformation, to 'Another part of the wood'[10]: Act Three, Scene Two. (For much of the scene, as the work became intenser, Brook continued to jingle the money in his pockets.) 'I wonder if Titania be awaked'[10], said Oberon, standing above us on the topmost gallery of the scaffold and peering down, free and remote, into the confined world below of mortals and groundlings. How much of this will be lost in the auditorium? The spectator will no longer be able to gaze upwards, as now, into an imagined heaven. Instead, he will stare square-on at its flattened and picture-frame reduction. Will this vertical and soaring sense of height then become a blockish set of horizontals in the final production? Will the imagined poetry of this space become merely prosaic in that one? For here Oberon's 'How now, mad spirit!'[11], all heads craning up to, seems to call across to Puck from a spire or steeple, high above the humdrum; while Puck's balance, on the same level, is vertiginous, and his words seemingly plucked from air in answer. But when they both take to trapezes and hurtle back and forth over the swaying arena, do Puck's 'wild geese' which 'sever themselves and madly sweep the sky'[11] gain an added resonance from such flying? Or is it nothing more than circus aerobatics?

The set invites to further climbing and swinging. Yet amidst it, the lovers' quartet must try to find an improvement in its dramatic relations. Indeed Hermia is now not merely driven 'past the bounds of maiden's patience'[12] into a thicket of metal, but overhung by ropes and iron. In turn, Lysander's vows and tears[13], and Helena's hurts and fears, spend their time climbing up and down ladders. Brook, impatient, halts it. 'This must be taken out of the geometry of the set' (which he himself has had constructed), he tells them, 'and towards

Oberon: This is thy negligence. Still thou mistak'st,
    Or else committ'st thy knaveries wilfully.
  Puck: Believe me, king of shadows, I mistook.
    Did not you tell me I should know the man
    By the Athenian garments he had on?

(III.ii.345–349)

humanity.' In fact, paraphernalia and artifice, once their novelty has faded, have conspired to block both feeling and invention. And it is as if the linearities of the scene's regular rhyming, within this setting and its formal outline, have also been heightened. The verse's recurring balance, and the repeated cadence of voices and gestures, seem to have become straitened within these vertical uprights and right angles: less poetry, than verbal theorems.

But, after the rehearsal, Demetrius told me that it was 'a great help to us having this set. We were making geometrical moves before, without it. We have been freed from artificiality,' he added. Yet in the next moment, he said that the setting was 'more confining.' Brook, on the one hand, finds their movements geometrical, and the actor feels 'freer', on the other. What do these apparent contradictions mean, if anything? Could it be that the set's constraints, and its now sharply-defined spaces, have liberated the actor from the fear of movement without focus, in a studio where little was fixed and nothing certain? Does the symmetry of this set, inspiring its own order, free the actors from movements prescribed and plotted by the director? And freed of anxiety about *where* they are, might not their sense of identity – of *who* they are – become stronger? Certainly, there is no such thing as an 'empty space', either in the physical world or the dramatic.

'This is thy negligence'[14], Oberon angrily tells Puck of the lovers' uncertainties and confusions. (Brook had blamed Hermia first, and then Lysander for them.) Spoken from the topmost gantry, an eyrie as high as Olympus in relation to the benighted mortals, Oberon is eagle-eyed and sees Puck now hiding on earth below. He points him out with perspex, and brings him to heel with a voice like a winged arrow. 'Believe me, king of shadows,' says Puck, quaking among us, 'I mistook'[14]. Yet even before Oberon spoke, he had been quaking. Brook intervenes swiftly. 'The real life for Puck, as Spirit, resides only in the words,' he tells him; but I also hear it as Brook's oriental bow to the playwright. 'It does not start with something felt inside him,' he continues. 'If there are changes in the words, take the key to your feelings from them. Do not reverse the order.' Puck had quaked too soon, but it sounds like a reversal of Brook's own orders. 'In the beginning was the word?', Puck asks Brook with a felicity rare in such (equally rare) exchanges. 'In this case, yes,' Brook answers, visibly surprised at Puck's intervention.

Oberon, elevated beyond our reach, is both larger than life and dwarfed by distance. 'He is in one world,' Brook says, 'and Puck in

¹⁵ *Oberon:* Thou see'st these lovers seek a place to fight.
Hie therefore, Robin, overcast the night.
The starry welkin cover thou anon
With drooping fog, as black as Acheron;
And lead these testy rivals so astray,
As one come not within another's way.
Like to Lysander sometime frame thy tongue,
Then stir Demetrius up with bitter wrong;
And sometime rail thou like Demetrius
And from each other look thou lead them thus,
Till o'er their brows death-counterfeiting sleep
With leaden legs and batty wings doth creep . . .
While I in this affair do thee employ,
I'll to my queen and beg her Indian boy;
And then I will her charmèd eye release
From monster's view, and all things shall be peace.

(*III.ii.354–377*)

¹⁶ *Puck:* Up and down, up and down,
I will lead them up and down:
I am feared in field and town:
Goblin, lead them up and down.

(*III.ii.396–399*)

¹⁷ *Puck:* Thou coward, art thou bragging to the stars,
Telling the bushes that thou look'st for wars,
And will not come? Come, recreant! Come, thou child!
I'll whip thee with a rod.

(*III.ii.407–410*)

¹⁸ *Lysander:* He goes before me and still dares me on:
When I come where he calls, then he is gone.
The villain is much lighter-heeled than I.
I followed fast, but faster he did fly,
That fallen am I in dark uneven way,
And here will rest me. (*Lies down*) Come, thou gentle day!
For if but once thou show me the gray light,
I'll find Demetrius, and revenge his spite.

(*Sleeps*)
(*III.ii.413–420*)

another.' In truth, and in the text, they are in the same one. Even at a far cry or near-whisper, Oberon's voice carries. 'Thou see'st these lovers seek a place to fight,'[15] he says, with a bird's-eye view but as if at Puck's elbow. 'Hie therefore, Robin,' he tells him, pacing the highest catwalk, while Puck moves at an echoing pace and stride below him, 'overcast the night'[15]. Order upon order – to undo the mortals' confusion – is given to Puck; 'and all shall be peace'[15], Oberon says, in a hollow stage-whisper. 'Remember the links with this line elsewhere in the play,' Brook tells him. And, as if with ease, Oberon's voice sounds its endless echo.

Moments later, 'Up and down, up and down/ I will lead them up and down'[16] sets Puck off, now without stilts, upon a crab-like sideways striding, his speech and movement expanded too, to greet the deep sense of a pending resolution. But Puck is merely recalling and reproducing (copying) old gesture and old inspiration. It is the passage on stilts, and stilted even without them. Brook, though visibly struck by it, stops him abruptly. The actor answers before Brook forms the question. 'I was playing a demonic power which almost took Puck over,' he tells Brook, without conviction. Brook rejects it. 'The words,' he repeats, 'are the most intimate thing to him. An inner change on this scale isn't possible for a spirit. The impulse must come to him wholly from the outside, wholly from the words he is speaking.'

Puck makes a second attempt. And, this time, he is led by the words as if led by the nose, visibly and audibly impelled and shaken back and forth, up and down, by what he is saying. He seems to be buoyed up by words[17], with a fire blazing in his eyes only. And as the work grew intenser, Lysander's voice and appearance – frequently pallid and without dimension – seemed to close-in on the rehearsal spectators. With his re-entrance at 'He goes before me and still dares me on'[18], his merely speaking figure had grown into a presence which confronted the small audience in close-up. It was as if for the first time we had to face him, both as man and actor. 'The villain is much lighter-heeled than I'[18] instantly drew the eye to question in detail his physical *persona*. At this moment, however fleeting, he was not merely speaking his lines and inviting a half-hearted attention to them, but filling a role and forcing his dimensions of mind and body upon us.

Moreover, 'Fallen am I in dark uneven way'[18] now reached that tragic pitch of loss which, three weeks ago, had been asked for without avail. His sorrows were simply taken in hand, and held out before us. His demands of us, and Brook's demands of him, had

¹⁹ *Helena:* O weary night, O long and tedious night,
   Abate thy hours! Shine comforts from the east,
   That I may back to Athens by daylight,
   From these that my poor company detest:
   And sleep, that sometimes shuts up sorrow's eye,
   Steal me awhile from mine own company.

(Sleeps)

  Puck: Yet but three? Come one more.
   Two of both kinds makes up four.
   Here she comes, curst and sad:
   Cupid is a knavish lad,
   Thus to make poor females mad.

(III.ii.431–441)

²⁰ *Hermia:* Never so weary, never so in woe;
   Bedabbled with the dew and torn with briers,
   I can no further crawl, no further go;
   My legs can keep no pace with my desires.
   Here will I rest me till the break of day.
   Heavens shield Lysander, if they mean a fray!

(Lies down and sleeps)

  Puck: On the ground
   Sleep sound:
   I'll apply
   To your eye,
   Gentle lover, remedy.

(Squeezing the juice on LYSANDER's eye)

   When thou wak'st,
   Thou tak'st
   True delight
   In the sight
   Of thy former lady's eye:
   And the country proverb known,
   That every man should take his own,
   In your waking shall be shown,
   Jack shall have Jill;
   Nought shall go ill;
   The man shall have his mare again, and all shall be well.   *(Exit)*

(III.ii.442–463)

suddenly come to fruition. 'Come, thou gentle day!'[18] is no longer a remote and lonely plea, at best lent enchantment by distance. Instead, it is shared with the spectator, who is taken, in thought, into Lysander's nightmare. And when he 'sleeps' against the grey-white flat, upright, arms apart and as if pinned, his wings seemed to spread as wide as the span of the whole play's meaning.

Now each successive lover's speech of wearied grief seems to be spoken both with and for the others. There is developing today a unison of thought and a harmony of gesture in their side-by-side speaking and sleeping, which for weeks has been elusive. At Helena's 'O weary night, O long and tedious night'[19] – now also sounding the unspoken thoughts of the sleeping Lysander and Demetrius – Brook tells her that it 'must have the simple feeling of the end of the road'. He wants from her 'the sense of time stopping'. To get to it, he asks her to 'try a simple sung prayer'; and her singing invocation to sleep, which 'shuts up sorrow's eye'[19], is now a mournful lullaby for all the lovers. ('Shine comforts from the east,'[19] she sings, looking to the orient on Brook's behalf for solace and inspiration, dressed in a *kimono*.)

'Yet but three? Come one more,'[19] says Puck, his voice and body still and watchful. But now his calm is edged with an idle menace. And 'Here she comes, curst and sad' seems, for the first time, a knell tolling for all lovers; while 'Cupid is a knavish lad,/ Thus to make poor females mad'[19] suddenly itself plumbs an eerie register where it is not enchantment by spirits, but Ophelia's madness which beckons. The three lovers, divided awake, are now united in one sleep, impaled together. Hermia's approach is to a lovers' cross, where love seems to lie not sleeping, but bleeding. 'Never so weary, never so in woe;/ Bedabbled with the dew and torn with briers'[20], she is now a fourth romantic pilgrim come, as if from a Gethsemane of the heart to a collective crucifixion, with pathos (and Puck) standing watch on the one hand, and bathos (and Brook) on the other. 'As you walk forward, suggest without gesture that you can "no further go",' he tells her. And so she does; and so it seems.

At the scene's end[20] Puck rolled a tennis ball across the acting area, at the very moment of sounding its deepest note of resolution: that 'every man should take his own' at waking, and that 'Jack shall have Jill ... and all shall be well'[20]. These might be the struck chords of a poetic justice – and struck quietly lest he wake the lovers – yet a tennis-ball was also being rolled slowly across our line of vision, at the (eight) feet of a dream-laden crucifixion, in *kimonos*. As Puck's parting and well-

²¹ (*ACT FOUR. Scene One. The wood. LYSANDER, DEMETRIUS, HELENA and HERMIA, lying asleep. Enter TITANIA, BOTTOM and FAIRIES; and OBERON behind, unseen*)

Titania: Come, sit thee down upon this flow'ry bed,
　　While I thy amiable cheeks do coy,
　　And stick musk roses in thy sleek smooth head,
　　And kiss thy fair large ears, my gentle joy.

Bottom: Where's Peaseblossom?

Peaseblossom: Ready.

Bottom: Scratch my head, Peaseblossom. Where's Mounsieur Cobweb?

Cobweb: Ready.

Bottom: Mounsieur Cobweb, good mounsieur, get you your weapons
　　in your hand, and kill me a red-hipped humblebee on the top of a
　　thistle; and, good Mounsieur, bring me the honey bag.

(*IV.i.–13*)

²² *Titania:* Or say, sweet love, what thou desirest to eat.

Bottom: Truly, a peck of provender. I could munch your good dry
　　oats. Methinks I have a great desire to a bottle of hay. Good hay,
　　sweet hay, hath no fellow.

(*IV.i.28–31*)

184

placed shot in the long symbolic passage of objects and feelings (what feelings?), it was either apt and moving, or merely a rolling tennis-ball. Inveigled by the dangerous illusion of significant meaning in every gesture, it was the first; uninveigled, it was the second. But the more arresting and rapt the performance, the easier now for a bush to seem a bear, or the rolling of a tennis-ball to become the silent music of the spheres, or a spirit in movement. There is a new moment of truth in this; in which a Rubicon of achievement having been crossed, sleight-of-hand could get away with murder.

Now Titania and Bottom enter[21] – today, to Mendelssohn's *A Midsummer Night's Dream* – she dancing and in a flustered passion, Brook jingling money in his pocket. He tells Bottom: 'Make your entrance badger-like'; while Titania is now as busy about him as Brook had long ago wanted. 'Come, sit thee down upon this flow'ry bed,'[21] she tells him, fussing. Caressing his (imagined) ass's cheeks, she calls him 'my gentle joy', adorning him with flowers, as sentiment and sensuality, tenderness and horror, curdle and seethe together. 'Mounsieur Cobweb, good mounsieur,'[21] says Bottom, his voice resonant and ripening to each cadence, 'get you your weapons in your hand, and kill me a red-hipped humblebee.'[21] His gestures, too, are as sure – and half-human – in their touch as his voice, half-neighed, is settled in its balance of ass and Bottom.

Less flexible and inventive but more thoughtful, less mobile and less responsive but more experienced, Bottom has seemingly built his role according to his own methods. His grasp of his part has grown at its own pace and rhythm (rather than that of Brook or the other actors), without obvious improvisation from day to day, and without renewal. What he has found he has kept, and polished. Brook has attended to him relatively little. He has let him go his own way, and Bottom has gone it, as if in private. Maladroit as an acrobat and discreetly withdrawn in the search for the pre-verbal, he nevertheless now stands shoulder-to-shoulder with the overt explorers of hidden impulse, inner truth and shared rhythm. Is he more honest, reaching old truths by old methods, rather than pretending to reach new truths by new ones? Acted upon, particularly as ass, rather than acting, has he perhaps taken his cue entirely from the other actors? Or is there a simple truth in this Bottom, both in the play and out of it, which is complex masquerade in the others?

'Methinks,' he says ruminant, 'I have a great desire to a bottle of hay.'[22] His broadened vowels, slowed intonation and the movement of

185

²³ *Oberon:* But first I will release the Fairy Queen.
    Be as thou wast wont to be;
    See as thou wast wont to see.
    Dian's bud o'er Cupid's flower,
    Hath such force and blessèd power.
    Now, my Titania, wake you, my sweet Queen.
Titania: My Oberon, what visions have I seen!
    Methought I was enamored of an ass.

                                                  (IV.i.67–74)

²⁴ *Oberon:* Come, my Queen, take hands with me,
    And rock the ground whereon these sleepers be.   *(Dance)*
    Now thou and I are new in amity,
    And will tomorrow midnight solemnly
    Dance in Duke Theseus' house triumphantly,
    And bless it to all fair prosperity.
    There shall the pairs of faithful lovers be
    Wedded, with Theseus, all in jollity.
Puck: Fairy King, attend, and mark:
    I do hear the morning lark.
Oberon: Then, my Queen, in silence sad,
    Trip we after night's shade.
    We the globe can compass soon,
    Swifter than the wand'ring moon.
Titania: Come, my lord; and in our flight,
    Tell me how it came this night,
    That I sleeping here was found
    With these mortals on the ground.   *(Exeunt)*

                                                  (IV.i.82–99)

his feeling are in full accord with one another. 'A bottle of hay' is spoken with a mouth-watering anticipation of asinine pleasure. But upon 'Good hay, sweet hay'[22] there came, straight from the horse's mouth, a neighing speech and a spoken neighing of 'hay' and its broad vowel, to stop both ass and man in their tracks. It had been arrived at by Bottom's own route, a jest beyond mere gesture, and an invention both pure and simple. Moreover, it stood in sharpened contrast to the artifice which followed: Oberon rolling a ball down Titania's forehead, as he commands his 'sweet Queen'[23] to wake from her slumbers, and she catching it as her eye opens.

Now, with the long day's work drawing to an end, Oberon and Titania advanced hand-in-hand ('Come, my Queen, take hands with me')[24] towards the half-dozen spectators. 'Find a rhythm for walking,' Brook called out, 'like the Japanese.' And in their sudden undulation, a near-gliding stride, old rehearsal demands were achieved, or were near-achieving. Here was, once more, an almost heraldic orientalism, a world away from Bottom's farmyard idyll. And as Titania summoned Oberon to flight[24], a new and more various movement was promised.

Brook told her that in the final production she would be 'lifted off in a feather hammock', and rise, winged, above the world of the mortal. Yet, today, the mundane had for long periods been held at a distance, or kept at bay, without benefit of flying. There had been a search for truth at arm's length, and a new soaring of illusion.

Fifth week, fourth day

This lonely dream in a rehearsal room of what reality might be, again paled and faded today before the life which will always be beyond it. I came as far as the theatre door, turned about, and went away again. I wandered around the town streets, watching the summer crowds go by, and returned home without attending the rehearsal. In any case, to whose Dream, or dream, am I being invited? Is it merely my own dream which, just like everyone else, I am trying to dream at these rehearsals? Is the only difference between us that they have earned the right, while I have not, to impose their fancies, or their nightmares, upon an audience?

And has anyone from these teeming streets, from *this* Stratford audience, been present, if not in body then at least in mind or spirit? Trampling the pavements, the crowds, sweating in the sun, seem from

(*Wind horn. Enter THESEUS, HIPPOLYTA, EGEUS, and train*)

    Theseus: Go, one of you, find out the forester,
    For now our observation is performed;
    And since we have the vaward of the day,
    My love shall hear the music of my hounds . . .
    We will, fair Queen, up to the mountain's top,
    And mark the musical confusion
    Of hounds and echo in conjunction.
    Hippolyta: I was with Hercules and Cadmus once,
    When in a wood of Crete they bayed the bear
    With hounds of Sparta. Never did I hear
    Such gallant chiding; for, besides the groves,
    The skies, the fountains, every region near
    Seemed all one mutual cry. I never heard
    So musical a discord, such sweet thunder.

                                (*IV.i.100–115*)

some angles – against the aerial Puck and the cool puppet-master – like beasts hot for the shambles. But from other angles, it is a (Japanese) padded-cell which is being constructed on the banks of the Avon, which few of them will choose to enter. Beckoned for yet another day within its vertical and thudding confinements, my own step had faltered. The flying trapeze, heaven-bound, was lost in the roaring traffic.

Fifth week, fifth day

Today I open the door upon volleys of thunderous drumming, the scaffolding swarming with actors in motley, swinging and climbing. Blown bubbles – as if to mock (or echo?) yesterday's world at its purchases and commons – cascade from the gantries, to the juggling of rings and hoops, and the stilts' gawky dancing. Pennants are flying, and plates spinning; the builders' yard heaving with a clangorous labour. The floor is now squared and padded, geometrized, and with a wrestler's mat as its centre and focus. On it, a mêlèe of lovers and mechanicals tumbles in horse-play and headstands. It is a nursery of adults, tin-drums beating. Brook shouts them to a halt. 'Stop wasting time!! (angrily) Don't bring low levels of work to rehearsal!!' Hands smacked, they are – or look – crestfallen.

'You must use all the best possibilities that you have discovered,' he continues. 'Working together as a group, each of you must by now know his own needs and problems. Use the time fully.' Outside, time runs in other channels. 'In ten days,' he tells them, 'you will be regretting the opportunities you wasted.' The actors return to their climbing, juggling, somersaults and prancing; Bottom, among them, alone in an awkward lolloping and rubbery kicking, an ass dancing. 'This morning,' Brook again shouts into the bedlam, 'I want everyone to feel out the differences of the heights.' The scaffolding is tiered. There are, in all, three levels for enactment. 'At each height,' he tells them, 'there is something gained and something lost. Find out, for example, what the third level can do for us.' Theseus' entry in Act Four[25], with his train and to the 'winding of horns', is to be the scene of the experiment.

From now on, the geometry of heights and levels, planes and symmetries, sequences and balances, exits and entrances, govern the rehearsal. Today's concern is with the relations of sound and distance,

189

²⁶ *Lysander:*   Our intent
     Was to be gone from Athens, where we might,
     Without the peril of the Athenian law –
     Egeus: Enough, enough, my lord; you have enough.
     I beg the law, the law, upon his head.

                                                    (*IV.i.148–152*)

²⁷ *Theseus:* Begin these wood birds but to couple now?
     Lysander: Pardon, my lord.
     Theseus: I pray you all, stand up.

                                                    (*IV.i.137–138*)

²⁸ *Theseus:* Away with us to Athens. Three and three,
     We'll hold a feast in great solemnity.
     Come, Hippolyta.
           (*Exeunt THESEUS, HIPPOLYTA, EGEUS, and train*)
     Demetrius: These things seem small and undistinguishable,
     Like far-off mountains turnèd into clouds.
     Hermia: Methinks I see these things with parted eye,
     When everything seems double.

                                                    (*IV.i.181–187*)

²⁹ *Bottom:* Heigh-ho! Peter Quince? Flute, the bellows mender? Snout,
     the tinker? Starveling? God's my life, stol'n hence, and left me
     asleep? I have had a most rare vision. I have had a dream, past the
     wit of man to say what dream it was. Man is but an ass, if he go
     about to expound this dream. Methought I was – there is no man
     can tell what methought I was – and methought I had – but man is
     but a patched fool if he will offer to say what methought I had.
     The eye of man hath not heard, the ear of man hath not seen,
     man's hand is not able to taste, his tongue to conceive, nor his
     heart to report, what my dream was.

                                                    (*IV.ii.198–210*)

the architectonics of appearance, the music of voices and spaces. When Theseus and Hippolyta enter at the topmost level, his 'Go one of you, find out the forester,/ For now our observation is performed'[25] is spoken into space, rangingly, while Hippolyta's 'I was with Hercules and Cadmus once'[25] floats from distance into the roof's upper reaches. They speak of echoes: he of 'the musical confusion of hounds and echo in conjunction', and she of 'one mutual cry . . . so musical a discord'. Their own voices, given height and resonance, seem to sing the words from the scaffold. At ground level, the bells of their trumpets upraised, horns 'wind' in consort with Hippolyta's 'gallant chiding' from the heights, baying out the sound of the 'hounds of Sparta'[25], and the 'sweet thunder'[25] she speaks of. Demetrius and Helena wait in mid-air, or at the second level.

Egeus, stranded below in his anger, is forced to talk up to Theseus and Hippolyta high above him[26]. His ire is launched into the heavens, his neck muscles straining; while Lysander, also at ground level, must call 'Pardon, my lord'[27] up two tiers. Demetrius and Helena, however, needing to intercede in the action, come quickly down a rope to do so, like firemen to a fire. With one eye of the mind closed (and the other cocked to judge the impact of such artifice) I can see that, well-lit and with the wind of favour behind it, the absurd could become heavy with portent, and some of these devices be perceived as significant gesture. That *A Midsummer Night's Dream* would then be suffocated beneath a mountain of piled-up effects, Pelion-upon-Ossa, is another matter.

Yet, at the departure of the court[28], the four lovers' responses are newly economical, newly measured. 'Count the squares,' Brook tells them, 'to keep your distance.' Today, there is a new equipoise and the long hoped-for coolness in their exchanges. 'These things seem small and undistinguishable,'[28] says Demetrius. And in his careful gesture and calculating sense of space, there is a precise – or precious – mathematics of voice and movement, a new refinement. Into this delicacy of feeling, Bottom's rude awakening now erupts[29]. 'He will be up in the flies,' Brook tells the actors, and will be lowered into this geometry, to lie across it in a gross asymmetry.

Perhaps the collision of rhythms sparked the moment. For, suddenly, the play's drying timber took fire. The court and the lovers, still poised, stand on the newly-painted side-lines. Bottom stirs fatly to the dawn-chorus. 'Heigh-ho! Peter Quince?'[29], he says, half-asleep; and Brook calls for echoing voices and bird-calls in answer. But as Bottom slowly came to, yawning, Brook swiftly stopped all impulse to

30

ACT FOUR. Scene Two. Athens. QUINCES'S house. Enter
   QUINCE, FLUTE, SNOUT and STARVELING.

Quince: Have you sent to Bottom's house? Is he come home yet?

Starveling: He cannot be heard of. Out of doubt he is transported.

Flute: If he come not, then the play is marred. It goes not forward,
   doth it?

Quince: It is not possible. You have not a man in all Athens able to
   discharge Pyramus but he.

Flute: No, he hath simply the best wit of any handicraft man in
   Athens.

Quince: Yea, and the best person too; and he is a very paramour for a
   sweet voice.

Flute: You must say 'paragon'. A paramour is, God bless us, a thing
   of nought.

(IV.ii.1–14)

31

(Enter SNUG)

Snug: Masters, the Duke is coming from the temple, and there is two
   or three lords and ladies more married. If our sport had gone
   forward, we had all been made men.

Flute: O sweet bully Bottom! Thus hath he lost sixpence a day during
   his life. He could not have scaped sixpence a day. An the Duke had
   not given him sixpence a day for playing Pyramus, I'll be hanged.
   He would have deserved it. Sixpence a day in Pyramus, or nothing.

(Enter BOTTOM)

Bottom: Where are these lads? Where are these hearts?

Quince: Bottom! O most courageous day! O most happy hour!

Bottom: I am to discourse wonders: but ask me not what; for if I tell
   you, I am not true Athenian. I will tell you everything, right as it
   fell out.

Quince: Let us hear, sweet Bottom.

Bottom: Not a word of me. All that I will tell you is, that the Duke
   hath dined. Get your apparel together.

(IV.ii.15–30)

continue the accompanying sound. For Bottom is returning, alone, to the world of mortals, and without dream-echoes. His voice suddenly isolated and as if baring itself for confession, 'I have had a most rare vision,'[29] he announced. His limbs and senses, heavy and sprawling, struggled to be free from slumber in the balanced silence and ordered space created for him; while his head tossed and shook, as if trying to throw off its asinine traces.

'The eye of man hath not heard,' he said, standing disordered within a geometer's right angles . . . 'the ear of man hath not seen,' he said, slowly but surely recovering his sense of touch and blind good humour . . . 'man's hand is not able to taste, his tongue to conceive, nor his heart to report, what my dream was.'[29] Bottom is restored, as confidently re-entered into his role – and once more by his own route – as ever. But today, his bluff assurance, in this muddle of his senses and the freezing symmetries which surround him, had become both tense and poignant in its contradictions.

The mechanicals' melancholy Fourth Act appearance is now also explored at different levels[30]. They move up and down the scaffolding like hod-carriers on a work-site, either in mockery or echo of the real world of labour. (These are no longer Jacob's ladders, and this is no passage from earth to heaven.) The moment is busy. Quince is at ground-level, calling up to ask if Bottom is 'come home yet'[30], while Starveling the tailor answers as if from an upper window, with Flute descending – as the scene begins – to the middle storey. Brook had at first called for the sound of a 'single metallic stroke' when the scene opens. As a second thought, it should be 'a solitary hammering'. Finally, he asks the mechanicals and the other actors in the scaffolding to 'make an enormous working noise'.

The scene is taken at a slow speed, at Brook's dictation. And between each speech[30] there is a miserable silence of comic despair at Bottom's absence, and a doom-laden expectation. There is space too, today, for the actors' inward but visible preoccupation with their roles in *Pyramus and Thisby*. Moreover, the exchanges between them are now discovered to be no conversation, but a spoken series of solitary tensions and sorrows, fearful for Bottom's passing. The entry of Snug the joiner[31] is made solitary also, and prepared for both in slow motion and in silence. And what he has to say is listened to in a gloomy distraction, near to weeping; so gloomy that only an explosion of laughter could relieve it.

After Snug's speech, Brook suddenly suggests that in their despair

20 Theseus: 'What masque? What music? How shall we beguile/The lazy time, if not with some delight?' (Act Five, Scene One); (l. to r.) Alan Howard (Theseus), John York and Hugh Keays Byrne (Attendants), Sara Kestelman (Hippolyta), John Kane (Philostrate), Mary Rutherford (Hermia), Christopher Gable (Lysander), Frances de la Tour (Helena), Ben Kingsley (Demetrius), Celia Quicke and Ralph Cotterill (Attendants).

they should begin to destroy their cherished properties for the court performance – so that Bottom's approaching reappearance will become a tragi-comic disaster of dire proportions. And so they do, while Flute sings in close but sad harmony with the others, of their 'sweet bully Bottom'[31]. Their feelings and their props have together been reduced to tatters, as Bottom makes his jovial re-entry[31]. It is a rare moment of pure bliss and comic consternation, which deepens into fright at Bottom's 'Get your apparel together . . . our play is preferred'[31]. Their grief at lost opportunity has been replaced by mute terror at the catastrophe which now awaits them. And as blank prose is brought to life by a lyric invention, attention is also drawn closer to detail. 'I will tell you everything,' says Bottom. 'Let us hear, sweet Bottom,' says Quince. 'Not a word of me,' says Bottom[31], in an absurd and jolly contradiction. It is played now to the hilt of a comic gusto, in which tears and laughter together make light of disaster.

There was now a break of one and a half hours, during which the actors and stage technicians moved into the main theatre. It was set (as if) in panelled mahogany for a performance of *Measure for Measure*; with a trapeze added for today's try-out. In this Star Chamber, the mechanicals, courtiers and fairies of *A Midsummer Night's Dream* seemed like fairground grotesques, harlequins and tumblers, come to stand trial. They were a spangled pantomime or a roaring circus, bodies not spirits. The trapeze, built for a Tarzan, flew in a space which was dark-brown and baronial.

Here, in the yawningly empty auditorium, flights were gauged and heights measured (with the marked pole of a vaulter or surveyor), lighting was tried and sight-lines examined. But how to translate oriental rites into this suburban plush and velvet? How to dream sylvan dreams under these chandeliers and on this fitted carpet? And how, at this distance in the Rear Stalls, confront the truth of the actors and hear their lines' hidden impulse? Meanwhile, the mechanicals seemed to stand forlorn beneath the flying figures – earthbound proletarians who will have to act the goat in a petit-bourgeois mansion.

What is now fixed in the actor's movement and gesture can also be clearly seen, for the first time, in this technical trial. They are put repeatedly through their paces for the technicians, along lines of thought which are already firmly established. There will be new invention to come in the remaining rehearsal time, but now new constraints, too, will be imposed both by the set's apparatus and by the technology of production. Technique, or technics, is now being

³² *ACT FIVE. Scene One. Athens. The palace of Theseus. Enter*
  THESEUS, HIPPOLYTA, PHILOSTRATE, Lords and
  Attendants)
Hippolyta: 'Tis strange, my Theseus, that these lovers speak of.
Theseus: More strange than true. I never may believe
  These antique fables, nor these fairy toys.
  Lovers and madmen have such seething brains . . .
  . . . And as imagination bodies forth
  The forms of things unknown, the poet's pen
  Turns them to shapes, and gives to airy nothing
  A local habitation and a name.
  Such tricks hath strong imagination,
  That, if it would but apprehend some joy,
  It comprehends some bringer of that joy;
  Or in the night, imagining some fear,
  How easy is a bush supposed a bear!

                                                              (*V.i.1–22*)

³³ *Theseus:* Such tricks hath strong imagination,
  That, if it would but apprehend some joy,
  It comprehends some bringer of that joy;
  Or in the night, imagining some fear,
  How easy is a bush supposed a bear!
Hippolyta: But all the story of the night told over,
  And all their minds transfigured so together,
  More witnesseth than fancy's images,
  And grows to something of great constancy;
  But, howsoever, strange and admirable.

                                                              (*V.i.18–27*)

installed around the actors, with its own house-rules and regulations. However, I notice that Brook himself uses very little of the technical jargon of theatre geography and dramatic science. Just as he seems to have no vocabulary of his own gesture and intonation, with which to display his intentions to the actors, so he avoids the 'man-of-the-theatre's' professional *argot* also. Sets are rarely 'struck' in his parlance, 'upstage' is 'over there', and 'moving downstage' is simply 'coming nearer'. Is this art which is artless, or the unease with his métier which I have already noticed? As for me, unseen in the dark of the auditorium, I am a sombre Elijah at a fairy-lit banquet; a mere bystander, passive among so many actors.

The rehearsal now resumed where it had left off, but with a new physical energy which seemed to have been found in the main theatre, and had been brought back with the actors. It is the beginning of Act Five, in the darkened palace of Theseus[32]. The courtiers once more gather in candlelight, beneath the heights of the scaffold. 'Play it high,' Brook tells them, being photographed for the archive as he does so. 'Theseus,' he says, 'is a man throwing a party.' A bank of candles has also been set out, in our absence, placed to serve as footlights. The faces of the actors are flickeringly lit, as in a dark Rembrandt interior, their bodies casting a deep shadow behind them.

Against such fitful light and rearing darkness, Theseus speaks with a regal power of the strange work of the 'seething brain'[32]. Moreover, his imagination at last seems as capable as the poet's of investing the 'airy nothing' before him with a 'local habitation and a name'; his voice as capable as the poet's of conjuring up 'some fear'; and 'in the night' of precisely such a dark moment as this one. 'How easy,' Theseus says, with an ease of authority which has become majestic, 'is a bush supposed a bear'[32].

Yet there was now also attempted a gratuitous interpolation into the text, the first of its kind, and brutal. (Whose is this invention? Can it be Brook's, or is it the actor's?) An off-stage voice, at Brook's signal seizing this moment of Theseus' greatest inwardness and concentration, suddenly intoned Prospero's lines from Act Three of *The Tempest*. 'We are such stuff as dreams are made on,' the voice said darkly, interrupting Hippolyta[33] with its breath bated. It was precisely the 'awful awesome', straining for effect, which Brook had himself berated. But how can it be that in this very scene, where Shakespeare's invention reaches such heights, anyone might think by these means to elevate it further? Is it perhaps intended as a bold sign – which will

197

34 *Theseus:*   Is there no play,
   To ease the anguish of a torturing hour?
   Call Philostrate.
Philostrate: Here, mighty Theseus.
Theseus: Say, what abridgment have you for this evening?
   What masque? What music? How shall we beguile
   The lazy time, if not with some delight?
Philostrate: There is a brief how many sports are ripe:
   Make choice of which your Highness will see first.
                                        (*Giving a paper*)
Theseus: 'The battle with the Centaurs, to be sung
   By an Athenian eunuch to the harp.'
   We'll none of that. That have I told my love,
   In glory of my kinsman Hercules.
   'The riot of the tipsy Bacchanals,
   Tearing the Thracian singer in their rage.'
   That is an old device; and it was played
   When I from Thebes came last a conqueror.
   'The thrice three Muses mourning for the death
   Of Learning, late deceased in beggary.'
   That is some satire, keen and critical,
   Not sorting with a nuptial ceremony.
   'A tedious brief scene of young Pyramus
   And his love Thisby; very tragical mirth.'
   Merry and tragical? Tedious and brief?
                                        (*V.i.36–58*)

35 *Philostrate:* It is not for you. I have heard it over,
   And it is nothing, nothing in the world;
   Unless you can find sport in their intents,
   Extremely stretched and conned with cruel pain,
   To do you service.
Theseus: I will hear that play . . .
   Go, bring them in: and take your places, ladies.
                                        (*Exit PHILOSTRATE*)
Hippolyta: I love not to see wretchedness o'ercharged,
   And duty in his service perishing.
Theseus: Why, gentle sweet, you shall see no such thing.
Hippolyta: He says they can do nothing in this kind.
Theseus: The kinder we, to give them thanks for nothing.
                                        (*V.i.77–89*)

not itself survive – of inventive life surviving into the rehearsal's later stages? Or is it the taste for artifice, become tasteless?

But in new moments of incomparable richness, this poor moment is overtaken and cancelled. It is the work of Hippolyta, Theseus and Philostrate – lately Titania, Oberon and Puck – who are not attempting to disguise the fact that *ego* and *alter ego* are one and the same person. (In the final production, costume changes notwithstanding, the audience will instantly recognize Titania in Hippolyta, Oberon in Theseus, and Puck in Philostrate). 'Call Philostrate,'[34] says this Oberon-Theseus. And, now, in Philostrate's 'Here, mighty Theseus' is a Puck returning to earth, as submissive and prepared to do Theseus' bidding as Puck had been to obey Oberon. Brook chooses this moment, with unerring judgment, to tell Philostrate to speak the line from Puck's spirit-place, high upon the scaffold. 'That will work very well,' he tells his Puck-Philostrate.

Almost every question which has been asked of the play's meaning is now suddenly reinforced and redoubled. Who, or what, is Oberon? Isn't the Duke of Athens as much a figment of the imagination as the King of the Fairies? And in the text itself there are newly resonating questions. 'Say, what abridgment have you for this evening?'[33], Theseus asks Philostrate, 'What masque? What music?' And Philostrate, just as Puck would have done, serves his master with a bill of fare to choose from[34]. Moreover, at this moment, there came a new improvisation from the actors, a true invention. Brook eagerly seizes upon it. For Theseus, accompanied by Philostrate – Oberon and Puck down to their very shadows – now took this bill of theatrical fare in a circuit of the lolling courtiers. And on the instant, they ceased to be idle extras of a royal household, speaking in the low voices of a campfire darkness, but men freely discoursing together[34] of *The Battle of the Centaurs*, *The Plot of the Bacchanals*, *The Three Muses* and *Pyramus and Thisby*, with animated and open gestures.

Hippolyta – shades of Titania! – is less angry than cross and impatient with Theseus' choice, against the advice of Philostrate[35], of the play of *Pyramus and Thisby*. In her 'I love not to see wretchedness o'ercharged,/ And duty in his service perishing'[35], there seems now to resound again the very rhythm of Titania's and Oberon's quarrels. Brook gets the other actors to freeze, as they listen to these exchanges. Our attention is thus concentrated, through them, upon a deep and inward echo which is being newly discovered.

Today, too, when the court has settled to the play which Theseus

³⁶ *Prologue:* This man is Pyramus, if you would know;
This beauteous lady Thisby is certain.
This man, with lime and roughcast, doth present
Wall, that vile wall which did these lovers sunder . . .
This man, with lantern, dog and bush of thorn,
Presenteth Moonshine . . .
This grisly beast, which Lion hight by name,
The trusty Thisby, coming first by night,
Did scare away, or rather did affright;
And, as she fled, her mantle she did fall,
Which Lion vile with bloody mouth did stain.

(*V.i.128–142*)

³⁷ *Theseus:* I wonder if the lion be to speak.
Demetrius: No wonder, my lord. One lion may, when many asses do.

(*V.i.152–153*)

³⁸ *Pyramus:* O wicked wall, through whom I see no bliss!
Cursed be thy stones for thus deceiving me!
Theseus: The wall, methinks, being sensible, should curse again.
Pyramus: No, in truth, sir, he should not. 'Deceiving me' is Thisby's
cue. She is to enter now, and I am to spy her through the wall.
You shall see it will fall pat as I told you. Yonder she comes.

(*V.i.178–185*)

³⁹ *Pyramus:* I see a voice: now will I to the chink,
To spy an I can hear my Thisby's face.
Thisby!
Thisby: My love thou art, my love I think.
Pyramus: Think what thou wilt, I am thy lover's grace;
And, like Limander, am I trusty still.
Thisby: And I like Helen, till the Fates me kill.
Pyramus: Not Shafalus to Procrus was so true.
Thisby: As Shafalus to Procrus, I to you.
Pyramus: O kiss the wall's hole, not your lips at all.
Pyramus: Wilt thou at Ninny's tomb meet me straightway?
Thisby: 'Tide life, 'tide death, I come without delay.

(*Exeunt PYRAMUS and THISBY*)

Wall: Thus have I, Wall, my part dischargèd so,
And, being done, thus wall away doth go.

(*Exit*)
(*V.i.190–205*)

has chosen for them, Quince entered more deeply than ever before into his Prologue. 'This man is Pyramus'[36], he says to the courtiers, his manner inviting. 'Introduce them one at a time, as you speak,' Brook – again in perfect accord with the moment – tells him. And after these introductions Theseus, turning in an airy aside to a courtier, can be heard to say, lip curling, 'I wonder if the lion be to speak'[37]. Snug, ineffably stupid, and who has found his way to a now fixed and slow-spoken Northern accent, is here motioned to by Brook to come forward. 'It is as if he stupidly thinks,' Brook suggests to him, 'that Theseus' question is his cue to speak.' The laughter, on-stage as well as off it, which greets Snug's double-take celebrates a moment of the action, though not of the text, which has been discovered together. It is a small moment of true sharing.

The enactment of *Pyramus and Thisby* is today also entered into more deeply. Brook taps out on a drum two differentiated rhythms, which he wants respectively from the mechanicals and the courtiers. As a result, Theseus' 'The wall, methinks, being sensible, should curse again'[38] has the heightened arrogance of a swift and (as if) princely wit, while Pyramus' reply 'No, in truth, sir, he should not'[38], with its heavy round vocables, has more than ever the pedestrian gait of the sturdy Bottom. Or, as Brook puts it, 'The key to the nature of the court's interventions is that their laughter and responses are sharper than those of the mechanicals. Remember,' he continues, 'that the scene cannot exist if the actors in *Pyramus and Thisby*, and their audience, are *both* hesitant. In the court, there must be assurance and mutual understanding. Their exchanges are not primarily for the purpose of sending up the actors, but to display their life at court as free and open.' A new note is being struck on Brook's drum. It is as if a sense of enclosure and introspection in this scene is today beginning to give way to a mood which is itself lighter and more open. I think Brook is in search of a movement from the major key to the minor, as the common *cadenza* of both plays approaches.

'I see a voice,'[39] says Pyramus to Thisby, in echo of Bottom's own confusions, and of the lovers' enchantments. 'My love thou art, my love I think,' replies Thisby, certainty confounded by doubt in a single moment. 'I kiss the wall's hole, not your lips at all,'[39] says Thisby to Pyramus, as a hard truth cancels art's illusion. To point up the parallels, and on a seeming impulse, Brook had asked the four court-lovers to go into their pairs – Demetrius with Helena, and Hermia with Lysander – and walk with each other, whispering and

40 *Hippolyta:* This is the silliest stuff that ever I heard.

Theseus: The best in this kind are but shadows; and the worst are no worse, if imagination amend them.

Hippolyta: It must be your imagination then, and not theirs.

Theseus: If we imagine no worse of them than they of themselves, they may pass for excellent men.

(V.i.208–214)

kissing, as Pyramus and Thisby exchange their comic vows and make their tragic assignation. 'Wilt thou at Ninny's tomb meet me straightway?' asks Pyramus of Thisby. ''Tide life, 'tide death, I come without delay,'[39] Thisby tells him. But now Brook suggests that Pyramus should here sing to Thisby, and she to him, while the four lovers counterpoint them with the echoes of their own songs of nocturnal enchantment.

In a sudden crescendo of *kitsch*, Brook himself strums on a guitar, as the six lovers, in intended close harmony, but caterwauling, sing their way to this shotgun marriage. As their improvised song ends, Brook asks Richard Peaselee, court-musician to *A Midsummer Night's Dream*, to find an accompaniment for the new duet of Pyramus and Thisby, and for the madrigal of the court-lovers. The sextet – which Brook describes as 'an appropriate term' – is, as it stands, like a cat's chorus. But there is a new-found assonance in it, its *kitsch* notwithstanding, which seems likely to join the other harmonies of the production.

It is also plain that, whereas in earlier rehearsals Brook and the actors strove deliberately for profundity in the melancholy tale of *Pyramus and Thisby*, it is now a love which will be guyed and foolish, more ludicrous than tragic. Yet, played not for awe but for innocent laughter, the passion of Pyramus and Thisby will perhaps seem the deeper for being thus transferred at one remove to the courtly partners. The latter, lovers not actors, will now act out their own feelings in dumbshow, while Pyramus and Thisby, actors not lovers, swear undying love for one another. 'Everything Pyramus and Thisby say,' Brook tells them, 'is of enormous importance to the court of Athens.' Moreover, Hippolyta's 'This is the silliest stuff that ever I heard,'[40] will now act against this sense, and be the more striking for it. 'Make this a freeze,' says Brook, 'so that everyone watches and listens to Hippolyta and Theseus.' In a fine stroke, Brook also wants the actor-mechanicals to be rooted to the ground by what is being said about them. Their dumbness and confusion, stalled and halting both within their own play and the play which is beyond them, are thus brought even closer to our attention. Their pains as actors are now appalling. Quince is in despair, as the taunts of the court bring his play to a standstill. Brook in addition tells the mechanicals to 'come right forward and listen to the show, forgetting what you're there for.'

The cast of *Pyramus and Thisby* now become spectators in their own play. They even begin, gradually, to smile at the court's sallies against

⁴¹ *Moonshine:* This lanthorn doth the hornèd moon present –
   Demetrius: He should have worn the horns on his head.
   Theseus: He is no crescent, and his horns are invisible within the
      circumference.
   Moonshine: This lanthorn doth the hornèd moon present;
      Myself the man i' th' moon do seem to be.
   Theseus: This is the greatest error of all the rest. The man should be
      put into the lanthorn. How is it else the man i' th' moon? . . .
   Lysander: Proceed, Moon.
   Moonshine: All that I have to say is to tell you that the lanthorn is the
      moon; I, the man i' th' moon; this thorn bush, my thorn bush; and
      this dog, my dog.

                                              (*V.i.237–252*)

⁴² *Pyramus:* Sweet Moon, I thank thee for thy sunny beams;
      I thank thee, Moon, for shining now so bright;
      For, by thy gracious, golden, glittering gleams,
      I trust to take of truest Thisby sight.
      But stay, O spite!
      But mark, poor knight,
      What dreadful dole is here!
      Eyes, do you see?
      How can it be?
      O dainty duck! O dear!
      Thy mantle good,
      What, stained with blood!

                                              (*V.i.266–275*)

⁴³ *Pyramus:* Thus die I, thus, thus, thus.
      Now am I dead,
      Now am I fled;
      My soul is in the sky.
      Tongue, lose thy light;
      Moon, take thy flight. (*Exit MOONSHINE*)
      Now die, die, die, die. (*Dies*)
   Demetrius: No die, but an ace for him; for he is but one.
   Lysander: Less than an ace, man; for he is dead, he is nothing.
   Theseus: With the help of a surgeon he might yet recover, and yet
      prove an ass.

                                              (*V.i.292–302*)

them, piteously neglecting their own struggle for self-possession in face of their superiors. And in the very generosity of the humble mechanicals before the court, as a gilded repartee tears their poor offering to shreds, the ludicrous itself becomes tragic[41]. Only Pyramus himself can restore the play's illusion. Only his speech 'Sweet Moon'[42] can, and does, halt the flow of courtly interruption. At the very moment of it, Brook says that 'Here, suddenly, a real miracle comes into the scene. Pyramus has the opportunity to make something authentic of their drama, and bring the court to silence.' Indeed, with his 'But stay, O spite!/ But mark, poor knight'[42], Pyramus can be heard for the first time addressing the court directly, specifically staying interruption and recalling his audience to attention. 'Eyes, do you see?' he asks them. And it is as if in despite of their disdain that Pyramus, at last, becomes visible to them[42], while the recovered silence restores the actors to themselves, and *Pyramus and Thisby* to its audience.

Now, new value was being given to many still unknown moments. Thus, at the death of Pyramus[43], Oberon is again remembered in Theseus, and Bottom fleetingly reappears also. 'With the help of a surgeon,' Theseus laconically mutters, 'he might yet recover, and yet prove an ass.'[43] The deaths of both Pyramus and Thisby, today acted without ostentatious straining for meaning or a Lear-like echo, are heard in a deeper silence for it. Indeed, today it was as if the court was not acting, but giving, its attention to the play's tragic resolution.

Moreover, a few minutes later, at the resolution of that other drama of Oberon and Titania, Brook was again working for emphatic parallel and echo. 'To the best bride-bed will we,/ Which by us shall blessèd be'[44], Oberon tells her, 'So shall all the couples three/ Ever true in loving be.' Brook asks them to hold each other close as they speak, and the two pairs of court-lovers to do likewise. And as Oberon, or Theseus, prays that 'Never mole, harelip, nor scar,/ Nor mark prodigious . . . shall upon their children be,'[44] he delicately traces with his fingertips upon the face of Hippolyta, or Titania, the last quiet echoes of a Shakespearian nightmare. They end forehead to forehead – and the other lovers also – as if sleeping, their quarrels reconciled and once more dreaming.

'So, good night unto you all,'[44] says Puck to the small knot of spectators, 'give me your hands, if we be friends.' But at his words, it is the lovers who take hands: Demetrius and Helena, Lysander and Hermia, Oberon and Titania. They stood still, looking out into a long hushed silence.

⁴⁴ *Oberon:* Now, until the break of day,
      Through this house each fairy stray.
      To the best bride-bed will we,
      Which by us shall blessèd be;
      And the issue there create
      Ever shall be fortunate.
      So shall all the couples three
      Ever true in loving be;
      And the blots of Nature's hand
      Shall not in their issue stand.
      Never mole, harelip, nor scar,
      Nor mark prodigious, such as are
      Despised in nativity,
      Shall upon their children be.
      With this field-dew consecrate,
      Every fairy take his gait,
      And each several chamber bless,
      Through this palace, with sweet peace,
      And the owner of it blest
      Ever shall in safety rest.
      Trip away; make no stay;
      Meet me all by break of day.

                                                      (*Exeunt all but PUCK*)

  Puck: If we shadows have offended,
      Think but this, and all is mended:
      That you have but slumb'red here,
      While these visions did appear.
      And this weak and idle theme,
      No more yielding but a dream,
      Gentles, do not reprehend:
      If you pardon, we will mend.
      And, as I am an honest Puck,
      If we have unearnèd luck
      Now to scape the serpent's tongue,
      We will make amends ere long;
      Else the Puck a liar call:
      So, good night unto you all.
      Give me your hands, if we be friends,
      And Robin shall restore amends.   (*Exit*)

                                                      (*V.i.390–427*)

Sixth week, first day

The actors' first audience is coming this afternoon. It will consist of seventy children, between the ages of eight and thirteen. The morning session is therefore to be abbreviated, and Brook now prepares the actors for this first rehearsal-performance. He is wearing his familiar denim suit – the battle-dress of the director. 'Let us work out very clearly the day which is ahead,' he tells them. 'Last week was a narrative week. [It was, but only intermittently.] Today's rehearsal before an audience must be its completion. We must ask ourselves,' he says, 'whether today we can put together freely, and in an improvised way, what we have done so far in rehearsal. Today there will be no such thing as something "going wrong",' he adds, 'for there will be no formality of performance.' Brook stands before them strangely dwarfed; composed, and pallid.

'In fact,' he says, 'we will be going right back to the conditions of the first week's big improvisations. The difference now, after five weeks, is that the story-line is known, rather than an inner secret.' What this means is not clear; perhaps that 'plot', revealed and spoken, has now been fully freed from the silences of the written. Or perhaps not. 'Of course,' Brook continues, 'we have arrived at only a small, sketchy, fragmentary amount of firm work for each scene. [This is not true. Much of the enactment is settling, or already settled.] But what we have, we must keep. Do not continually look for something new during the performance. We have at least the basis, and the story which this basis tells. Today will in effect be a very free run-through of this material, using as your guides the layout of the set, the props, and the different levels. And do not forget that your first audience will demand a sense of narrative, that the story be told in a way which is clear, lively and amusing.' The mood is leaden.

'This cannot be done without an audience,' Brook says, his stride lengthening over the Monday morning hurdles. 'We're using the

21 Prologue: 'Gentles, perchance you wonder at this show;/But wonder on, till truth make all things plain' (Act Five, Scene One); (l. to r.) John Kane (Philostrate) and Philip Locke (Prologue).

children, but it is no use using someone without making a fair exchange.' (Is this de Sade crossed with Bentham, or the simple *quid pro quo* of the market?) 'If we do not keep them interested,' he adds, 'we will be exploiting them. So an ass's head has been run-up for Bottom's transformation, since it would be unreasonable to deprive them of it. Our first obligation is to keep a life going for the children.' The rehearsal-hall is lifeless. 'And since there is no pretence that this is anything but a rehearsal, we must find a shared improvisatory technique,' Brook goes on, as contradiction threatens to dog and snap at the actors' footsteps. 'You may have to do something twice, break off, explain something, when you feel the tension going. The comic actors will have a choice of making a series of improvised gags off the cuff, or of following the broad strokes worked out in rehearsal.' The strokes have been fine throughout, and getting finer.

'There are no rules for today's event,' Brook continues, multiplying the rules with each sentence, 'except that it is no good doing something for kids of eight which would arouse adult laughter. You can talk to a child and ask him a question,' Brook says, while a new pall of expectation descends on the actors' shoulders; 'or stop, and correct a loss of interest and your own feelings of panic, if the children become restless.' There is a stony silence into which Brook speaks, again beginning to jingle the money in his pockets. 'Two standards must govern the work,' he tells them; 'the preservation of the children's interest, and the preservation of their interest in relation to the story.' Eyes wander. The mood is a cold one.

'They should come into a warm-up,' Brook says, 'into a working area. There should be no suggestion of a barrier between the audience and the actors. They should be allowed to come close, and to touch. The beginning of the play's action should come out of this touching. There should, however, be a new prologue, a free-form introduction, invented and spoken by Quince.' Ruffled, Quince blinks rapidly, balking. Brook's stone has been dropped suddenly like a lead weight into his glassy and vacant expression. 'Among other things, it will have to explain the doubling of parts to the audience,' Brook tells him, 'since there will be no costume changes. It must avoid talking of fairies, since this would be imagination-destroying. And after the prologue, the flavour of the afternoon's event must be created within a few seconds.' These are tall orders. 'It will be,' Brook finally reminds them (impassive), 'the original exercise of putting on the first performance of a new play.' That is, it will be the first performance of a

22 Wall: 'This loam, this roughcast, and this stone, doth show/That I am that same wall; the truth is so' (Act Five, Scene One); Norman Rodway (Wall).

first performance. And at its end, Brook asks that they 'feel naturally how it should break off, as you take hands together.'

But the afternoon was a disaster. Lit warmly for the first time – the structure's middle level now cancelled by hanging canvas – with the cast in improvised costumes, it was as if a patchwork pierrot show, or a human Punch-and-Judy in close-up, awaited the excited children. Eyes and faces were shining with expectation. Milling about in the playing area, to the strange sounds of whirling and drumming, they looked up agog to the strutting and looming actors, and craned and pointed at the topmost (cloaked) figures standing upon the scaffold, plates and hoops spinning. There was a dreadful promise of wonders in the air; and all the breaths which were being held, to stifle a terrible joy and panic, slowly inflated the hall to bursting. Yet nothing happened. Instead, there was a long exhalation of disappointment and the let-down, in a slow puncture, of every childish exhilaration.

Ill-at-ease, Quince's new prologue was a lecture, not an invitation; not invention, but instruction; not an opening into a child's world of dreams and fancies, but adult inhibition and closure. 'We are actors,' he announced, 'we need your imaginations.' And pulling back and forth at his feelings – his hands twisting like an onanist – 'without you we are nothing,' he said to the noisy ranks of giggling and nudging children. 'We will try to be good actors,' he continued, 'but you must use your imaginations. Just as when you have stories read to you, you see things in your mind's eye,' he went on, floundering in the gulf he had within seconds created between himself and the children, 'so now, when we tell you the story of *A Midsummer Night's Dream*, you must try to imagine the Palace of Athens, the woods and the spirits.' Then, solemnly, his voice and gesture uninventive and forbidding, he introduced the characters to their (whispering) audience. They stood rigid and awkward before the children: on the one hand, experience in a funk and gravely presented, and, on the other, innocent excitement, wide-eyed but already waning.

Now the play became no 'play' at all, but dead earnest. Laughter died. Each smile seemed a *rictus*, and every lament a stretched grimace. All emphasis seemed nagging, every prop an obstacle, banter raucous, love unlovely and cloying, and the lyrical without meaning. Even echo sounded like mere reiteration. The spirits, or fairies, were now hirsute men in gym-shoes and leaden-footed, their magic no magic, their spinning plates nothing more than plates spinning. The narrative line was lost also, while the volleys of drumming were now

1 *(Enter THISBY)*

Thisby: This is old Ninny's tomb. Where is my love?
Lion: Oh – *(The lion roars. THISBY runs off)*
Demetrius: Well roared, Lion.
Theseus: Well run, Thisby.
Hippolyta: Well shone, Moon. Truly the moon shines with a good
    grace.
                                  (The Lion tears Thisby's mantle, and exit)
Theseus: Well moused, Lion.
Demetrius: And then came Pyramus.
Lysander: And so the lion vanished.

                                               (V.i.255–261)

2 *Puck:* We will make amends 'ere long;
    Else the Puck a liar call:
    So, good night unto you all.
    Give me your hands, if we be friends,
    And Robin shall restore amends.   *(Exit)*

                                               (V.i.422–427)

3 *Puck:* I am that merry wanderer of the night.
    I jest to Oberon, and make him smile,
    When I a fat and bean-fed horse beguile,
    Neighing in likeness of a filly foal:
    And sometime lurk I in a gossip's bowl,
    In very likeness of a roasted crab;
    And when she drinks, against her lips I bob
    And on her withered dewlap pour the ale.
    The wisest aunt, telling the saddest tale,
    Sometime for three-foot stool mistaketh me;
    Then slip I from her bum, down topples she,
    And 'tailor' cries, and falls into a cough;
    And then the whole quire hold their hips and laugh,
    And waxen in their mirth, and neeze, and swear
    A merrier hour was never wasted there.

                                               (II.i.43–57)

4   *(Enter OBERON at one door, with his train; and TITANIA at*
                                         another, with hers)
Oberon: Ill met by moonlight, proud Titania.

                                               (II.i.60)

such torment that the ear yearned, aching, for silence. 'Acting,' unrelated to the audience it was addressing, failed to reach it; seemed, often, to have abandoned the audience to its own restless devices.

And, abandoned, the children – blighted – eventually fell dully quiet. All the miseries of the drama seemed to conspire to bring the actors and their audience into one mutual discord: of random noise, sound without music on the one hand, and a bored silence on the other. Only when Lion, in dumb desperation late in the play[1], crawled roaring among the children was there laughter, and a wildfire release (swiftly doused) from numbness. And only at the very last, at Puck's 'Give me your hands, if we be friends'[2], when he led the cast deep into the audience to take the children by their hands, was there a moment of contact. Inhibition had seemed to catch the actors by their throats from the first moment of the impromptu Prologue. What had followed was neither dream nor nightmare, neither bush for adults nor bear for children, but two hours of withered impulse and withdrawal. It had been the actors' cold turkey, and a sudden failure.

Brook was undisturbed, and even cheerful. The inhibition – which he described to me then and there as 'prissy' – had not been in the actors, he said, but in the children. It had been a 'barrier' to performance. He seemed to wave away all sense of failure ('this is not a play for children'); the melancholy prologue and the young audience's disappointed departure were of equal unimportance. Yet the disparate elements of the production had come apart at the seams. What had been bared had seemed a mere pastiche, layer-upon-layer. And as meaning had lost itself in a labyrinth of confused impulses and the children's long silence, each actor had struggled against the text, the other actors, and the audience, striving for his or her own responses.

Thus, Puck's 'I am that merry wanderer of the night'[3] had been jazzed up under pressure, and driven without music to a climax. With the spirits bucking and bending to his rhythm, it became a desperate virtuoso performance, unrelated to what preceded and followed. The tapped side-drums, finger-bells, and Eastern arpeggios which had greeted Titania's entrance 'with her train'[4] and Oberon's 'Ill met by moonlight'[4], were (what they always were?) merely coy oriental effects without moment. Under the scrutiny of children, this Emperor – and his fey Empress – had no clothes. And not even Thai hand-and-neck movements, in perfect temple unison, could cover the actors' cross-rhythms and cross-purpose.

In the Third Act quartet, Helena's eyes and gestures pleaded for

⁵ *Helena:* O spite! O hell! I see you all are bent
   To set against me for your merriment:
   If you were civil and knew courtesy,
   You would not do me thus much injury.
   Can you not hate me, as I know you do,
   But you must join in souls to mock me too?

(III.ii.145–150)

⁶ *Hermia:* O me! You juggler! You canker blossom!
   You thief of love! What, have you come by night
   And stol'n my love's heart from him?
   Helena: . . . Fie, fie! You counterfeit, you puppet, you!
   Hermia: Puppet? Why so? Ay, that way goes the game.
   Now I perceive that she hath made compare
   Between our statures . . .
   How low am I, thou painted maypole? Speak!
   How low am I? I am not yet so low
   But that my nails can reach into thine eyes.

(III.ii.282–298)

⁷ *Lysander:* The villain is much lighter-heeled than I.
   I followed fast, but faster he did fly.
   That fallen am I in dark uneven way,
   And here will rest me. (*Lies down*) Come, thou gentle day!

(III.ii.415–418)

⁸ *Theseus:* My hounds are bred out of the Spartan kind,
   So flewed, so sanded; and their heads are hung
   With ears that sweep away the morning dew;
   Crook-kneed, and dew-lapped like Thessalian bulls;
   Slow in pursuit, but matched in mouth like bells,
   Each under each.

(IV.i.116–121)

responses[5]; Hermia tried in vain to turn from vixen to tiger[6]; Lysander fell deeper than ever into his dark, uneven way; and tore his grief to tatters[7]. Theseus' hounds were now so 'crook-kneed' and 'dew-lapped'[8] that they tumbled over each other. Was it gross misjudgement that tripped them, or the finest margin of error? Even the mechanicals and spirits lost their touch and bearings, as jokes misfired and plates tumbled, while the lovers lost their sex as the fairies lost their magic. Feet were snared, tongues tied and feelings manhandled. And as care and caution were thrown to the winds, both speech and movement became coarser. Ill-considered gesture and rhythmless intonation stranded the actors, catching them often in slovenly and cruel exposure; and as the actors' *élan* failed, effort failed with it.

It was as if Brook's reliance – or dependence – upon the actors' largely untrained capacity for refinements of control and balance had betrayed him. Lacking the physical resources himself to demonstrate to them in rehearsal what he wanted, his promptings alone (however instructive) seemed to have proved insufficient. Today, it was also as if the actors' performance had paid a heavy price for the director's impositions; as if his whims had suffocated their fancies, while imagination had gone a-begging, rattling an empty tin, among actors and audience. The actors, their old isolation in the ascendant, had been unwilling (or unable) to rescue one another. Their 'ensemble' suddenly seemed a five-week-old chimera, as evanescent as a casting department and a summer season can make it. Movement and action, having lost their point and direction, had become, like the box-office itself, nothing but 'business'. And, at the last, Theseus failed to become Oberon, or Hippolyta Titania. Untransmuted, the real refused to become ideal, or the humdrum magic; and, under the stern gaze of children, the truth resisted the embrace of illusion. The ass was Bottom.

Suddenly – with the first night closing in – the rehearsal period seems to have been too short for the production. The actors' resources, both physical and intellectual, appear limited, and strained to their limits. Today, it seems as if the parts of the whole had been sundered scene from scene, and act from act, with the actors' technique and the director's devices insufficient to hold them together. Is Brook about to prove to his own satisfaction that English actors are only capable of speaking and walking through Shakespeare as to the manner born, playing the milord and the bumpkin in fancy dress for the tourist? Or could it be that under the oriental veneer and French polish of

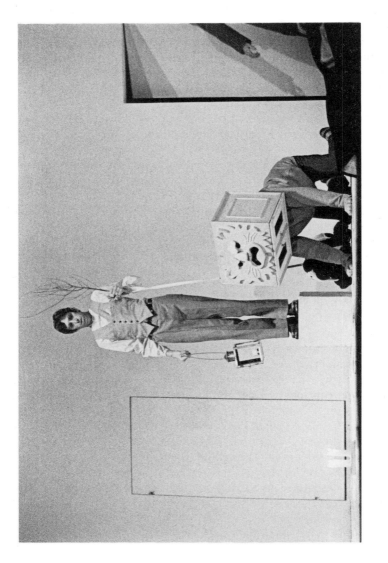

23 Enter Lion and Moonshine (Act Five, Scene One); (l. to r.) Terrence Hardiman (Moonshine) and Barry Stanton (Lion).

Brook's production, the old Adam (and Eve) of the English theatre is putting up a rearguard resistance? Alternatively, might this production at heart be merely a cynical liaison, a *ménage à trois*, between the professional actor's reflexes, the technology of a modern theatre and an old play's modish re-direction? And will it be a 'success' or a 'failure'? Certainly, the actors today seemed assailed by the demands placed upon them; unable simultaneously to speak and to juggle, to love encircled by wire, to think and climb a ladder. Preoccupied and distracted, passing in and out of the action, the actors were ill-at-ease and out-of-patience, reduced by the various tasks and styles of the production. I watched them leaving; wearied.

Sixth week, second day

Today, as I come in, Brook and the actors appear bemused with each other. As they begin once more to piece the play together, the atmosphere becomes oppressive; too late now for a re-working, too soon for a *post-mortem*. I even feel my own presence at this wake to be predatory in the eyes of the actors – not so much a fly-on-the-wall, as a perching vulture; eyes hooded in boredom and talons sharpened. Yet Brook's efforts at salvage in a débacle require all hands on deck. Even the sympathy of the lone spectator might be needed. In any case, in the struggle to raise a light, no one can stand for its extinction.

'Because of this open space we're rehearsing in,' Brook is saying, his tone and manner clipped and uncertain, and quickly moving to blame the actors, 'you are not instinctively able to return to tension in your acting, after eruptions of noise and music. This place,' he says with an inhibited gesture, 'is more like a railway-station than anything else.' (It is nothing like a railway-station.) 'Work becomes more diffuse here,' he tells them, 'because of the distractions.' (There are few distractions.) 'We must go beyond any point so far reached,' he continues bravely, 'to the life behind the text, and to a shared logic. There is nothing more destructive,' he says, dividing the actors, 'than a situation where one or two people get out of tune with the others.' Nobody is specified, but suspicion and guilt, insecurity and isolation, are, in one *coup de main*, deepened.

Brook now calls the actors to sit in a circle, and to 'do the first stretch of the play, without referring to the text and without action'. Lips pursed with determination, he asks the actors to 'take up positions

9 (*ACT ONE. Scene One. The palace of Theseus. Enter THESEUS,*
  HIPPOLYTA, PHILOSTRATE and Attendants)
  Theseus: Now, fair Hippolyta, our nuptial hour
    Draws on apace. Four happy days bring in
    Another moon; but, O, methinks, how slow
    This old moon wanes! She lingers my desires,
    Like to a stepdame, or a dowager,
    Long withering out a young man's revenue.
  Hippolyta: Four days will quickly steep themselves in night,
    Four nights will quickly dream away the time;
    And then the moon, like to a silver bow
    New-bent in heaven, shall behold the night
    Of our solemnities.

                                                    (*I.i.1–11*)

10   (*Enter EGEUS and his daughter HERMIA,*
                              LYSANDER and DEMETRIUS)
  Eegeus: Happy be Theseus, our renownèd Duke!
  Theseus: Thanks, good Egeus. What's the news with thee?
  Egeus: Full of vexation come I, with complaint
    Against my child, my daughter Hermia.
    Stand forth, Demetrius. My noble lord,
    This man hath my consent to marry her.
    Stand forth, Lysander. And, my gracious Duke
    This man hath bewitched the bosom of my child.
    Thou, thou, Lysander, thou hast given her rhymes,
    And interchanged love tokens with my child.
    Thou hast by moonlight at her window sung,
    With feigning voice, verses of feigning love,
    And stol'n the impression of her fantasy
    With bracelets of thy hair, rings, gauds, conceits,
    Knacks, trifles, nosegays, sweetmeats, messengers
    Of strong prevailment in unhardened youth.

                                                    (*I.i.20–35*)

11 *Theseus:* What say you, Hermia? Be advised, fair maid.
    To you your father should be as a god . . .
  Hermia: . . . I would my father looked but with my eyes.
  Theseus: Rather your eyes must with his judgment look.

                                                    (*I.i.46–57*)

where you can see those with whom you are involved in the play'. He is ordering them to find their way back to a lost *éclat* and intensity of purpose, sitting. Criticism is to take the form of first attacking problems of verbal rhythm and precision, not of physical movement. Brook also tells an ASM to draw habitual verbal errors to the actors' attentions. Revival is thus being made to depend less on new invention, than on the renewed recognition and orchestration of impulse and feeling. Above all, it is through the words that a Phoenix will rise from the ashes.

'Mark the pulse of the line,' Brook tells Theseus, interrupting him with a terse impatience often only six words of the first scene[9]. This is tugging at the actor's leash with a vengeance, and Theseus bridles on the instant. Within seconds, Hippolyta's 'And then the moon . . . shall behold the night/ Of our solemnities'[9] has also been jerked to a standstill. 'Avoid strain and stress,' Brook tells her curtly, calm biting its tongue in exasperation. 'You picked out the word "night" yourself,' she says rounding on him, eyes flaring. 'Sense the pulse and melody,' Brook replies flatly, without expression. In the clashing of nervous moods and shared apprehension, every voice is coloured by vexation, and by exaggerated or bruised feeling. All is action and reaction, in *staccato* rhythm.

Now Egeus' entrance[10], Brook declares harshly, 'brings on something nauseously assertive.' But this is in Brook, not Egeus. Now, too, Egeus' complaints[10] against Lysander, for 'bewitching' his daughter with 'conceits', 'knacks' and 'trifles', are – according to Brook – 'a denunciation of the force of imagination.' But this is in Brook, not Shakespeare. Moreover, anger takes the cue from anger, as the actors stumble under pressure. 'What say you, Hermia?'[11] says Theseus, his accent and gesture now browbeaten by Brook's interruptions. He has become impatient in the role and out of it; the tempo of his speaking is both roughshod and overridden. The exchange of swift glances between the actors has little now to do with the pre-verbal. 'I would my father looked but with my eyes,'[11] says Hermia. He just has, but it is a different complicity, and one which Brook does not seem to have noticed. 'Find something in your eyes which Theseus can pick up,' Brook tells her. The advice is superfluous.

In such turbulence, the exchanges between Lysander and Hermia, which last week were becoming fluent, quickly founder. In 'How now, my love! Why is your cheek so pale?'[12], there is less love than irritation, and less lovers' greeting than interrogation. 'Try to sense

¹² *Lysander:* How now, my love! Why is your cheek so pale?
How chance the roses there do fade so fast?
Hermia: Belike for want of rain, which I could well
Beteem them from the tempest of my eyes.

(*I.i.128–131*)

¹³ *Puck:* I am that merry wanderer of the night.
I jest to Oberon, and make him smile,
When I a fat and bean-fed horse beguile,
Neighing in likeness of a filly foal:
And sometime lurk I in a gossip's bowl,
In very likeness of a roasted crab;
And when she drinks, against her lips I bob,
And on her withered dewlap pour the ale.

(*II.i.43–50*)

¹⁴ *Oberon:* My gentle Puck, come hither. Thou rememb'rest
Since once I sat upon a promontory,
And heard a mermaid, on a dolphin's back,
Uttering such dulcet and harmonious breath,
That the rude sea grew civil at her song,
And certain stars shot madly from their spheres,
To hear the sea maid's music.
Puck: I remember.
Oberon: That very time I saw, but thou couldst not
Flying between the cold moon and the earth,
Cupid all armed. A certain aim he took
At a fair vestal thronèd by the west,
And loosed his love shaft smartly from his bow,
As it should pierce a hundred thousand hearts.

(*II.i.148–160*)

¹⁵ *Oberon:* Fetch me that flow'r; the herb I showed thee once:
The juice of it on sleeping eyelids laid
Will make a man or woman madly dote
Upon the next live creature that it sees.
Fetch me this herb, and be thou here again
Ere the leviathan can swim a league.
Puck: I'll put a girdle round about the earth
In forty minutes.   (*Exit*)

(*II.i.169–176*)

the rhythms here in a more subtle way,' Brook insists with equal irritation; 'it is sluggish and unaware.' The actors stare at him in a silence which seems near to accusation. 'After the courtly formalities,' he warns them, leaden and grounded, 'this must be a flying into one another's arms.' Flight seems more likely than flying; a dead horse has been flogged to a standstill. And as poetry became prose, and words lost their meanings, 'you are not listening to one another,' Brook told them. More to the point, they seemed not to be listening to Brook either. Effort had now become hard labour, and every step pedestrian. Depressed, the lovers were half-hearted, the spirits dispirited, Bottom mechanical and all his fellows lifeless.

Only Puck recovered his vivacity, and Oberon his pride: the first ('And sometime lurk I in a gossip's bowl')[13] finding his mischievous stride, and the second ('Flying between the cold moon and the earth')[14] his majestic rhythm. But in today's longueurs, even Puck's promise to 'put a girdle round about the earth in forty minutes'[15] seemed too long by half. Finally, in Act Two, Scene Two, when only Brook's patience appeared unexhausted, instead of singing[16] the Fairies struck – and struck hard, for the bored and frustrated actors. 'Every time we work on this,' their shop steward told Brook belligerently, 'there are four different views among us of what you would approve of.' There is a silence; and a moment of heavy-breathing. Was this the albatross of director's theatre coming home to roost, or a real cuckoo in the nest of illusion? Brook covered his face with his hands, as if despairing.

This midsummer night's dream had been both moonless and airless. Leaving, asphyxiated, in the dark of it, I collided with a Japanese gong while making my own laborious exit.

Sixth week, third and fourth days

I felt sated and wearied with the tangled process of rehearsals, and stayed at home. But writing out in a fair copy my own scribbled notes and verbatim transcriptions seemed to give shape to the shapeless. It was as if finding the *mot juste* for transient impression brought order, with its own artifice, into the chaos of my responses. At worst it was remedial exercise; basket-weaving, with words.

The rehearsals had become becalmed and energyless. And with that strange osmosis of feeling which not only links actor to actor, and

1st Fairy: You spotted snakes with double tongue,
 Thorny hedgehogs be not seen;
 Newts and blindworms, do no wrong.
 Come not near our Fairy Queen.

         (*II.ii.9–12*)

17 *Puck:* The shallowest thickskin of that barren sort,
 Who Pyramus presented in their sport,
 Forsook his scene, and entered in a brake.
 When I did him at this advantage take,
 An ass's nole I fixèd on his head.

         (*III.ii.13–17*)

spectator to spectator, but also actor to spectator and spectator to actor, I was as bored and exasperated as they were. I had abandoned the rehearsals, too, at the point (or pointlessness) of a 'sweet lullaby',[16] sung by disaffected 'spirits'. The wasteful absurdity of it seemed, during this two-day hiatus of silent consideration, to be an outrage.

After all, what has any adult, ostensibly sound in mind and body, to do with 'spotted snakes with double tongue', 'beetles black', 'weaving spiders' and all the rest of it? What have Philomele and 1970 in common? Who cares or can care for the infantile safety, threatened by 'thorny hedgehogs', of 'our Fairy Queen', when the real world is menaced? Who can there be foolish enough to sing 'Lulla, lulla, lullaby', in sympathetic chorus with a bunch of hard-pressed Fairies? On which side of the footlights are the 'blindworms'? Or are they on both sides, in equal numbers?

And if so, why should I, or anyone else, bother to join them?

Sixth week, fifth day

When I return – the moth always returns to the flame, even if its wings are burning – Brook is still sitting where he was sitting before, and still talking. But I can hear immediately that the sense of oppression and mistrust has lifted; as has that enforced calm in Brook which betokens tension and trouble. The subject of discourse is Bottom's transformation, and the day's work is to concentrate on its re-exploration. It is plainly seen by Brook as the pivot and focus of the drama. How far is this emphasis itself the product of Brook's dependence, in crisis, on the stalwart and dependable Bottom as the sheet-anchor of the production? (To the extent that it is, it is a paradox, since Bottom alone of the cast seems to have formed his role, and grown in assurance, according to his own, not Brook's, methods.)

Bottom's asinine 'nole'[17] has now been made in its finished form by the Wardrobe Department. Brook is saying, as I enter, that 'the prop of the ass's head cannot be more than a token'. The subterranean scepticism which had been growing among some of the actors, and had broken surface three days ago, has now visibly and audibly abated. Attention and concentration have returned to the actors' voices and bodies. 'No conceivable object,' Brook is calmly telling them, 'can turn a man into a believable animal.' True or not, it seems that the children have taught Brook a lesson.

(*ACT THREE. Scene One. The wood. TITANIA lying asleep. Enter*
   QUINCE, SNUG, BOTTOM, FLUTE, SNOUT and
   STARVELING)
   Bottom: Are we all met?
   Quince: Pat, pat; and here's a marvellous convenient place for our
      rehearsal. This green plot shall be our stage, this hawthorn brake
      our tiring house, and we will do it in action as we will do it before
      the Duke.
   Bottom: Peter Quince?
   Quince: What sayest thou, bully Bottom?
      Bottom: There are things in this comedy of Pyramus and Thisby
      that will never please. First, Pyramus must draw a sword to kill
      himself; which the ladies cannot abide. How answer you that?
                                                               (*III.i.1–11*)

19   (*Enter PUCK*)
   Puck: What hempen homespuns have we swagg'ring here,
      So near the cradle of the Fairy Queen?
      What, a play toward! I'll be an auditor;
      An actor too perhaps, if I see cause.
                                                               (*III.i.68–71*)

20 *Thisby:* Most radiant Pyramus, most lily-white of hue,
      Of colour like the red rose on triumphant brier,
      Most brisky juvenal, and eke most lovely Jew,
      As true as truest horse, that yet would never tire,
      I'll meet thee, Pyramus, at Ninny's tomb.
   Quince: 'Ninus' tomb,' man. Why, you must not speak that yet.
      That you answer to Pyramus. You speak all your part at once, cues
      and all. Pyramus enter. Your cue is past; it is 'never tire'.
   Thisby: O − as true as truest horse, that yet would never tire.
                        (*Re-enter PUCK, and BOTTOM with an ass's head*)
                                                               (*III.i.83–92*)

21 *Puck:* I'll follow you, I'll lead you about a round,
      Through bog, through bush, through brake, through brier,
      Sometime a horse I'll be, sometime a hound,
      A hog, a headless bear, sometime a fire;
      And neigh, and bark, and grunt, and roar, and burn,
      Like horse, hound, hog, bear, fire, at every turn.
                                                               (*III.i.96–101*)

Great expectation – in actors, director, technicians, spectators – once more begins to flower, in ground which a little while ago had seemed so stony. Brook says (without hectoring) that 'no water colour interpretation of the play will be possible at any point.' The struggle against the dilute and the sentimental, to be centred by Brook upon the apocalypse of Bottom's transformation, will hopefully drive the actors back to the higher ground of effort and revelation, which they had earlier begun to capture. 'We are not yet bringing out at all,' he adds, his own confidence restored to his manner, 'that the whole play is about couples, of whom Titania and The Ass are a crucial example.' The rehearsal is to begin in the wood at the start of Act Three[18], with Titania sleeping and at the entrance of 'the clowns', Bottom among them. It is close to the point where rehearsal (and I) left off three days ago.

'The mechanicals' relationship to the unknown,' Brook says, as they feel their way forward like blind men, 'will be immediately raised here, when they enter a pool of moonlight, surrounded by darkness.' Both the spot and the spotlight must be, and today can be, imagined. Their voices, too, have a new resonance. You can hear the echo, if you listen. 'What hempen homespuns have we swagg'ring here?'[19], Puck asks himself and them and us, in one all-embracing question (and answer). Today, it once more seems to dissolve every distinction between actors and audience, even if it cannot answer yesterday's bitter questions. 'What, a play toward!' Puck exclaims. 'I'll be an auditor,/ An actor too, perhaps,'[19] he says, speaking for himself and the spectator. Or, as Brook puts it, 'only through the instrumentality of a "play", can a step towards the truth be taken.'

The truth which Brook wants to find, in his urgent need to re-arouse invention, is an animal one. The sleeping dog must be reawakened. That Thisby in her transports declares herself 'as true as truest horse'[20] now becomes a cue for both rehearsals, Brook's and Quince's. For in this absurd image of the perfect lover, emphatically repeated by Shakespeare at the point of Pyramus' re-entrance[20], Brook declares that there is 'a sense of sexual preparation for Bottom's reappearance as an ass.' Moreover, Puck's urge to haunt and bedevil the mechanicals, and his threat that 'sometime a horse I'll be, sometime a hound . . ./ And neigh, and bark, and grunt, and roar, and burn,'[21] signifies, Brook tells the actors, that 'everything in Puck will be released at an animal level.' As for Bottom, 'the deepest things are freed in him' as he loses his head and returns, hairy and neighing, to the action[22]. These

22 *(Re-enter PUCK, and BOTTOM with an ass's head)*
Pyramus: If I were fair, Thisby, I were only thine.
Quince: O monstrous! O strange! We are haunted. Pray, masters! Fly,
masters! Help!

(Exeunt all but BOTTOM and PUCK)
(III.i.93–95)

23 *Snout:* O Bottom, thou art changed! What do I see on thee?
Bottom: What do you see? You see an ass head of your own, do
you? *(Exit SNOUT)*

(Enter QUINCE)
Quince: Bless thee, Bottom! Bless thee! Thou art translated. *(Exit)*
Bottom: I see their knavery. This is to make an ass of me; to fright
me if they could.

(III.i.105–111)

24 *Titania:* (*Awaking*) What angel wakes me from my flow'ry bed?
Bottom: (*Sings*) The finch, the sparrow, and the lark,
The plain-song cuckoo gray,
Whose note full many a man doth mark,
And dares not answer nay –
for, indeed, who would set his wit to so foolish a bird? Who would
give a bird the lie, though he cry 'cuckoo' never so?
Titania: I pray thee, gentle mortal, sing again.

(III.i.118–125)

25 *Oberon:* What thou seest when thou dost wake,
Do it for thy truelove take;
Love and languish for his sake.
Be it ounce, or cat, or bear,
Pard, or boar with bristled hair,
In thy eye that shall appear
When thou wak'st, it is thy dear.
Wake when some vile thing is near. *(Exit)*

(II.ii.27–34)

26 *Oberon:* Ill met by moonlight, proud Titania.
Titania: What, jealous Oberon! Fairy, skip hence.
I have forsworn his bed and company.
Oberon: Tarry, rash wanton; am not I thy lord?
Titania: Then I must be thy lady.

(II.i.60–64)

226

are also moments of arrest by fear, a fear which, Brook says, 'cannot be found by technical analysis of how to stage it. Its true source and nature must be set in motion each time, on sight of Bottom.'

'O monstrous! O strange!'[22] exclaims Quince at the animal apparition – and, before fleeing in terror, 'Bless thee, Bottom! Bless thee! Thou art translated.'[23] Brook stops the actors once more to tell them that, in contrast to the bestial, Quince is 'the only character with a kind of intellectual existence', and 'with an interest in the theory of things'. Quince, taking the hint swiftly, straightaway steps out of Shakespeare's rehearsal into this one. The actor speaks, *in propria persona*. He declares that 'having tried to do a "play" with its own transformations, Quince has suddenly seen a "real" transformation going on in front of him'. (Snug's transformation into a Lion is nothing compared with Bottom's.) This is finely said, and seems to galvanize the whole cast to action.

As Brook had intended, the actors now become all animal impulse, the beast in man the spur to renewal. 'What do I see on thee?'[23] says Snout quiveringly to Bottom. 'You see an ass head of your own,' Bottom roaringly tells him. Bottom, made an ass of and an ass to us, in turn sees an ass in Snout the tinker, as animal imagination runs riot. Bottom's dander is now, once more, fully aroused. 'I see their knavery,'[23] he says, his voice charged and his body swelling; 'this is to make an ass of me, to fright me if they could.' Brook tells him that his fear 'has to do with finding that everything has changed around him'. Bottom has 'a feeling of liberation'; it is 'a fear which is combined with pleasure.'

All ears now prick to Titania's voluptuous waking[24]. 'What angel wakes me from my flow'ry bed?' she whispers, her body stirring. 'Titania,' says Brook, 'is not seeing an ass pure and simple, but a man with the head of an ass. The worlds of spirit and flesh are intertwining.' (Oberon had invoked a bestiary[25] to plague Titania, but not an ass, nor Bottom.) And as Bottom, gross and tumescent, sings[24] to her – lithe, and uncoiling – it is lust, not love, which seems to prompt her to a newly lascivious motion. 'She is slowly descending from spirit to woman,' Brook tells her, as the sexual pulse of the scene quickens. 'Sex between them,' he adds, 'will be at a wholly mortal and human level.' Moreover, 'it is not the first time for her'[26], so that though it is Beauty and the Beast who will soon couple, this Beauty is a 'rash wanton', and not a virgin. 'Oberon himself,' Brook says to Titania, her body as if

²⁷ *Titania:* Thou art as wise as thou art beautiful.
  Bottom: Not so, neither; but if I had wit enough to get out of this
    wood, I have enough to serve mine own turn.
  Titania: Out of this wood do not desire to go.
    Thou shalt remain here, whether thou wilt or no.
    I am a spirit of no common rate.
    The summer still doth tend upon my state;
    And I do love thee. Therefore, go with me.
    I'll give thee fairies to attend on thee,
    And they shall fetch thee jewels from the deep,
    And sing, while thou on pressèd flowers dost sleep.

                                              (*III.i.135–145*)

²⁸ *Bottom:* Your name, honest gentleman?
  Peaseblossom: Peaseblossom.
  Bottom: I pray you, commend me to Mistress Squash, your mother,
    and to Master Peascod, your father. Good Master Peaseblossom, I
    shall desire you of more acquaintance too. Your name, I beseech
    you, sir?
  Mustardseed: Mustardseed.
  Bottom: Good Master Mustardseed, I know your patience well. That
    same cowardly, giantlike ox-beef hath devoured many a gentleman
    of your house. I promise you your kindred hath made my eyes
    water ere now. I desire you of more acquaintance, good Master
    Mustardseed.
  Titania: Come, wait upon him; lead him to my bower.
    The moon methinks looks with a wat'ry eye;
    And when she weeps, weeps every little flower,
    Lamenting some enforcèd chastity.
    Tie up my lover's tongue, bring him silently.
                        (*Exit TITANIA, with BOTTOM and Fairies*)
                                              (*III.i.170–186*)

²⁹ *Puck:* A crew of patches, rude mechanicals,
    That work for bread upon Athenian stalls,
    Were met together to rehearse a play,
    Intended for great Theseus' nuptial day.
    The shallowest thickskin of that barren sort,
    Who Pyramus presented in their sport,
    Forsook his scene, and entered in a brake.
    When I did him at this advantage take,
    An ass's nole I fixèd on his head.

228

opening to Bottom, 'has already provided you with the most earthy experience.' It is 'something for which you could not feel nostalgia'; while what faces her now is 'not a romance, but animal copulation'.

Feelings fully erected, all is now a dalliance[27] to elongate the sexual tension, beyond bearing. It is held at a point of arousal close to a dream's orgasm. Even Bottom's languorous and slow-witted exchanges[28] with Cobweb, Mustardseed and Peaseblossom, which Brook describes as 'coarse with the confidence of keeping Titania waiting', seem to tremble now upon the very apex of desire. In their very inconsequence, they seem today a form of terminal sexual petting. To Brook, however, they are something different. They are, he says, 'part of the sliding, shifting, relations between Bottom and the others, where anything is possible between them, from having a drink to committing buggery together'. This itself is a perverse reading. 'Come,' says Titania, as if no longer able to wait to be covered, 'lead him to my bower.'[28] And as they leave to their (imagined) pleasures, (as if) to couple, no moon (this mid-morning) looks on 'with a wat'ry eye', nor 'weeps every little flower'[28], as Shakespeare seemingly intended. For in Titania's and Bottom's embraces, no lost or violated chastity will be lamented. Indeed, these lovers will not even 'make love'. They will 'have sex', and *a tergo* in the bargain.

Meanwhile, in 'another part of the wood', Puck tells Oberon of what has happened[29], from the commencement of the mechanicals' rehearsal in the previous scene to the moment at which 'Titania waked and straightway loved an ass'[29]. For the first time – a strangely belated discovery – Puck's speech, with its vivid account of the alarm of the actors, is seen as providing what Brook today calls a 'retrospective description of the transformation of Bottom, to guide the actual enactment of it'. And as the morning's work comes to an end, Puck's images of flight are heard – also for the first time – to echo Quince's desperate 'Fly, masters!'. In addition, Puck's observation that 'senseless things', such as briers and thorns, had then begun to 'do them wrong'[29], snatching at their sleeves and hats, is described by Brook as the 'great theme of the play'. (It is also now clear that those briers have become these wires, and those thorns are these coils of metal.)

Why so? Because, says Brook, there is adumbrated here the question of 'the goods and ills of the imagination', which transitively catch at our sense of reality and ensnare us in illusion. It is 'something

Anon his Thisby must be answerèd,
And forth my mimic comes. When they him spy,
As wild geese that the creeping fowler eye,
Or russet-pated choughs, many in sort,
Rising and cawing at the gun's report,
Sever themselves and madly sweep the sky,
So, at his sight, away his fellows fly;
And, at our stamp, here o'er and o'er one falls;
He murder cries, and help from Athens calls.
Their sense thus weak, lost with their fears thus strong,
Made senseless things begin to do them wrong,
For briers and thorns at their apparel snatch;
Some sleeves, some hats, from yielders all things catch.
I led them on in this distracted fear,
And left sweet Pyramus translated there;
When in that moment, so it came to pass,
Titania waked, and straightway loved an ass.

(*III.ii.9–34*)

to brood upon', Brook tells the actors as they break, 'for it goes to the root of the play's meaning'. Likewise, imagination can now leave Bottom to his (half-human) devices, lost offstage in the arms of Titania, and translated; or – if it chooses – walk off with David Waller for a beer and sandwich.

During the lunch-break, I had a long conversation with Brook, the first for some time. He confessed that he had been 'dispirited' by the performance for the children, but said that 'much had been learned from it'. In particular, the actors had gained a sense of their 'inadequacies' from the experience. And on the basis of this new understanding, the 'beginnings of good work' were now possible. 'Something can now happen,' he said. (It has, as he knows, already begun to happen.) Yet the cast – and the Royal Shakespeare Company, which he described with thinly concealed sarcasm as 'supposedly the best Shakespearian company in the world' – was 'uninventive'. The exhilaration which comes from finding unlimited creative potential in a theatrical troupe was, he said, 'rarely present'. (In the cast of *A Midsummer Night's Dream*, he singled out only Frances de la Tour and Alan Howard.) The essential prerequisite for developing such creativity was to 'take the promising actors' and 'give them a strongly-led, consistent and imaginatively-intensive training'. The leadership, the imagination and the training were all lacking in the company. The rest of the season's work, he said, was in consequence 'terrible'.

He said, too, that the problem of the 'really talented' young actor or actress was a 'technical' one. Whatever the actor's gifts, and however these might manifest themselves in non-Shakespearian plays, 'technical anxieties' often all but extinguished their creative potential in Shakespeare. Only actors 'like Paul Scofield or Irene Worth' fully possessed the combination of technical mastery and imagination which Shakespearian acting demanded. Today's actors of Shakespeare were not adequately trained to it, not even at the R.S.C. where it could have been expected. (Later, in a separate conversation with Michael Bogdanov, an 'assistant director' of this production – but whose role and presence seem vestigial – I was told that there was both exhaustion from overwork and disaffection among the actors. There was exhaustion with an eight-play season, disaffection with the company's general artistic direction, and a constant stream of actors petitioning Brook for work at his new 'International Theatre Research Centre' in Paris.)

30 *Puck:* What hempen homespuns have we swagg'ring here,
So near the cradle of the Fairy Queen?
What, a play toward! I'll be an auditor;
An actor too perhaps, if I see cause.
Quince: Speak, Pyramus. Thisby, stand forth.
Pyramus: Thisby, the flowers of odious savours sweet –
Quince: Odours, odours.
Pyramus: – odours, savours sweet:
So hath thy breath, my dearest Thisby dear.
But hark, a voice! Stay thou but here awhile,
And by and by I will to thee appear. (*Exit*)
Puck: A stranger Pyramus than e'er played here! (*Exit*)
Thisby: Must I speak now?
Quince: Ay, marry, must you. For you must understand he goes but
to see a noise that he heard, and is to come again.
Thisby: Most radiant Pyramus, most lily-white of hue,
Of colour like the red rose on triumphant brier,
Most brisky juvenal, and eke most lovely Jew,
As true as truest horse, that yet would never tire,
I'll meet thee, Pyramus, at Ninny's tomb.

(*III.i.68–87*)

Brook complained of many things: of the theatre building, of ticket-prices ('scandalous', 'inhibiting'), of the lack of ensemble, of actors' training. His geniality, such as it is, is wary and always uneasy. And however he keeps his distance, at close conversational quarters he seems intellectually secure only in his immediate tasks as director. Bogdanov says that, unlike other directors who 'lack his modesty', he is responsive to, and ready to accept, advice and suggestion. Unlike *his* productions, theirs in consequence are 'simply a projection of their hang-ups and personal problems'. I told Brook that I thought he had given up his attempt to overcome the 'suburbanism' of the lovers, and had accepted it. I added that though it was now overlaid with other discoveries and insights, it was still there, always threatening to disable invention with artifice, and feeling with sentiment. He is irritated at the suggestion that he has 'accepted' anything. The production, he says briskly, is 'still open to every possibility'. I also tell him of what I myself have heard, several times in the last weeks, at Quince's 'Bless thee, Bottom! Bless thee! Thou art translated'. Quince's present astonishment is 'banal', I say to him. It ought to be, instead, a 'benediction for Bottom's transformation', a '*Salve!*' at his entrance into a heaven of midsummer dreams and pleasures.

The rehearsal resumes. Brook asks the actors to go back to Puck's intrusion upon the mechanicals' rehearsal[30]. The entire transformation of Bottom, the production's source of renewal, is to be re-enacted. And as Puck asks 'What hempen homespuns have we swagg'ring here,/ So near the cradle of the Fairy Queen?'[30], the mechanicals continue their actors' work, deeply absorbed in their own problems. They can neither see nor hear him. But Bottom, suddenly afraid, draws his sword, roaring into the (imagined) darkness at (imagined) voices. His weapon, brandished like a phallus, is seized by the (as if) invisible Puck; who now leads Pyramus (or Bottom) by the sword (or penis-tip) away into that off-stage limbo, or magical tiring-house, where he will be fitted out to fright the mechanicals, and to pleasure Titania.

Quince tells us, and the other actors, that Bottom has gone 'but to see a noise that he heard'[30]. It is itself a sentence only partially heard before, and anticipates Bottom's own confusion of mind and senses one act later. 'Most radiant Pyramus,' says Thisby of her temporarily absent lover, swallowed up into the engulfing darkness, 'most lily-white of hue, of colour like the red rose on triumphant brier'[30] – she, too, losing her wits and senses, colour-blind in this moonlight.

31   (*Re-enter PUCK, and BOTTOM with an ass's head*)

Pyramus: If I were fair, Thisby, I were only thine.

Quince: O monstrous! O strange! We are haunted. Pray, masters! Fly, masters! Help!

(*Exeunt all but BOTTOM and PUCK*)

(*III.i.93–95*)

32   (*Enter QUINCE*)

Quince: Bless thee, Bottom! Bless thee! Thou art translated.   (*Exit*)

Bottom: I see their knavery. This is to make an ass of me; to fright me, if they could. But I will not stir from this place, do what they can. I will walk up and down here, and will sing, that they shall hear I am not afraid.   (*Sings*)

> The woosel cock so black of hue,
> With orange-tawny bill,
> The throstle with his note so true,
> The wren with little quill –

Titania: (*Awaking*) What angel wakes me from my flow'ry bed?

(*III.i.109–118*)

Meanwhile, neighings and Thisby's 'truest horse' presage the imminence of Bottom's terrifying reappearance[31]. For when he enters, his 'nole' nodding and eyes starting, there is a slow descent into a varied and frozen terror. Snout is laughing his way towards a lock-jawed grimace, Quince crossing himself in a double-take redoubled, Starveling backing away, open-mouthed, from puzzlement to a silent horror. And then a collective frisson, its hair on end, breaks out yelling into the open, the spirits cornering the mechanicals and putting them to flight up and down ladders in a frenzied running, fright running wild with them.

'Bless thee, Bottom! Bless thee! Thou art translated,'[32] says Quince, astounded as ever. Brook stops him. 'This is a line,' he says, echoing our earlier conversation, 'different from the others.' In it, he tells Quince, 'fear is mingled with adoration'. And so it is in the enactment, which is now rapt not stricken, and become devout as prayer. 'I see their knavery,'[32] says Bottom, his coarse voice counterpointing Quince's reverential gesture, as the Fairies, blacksmith-like, fit his feet with clogs, or his hoofs with iron. Now, Bottom's 'the woosel cock so black of hue'[32], at its first rehearsing in a changed context, seems – the cock notwithstanding – a chanted plainsong; while Titania's 'What angel wakes me from my flow'ry bed?'[32] has become a matins sung to the god of love, or lechery's sexual orison.

But Bottom, in the increasing stress of invention, is now also searching for an impulse which seems beyond reaching. 'I will walk up and down here, and will sing,' he says, 'that they shall hear I am not afraid.'[32] And he goes up and down, (as Puck will later), strangely pacing back and forth over the lines, at his own compulsive dictation. The rehearsal makes way for him, and comes to a standstill. Repeating the words over and over, he seems to be driven by his own tension to find in 'the woosel cock so black of hue' words which he can hear, but not yet utter. There is in him both the desire to sing and the need for neighing. It is as if man and animal were struggling to express their fears and joys in an impossible communion – or a desperate actor were looking for dipthongs which might bring ass and man together. And suddenly it is the very sounds and syllables of 'the woosel', 'of hue', 'tawny' and 'so true'[32] which take the convulsive stress of his hee-hawing and crooning. In its indeterminateness, lost between worlds, and with the rehearsal fallen into an unprecedented silence for him, this canticle of braying now suggests the most terror-struck and

³³ *Titania:* Be kind and courteous to this gentleman;
 Hop in his walks, and gambol in his eyes;
 Feed him with apricocks and dewberries,
 With purple grapes, green figs, and mulberries;
 The honey bags steal from the humblebees,
 And for night tapers crop their waxen thighs,
 And light them at the fiery glowworm's eyes,
 To have my love to bed and to arise;
 And pluck the wings from painted butterflies,
 To fan the moonbeams from his sleeping eyes.
 Nod to him, elves, and do him courtesies.
Peaseblossom: Hail, mortal!
Cobweb:　　　　Hail!
Moth:　　　　　　　　Hail!
Mustardseed:　　　　　　　　Hail!
Bottom: I cry your worships mercy, heartily: I beseech your worship's
 name.
Cobweb: Cobweb.
Bottom: I shall desire you of more acquaintance, good Master
 Cobweb: if I cut my finger, I shall make bold with you. Your name,
 honest gentleman?
Peaseblossom: Peaseblossom.
Bottom: I pray you, commend me to Mistress Squash, your mother,
 and to Master Peascod, your father. Good Master Peaseblossom, I
 shall desire you of more acquaintance too. Your name, I beseech
 you, sir?
Mustardseed: Mustardseed.
Bottom: Good Master Mustardseed, I know your patience well. That
 same cowardly, giantlike ox-beef hath devoured many a gentleman
 of your house. I promise you your kindred hath made my eyes
 water ere now. I desire you of more acquaintance, good Master
 Mustardseed.
Titania: Come, wait upon him; lead him to my bower.
 The moon methinks looks with a wat'ry eye;
 And when she weeps, weeps every little flower,
 Lamenting some enforcèd chastity.
 Tie up my lover's tongue, bring him silently.
　　　　　　　　　(*Exit TITANIA, with BOTTOM and Fairies*)
　　　　　　　　　　　　　　(*III.i.150–186*)

236

discordant of all propositions yet put to our imaginations: that man and animal may merge one into the other. The ass's 'nole' has not merely been set upon a human body, but a new and fantastic creature is struggling to be born from Bottom and the actor's invention, which is both horse-shod and human-hearted.

'Be kind and courteous to this gentleman,'[33] says Titania to the Fairies, her voice as if trembling with desire. And Bottom, as if in heat, is hoisted on to their shoulders. 'Hop in his walks, and gambol in his eyes,'[33] she tells them swooningly, as they gather around him in a bee-cluster, toying with him. One of them has his arm extended and raised between Bottom's legs, his fist clenched into a bursting knob or *corona*. 'Feed him with apricocks,'[33] Titania tells the Fairies, holding the fist cupped in her hands, her voice fainting. 'Hail, mortal! Hail!'[33] they whisper, pandering to Bottom, and playing the pander. 'I pray you, commend me to Mistress Squash . . . and to Master Peascod,'[33] Bottom says to Peaseblossom, his slow and nodding courtesies painfully postponing, as if in *coitus interruptus*, the moment's bulging climax. The rest of the cast has gathered on the topmost gantry, voyeurs watching Bottom riding into heaven. This heavy beast – Ass, Pyramus, Waller, Bottom and soon to have two backs in the bargain – is now raised higher, a man's legs locked around the naked shoulders of the spirits, and the clenched fist at its fullest, near-vertical, erection.

To Mendelssohn's *Wedding March*, sent-up in a sardonic gesture, Titania strokes this (as if) standing phallus amid a lascivious clutch of fairies, who seem to hang upon every sexual impulse and erotic gesture. Mendelssohn's sentimental ghost is also about to be laid, as if for ever. On this triumphal carriage – Lust's, not Cupid's – Bottom is exalted, and Titania transported[33]. And as it resumes its course towards an imagined union, in a cascade of flying discs and floating bubbles, so Puck and Oberon on trapezes resume their back and forth and side to side swinging above it. But it is an earthy, not aerial, rhythm; and, below them, it is not heavenly but earthly bodies which are in motion. 'The men,' says Brook wryly, 'will be relating to Bottom. He is about to do it to Titania. For all of them.' The impulse is harsh and down-to-earth; in a froth of bubbles.

Sixth week, sixth day

The morning's exercises were in progress when I arrived. In the hall,

[34] *ACT ONE. Scene One. The palace of Theseus. Enter THESEUS, HIPPOLYTA, PHILOSTRATE and Attendants.*

Theseus: Now, fair Hippolyta, our nuptial hour
Draws on apace. Four happy days bring in
Another moon; but, O, methinks, how slow
This old moon wanes! She lingers my desires,
Like to a stepdame, or a dowager,
Long withering out a young man's revenue.
Hippolyta: Four days will quickly steep themselves in night,
Four nights will quickly dream away the time;
And then the moon, like to a silver bow
New-bent in heaven, shall behold the night
Of our solemnities.

(I.i.1–11)

there was a heightened sense of expectation, of effort without tension, of elevation. At the centre of a wide circle of actors stood a single figure, in the role of conductor. He was making an improvised series of his own movements which, in Brook's words, had to be 'taken up' by the others. First gestures, and then sounds, and then gesture-and-sound together, had to be reproduced 'without interval' by the circle of actors. The actor at the centre was told to rely on 'awareness' of his 'presence' on the part of the others; they in their turn were only to 'half-watch' him, but what he did was to be 'instantly followed'. And as actor or actress took over, one after the other, at the centre, it was to be done 'without hesitation or inhibition'.

Today, in the shared alertness, there was swiftness of communication and immediacy of feeling. But are these exercises to produce ensemble, or to reproduce the *effects* of ensemble in ensemble's absence? I notice also that two company actresses, not in the cast but visibly eager to attract his attention, were allowed by Brook to join the circle of familiars. (A third actor was later waved away with irritation.) Yet how can this be, if the purpose of the exercise is to achieve the deepest intimacy of impulse among the actors of *A Midsummer Night's Dream*? Their unexpected presence, together with that of new spectators from within the R.S.C. – including John Barton, sourly watchful of Brook and studiously ignored by him – suggests something different: that new hopes and interests are being aroused in the company by report of this process of rehearsal, and of its promise.

The note immediately struck, as the day's rehearsal-performance commences, is of a passionate and melancholy anger. It too is unexpected. But in tone and timbre, it straightaway reaches into the play's deepest currents of dream and nightmare. How is this? Now, Act One, Scene One is not solemn, but still; pregnant with the play's event and also heavy with menace. It contains the very promise of riches which has brought today's company spectators to it. The actors seem to tell us, as the play begins[34], that we are standing together on the threshold of illusion, at the point of day–dream, and on the verge of danger. Uneasy but compelling, the mood they are creating is of that strange half-light which precedes storm, and the opening of the heavens.

It is a half-light – 'how slow this old moon wanes!'[34] – which seems to have been translated into sound and appearance. The dream we are being promised is a dream dreamed in solitude and passionate discontent, and expressed in longing and anger. 'I beseech your

35 *Hermia:* I beseech your Grace that I may know
   The worst that may befall me in this case,
   If I refuse to wed Demetrius.
Theseus: Either to die the death, or to abjure
   Forever the society of men.
   Therefore, fair Hermia, question your desires;
   Know of your youth, examine well your blood,
   Whether, if you yield not to your father's choice,
   You can endure the livery of a nun,
   For aye to be in shady cloister mewed,
   To live a barren sister all your life,
   Chanting faint hymns to the cold fruitless moon.

                                              (I.i.62–73)

36 *Lysander:* I am beloved of beauteous Hermia.
   Why should not I then prosecute my right?
   Demetrius, I'll avouch it to his head,
   Made love to Nedar's daughter, Helena,
   And won her soul; and she, sweet lady, dotes,
   Devoutly dotes, dotes in idolatry,
   Upon this spotted and inconstant man.
Theseus: I must confess that I have heard so much,
   And with Demetrius thought to have spoke thereof;
   But, being overfull of self-affairs,
   My mind did lose it. But, Demetrius, come;
   And come Egeus. You shall go with me;
   I have some private schooling for you both.
   For you, fair Hermia, look you arm yourself
   To fit your fancies to your father's will;
   Or else the law of Athens yields you up –
   Which by no means we may extenuate –
   To death, or to a vow of single life.
   Come, my Hippolyta. What cheer, my love?
   Demetrius and Egeus, go along.
   I must employ you in some business
   Against our nuptial, and confer with you
   Of something nearly that concerns yourselves.
Egeus: With duty and desire we follow you.
                    (Exeunt all but LYSANDER and HERMIA)
Lysander: How now, my love! Why is your cheek so pale?
   How chance the roses there do fade so fast?

                                              (I.i.104–129)

Grace,'[35] Hermia says, distant in her own despairs and as if sleep-walking, 'that I may know the worst that may befall me . . . if I refuse to wed Demetrius.' The mood darkens. 'Either to die the death,' replies Theseus, stern in his melancholy and pausing in his own sombre speculation, '. . . or to abjure forever the society of men.'[35] (He had paused so long that he was interrupted by the prompter.) The play's opening scene is now steeped in a deep inward isolation of the characters, one from the other. And it is as if these exchanges are for the mind's ear and these sights for the mind's eye only, as they are in a dream for the dreamer.

'I must confess,'[36] says Theseus, his voice and gesture faded with preoccupation, 'that I have heard so much . . . but, being overfull of self-affairs, my mind did lose it.' He speaks wearily, as if out of duty; speech an eerie intrusion, silence a return to dreaming. The spectators – whether unmoved actors leaning at the topmost rail of the gantry, or marooned witnesses sitting in the audience – watch in the same silence. Ambiguous observers of a 'play' and of each other, it is as if we are all absently held in the same long vistas of the reflective imagination; mirror-images which recede into the deepest introversion, or a tragic oblivion. 'Or else,'[36] says Theseus, as though some other inaccessible thought were being interrupted, 'the law of Athens yields you up to death, or to a vow of single life.' Now each pause becomes an inward moment, long enough for thought to speculate at large (or minds to wander), and for the actors to become their own audience. 'Come, my Hippolyta,'[36] says Theseus, starting suddenly and on a fitful impulse, as if the 'play' and his 'role' in it had been for a while forgotten. 'What cheer, my love?'[36] he asks her. The question, idle or lonely, is asked out of a deep and fretful longing. Theseus, solitary, angered, receives no answer.

It is this dark and louring mood, its brow furrowed, which now takes up and sustains all the actors. Lysander's 'How now, my love! Why is your cheek so pale?'[36] is impatient with the same passion, and 'How chance the roses there do fade so fast?' less solicitous than irritated and anxious. His speech on the brevity of love[37], freed of its Home Counties cadence, is darkened with spleen and sexual frustration. Its melancholy is thwarted desire's black humour. 'Let us teach our trial patience, because it is a customary cross,' Hermia tells him[37]. And despite her own despondency, she rallies him from despair with good counsel, and with a strength of will which is beyond him. Yet there is as much reciprocity in this as in the preceding exchanges

³⁷ *Lysander:* Or, if there were a sympathy in choice,
    War, death, or sickness did lay siege to it,
    Making it momentany as a sound,
    Swift as a shadow, short as any dream . . .
    So quick bright things come to confusion.
  Hermia: If then true lovers have been ever crossed,
    It stands as an edict in destiny;
    Then let us teach our trial patience,
    Because it is a customary cross.

(I.i.141–153)

³⁸ *Hermia:* My good Lysander!
    I swear to thee, by Cupid's strongest bow,
    By his best arrow with the golden head . . .
    And by that fire which burned the Carthage queen,
    When the false Troyan under sail was seen,
    By all the vows that ever men have broke,
    In number more than ever women spoke,
    In that same place thou hast appointed me,
    Tomorrow truly will I meet with thee.

(I.i.168–178)

³⁹ *Hermia:* God speed fair Helena! Whither away?
  Helena: Call you me fair? That fair again unsay.
    Demetrius loves you fair. O happy fair!
    Your eyes are lodestars, and your tongue's sweet air
    More tunable than lark to shepherd's ear,
    When wheat is green, when hawthorn buds appear.
    Sickness is catching. O, were favour so,
    Yours would I catch, fair Hermia, ere I go.

(I.i.180–187)

⁴⁰ *Hermia:* I give him curses, yet he gives me love.
  Helena: O that my prayers could such affection move!
  Hermia: The more I hate, the more he follows me.
  Helena: The more I love, the more he hateth me.
  Hermia: His folly, Helena, is no fault of mine.
  Helena: None, but your beauty: would that fault were mine!
  Hermia: Take comfort. He no more shall see my face;
    Lysander and myself will fly this place.

(I.i.196–203)

between them. For it is against the weight of Lysander's own dark and newly-discovered foreboding that this energy and passion of Hermia's have themselves been aroused, and the support he needs has been found and given. The strength of conviction and firmness of address which she now brings to 'My good Lysander! I swear to thee . . ./ By all the vows that ever men have broke'³⁸ are responses awakened in her by the fainting of his spirits. And in it there seems to be, against whatever odds, the truest feeling.

It is now as friend to friend that Hermia greets her jealous foe with a 'God speed fair Helena!'³⁹ 'Call you me fair?' the other answers near to tears. And when Hermia takes her hand, against the rivalry of the lines⁴⁰, to console her for her bitterness at failing to win the love of Demetrius, it is now a tender sympathy in the midst of contention which Helena finds in Hermia. Against frustrated male anger, here is a sisterhood in sorrow, and in Hermia's seemingly slender role, a largeness of hitherto unsuspected feeling. That Demetrius loves her and not Helena, Hermia says, is 'his folly' and 'no fault of mine'⁴⁰. 'None, but your beauty,' says Helena sadly, slipping Hermia's handclasp, as physically solitary now and as deep in longing as was Theseus. 'Take comfort,'⁴⁰ Hermia tells her – and in the poignant simplicity of it, is a passionate and loving gesture of reassurance.

Watching it in silence, and cloaked on their scaffold like vultures in a tree's topmost branches, wings folded, the other actors' presence heightens expectation further. It sharply narrows the focus of concentration, to what now seem tragically doomed movements below them. Within the vulnerable artifice of a 'play', it is as if we are being presented with the irony of 'acting' and love's illusion together. Moreover, it is not *Pyramus and Thisby* but *A Midsummer Night's Dream* which is, or has become, the 'lamentable comedy'. And when Bottom asks 'What is Pyramus?'⁴¹, Quince's desolate reply – 'A lover that kills himself . . . for love'⁴¹ – is of a melancholy which for the first time answers fully to the other lovers' darkest impulses. 'That will ask some tears in the true performing of it,' Bottom comments. Today, it is as true of one play as of the other.

The long weeks of rehearsal are coming to new fruition. The listeners on their gantry do not merely overlook, but seem to threaten, the actors on *terra firma*. 'The raging rocks/ And shivering shocks/ Shall break the locks/ Of prison gates,'⁴¹ Bottom declaims giddily, his virtuosity rushing to his head and greeted with applause by the other mechanicals. But above them, other hands now move in unison. It is a

41 *Bottom:* What is Pyramus? A lover, or a tyrant?
   Quince: A lover that kills himself, most gallant, for love.
   Bottom: That will ask some tears in the true performing of it . . . yet
   my chief humour is for a tyrant. I could play Ercles rarely, or a
   part to tear a cat in, to make all split.
                    The raging rocks
                    And shivering shocks
                    Shall break the locks
                    Of prison gates;
                    And Phibbus' car
                    Shall shine from far,
                    And make and mar
                    The foolish Fates.
   This was lofty! Now name the rest of the players.

                                                          (*I.ii.18–33*)

42 *Snug:* Have you the lion's part written? Pray you, if it be, give it me,
   for I am slow of study.
   Quince: You may do it extempore, for it is nothing but roaring.
   Bottom: Let me play the lion too. I will roar that I will do any man's
   heart good to hear me. I will roar, that I will make the Duke say,
   'Let him roar again, let him roar again.'
   Quince: An you should do it too terribly, you would fright the
   Duchess and the ladies, that they would shriek; and that were
   enough to hang us all . . .
   Bottom: . . . I will aggravate my voice so that I will roar you as gently
   as any sucking dove; I will roar you an 'twere any nightingale.
   Quince: You can play no part but Pyramus, for Pyramus is a sweet-
   faced man; a proper man as one shall see in a summer's day; a most
   lovely, gentlemanlike man: therefore you must needs play Pyramus.
   Bottom: Well, I will undertake it. What beard were I best to play it
   in?
   Quince: Why, what you will.
   Bottom: I will discharge it in either your straw-colour beard, your
   orange-tawny beard, your purple-in-grain beard, or your French-
   crown-colour beard, your perfit yellow.
   Quince: Some of your French crowns have no hair at all, and then
   you will play barefaced. But, masters, here are your parts; and I am
   to entreat you, request you, and desire you, to con them by
   tomorrow night; and meet me in the palace wood, a mile without
   the town, by moonlight . . .

menacing motion, and soundless at a distance, as if an incubus, hydra-headed, were brooding upon innocence at its harmless pleasures. Now, shadows deepen even around Snug's pitiably small part as Lion. It is 'nothing but roaring,'[42] Quince apologetically tells him. Downcast, but as passionate as a lover, the slow-witted Snug sets to roaring. But Bottom, greedy for the Lion's share also, roars against him[42]. Absurdly, they pit their roars against each other in crescendo. And into Snug's roaring comes, or seems to come, the same pent-up anger of a will frustrated which has today seemed to darken all expression. Snug, heart in mouth, seems to be fighting for his lonely life as actor, just as thwarted love in the previous scene despaired for its requital.

Quince stops the contest. But now his warning to Snug, heard in silence by the dark and unmoving figures above them, that 'an you should do it too terribly, you would fright the ladies . . . and that were enough to hang us all,'[42] is no longer either solicitous or comic. It is instead an admonition spoken with an anxiety momentarily close to tragic despair, in which Quince's authority seems as solitary and melancholic as that of the Duke of Athens himself. And, today, as he refuses the part of Lion to Bottom, there is in Quince's preoccupation an echo of that very inwardness and distance which had earlier seemed to isolate Theseus from his fellow-actors. 'You can play no part but Pyramus,' Quince says, distracted and withdrawing, 'for Pyramus is a sweet-faced man.'[42] Now, the cajolery[42] of Bottom (who needs no persuading) into the part of Pyramus is all the more light-hearted for the dark moments which preceded it; as if feeling itself were being deepened by the *chiaroscuro*, and every impulse heightened.

Now, too, the merriment which greets Quince's and Bottom's jests on the subject of beards, syphilis and baldness[42], is as full-bodied as the answering laughter from the heights above them is hollow. Every tone, light and dark, seems enriched, not coarsened, by its partner. The innocence of the mechanicals and the spirits' menace gain in force from each other, the comic sharpens its wits on the tragic, while the real and the imagined dance attendance on the spectators together. The mechanicals are in the very highest of spirits at the end of the First Act[42]; there is a bedlam of yelling and heedless laughter, watched in silence from the scaffold. Snug roars to his heart's content, the jovial Bottom – climbing a ladder – roisters with his fellows, and the busy Quince fixes the time and place for their next rehearsal. Melancholy and anger are being held at bay in a storm of shouting. 'Enough!'

Bottom: We will meet; and there we may rehearse most obscenely and courageously. Take pains; be perfit; adieu.

Quince: At the Duke's Oak we meet.

Bottom: Enough; hold or cut bowstrings. (*Exeunt*)

(*I.ii.58–98*)

43 (*ACT TWO. Scene One. A wood near Athens. Enter a FAIRY at one door, and PUCK at another*)

Puck: How now spirit! Whither wander you?

Fairy: Over hill, over dale,
   Thorough bush, thorough brier,
   Over park, over pale,
   Thorough flood, thorough fire,
   I do wander everywhere,
   Swifter than the moon's sphere.

(*II.i.1–7*)

44 *Fairy:* Farewell, thou lob of spirits; I'll be gone.
   Our Queen and all her elves come here anon.
Puck: The King doth keep his revels here tonight.
   Take heed the Queen come not within his sight.
   For Oberon is passing fell and wrath,
   Because that she as her attendant hath
   A lovely boy, stolen from an Indian king.

(*II.i.16–22*)

45 *Puck:*   Thou speakest aright;
   I am that merry wanderer of the night,
   I jest to Oberon, and make him smile,
   When I a fat and bean-fed horse beguile,
   Neighing in likeness of a filly foal:
   And sometime lurk I in a gossip's bowl,
   In very likeness of a roasted crab;
   And when she drinks, against her lips I bob . . .
   . . . But, room, fairy! Here comes Oberon.
Fairy: And here my mistress. Indeed that he were gone!
            (*Enter OBERON at one door, with his train;*
                and TITANIA, at another, with hers)
Oberon: Ill met by moonlight, proud Titania.

(*II.i.42–60*)

shouts Bottom into the clamour. 'Hold!' he says, as the noise and movement engulf him, 'or . . . cut bowstrings'[42]. His voice is resonant, but today his glance is strangely withdrawn and distant. There is in turn a split-second of slack-jawed incomprehension in the actors, stunned (for the first time, here) at words which appear to be, and perhaps are, beyond meaning. It is a sudden and eerie stroke of dumbfounded invention, this instant of astonishment and hesitation. And in it, there swiftly opens up for the spectator too a gaping prospect – mouths blackened 'O's – in which all the senses might lose their focus, and the whole stricken world its bearings.

That even the entry of Puck, as the Second Act begins[43], should be overseen by courtiers calmly watching from their heights, now seems a deeper irony than ever. This is not man observed by spirits, but vice-versa; is masquerade upon masquerade, vista within vista. For the courtiers are, like us, being made knowing familiars of a world, Puck's world, which is designed to deceive them. Yet they are strangely insouciant and smiling, witnesses who must look – or so we, watching *them*, imagine – without seeing. Moreover, as if suspended in air, these earthlings look down upon aerial spirits, grounded before us; elevated humans, standing in judgment over the (as if) superhuman beneath them. Puck is overheard and under surveillance. 'How now, spirit! Whither wander you?'[43], he peremptorily asks of the Fairy. A demand, not a greeting, it also is spoken under pressure of the First Act's passions, and charged with the same melancholy anger; there is a rage of the mind coursing, and it is driven 'thorough flood, thorough fire . . ./ Swifter than the moon's sphere'[43]. And that 'the King doth keep his revels here tonight'[44] is today not a promise of joys, but a forewarning of tempest, while in Oberon's temper, 'passing fell and wrath', is a new truth and a new rightness.

Even Puck's wit is now edged with spleen, and his jests laced with ill-humour. 'Thou speakest aright;/ I am that merry wanderer of the night'[45] seems mordant and world-weary; Puck's very voice is biting. 'I jest to Oberon, and make him smile,/ When I a fat and bean-fed horse beguile'[45] has turned (or been twisted) to a wry and cruel grimace. There is wincing and spite in it, not laughter; not mirth, but anger. 'Room, fairy! Here comes Oberon'[45] is no faery and breathless whisper (fairy to fairy), but a spat of Puck's fear for his fierce master; and 'Ill met by moonlight, proud Titania'[45] a spiked crown of thorns, spleen's black flower.

This is all in a dark key, its rhythm irritated by dissension and

46 *Oberon:* How canst thou thus for shame, Titania,
    Glance at my credit with Hippolyta,
    Knowing I know thy love to Theseus?
    Didst not thou lead him through the glimmering night
    From Perigenia, whom he ravishèd?
    And make him with fair Aegles break his faith,
    With Ariadne and Antiopa?
  Titania: These are the forgeries of jealousy . . .
    . . . with thy brawls thou hast disturbed our sport . . .
    The ox hath therefore stretched his yoke in vain,
    The plowman lost his sweat, and the green corn
    Hath rotted ere his youth attained a beard;
    The fold stands empty in the drownèd field,
    And crows are fatted with the murrion flock . . .
    Therefore the moon, the governess of floods,
    Pale in her anger, washes all the air,
    That rheumatic diseases do abound.
    And thorough this distemperature we see
    The seasons alter . . .
    . . . The spring, the summer,
    The childing autumn, angry winter, change
    Their wonted liveries; and the mazèd world,
    By their increase, now knows not which is which.
    And this same progeny of evils comes
    From our debate, from our dissension:
    We are their parents and original.

                                (*II.i.74–117*)

47 *Oberon:* Why should Titania cross her Oberon?
    I do but beg a little changeling boy,
    To be my henchman.
  Titania: Set your heart at rest.
    The fairy land buys not the child of me.
    His mother was a vot'ress of my order . . .
    And sat with me on Neptune's yellow sands,
    Marking th' embarkèd traders on the flood;
    When we have laughed to see the sails conceive
    And grow big-bellied with the wanton wind . . .
    And for her sake do I rear up her boy,
    And for her sake I will not part with him.

discord. Oberon's 'How canst thou thus for shame, Titania,/ Glance at my credit with Hippolyta,/ Knowing I know thy love to Theseus?'[46] is now a jaded lovers' quarrel, streaked through with a lover's hatred. Titania's response is a swift riposte, not an answer. 'These are the forgeries of jealousy!'[46] she shouts at him. Fiery and watched over with a cool nonchalance from the gantry, she is being carried on a jagged impulse and a tide of hot blood towards Oberon's revenge, and Bottom's animal embraces. Her seething speech, of 'brawls' and 'diseases', of 'mockery' and 'evil', makes her now as 'pale in her anger'[46] as the moon she speaks of. Her compassion, a melancholy humour, for the ox who has 'stretched his yoke in vain'[46] and for the toiling plowman in a distempered season, when the corn rots and 'the fold stands empty'[46], is pity come to grief and poetry turned to anguish.

Today Oberon folds her in his arms for comfort, as 'we see the seasons alter'[46] in her own turbulent voice and gesture. Shielding her, in heat, from 'hoary-headed frosts' and 'angry winter'[46], she arches herself, chafing, against him. A 'Queen of the Fairies' with a body all-too-human, sexuality and hatred, anger and sorrow, have here come to their tautest conjunction: 'hot ice' enflamed, but unmelting. 'And this same progeny of evils,' Titania whispers, recoiling (and still under surveillance), 'comes . . . from our dissension.'[46] She is as if horror-struck at this conjuring-up of a 'mazèd' world, unhinged by conflict. For, like us, she fears truth's dissolution, when season is entwined with season, daylight's clarities with night's dreaming, and – on the verge of her own bewitching – reality with illusion.

Today, there is a knife-to-throat tension in it which briefly stills all urge to superfluous movement. It holds the spectator-actors on their scaffold to a fixated staring; it makes us, through them, hang upon each fleeting shift of emotion and change of cadence, as if life itself depended upon it.

'Set your heart at rest,'[47] says Titania, and for an instant a perfect comfort overflows us. But, in the very next, 'the fairy land buys not the child of me'[47] seems to dash the prospect of concord for ever. Her rejection of Oberon's strange request for 'a little changeling boy, to be my henchman'[47] is now as cold and harsh as the solace of their bodies, moments before, was warming: swift mood-swings which carry explosively pent-up feeling back and forth with them, in a fixed arc from anger to anger. (It is drawing new truths from the text, while at the same time taxing the actors' invention and endurance.) 'The sails'

. . . *Oberon:* Give me that boy, and I will go with thee.
Titania: Not for thy fairy kingdom. Fairies, away!
   We shall chide downright, if I longer stay.
                          (*Exeunt TITANIA with her train*)
Oberon: Well, go thy way. Thou shalt not from this grove
   Till I torment thee for this injury.
   My gentle Puck, come hither.

                                           (*II.i.119–148*)

48 *Oberon:*   Thou rememb'rest
   Since once I sat upon a promontory,
   And hear a mermaid, on a dolphin's back . . .
   . . . That very time I saw, but thou couldst not,
   Flying between the cold moon and the earth,
   Cupid all armed. A certain aim he took
   At a fair vestal thronèd by the west,
   And loosed his love shaft smartly from his bow,
   As it should pierce a hundred thousand hearts . . .
   It fell upon a little western flower,
   Before milk-white, now purple with love's wound,
   And maidens call it love-in-idleness.
   Fetch me that flow'r.

                                           (*II.i.148–168*)

49 *Oberon:* I'll watch Titania when she is asleep,
   And drop the liquor of it in her eyes.
   The next thing then she waking looks upon,
   Be it on lion, bear, or wolf, or bull,
   On meddling monkey, or on busy ape,
   She shall pursue it with the soul of love.
   And ere I take this charm from off her sight . . .
   I'll make her render up her page to me.
   But who comes here? I am invisible . . .
                    (*Enter DEMETRIUS, HELENA following him*)
Demetrius: I love thee not, therefore pursue me not . . .
   Hence, get thee gone, and follow me no more.

                                           (*II.i.177–194*)

50 *Demetrius:* Do I entice you? Do I speak you fair?
   Or, rather, do I not in plainest truth
   Tell you, I do not nor I cannot love you?

                                           (*II.i.199–200*)

which today 'conceive' upon Titania's tongue, and 'grow big-bellied with the wanton wind' now move to her sensuous rhythm – only to be wrecked in rage, at the tide's quick turning. 'I will not part with him!'[47] Titania declares, angered by Oberon's own angry longing. 'Give me that boy!'[47] he demands fiercely, as she makes to leave, her feelings not merely aroused but rampant, and her disdain for him itself become sexual.

Now there is as wild a craving in Titania as there is in Oberon. Suddenly kissing him with a desire near to devouring, she clasps his head in her hands as if she were Salome, and he John the Baptist. The Sugar-Plum Fairy has been transfigured. It is as if, too, there is a lust in all this which can only be satisfied with pleasures which are forbidden. 'Thou shalt not from this grove,'[47] Oberon says when she has gone, 'till I torment thee for this injury.' And as he summons Puck to do his bidding, his fellow-actors look down upon his plans for vendetta. Today, his voice and demeanour are fresh with menace. But there is once more the deep tone of melancholy in his anger, as well as of a fierce calculation. It is cruelty with a vengeance, yet with a harsh passion in it which Oberon will sate vicariously, and Titania directly, through the innocent Bottom – with two sets of spectators to attend upon them. 'My gentle Puck, come hither,'[47] Oberon commands, a controlled violence in his gesture and his voice's coldly jesting tone threatening to bring down the heavens. It is speech as hard and cutting as a diamond, his 'flying between the cold moon and the earth'[48] as piercing as the 'fiery shaft' of Cupid which is its subject.

For the first time, too, Oberon's anger is ridden, or driven, beyond mere bad temper, as if a sexual rage, 'purple with love's wound',[48] were bleeding before us. 'I'll watch Titania when she is asleep,'[49] Oberon tells Puck, his eye glinting to the mounting of his desire, as if he were an Othello with his Iago. And when she awakes enchanted, he will gloatingly see her dote 'on lion, bear, or wolf, or bull'[49]; and force her, thus transported, to 'render up her page to me'[49]. Flower both of desire and melancholy, as confounded in him as in his double, Theseus, this has become more devilry than enchantment. In the quick of Oberon's satanic anger and excitement, there is now no sprite, and nothing spritely. Even 'I am invisible'[49] is Oberon-as-Prospero, or Magus.

At the lovers' entrance[49], the long spell – too long – remains unbroken. Demetrius 'I love thee not, therefore pursue me not'[49] and 'Do I entice you? Do I speak you fair?'[50] are not merely caught by the

51 *Helena:* The more you beat me, I will fawn on you.
   Use me but as your spaniel, spurn me, strike me.
   Neglect me, lose me; only give me leave,
   Unworthy as I am, to follow you . . .
   Demetrius: Tempt not too much the hatred of my spirit,
   For I am sick when I do look on thee.

(*II.i.204–212*)

52 *Oberon:* A sweet Athenian lady is in love
   With a disdainful youth. Anoint his eyes . . .
   And look thou meet me ere the first cock crow.
   Puck: Fear not, my lord, your servant shall do so.

(*Exeunt*)
(*II.i.260–268*)

53   (*Enter OBERON and squeezes the flower*
                        on TITANIA's eyelids)
Oberon: What thou seest when thou dost wake,
   Do it for thy truelove take . . .
   Be it ounce, or cat, or bear,
   Pard, or boar with bristled hair,
   In thy eye that shall appear
   When thou wak'st, it is thy dear.
   Wake when some vile thing is near.   (*Exit*)

(*II.ii.27–34*)

54 *Hermia:* So far be distant; and, good night, sweet friend.
   Thy love ne'er alter till thy sweet life end!
   Lysander: Amen, amen, to that fair prayer, say I,
   And then end life when I end loyalty!
   Here is my bed. Sleep give thee all his rest!
   Hermia: With half that wish the wisher's eyes be pressed!

(*They sleep*)
(*II.ii.57–65*)

55 *Puck:* Churl, upon thy eyes I throw
   All the power this charm doth owe.
   When thou wak'st, let love forbid
   Sleep his seat on thy eyelid.
   So awake when I am gone,
   For I must now to Oberon.

(*II.ii.78–83*)

heels in hanging wire, but white-hot with hatred. And suddenly Brook, silent for nearly an hour, shouts them to silence. Once more, the lovers have become *bêtes noires* all, and sitting targets. What was proper to Oberon and Titania is in them a thoughtless display of 'generalized feeling'; what was passion in the spirits is 'emotionalism' in the lovers. 'I feel terror blocking my response,' Demetrius apologetically tells Brook. Brook ignores him. They are 'wasting their time,' Brook tells them. What he knows, but does not say, is that there must now be tranquil moments, *andante*, after such intensely sustained invention. There must be love, not mania, in Demetrius and Helena; hurt, but not anger. It is the minor key, not the major. Helena's 'The more you beat me, I will fawn on you'[51] is not Masoch's perversion but plain love's pleading. And Demetrius' 'Tempt not too much the hatred of my spirit,/ For I am sick when I do look on thee'[51] is unhappy youth's excess, not a Grand Guignol passion.

But Brook, tiring together with the actors, has stopped their momentum with his intervention. In any case, tension has its own apogee, beyond which lies only satiety and impatience. Instead, there are technical variations to work on, which serve to relieve the pressure. Oberon and Puck will be raised up at the end of Act Two, Scene One ('And look thou meet me ere the first cock crow'[52]), and fly away for their *exeunt* – to return by air for the 'flower squeezing'[53], as Brook puts it. He now suggests that this bewitching of Titania should itself take place upon trapezes, with Oberon, Puck and Titania suspended all three, and floating. (It will make a pretty picture of it, or a pantomime tableau on pulleys.) And as the drops of 'love-in-idleness', the 'little western flower', are laid upon her 'sleeping eyelids', and Oberon prays that she 'wake when some vile thing is near'[53], it is the sound of a 'pard, or boar with bristled hair'[53] which we will hear. A 'sexual roar', Brook decides, not a high-pitched scream, will now signal the moment of Titania's enchantment, or undoing.

Gone too, after peremptory discussion, are Hermia's and Lysander's sung exchanges which follow, as Titania sleeps close by them. 'Amen, amen, to that fair prayer, say I,'[54] chanted (tunelessly) by Lysander since the early days of rehearsal, has gone for a burton. The long-discovered impulse has been as quickly discarded. Now, when the sleeping Lysander is in turn bewitched[55], he will clutch at Puck's legs and thighs, as if starting in fear from his fitful slumbers: a troubled gesture which will speak in the play's darkest and most anxious rhythms, and tell us – again – of Shakespeare's (or Brook's) nightmarish dreaming.

56 *Helena:* O, I am out of breath in this fond chase!
  The more my prayer, the lesser is my grace.
  Happy is Hermia, wheresoe'er she lies,
  For she hath blessèd and attractive eyes.
  How came her eyes so bright? Not with salt tears.
  If so, my eyes are oft'ner washed than hers.
  No, no, I am as ugly as a bear,
  For beasts that meet me run away for fear . . .
  But who is here? Lysander! On the ground!
  Dead? Or asleep? I see no blood, no wound.
  Lysander, if you live, good sir, awake.
  Lysander: (*Awaking*) And run through fire I will for thy sweet sake.
  (II.ii.88–103)

57 *Helena:* Wherefore was I to this keen mockery born?
  When at your hands did I deserve this scorn? . . .
  O, that a lady, of one man refused,
  Should of another therefore be abused! (*Exit*)
  Lysander: She sees not Hermia. Hermia, sleep thou there,
  And never mayst thou come Lysander near!
  For as a surfeit of the sweetest things
  The deepest loathing to the stomach brings . . .
  So thou, my surfeit and my heresy,
  Of all be hated, but the most of me!
  (II.ii.123–142)

58 *Hermia:* (*Awaking*) Help me, Lysander, help me! Do thy best
  To pluck this crawling serpent from my breast!
  Ay me, for pity! What a dream was here!
  Lysander, look how I do quake with fear . . .
  Lysander! What, removed? Lysander! Lord!
  What, out of hearing? Gone? No sound, no word?
  Alack, where are you?
  (II.ii.145–153)

59 *ACT THREE. Scene One. The wood. TITANIA lying asleep.*
  Enter QUINCE, SNUG, BOTTOM, FLUTE, SNOUT and
  STARVELING.
  Bottom: Are we all met?
  Quince: Pat, pat; and here's a marvellous convenient place for our
  rehearsal. This green plot shall be our stage, this hawthorn brake
  our tiring house.
  (III.i.1–4)

The technical *intermezzo* is over; and Brook's exasperation, with it. Indeed, Helena's 'O, I am out of breath in this fond chase'[56] rejoins us, now without demur, to the moods reached earlier by Oberon and Titania. For the first time, it is deepening towards the tragic. 'How came her eyes so bright?'[56] is no longer mere rivalry, pert and petty, but touched at its heart with melancholy; 'I am as ugly as a bear,'[56] a painful passion, closer to anguish than to self-pity. And in Helena's fearful discovery, lest it be Demetrius, of a man's body – 'But who is here? Lysander! On the ground! Dead? Or asleep?'[56] – there is no conventional 'female' alarm, coyly frightened, but for the briefest moment death's shadow and love's bereavement. Lysander's waking and his embrace of Helena is now a relief to us also, so close to us is such feeling; his enchanted fondness for her, though she does not share it, a solace which touches the spectator. That contention follows, as fierce as that between Oberon and Titania, is now also a tragic irony. For love, mistaking, is making 'keen mockery'[57] of Helena's longings for her lover. 'O, that a lady, of one man refused,/ Should of another therefore be abused!' is now spoken in sexual anger, the anger (and sadness) of a woman who thinks that her ill-favour and isolation are being exploited by Lysander.

In turn, Lysander's bewitched anger and hatred for Hermia, innocently sleeping, is now fired with a cruel energy far beyond reason[57]. Today, this mistaking evokes only pity for Hermia. For she, in her turn, awakes as alone as Helena[58], pleading for help from Lysander, who has already left her. 'Lysander,' she says, today quiet and trusting in him, 'look how I do quake with fear!'[58] But he has gone, leaving her to her needs, and to our compassion. And though she now fumbled over her discovery[58] of Lysander's desertion, missing her way from intimacy to isolation, and from fear to sorrow, there will be a new truth in these moments. As the act ends, Brook tells her that 'we will work on it together' – and then, as if he were Alice, calls for Max Reinhardt's rabbit.

The casual proposal of an earlier rehearsal that a real animal should be introduced into 'the wood' of Act Three[59] (made of wire and gantries), is now met by a grey rabbit. It is set down, with something close to a simper, by one of the more tender-hearted fairies. Nose twitching, it faces the clownish onrush of Quince, Bottom and the others for only a moment . . . and then bolts for it, tail bobbing. Its custodian must recover it. He revolts, aghast and pouting. He will not do it. He is in a pet over it, indignant and sulking. He will not, he says to

⁶⁰ *Quince:* Then, there is another thing: we must have a wall in the great
chamber; for Pyramus and Thisby, says the story, did talk through
the chink of a wall.

Snout: You can never bring in a wall. What say you, Bottom?

Bottom: Some man or other must present Wall: and let him have
some plaster, or some loam, or some roughcast about him, to
signify Wall; and let him hold his fingers thus, and through the
cranny shall Pyramus and Thisby whisper.

(*III.i.54–63*)

⁶¹ *Snout:* O Bottom, thou art changed! What do I see on thee?

Bottom: What do you see? You see an ass head of your own, do you?

(*Exit SNOUT. Enter QUINCE*)

Quince: Bless thee, Bottom! Bless thee! Thou art translated. (*Exit*)

(*III.i.105–109*)

⁶² *Titania:* And I do love thee. Therefore, go with me.
I'll give thee fairies to attend on thee,
And they shall fetch thee jewels from the deep,
And sing, while thou on pressèd flowers dost sleep:
And I will purge thy mortal grossness so,
That thou shall like an airy spirit go.

(*III.i.142–147*)

⁶³ *Titania:* Come, wait upon him; lead him to my bower,
The moon methinks looks with a wat'ry eye;
And when she weeps, weeps every little flower,
Lamenting some enforcèd chastity.
Tie up my lover's tongue, bring him silently.

(*Exit TITANIA with BOTTOM and Fairies*)

(*III.i.182–186*)

Brook, 'submit him to these frights'. There is oafish laughter from the other actors. 'His terrors,' he announces, mouth puckering and near to stamping his foot, 'were not funny.' Arms akimbo, the mechanicals bellow at these fairy flounces. But it is the end of Brook's rabbit.

'Are we all met?'[59] asks Bottom, subsiding. 'Pat, pat,' says Quince, as off-stage the rabbit is noisily recaptured. Both rehearsals are distracted. Yet it is also as if the actors are relieved to have come down at last from their high tension. In low-key and *sotto voce*, they seem to draw away from engagement with their complex roles, as well as from their audience. But the result of their seeming unconcern paradoxically rivets the attention. Preoccupied with the technical problems of *Pyramus and Thisby*[60], their acting appears to be unaware of itself. And the lines, only half-articulated, seem theirs not Shakespeare's. They stand on the stage, speak and move, but as if they were not actors. Is this closer to the 'real', or a bad rehearsal? (Might it be both together?) Are they even aware of their own introversion? Is it lapse or achievement? Is it the result of preceding artifice and contrivance, or its negation? Are they catching their breaths, or is it inspiration?

Once again, it is Bottom who extricates both actor and spectator from such passivity and speculation. A clown's red nose is stand-in for the ass's nole. But today so changed is he by it – or so we wish to imagine – and so fearstruck his fellows, that in our eyes it will make-do for all the world's terrors, both childish and adult. 'Bless thee, Bottom! Bless thee! Thou art translated'[61] is, once more, a sacramental response to his monstrous appearance. It is Shakespeare's words made (horse)flesh, a red-nosed transubstantiation. 'And I do love thee. Therefore go with me,'[62] Titania tells this satyr, her sexual anguish now drawn from those nether regions where a Bosch could couple man with monster. Kissing him, Titania seems as if she might dissolve the hardy Bottom into a liquefaction. 'I will purge thy mortal grossness so,/ That thou shalt like an airy spirit go'[62], now seems a plain promise of sexual release in the bliss of orgasm.

And as the scene carries Titania and Bottom to the acme of their pleasures,[63] so today's sexual anger and melancholy also reach their highest point of tension. The ass's phallus – or spirit-arm erected – is fiercely celebrated. The crowd of actors serves as swarming acolytes at this sexual worship; with spinning plates, jugglery and streamers; with merriment on trapezes and Mendelssohn swirling about them. Bottom, arms raised in heroic conquest, rides above it; grimacing man, transported.

257

Seventh week, first day

It is the beginning of the final week of rehearsal. The exercises are slack and listless. 'Everyone,' Brook is saying, sitting at a table, 'should go quickly to a physical manoeuvre or challenge, with an instinctive pleasure.' Last week's rehearsals ran the gamut from failure in performance to a triumph, in private – and had left Bottom in Titania's bower. Now, effort and pains-taking must resume, as if against the grain and on a tired Monday morning. (But the casualness is less listless than it seems. There is anticipation in it, and energy in reserve.) 'The difficulty about the play,' Brook tells the actors as they gather round him, 'is that the pouring out of a torrent of words, the act of writing, was a spontaneous act of physical joy in creation. [Nothing is more unlikely.] When the rehearsal began, I used the loose comparison with singing, to give an analogy with the form of this joy. But the problem in this theatre,' Brook says, his head gesturing with a barely perceptible nod to the building around him, is ' "How can you take a piece of writing which is not in contemporary forms, and find your way to that same kind of pleasure in the material?" '

The question, essentially just, nevertheless contains its own rhetoric. For it is grounded in a growing sense, on Brook's part, of potentiality in the actors and of confidence in the reach of this production. 'Compare any Irishman on a Saturday night after closing-time,' Brook continues, 'producing words for the pleasure of producing them.' This is a stage-Irishman in his cups, and full of blarney. 'I have seen improvisation of verse in Persia, where two men take alternate lines from each other, communicating with each other – and to others – through their pleasure in lyrical invention. So that looking at this play as something archaic or a matter of mere technique, a chore or work purely, is not the way. I cannot tell you to be joyful,' he says, 'I can only eliminate the useless solutions.'

The actors are calm and studied. There is now achievement behind

¹ *ACT THREE. Scene Two. Another part of the wood. Enter*
   OBERON and PUCK.
   Oberon: I wonder if Titania be awaked;
      Then, what it was that next came in her eye,
      Which she must dote on in extremity.

                                                        (*III.ii.1–3*)

² *Puck:* A crew of patches, rude mechanicals,
      That work for bread upon Athenian stalls,
      Were met together to rehearse a play,
      Intended for great Theseus' nuptial day.
      The shallowest thickskin of that barren sort,
      Who Pyramus presented in their sport,
      Forsook his scene, and entered in a brake.
      When I did him at this advantage take,
      An ass's nole I fixèd on his head.
      Anon his Thisby must be answerèd,
      And forth my mimic comes. When they him spy,
      As wild geese that the creeping fowler eye,
      Or russet-pated choughs, many in sort,
      Rising and cawing at the gun's report,
      Sever themselves and madly sweep the sky,
      So, at his sight, away his fellows fly.

                                                        (*III.ii.9–24*)

³ *Demetrius:* O, why rebuke you him that loves you so?
      Lay breath so bitter on your bitter foe.
   Hermia: Now I but chide; but I should use thee worse,
      For thou, I fear, hast given me cause to curse.
      If thou hast slain Lysander in his sleep,
      Being o'er shoes in blood, plunge in the deep,
      And kill me too.
      The sun was not so true unto the day
      As he to me. Would he have stolen away
      From sleeping Hermia?

                                                        (*III.ii.43–52*)

⁴ *Demetrius:* You spend your passion on a misprised mood:
      I am not guilty of Lysander's blood;
      Nor is he dead, for aught that I can tell.
   Hermia: I pray thee, tell me then that he is well.
   Demetrius: An if I could, what should I get therefore?

and before them, and no demurral in glance or gesture. 'When the taste is there, the rhythm of the play is alive. When there is strain, the true rhythm, which is endlessly vital, is missing.' They no longer seem puzzled. 'Though physical exercises can animate the group,' Brook goes on, 'there is a trap there also. You cannot substitute physical movement for the pulse and life of a speech, though they eventually go together. Imagine one hundred blind people listening to you. The fact that you swing on a trapeze is irrelevant. But the impulse which takes you to the trapeze, should be in what you say. It should be audible.' There is a contented silence. The actors are not so much listening, as waiting.

Brook has begun to spread himself into this silence. Time and space for speech have been gained by the growth of promise in the production. Thus, when Oberon and Puck resume in 'Another part of the wood'[1] (Act Three, Scene Two) Brook is quick to comment. At Puck's description of Bottom as 'the shallowest thickskin of that barren sort'[2], Brook tells him to 'think how vivid this line is. It is as good as anything in Joyce. Don't take it for granted. An Irishman,' he adds, 'would be smiling with pleasure if he'd thought of it.' And as the scene's simple rhyme-scheme resumes and begins to gather momentum[2], Brook interrupts the actors again to warn them against a carefully-stressed reading ('mechanical stress is the wrong route'), which 'replaces the life of the words.' He tells Puck instead to 'ask what particular virtue there is in rhyme'. He must not 'apologize for the verse, throwing away the rhyming words as if you preferred that they weren't there', but 'find in them a positive virtue and a source of joy'.

The rehearsal has been halted by the intervention, and Brook expands the moment. 'This is a surrealist situation,' he says comfortably, 'for all of us to be avoiding the rhyming, when it occurs throughout the play. We must ask rather: "In what way can repeated rhyming lines give strength to the character speaking them?" If the question is not answered, trapezes and so forth will be substitutes, into which something which is not alive will be fitted. The play also steps in and out of rhyme[3]. Since nothing is there by accident, why is this?' he asks the actors. 'What purposes and strengths are there in it? This must be discovered.' In this reading, the play is as much a score as a text – and not mere rhyming couplets, but a verbal music. The spoken word's prosaic limits are being challenged; verse, blank or rhyming, demands poetic justice. And it is not 'heightened' speech, nor a sung performance (neither Gilbert and Sullivan, nor Schoenberg's *Moses*

Hermia: A privilege, never to see me more.
And from thy hated presence part I so.
See me no more, whether he be dead or no.

(*Exit*)
(*III.ii.74–81*)

5 *Oberon:* What hast thou done? Thou hast mistaken quite,
And laid the love juice on some truelove's sight.
Of thy misprision must perforce ensue
Some true love turned, and not a false turned true.
Puck: Then fate o'errules, that, one man holding troth,
A million fail, confounding oath on oath.
Oberon: About the wood go swifter than the wind,
And Helena of Athens look thou find.
All fancy-sick she is and pale of cheer,
With sighs of love, that costs the fresh blood dear:
By some illusion see thou bring her here.
I'll charm his eyes against she do appear.
Puck: I go, I go; look how I go,
Swifter than arrow from the Tartar's bow.

(*Exit*)
(*III.ii.88–101*)

6 (*Enter LYSANDER and HELENA*)

Lysander: Why should you think that I should woo in scorn?
Scorn and derision never come in tears:
Look, when I vow, I weep; and vows so born,
In their nativity all truth appears.
How can these things in me seem scorn to you,
Bearing the badge of faith, to prove them true?
Helena: You do advance your cunning more and more.
When truth kills truth, O devilish-holy fray!
These vows are Hermia's: will you give her o'er?
Weigh oath with oath, and you will nothing weigh.
Your vows to her and me, put in two scales,
Will even weigh; and both as light as tales.
Lysander: I had no judgment when to her I swore.
Helena: Nor none, in my mind, now you give her o'er.
Lysander: Demetrius loves her, and he loves not you.
Demetrius: (*Awaking*) O Helen, goddess, nymph, perfect, divine!
To what, my love, shall I compare thine eyne?
Crystal is muddy. O, how ripe in show
Thy lips, those kissing cherries, tempting grow!

262

and Aaron), which Brook seeks from the actors, but a lyric-speaking which will open itself to the words' rhymes, as well as to their rhythms.

Rhyme in this scene means, too, that 'there is a constant wit and humour in it. Thought,' Brook says, 'is here more alive for being in rhyme. These rhyming exchanges are a source of life. They cannot be avoided.' Today, the actors will not be left to their own devices. 'The line as written,' Brook continues, 'must seem the only possible way of saying what is said. If you say it in such a way that it would be capable of paraphrase, you cannot communicate the life of it.' The actors' shoulders are once more being loaded – such fidelity to The Word is an onerous business. 'Every stress you give to a line,' Brook tells them, 'must be a commitment, not an accident nor a mechanical habit. It requires deep concentration from everyone, and increasing rigour.'

Within moments, the actors are again halted. 'Rhyme provides its own punctuation,' Brook says to Hermia and Demetrius[4]. If you know and feel the rhyme, let its finality fall into place. There is no need to stress it.' Rhyme had first been avoided, then chased and chivvied. Now it begins to find its own feet, as the actors move (spiritedly) from one rhymed response to another[5]. 'Stressing a word,' Brook adds for good measure, 'mechanically closes it. Expand the word from the inside. Try to find the thought within it. Then it will open,' he promises, 'and spread outwards across the other words around it.' The actors seem undaunted. Today, themselves translated, what Brook is saying seems both crystal-clear and true, rather than an opaque vision.

One word may even bear another word within it. This is not so much The Word made flesh, as pregnant with meaning. Thus, Lysander's 'Bearing the badge of faith to prove them true'[6], Brook now tells him, is not a matter of the 'badge of faith alone.' The word 'bearing', he says, 'brings it in'. The 'badge of faith' is enclosed or contained within the word 'bearing'; or, perhaps, the 'badge of faith' is borne along by 'bearing'. This seems a metaphysic of speech, and hard for the listener to fathom. Yet, today, it appears to possess for the actors its own dense aura of signification.

And within a few lines, Brook intervenes again. 'The zest and youth' of the play lies in the way the characters 'keep something going in the air'. Hence, Brook explains, there is a 'continuous maintenance of impulse, tit-for-tat, between the lovers.' (Constantly interrupted, the actors themselves are losing their stride. They have found the rhyme, but have lost their rhythm.) Thus, at 'Why should you think that I should woo in scorn'[6], there are six lines for Lysander, followed by six

That pure congealèd white, high Taurus' snow,
Fanned with the eastern wind, turns to a crow
When thou hold'st up thy hand: O, let me kiss
This princess of pure white, this seal of bliss!

(III.ii.122–124)

7 *Lysander:* Why seek'st thou me? Could not this make thee know,
  The hate I bare thee made me leave thee so?
Hermia: You speak not as you think: it cannot be.
Helena: Lo, she is one of this confederacy!
  Now I perceive they have conjoined all three
  To fashion this false sport, in spite of me.
  Injurious Hermia! Most ungrateful maid!
  Have you conspired, have you with these contrived
  To bait me with this foul derision?
  Is all the counsel that we two have shared,
  The sister's vows, the hours that we have spent,
  When we have chid the hasty-footed time
  For parting us – O, is all forgot?

(III.ii.189–201)

8 *Helena:* And will you rent our ancient love asunder,
  To join with men in scorning your poor friend?
  It is not friendly, 'tis not maidenly.
  Our sex, as well as I, may chide you for it,
  Though I alone do feel the injury.
Hermia: I am amazèd at your passionate words.
  I scorn you not. It seems that you scorn me.
Helena: Have you not set Lysander, as in scorn,
  To follow me and praise my eyes and face?
  And made your other love, Demetrius,
  Who even but now did spurn me with his foot,
  To call me goddess, nymph, divine and rare,
  Precious, celestial?

(III.ii.215–227)

9 *Lysander:* Helen, I love thee; by my life, I do!
  I swear by that which I will lose for thee,
  To prove him false that says I love thee not.
Demetrius: I say I love thee more than he can do.
Lysander: If thou say so, withdraw and prove it too.
Demetrius: Quick, come!
Hermia: Lysander, whereto tends all this?

for Helena, similarly structured, which bring them deeper – and at an even pace – into a mutual mistaking. Likewise, in the swift and complementary alternation of single lines which follows[6] is 'an animated life', a life which is 'sustained between them'. Moreover, the enchanted Demetrius now wakes[6] not only to crossed love's tangled rhythms, but also to a rhyme which promises, and will later bring, a perfect reconciliation. 'O, let me kiss/ This princess of pure white, this seal of bliss!'[6] he exclaims to Helena. It is a rhyme, Brook tells Demetrius, which is also 'part of his exalted feeling', and in which the actor 'must catch the pleasure of this flight of inspiration'.

Today, rediscovered and – however haltingly – celebrated, the rigours of blank verse are giving way to rhyme's pleasures. As a result, the abrupt ending of rhyme in Helena's long and bitter accusation[7] of Hermia's supposed conspiracy against her, now contains its own more audible meaning. That is, without rhyme, 'something more spontaneous comes into the movement of feeling,' Brook tells Helena. 'You yourself must feel,' he says, 'the underlying necessity for this torrent of words. You must feel you have to open up for them.' And it is this impulse, Brook declares, which 'takes Helena out of rhyme' and into a freer rhythm. (Helena herself is addressed, but not consulted. It is as if she must speak on Brook's account, while Brook speaks on Shakespeare's.) 'A much greater inner animation is at work,' Brook warns her, which is 'fancy-sick' and now too disordered for the assurances and symmetries of the rhyming couplet.

No sooner said, than done: Helena's speech is a headstrong rush of emotion in turmoil, her thoughts and feelings tumbling headlong over one another[8]. 'I am amazèd at your passionate words,'[8] Hermia tells her; for it is a passion barely able to catch its breath, which has slipped rhyme's halter and bolted. Yet, as crossed love becomes a cat's cradle of riotously entangled impulses[9], Brook again impatiently stops the actors. Called on a few minutes ago to find 'pleasure' in words and 'joy' in their expression, they are now being restrained from their desire for freedom of speech and movement. It is as if Brook's own anxiety about the lovers has again begun to pace them, harrying them with instruction. The moment is uneasy, and sours under this constant pressure for correction.

And as has happened before, Brook himself tries to take irritated refuge from it in a spun web of new and obscure complication. 'We have now looked at the play from many different angles,' he tells them, 'using different approaches.' He composes himself, his voice speaking

Lysander: Away, you Ethiope!
Demetrius: No, no; he'll
  Seem to break loose; take on as you would follow,
  But yet come not: you are a tame man, go!
Lysander: Hang off, thou cat, thou burr! Vile thing, let loose,
  Or I will shake thee from me like a serpent!
Hermia: Why are you grown so rude! What change is this,
  Sweet love?
Lysander: Thy love! Out, tawny Tartar, out!
  Out, loathèd med'cine! O hated potion, hence!

(III.ii.251–264)

out of an enforced stillness. 'What would become increasingly plain, if we had five years to rehearse,' he says, his eyes gelid, 'is that verse is a concentration.' There is silence. 'In prose, the opposite is the case. There, expansion, diffusion, improvisation and "business" bring involvement. Verse requires greater and greater discipline, and concentration. Not technique, but commitment.'

His brow is like thunder. The actors, it becomes clear, are being newly blamed for their lyric shortcomings. 'Verse-plays are not more "beautiful", more "solemn" and so on.' His exasperated tone is cutting in the silence. 'In verse, the moment everything is in tune, something physical appears, a taste, something enjoyable.' This is too gnomic for words. The actors' eyes seem to cloud against it. 'Does this correspond with your own impressions?' he asks. There is an even denser silence, expression as blank as verse at its blankest. No one bats an eyelid, nor moves a muscle. 'Then we haven't got far enough,' Brook announces, from deep within his own emotional dug-out. He is stern and cold, the actors unconcerned and impassive.

But it is a shadow-play, and the distance between them is carefully measured. For energy is being conserved, as public performance approaches.

Seventh week, second day

A second, seemingly dangerous, day of lethargy and preoccupation. Brook sits at his table writing letters, while the actors exercise like sleep-walkers. It is a studied calm, for there is a tension and exertion near to hysteria beneath the surface. This balletically-posed slackness of gesture and movement is an antidote to taking fright, and running for it. It is not a relaxed preparation for effort, but a pent-up avoidance of it; not the recuperation of feeling, but its repression. Even the spectator now assumes a casual air, his heart beating faster for the actors – while thought, running amok, bites its nails as if idle.

Today, too, the actors appear more isolated than ever from one another; alone together. They have also never seemed more remote from the director. For they know (and so must he, writing letters) that the play is in their hands, not his. Its physical enchantments, both in the first and the last analysis, are a burden which rests essentially on their shoulders. Today, their introversion also shuts out their small audience from all relation with them. The actor, awaiting his moment

¹⁰ *Oberon:* I wonder if Titania be awaked;
Then, what it was that next came in her eye,
Which she must dote on in extremity.
Here comes my messenger. How now, mad spirit!
What night-rule now about this haunted grove?
Puck: My mistress with a monster is in love.
Near to her close and consecrated bower,
While she was in her dull and sleeping hour,
A crew of patches, rude mechanicals,
Were met together to rehearse a play.

(III.ii.1–10)

¹¹ *Puck:* And forth my mimic comes. When they him spy,
As wild geese that the creeping fowler eye,
Or russet-pated choughs, many in sort,
Rising and cawing at the gun's report,
Sever themselves and madly sweep the sky,
So, at his sight, away his fellows fly;
And, at our stamp, here o'er and o'er one falls;
He murder cries, and help from Athens calls.
Their sense thus weak, lost with their fears thus strong,
Made senseless things begin to do them wrong;
For briers and thorns at their apparel snatch;
Some sleeves, some hats, from yielders all things catch.
I led them on in this distracted fear,
And left sweet Pyramus translated there:
When in that moment, so it came to pass,
Titania waked, and straightway loved an ass.

(III.ii.19–34)

¹² *Demetrius:* O, why rebuke you him that loves you so?
Lay breath so bitter on your bitter foe.
Hermia: Now I but chide; but I should use thee worse,
For thou, I fear, hast given me cause to curse.
If thou hast slain Lysander
Being o'er shoes in blood, plunge in the deep
And kill me too . . .
It cannot be but thou hast murdered him.
So should a murderer look, so dead, so grim.
Demetrius: So should the murdered look; and so should I
Pierced through the heart with your stern cruelty.

(III.ii.43–59)

268

and with the play on the tip of his tongue, recedes into himself beyond all reaching. He, or she, is suddenly no longer your familiar, but merely a still, or moving, figure. It is as if a vacancy of mind and body has overtaken the actors. They are without animation; *incommunicado*, or dreaming.

'I wonder,' Oberon says idly, 'if Titania be awaked.'[10] Today, it is an inward question: thinking aloud, not acting. 'Then,' he says, musing, 'what it was that next came in her eye,/Which she must dote on in extremity.'[10] It is speculation not enactment, and there is less sound in it than silence. It barely ripples the surface of feeling. 'Here comes my messenger,' Oberon says, as if himself starting from sleep, all but rubbing his eyes and yawning. 'How now, mad spirit!'[10] is pure bluff. For today, Oberon is a day-dreamer, pulling himself together. 'My mistress with a monster is in love,'[10] Puck answers, sibilants busy but feet dragging. This spirit seems deflated; and the manner of it promises rehearsal hours as 'dull and sleeping' as Titania's. Today, even the 'choughs . . . [which] madly sweep the sky'[11] are grounded, eyes shut and wings folded. 'He murder cries, and help from Athens calls'[11] falls on deaf ears; and these 'briers' are thornless.

Puck's is today a muffled rhythm. Accompanied by soft drum-beats (signalled by Brook standing, pen in hand, at his table), it is more a Dead March than Night-Music. Even 'When in that moment, so it came to pass,/ Titania waked, and straightway loved an ass'[11] slumbers. It is as if Titania had overslept, and Puck with her. Today, not even Brook's punctuations by percussion – drum, cymbal, and zither *arpeggio* – can awaken such dormant impulse. Demetrius and Hermia 'rebuke', 'chide' and 'curse' each other[12], are variously 'pierced through the heart'[12] or 'spend their passion'[13], but this is hand-wringing, not heart-felt; not ardour but hard labour, and heavy-going. To lighten the load of it, Brook changes the plotting of the lovers' hectic quartet[14], and reverts to the movement of an earlier rehearsal. Instead of standing their ground four-square, Brook directs them up the masts and into the set's rigging. Instead of a toe-to-toe exchange of leaden blows, until they (and we) are punch-drunk with it, they will run up and down ladders, bobbing and weaving – now not sitting, but moving, targets. The life of these exchanges is, at the last, *not* to come from the actors' words but from their actions. Rhythm and impulse, unfound in the lines, will be found in the ladders. It is a short cut, and for Brook an unkind one.

Today, whether on 'plainer ground'[15] or 'fallen . . . in dark uneven

¹³ *Demetrius:* You spend your passion on a misprised mood:
  I am not guilty of Lysander's blood.

(III.ii.74—75)

¹⁴ *Hermia:*   Lysander, whereto tends all this?
  Lysander: Away, you Ethiope.
  Demetrius: No, no; he'll
  Seem to break loose; take on as you would follow,
  But yet come not: you are a tame man, go!
  Lysander: Hang off, thou cat, thou burr! Vile thing, let loose,
  Or I will shake thee from me like a serpent!
  Hermia: Why are you grown so rude! What change is this,
  Sweet love?

(III.ii.256—262)

¹⁵ *Puck:* Where art thou?
  Lysander: I will be with thee straight.
  Puck: Follow me then,
  To plainer ground . . .
  Lysander: He goes before me and still dares me on:
  When I come where he calls, then he is gone.
  The villain is much lighter-heeled than I.
  I followed fast, but faster he did fly,
  That fallen am I in dark uneven way,
  And here will rest me. (*Lies down*) Come, thou gentle day!

(III.ii.402—418)

¹⁶ *Puck:* When thou wak'st,
  Thou tak'st
  True delight
  In the sight
  Of thy former lady's eye:
  And the country proverb known,
  That every man should take his own,
  In your waking shall be shown.
  Jack shall have Jill;
  Nought shall go ill;
  The man shall have his mare again, and all shall be well.

(III.ii.454—463)

way'[15], asleep or waking, there is little delight and less wonder. There is nothing aerial about the spirits and little life in the mortals. It is as if the text has been wrung to tatters. Speech itself seems worn-out, and emotion threadbare. Moreover the imagination of the spectator refuses implication in such proceedings, just as the courtiers refuse it to *Pyramus and Thisby*. As a result, comic invention becomes horseplay and love itself foolish. It is all, once more, pure moonshine. Worse, whether 'Jack shall have Jill' (or not), and whether 'all shall be well'[16] (or not), no longer seem to matter. It is 'play's' nadir that pretension should be so pricked, and near to expiring.

At the end of the day, the morning's inertia has got its final come-uppance. Energy is at its lowest ebb. The actors seem plain tired of the play, and of each other. Brook, who today has done nothing to prevent this descent into the doldrums, and has kept his own counsel for more than an hour, suddenly asks the lovers to go back to their (Third Act) quadrille of mis-spent passion. They are to perform the whole scene (Act Three, Scene Two) 'in ten minutes'; it is to be a 'speeded-up cinematic version' of the already-plotted action, racing through the words – and up-and-down ladders – *con brio*. They do it. With an enforced gusto, they whip-up for Brook every flagging impulse of mind and body, to a fever-pitch of movement and expression. Wild-eyed and breathless, the actors drive themselves to a standstill before him. 'It was the best rehearsal of that scene so far,' he tells them. (It was not, and they know it.) They are not looking, but staring. 'It gave a sense of people who can do things,' he says, 'quickly, at speed, and with pleasure.'

They seem hollow-eyed with exhaustion, clowns without make-up. These are dangerous moments, as the play stumbles at its last hurdle. The hall seems to darken with anxiety; truth, as well as illusion, becoming immaterial.

Seventh week, third day

I felt as weary of the play today, as the actors appeared to be yesterday, and stayed at home. It is a privilege unavailable to them. Bottom's 'No more words. Away! Go, away!'[17] at the end of Act Four, seemed a fitting epigraph for the rehearsals, as well as for my attendance at them. After weeks of work, and with the end in sight, the play was not merely becalmed, but appeared to have become tawdry to the actors. Even the question of 'success' or 'failure' was now a matter of dulled

¹⁷ *Bottom:* Masters, I am to discourse wonders; but ask me not what; for if I tell you, I am not true Athenian. I will tell you everything, right as it fell out.

Quince: Let us hear, sweet Bottom.

Bottom: Not a word of me . . . No more words. Away! Go, away!

(IV.ii.26–43)

¹⁸ *Puck:* Up and down, up and down,
 I will lead them up and down:
 I am feared in field and town:
 Goblin, lead them up and down.
 Here comes one.

(Enter LYSANDER)

Lysander: Where art thou, poor Demetrius? Speak thou now.

Puck: Here, villain; drawn and ready. Where art thou?

Lysander: I will be with thee straight.

Puck: Follow me, then,
 To plainer ground. (*Exit LYSANDER*)

(Enter DEMETRIUS)

Demetrius: Lysander! Speak again!
 Thou runaway, thou coward, art thou fled?
 Speak! In some bush? Where dost thou hide thy head?

Puck: Thou coward, art thou bragging to the stars,
 Telling the bushes that thou look'st for wars,
 And will not come? Come, recreant! Come, thou child!

(III.ii.396–409)

unconcern, 'audience', 'box office', 'critics' consigned alike to a limbo of unmeaning. 'Masters,' Bottom had said (time and again), 'I am to discourse wonders: but ask me not what.'[17] In yesterday's state of mind, it seemed as if no one would think to.

But what is 'success' and what 'failure'? If the line between them is as fine as that between invention and contrivance, between the significant and the pretentious, and even between sense and nonsense, then it is fine indeed. I have learned from these rehearsals that with one theatrical false step – which can sometimes not be traced, or even discovered – love can become sentiment, pathos bathos, and the tragic comic. Moreover, just as yesterday's jokes are today unfunny (especially if endlessly repeated), so today's realism is artifice tomorrow. In the theatre, relativity is all. There are no absolutes. Light and meaning can be bent at will, beyond the wit even of an Einstein. And what is climactic and revelatory to one, may be mere sound and fury to another.

We change too, at rehearsal, from day to day and even from moment to moment. A crisis which is cathartic in some moods may be merely overwrought in others; just as sound can swiftly become noise, or a clash of heroic wills become irritating and abrasive. At the drop of a hat we can be provoked to laughter, while pity can – in a moment – become terror, or vice-versa. As for the actor, the null and the void sometimes seem to lurk in every syllable and cadence, so tenuous and insubstantial is dramatic representation, so precarious its achievement. Yesterday, for the first time, it was also clear that neither the actors nor the director were aware of the impression they were making, or failing to make, on their small audience. It is as if their involved familiarity with the text, and with its hermetic motions, has been spun into a dense web of private and exclusive feeling between them.

Yet what was unclear in yesterday's light may become clear in tomorrow's. Today, it is only the unspoken words on the page which seem to possess substance – or a local habitation and a name – fixed and immovable against the actors' speech, and its evanescence.

Seventh week, fourth day

Brook is literally drumming-up the actors' energies. It is Act Three, Scene Two. Puck is drummed 'up and down, up and down'[18], drummed 'in field and town', drummed at his entrance, drummed at

¹⁹ *Puck:* On the ground
        Sleep sound:
        I'll apply
        To your eye,
        Gentle lover, remedy.

                    (*Squeezing the juice on LYSANDER's eye*)
                                    (*III.ii.448–452*)

²⁰ *Bottom:* Scratch my head, Peaseblossom. Where's Mounsieur
        Cobweb?
    Cobweb: Ready.
    Bottom: Mounsieur Cobweb, good monsieur, get you your weapons in
        your hand, and kill me a red-hipped humblebee on the top of a
        thistle; and good mounsieur, bring me the honey bag. Do not fret
        yourself too much in the action, mounsieur.

                                    (*IV.i.7–14*)

²¹ *Titania:* Sleep thou, and I will wind thee in my arms.
        Fairies, be gone, and be all ways away.

                                    (*Exeunt Fairies*)

        So doth the woodbine the sweet honeysuckle
        Gently entwist; the female ivy so
        Enrings the barky fingers of the elm.
        O, how I love thee! How I dote on thee!

                                    (*They sleep*)
                                    (*IV.i.37–42*)

²² *Oberon:* Now, my Titania, wake you, my sweet Queen.
    Titania: My Oberon, what visions have I seen!
        Methought I was enamoured of an ass.
    Oberon: There lies your love.
    Titania: How came these things to pass?
        O, how mine eyes do loathe his visage now!

                                    (*IV.i.72–76*)

²³ *Puck:* Fairy King, attend, and mark:
        I do hear the morning lark.
    Oberon: Then, my Queen, in silence sad,
        Trip we after night's shade.
        We the globe can compass soon,
        Swifter than the wand'ring moon.
    Titania: Come, my lord.

                                    (*IV.i.90–96*)

his departure. The drums, struck in a strict tempo to Brook's order, for a while seem to match – in pitch, in impulse and intonation – the actor's own voice and gesture. He strides the stage on stilts, as ever, terrorizing the dumbstruck Lysander and Demetrius[18], his nightmare step as huge as the be-scissored tailor's in *Strummelpeter*. 'Follow my voice,' Puck calls to them. Drummed and looming, he is carrying Demetrius on his back, yet Puck is invisible to him. But the stage is all clamour, the voice and its craft drowning in this *crescendo*. The ear is set on edge by it. In such circumstances not only sound, but physical effort also, becomes irksome to the spectator. It is now both the words ('On the ground/ Sleep sound')[19] and Puck's stooping gestures ('squeezing the juice on Lysander's eye')[19], which attract and promptly repel attention. The observer's eye seems to narrow to the very crease of his shirt and every ungainly fold of his body, before quickly recoiling.

Bottom's post-coital encounter with Peaseblossom, Cobweb and the others[20] has likewise lost its graces. Their attentions to him are now not assiduous, but frantic. Where there was once a passionate endeavour, there is now only frenzy. 'Do not fret yourself too much in the action,'[20] Bottom tells Cobweb, for the first time justly. But this fretting is strenuous and clumsy, and is not so easily abated. Is such 'business' a mere makeshift, a product of Brook's impulse, or that of the actors? Is this high-pitch of energy a symptom of increasing tension? Or, on a different day, will all this lose its desperation, and be applauded? Certainly, there is little self-control, and less 'coolness', about it. Instead, it is as if the long discipline of the rehearsal process is now being forgotten, and a frightened instinct is taking over.

Now Titania's contentments, as she lies down to a dreamy sleep, must do battle with the general disorder of feeling. 'O, how I love thee! How I dote on thee!'[21] is no longer her sigh of recollected pleasure, but edged with exasperation at the insensate scurrying and disturbance around her. And when she wakes to her disenchantment, 'O, how mine eyes do loathe his visage now!'[22] has become no more than conventional distaste, shorn of all vision. For there is nothing left of tumult in it; her feelings have been ruffled, rather, by the scene's failure. But within moments – all uneasy – Puck's 'Fairy King, attend and mark:/ I do hear the morning lark'[23] contains the first dawning presentiment of a key-change, and of a passage from darkness. For the words summon our attention, as they now summon Oberon's, despite their accompaniment by musical noises-off which are as high-pitched

²⁴ *Hippolyta:* I was with Hercules and Cadmus once,
When in a wood of Crete they bayed the bear
With hounds of Sparta. Never did I hear
Such gallant chiding . . .
Theseus: My hounds are bred out of the Spartan kind,
So flewed, so sanded; and their heads are hung
With ears that sweep away the morning dew;
Crook-kneed, and dew-lapped like Thessalian bulls;
Slow in pursuit, but matched in mouth like bells.

(*IV.i.109–120*)

²⁵ *Theseus:*   I pray you all, stand up.
I know you two are rival enemies.
How comes this gentle concord in the world,
That hatred is so far from jealousy,
To sleep by hate, and fear no enmity?
Lysander: My lord, I shall reply amazedly,
Half sleep, half waking: but as yet, I swear,
I cannot truly say how I came here.

(*IV.i.139–145*)

²⁶ *Bottom:* Heigh-ho! . . . I have had a most rare vision. I have had a
dream, past the wit of man to say what dream it was . . . The
eye of man hath not heard, the ear of man hath not seen, man's
hand is not able to taste, his tongue to conceive, nor his heart to
report, what my dream was.

(*IV.i.198–210*)

²⁷ *Quince:* Have you sent to Bottom's house? Is he come home yet?
Starveling: He cannot be heard of. Out of doubt he is transported.
Flute: If he come not, then the play is marred. It goes not forward,
doth it?
Quince: It is not possible. You have not a man in all Athens able to
discharge Pyramus but he.

(*IV.ii.1–8*)

²⁸   (*Enter BOTTOM*)
Bottom: Where are these lads? Where are these hearts?
Quince: Bottom! O most courageous day! O most happy hour!

(*IV.ii.23–24*)

276

as the actors' own tensions. It is the sudden note of a deep stillness in Puck's voice which arrests us, held ourselves by his recovery of concentration. Now, however reluctantly, we are ready to enter Hippolyta's wood with her and go hunting with Theseus[24] – even if his Spartan hounds 'slow in pursuit', must be drummed into it. And in the lovers' reconciliation which follows[25], we find ourselves once more reconciled to the action. For it seems (or we again allow it to seem) that they touch us too, however briefly, when they at last take hands together.

Only Bottom's waking[26] – his 'Heigh-ho!' become a 'hee-haw!' – is now proving constant in its achievement. Standing on solid ground, excavated by Stanislavsky, his role has been built to last, beyond all need (or possibility) of re-making. Change of mood and impulse, director's suggestion, the demands of ensemble and improvisation, seemingly cannot wither or stale it. 'I have had a most rare vision. I have had a dream, past the wit of man to say what dream it was'[26] is today as asinine and awestricken, as coarsely jocular and tenderly bewildered, as stupid and fearful as ever. And from him, the other mechanicals take heart for their rehearsal. 'He cannot be heard of,'[27] says Starveling the tailor; 'out of doubt he is transported.' Seemingly on an awakened impulse, Snout the tinker now crosses himself to hear it – and, by such sleight-of-hand, echoes Quince's earlier benedictions upon Bottom's translation.

But this is a momentary invention, in a mood which is deeply unsettled. At best, the play passes unheeded upon a plane surface. At most, the raised voice is raucous, gesture abrupt and movement ragged; all rough edges. Even the joyful reception of Bottom[28], restored to himself, has become strident. The smile of recognition, in actor and spectator alike, today fades swiftly under the assault of mere noise and unfeeling. Moreover the search for the lost chord again brings Brook to explore effects rather than causes. Thus when the court enters at the beginning of the Fifth Act[29], flying cushions fall (at Brook's orders) from the gantry's top level, swiftly thudding one by one into the arena. And as Theseus discourses, flatly, on the soaring of the imagination[29], a distant off-stage whirling and whirring accompanies his flights of fancy.

Yet, despite such devices, today every bush remains a bush, and every bear a bear. The lovers' 'joy and mirth'[30], unfelt, is a cold comfort, their outward smiles (teeth bared) merely grimacing. Today, it is Theseus' 'anguish of a torturing hour'[30] which rings truest. And

²⁹ *ACT FIVE. Scene One. Athens. The palace of Theseus. Enter*
   THESEUS, HIPPOLYTA, PHILOSTRATE, Lords and
   Attendants.
Hippolyta: 'Tis strange, my Theseus, that these lovers speak of.
Theseus: More strange than true. I never may believe
   These antique fables, nor these fairy toys.
   Lovers and madmen have such seething brains.

                                                                    (V.i.1–5)

³⁰   (*Enter LYSANDER, DEMETRIUS, HERMIA and HELENA*)
Theseus: Here come the lovers, full of joy and mirth.
   Joy, gentle friends! Joy and fresh days of love
   Accompany your hearts!
Lysander: More than to us
   Wait in your royal walks, your board, your bed!
Theseus: Come now, what masques, what dances shall we have . . .
   What revels are in hand? Is there no play
   To ease the anguish of a torturing hour?

                                                                  (V.i.28–37)

³¹ (*Enter PYRAMUS, THISBY, WALL, MOONSHINE and LION,*
                                                         as in dumbshow)
Prologue: Gentles, perchance you wonder at this show;
   But wonder on, till truth make all things plain.
   This man is Pyramus, if you would know;
   This beauteous lady Thisby is certain.
   This man, with lime and roughcast, doth present
   Wall, that vile Wall which did these lovers sunder.

                                                                (V.i.126–131)

³² *Pyramus:* O wicked wall, through whom I see no bliss!
   Cursed be thy stones for thus deceiving me!
Theseus: The wall, methinks, being sensible, should curse again.
Pyramus: No, in truth, sir, he should not. 'Deceiving me' is Thisby's
   cue. She is to enter now, and I am to spy her through the wall.
   You shall see it will fall pat as I told you. Yonder she comes.
                                                        ((*Enter THISBY*)
   . . . I see a voice: now will I to the chink,
   To spy an I can hear my Thisby's face.

                                                                (V. i. 179–191)

the relief he seeks in *Pyramus and Thisby*, we seek also. But now the melancholy and angry passion which once charged the moment, has been reduced to nothing more than anxiety and boredom. Nevertheless, when Prologue innocently presents the play's characters[31] to the courtiers, our hopes again spring up, eternal. 'Gentles,' he says, 'perchance you wonder at this show.'[31] That today we cannot wonder at it, and no more the actors, is itself as poignant as ever.

Brook, still bent *faut de mieux* upon 'business', now wants each of the *dramatis personae* of *Pyramus and Thisby* to strike a comic posture at his entrance, 'as in dumbshow'[31]. He also asks them to 'introduce something new and surprising into these poses on each night of performance', 'something genuinely comic and fresh', for the benefit both of their courtly and box-office audiences. Together, they now create a tableau of emblematic gesture, which depicts the 'very tragical mirth' to follow. Thus Pyramus and Thisby, stopped in their tracks before us, exchange transfixed but loving glances; whisper (in silence) through Wall's frozen fingers; to Moonshine's unmoving lantern and Lion's noiseless roaring. The lovers' death, as the tableau rearranges, is both mute and bloodless. Stabbed, Pyramus and Thisby expire without a murmur, eyes staring. But the spoken enactment of it which follows, is just as unmoving. Moreover, the courtiers, reclining on their fairy-flung cushions, seem beyond caring; or are merely actors, resting. Pyramus and Thisby themselves seem to pass out of sight, and out of mind, in the darkness of this inattention. They are shadows, unamended by imagination.

Yet this very neglect and unawareness – today, ironically, inadvertent – seems closer to the text's intention, than every contrivance. For when Pyramus absurdly steps out of his role, to correct an idle intervention by Theseus[32], the verity of the moment is in fact seen to lie in its casual unconcern for the craft of acting, for the integrity of the text, or the susceptibilities of the audience. Moreover, on the instant, Pyramus becomes David Waller, and Theseus Alan Howard. It is, what it always was, an argument between two actors. And that the other mechanicals for the first time now recoil from Pyramus' gaffe, in a show of disbelief and horror, itself signals a renewed engagement with their roles which might outlast the moment. Nevertheless, the confusions of Pyramus' 'I see a voice . . . I hear my Thisby's face'[32] also seem no more than the faltering of an ill-prepared actor in the role and out of it; or a comment from one confused rehearsal upon another.

Erased today, too, is the sense of the actor-mechanicals as working

³³ *Lion:* Then know that I, as Snug the joiner, am

A lion fell, nor else no lion's dam;

For, if I should as lion come in strife

Into this place, 'twere pity on my life.

Theseus: A very gentle beast, and of a good conscience.

Demetrius: The very best at a beast, my lord, that e'er I saw.

(V.i.220–225)

³⁴ *(Enter THISBY)*

Thisby: This is old Ninny's tomb. Where is my love?

Lion: Oh – *(The LION roars. THISBY runs off)*

Demetrius: Well roared, Lion.

Theseus: Well run, Thisby.

Hippolyta: Well shone, Moon. Truly, the moon shines with a good grace.

(The LION tears THISBY's mantle, and exit)

Theseus: Well moused, Lion.

Demetrius: And then came Pyramus.

Lysander: And so the lion vanished.

(V.i.255–263)

³⁵ *Bottom:* Will it please you to see the epilogue, or to hear a Bergomask dance between two of our company?

Theseus: No epilogue, I pray you; for your play needs no excuse. Never excuse, for when the players are all dead, there need none to be blamed. Marry, if he that writ it had played Pyramus and hanged himself in Thisby's garter, it would have been a fine tragedy: and so it is, truly; and very notably discharged.

(V.i.342–350)

³⁶ *Oberon:* Through the house give glimmering light,

By the dead and drowsy fire:

Every elf and fairy sprite

Hop as light as bird from brier;

And this ditty, after me,

Sing and dance it trippingly.

Titania: First, rehearse your song by rote,

To each word a warbling note:

Hand in hand, with fairy grace,

Will we sing, and bless this place.

(V.i.380–389)

craftsmen of Athens. Their identities, once painstakingly laboured over, have in the last days been dissolved by the depression of effort into mere figures of fun. They have been reduced to comic devices, lacking body and dimension. When Lion roars, and proclaims himself to be Snug the joiner[33], there is no man – as there once was – beneath the skin; nor is this a Lion either. Nonetheless, Theseus' benevolence towards him is princely. He is 'a very gentle beast, and of good conscience'[33]. But this is too generous by half, and to kill him with kindness. For this Lion, beaming in simple relief from terror, is today a comic cut-out, a cardboard figure. When he roars again[34], crawling into the ranks of the courtiers – as he once crawled, roaring, among the audience of children – it is a cartoon frolic. Yet the pantomime of it, if the truly tragi-comic were to embrace these moments, could touch us to the quick. For we are laughing, or failing to laugh, at the very heart and soul of all illusion, whether innocent or experienced.

It was only at the day's end, when Shakespeare himself put in a fleeting appearance at the rehearsal, that the fatal ebbing of energy and invention was for a few instants halted. 'Marry,' says Theseus as the play's *coda* approaches, 'if he that writ it had played Pyramus and hanged himself in Thisby's garter, it would have been a fine tragedy.'[35] In the jest, wry and biting at the play's 'failure', is the voice of the playwright, mocking himself (as well as Quince), the play, and his audience. At the same time, every cavil of ours is suddenly checked in its stride, and put to shame, by Shakespeare himself. 'For when the players are all dead,' Theseus says for him, 'there need none to be blamed.'[35]

Yet, paradoxically, it is *today's* miscarriage – of both plays – which has brought us to this truth, though too late to reclaim our attention. But, now, at the very last[36], when Oberon, Titania and Puck once more stand before us, in place of Theseus, Hippolyta and Philostrate, Spirit must step back into the shoes of mortals, without changing its costume. In the rehearsal's dying fall, therefore, we must believe first in the Duke of Athens, and then – within seconds – in the King of the Fairies. We are even being asked by Brook, in the play's closing moments, to annul the difference between them; while retaining our sense, distinct but connected in the mind's eye, of the worlds of play and earnest, of spirit and mortal, of shadow and of substance. And if *A Midsummer Night's Dream* is fully to 'work', the actors must conduct us from one world to the other.

Today they did not. Tomorrow is a public rehearsal-performance.

24 Lion: 'Then know that I, as Snug the joiner, am a lion fell' (Act Five, Scene One); (l. to r.) Terrence Hardiman (Moonshine), Barry Stanton (Lion), Philip Locke (Prologue), David Waller (Pyramus), Norman Rodway (Wall) and Glynne Lewis (Thisby).

There is an invited crowd of one hundred and fifty people in the rehearsal-hall. They seem strangers, come armed with their own expectations and inhibitions. 'They carry their own expectant hush with them,' Brook says hopefully, whispering and uneasy. There is alarm in the air, brought by the audience. The packed hall, benign or dull in rehearsal, tonight seems a furnace of tensions.

The actors, limbering up in full view of the spectators, have paled in the anticipation of effort, and are sweating like horses. Or, they saunter from pillar to post, casually trembling. Some, frightened into a feigned diffidence, are conversing to carefully-struck, but nerve-racked, midstage poses. The crowd seem predators, perching on their seat-edges; and in the teeth of this audience, now all eyes and with breaths bated, the actors are being visibly aroused to a fierce self-consciousness in every movement and gesture. Or is this the nervous self-awareness, as the crowd falls silent, which will bring back vitality and freshness to flagging performance?

Brook unexpectedly takes the floor, and faces the ranks of spectators. 'Tonight you are our guests, and are very welcome,' he says. His voice has a tremor in it. 'Our work is not yet finished. But it is useful to us to play a rough version of our performance. If you come again, you will have to pay two guineas. [In the crowd, 'Who's he?' forms itself, behind hands, in hurried whispers.] The difference will be that, for two guineas, all this' – gesturing behind him, to a thin scatter of laughter – 'will be white. The light will be roughly as it is now. In addition, there will be both total darkness and candlelit darkness, which cannot be achieved at this performance.'

The audience is now closely attentive. 'For two guineas,' he announces, 'the trapezes which you can see will also move up and down, as well as back and forth.' He is calmer, and more jovial. 'And when we have wigs and costumes, something mysterious will happen: Theseus, Hippolyta and Philostrate will turn into Oberon, Titania and Puck. But even without costumes, you will be able to find the connection between them.' All three stand, white-faced, beside him; acrobats, with their ringmaster. 'At the beginning, you will see Theseus and Hippolyta,' he says, and walks to his seat, the audience's hopes uncoiling, the ring rippling with expectation. There is readiness in the spectators, and fear in the actors; tension and good humour together, as court, spirits, clowns and lovers climb ladders to their

283

(*ACT ONE. Scene One. The palace of Theseus. Enter THESEUS, HIPPOLYTA, PHILOSTRATE and Attendants*)

Theseus: Now, fair Hippolyta, our nuptial hour
  Draws on apace. Four happy days bring in
  Another moon; but, O, methinks, how slow
  This old moon wanes! She lingers my desires,
  Like to a stepdame, or a dowager,
  Long withering out a young man's revenue.

Hippolyta: Four days will quickly steep themselves in night,
  Four nights will quickly dream away the time;
  And then the moon, like to a silver bow
  New-bent in heaven, shall behold the night
  Of our solemnities.

Theseus: Go, Philostrate,
  Stir up the Athenian youth to merriments,
  Awake the pert and nimble spirit of mirth,
  Turn melancholy forth to funerals;
  The pale companion is not for our pomp.

                                      (*I.i.1–15*)

                    (*Enter EGEUS and his daughter HERMIA,
                        LYSANDER and DEMETRIUS*)

Egeus: Happy be Theseus, our renownèd Duke!

Theseus: Thanks, good Egeus. What's the news with thee?

Egeus: Full of vexation come I, with complaint
  Against my child, my daughter Hermia.
  Stand forth, Demetrius. My noble lord,
  This man hath my consent to marry her.
  Stand forth, Lysander. And, my gracious Duke
  This man hath bewitched the bosom of my child . . .

Theseus: What say you Hermia? . . .
  Demetrius is a worthy gentleman.

Hermia: So is Lysander.

Theseus: In himself he is:
  But in this kind, wanting your father's voice,
  The other must be held the worthier.

Hermia: I would my father looked but with my eyes.

Theseus: Rather your eyes must with his judgment look.

Hermia: I do entreat your Grace to pardon me.

                                      (*I.i.20–58*)

places, or wait to make their entrances. Is this a serious or a frivolous moment? Will this network of devices and movements give us sight and sense of the tumults and exhilarations of the written? What is the role of the audience? Mere witnesses of 'success' or 'failure'? Judges? Or participants, with their own duties?

'Now, fair Hippolyta,'[37] Theseus begins (yet again), 'our nuptial hour draws on apace. Four happy days bring in/ Another moon; but O, methinks, how slow/ This old moon wanes.' Instantly audible is a tone brightened by contact with an audience. The introspective melancholy of private rehearsal has itself waned almost to disappearing. There is no passionate mooning in this, but a daylight feeling, lucid and open; neither gloom nor anger, but a plain prologue to the drama. It is as if a demand for 'light and yet more light' is being attributed, by actors' instinct, to the audience. Brook – who takes written notes for the first time, throughout the performance – strongly approves it. A dark passion here, he will say later, is a 'depressant'; 'lightness and delicacy' must inform the play's first moments.

Yet the text soon turns out to impose its own solemnities against an address so bright and simple. Egeus is stern[38], his pose rigid, his rhythm pedestrian. Shorn of its once-discovered passions, his speech is merely hieratic; the passage one of 'typically Shakespearian' scene-setting and declamation, the only such passage in the drama. Brook would like 'something Italianate', an 'eruption' in the First Scene, he says later. Instead, these are statuesque moments of formal plea and counter-plea, exclamation against exclamation[38].

The audience is already deeply-stilled. It is too early to gauge their responses. But their passive expressions are raked by salvoes of anxious glances. Are they just looking, or really watching? Listening, or merely hearing? Might they even keep their own counsel to the bitter end, sit on their hands, and file out in silence? Hermia, the 'Shakespearian' heroine, seems a slighter figure than ever. Her pleading[38] sounds bashful and winsome against the court's grey-beard sternness. And strangely she and the court, in their gestures and speaking, seem to be keeping closer to the stereotypes of the Shakespearian mode and its outward conventions, than to the ensemble search for the words' inner impulses. It is almost as if the audience has brought this convention in with them. Or are the actors trying to meet what they take to be the crowd's expectations? Theseus ('What say you, Hermia?')[38], even without his ermine, is stiffly magisterial; Hermia ('I do entreat your grace to pardon me')[38] has

³⁹ *Theseus:* For you, fair Hermia, look you arm yourself
      To fit your fancies to your father's will;
      Or else the law of Athens yields you up –
      Which by no means we may extenuate –
      To death, or to a vow of single life . . .
                    (Exeunt all but LYSANDER and HERMIA)
    Lysander: How now, my love! Why is your cheek so pale?
      How chance the roses there do fade so fast?

                                        (I.i.117–129)

⁴⁰ *Hermia:* Farewell, sweet playfellow. Pray thou for us;
      And good luck grant thee thy Demetrius!
      Keep word, Lysander. We must starve our sight
      From lovers' food till tomorrow deep midnight.
    Lysander: I will, my Hermia.   *(Exit HERMIA)*
                    Helena, adieu.
      As you on him, Demetrius dote on you!

                                        (Exit LYSANDER)
    Helena: How happy some o'er other some can be!

                                        (I.i.220–226)

⁴¹ *Helena:* For ere Demetrius looked on Hermia's eyne,
      He hailed down oaths that he was only mine . . .
      I will go tell him of fair Hermia's flight.
      Then to the wood will he tomorrow night
      Pursue her; and for this intelligence
      If I have thanks it is a dear expense:
      But herein mean I to enrich my pain,
      To have his sight thither and back again.

                                        (Exit)

(Scene Two. Quince's house. Enter QUINCE, SNUG, BOTTOM,
  FLUTE, SNOUT and STARVELING)
Quince: is all our company here?

                                        (I.i.242–251 and I.ii.1)

become a sweet young thing, and cowers before him. It is all male bearing on one side, and feminine frailty on the other – or darkness and light, without shadow. 'She plays the role as she sees herself: virginal and decent,' Brook said to me later. There is 'no charge' in her; he would have to 'turn her hesitations into some form of eccentricity,' he added. Growth from within will be abandoned for a surgeon's graft by the director.

And for all that Theseus' grim-visaged and deadly menace ('Or else the law of Athens yields you up . . ./ To death, or to a vow of single life')[39] strikes fear into the heart of tender maiden, it is a Shakespearian rite we are watching, not the re-creation Brook has fondly hoped for. 'He vests himself,' Brook said irritatedly later, 'with a generalized mysteriousness. Too much of his work is ill-considered.' Lysander, too, is merely – but clearly – the love-sick swain of copybook romances, yet lacking in both ardour and impatience. He is love-lorn, but joyless[39]. Hermia, in turn, is no longer Helena's comfort. For, as if pre-occupied tonight with her own stage-presence, she has little time and less sympathy to spare for another woman. But that she and Lysander should now laughingly leave Helena to her own plaintive devices[40] has the public virtue of a simple and cruel meaning, if not the depths of a more private and complex feeling.

Yet it also seems that what is lacking in the actors is already being partly made good by the audience. It is as if the leaden moment is being buoyed up by the spectators' presence, and a darker resonance given by them to the lightweight. Effect is paradoxically multiplied by being divided among them, and sound seems to be sustained, not diminished, when it pits itself to the echo against their silence. Moreover, at the mechanicals' first entrance[41], a new and true life comes with them, enhanced by Helena's novel conceit of leaving late and being caught up, running, among them. And theirs is no 'Italianate' nor Athenian eruption. In this arena, instantly stirring to greet them, they are local craftsmen and this is a comfortingly English bedlam.

Their clamour is deep-settled and complex with weeks of rehearsal, their 'business' practised to an artisan perfection. Indeed, for perilous moments, their skills arouse more silent admiration than welcoming laughter – as if comic response were being quelled by an attention to artistic detail. Here the director's judgment is under greatest pressure; if only the already-knowing laugh, he has lost his audience. But such fears are unfounded. Sympathy and connivance grow swiftly together.

287

⁴² *Puck:* How now, spirit! Whither wander you?
   Fairy: Over hill, over dale,
      Thorough bush, thorough brier,
      Over park, over pale,
      Thorough flood, thorough fire,
      I do wander everywhere
      Swifter than the moon's sphere.

                                          (II.i.1–7)

⁴³ *Puck:* I am that merry wanderer of the night.
      I jest to Oberon, and make him smile . . .
      And then the whole quire hold their hips and laugh,
      And waxen in their mirth, and neeze, and swear
      A merrier hour was never wasted there.
      But, room, fairy! Here comes Oberon.

                                       (II.i.43–58)

⁴⁴   *(Enter OBERON at one door, with his train,*
                            and TITANIA at another, with hers)
  Oberon: Ill met by moonlight, proud Titania.
  Titania: What, jealous Oberon! Fairy, skip hence. I have forsworn his
    bed and company.
  Oberon: Tarry, rash wanton; am not I thy lord?
  Titania: Then I must be thy lady: but I know
      When thou hast stolen away from fairy land
      And in the shape of Corin sat all day,
      Playing on pipes of corn, and versing love
      To amorous Phillida. Why art thou here,
      Come from the farthest steep of India?

                                       (II.i.60–69)

⁴⁵ *Titania:* These are the forgeries of jealousy:
      And never, since the middle summer's spring,
      Met we on hill, in dale, forest, or mead,
      By pavèd fountain or by rushy brook,
      Or in the beachèd margent of the sea,
      To dance our ringlets to the whistling wind,
      But with thy brawls thou hast disturbed our sport . . .
      And this same progeny of evils comes
      From our debate, from our dissension;
      We are their parents and original.

                                     (II.i.81–117)

These are gross and warm-hearted familiars, deeply reassuring if you have lost your bearings, from the start, in the Court of Athens. With their proletarian ground-bass to set against the rarefied music of the courtiers, they are (or seem to be) comrades-in-arms with the audience, rather than an aristocracy of the imagination.

But there is also a collective cacophony in their sounds and movements, such as to make both eye and ear restless. And it spreads, magnified by the noise of audience laughter. In the release of the actors' tensions, there is both exhilaration and disorder. There is no 'basic sound' – Richard Peaselee, the company composer, agreed later – 'to which other sounds relate, and to which they can return'. It is, rather, a rhythm disjointed by anxiety, excitement and effort, and unsettled by the new counterpoint of the crowd's responses. The Fairies, however, with no need to come to earth, find their feet more quickly. Under Puck's guidance, they wander 'over hill, over dale/ Thorough bush, thorough brier'[42] with a fleetness of foot, and sureness of touch, which sets the pulse of the words and of the audience racing together. But, now, with a spring in its stride such as this, there can be no anger, no melancholy, and little passion. Instead, 'I am that merry wanderer of the night'[43] is refined (or thinned out) gossamer; a spider's web of faery convention, and light music.

In contrast, Titania is not so much 'Ill met by moonlight'[44], as drawn into the arena, via the players' entrance, to a hail of fairy-flung – and mishandled – missiles. And this is less a train of her fairy attendants than a jaded bunch of team-spirits. To accompany them there is no music of the gyrating spheres, but the whirling and whistling clamour of the football-terrace, armed with klaxons and rattles. Yet there may be a visible splendour to come in it, too, when it is lit and costumed. For Titania might then become a gaudy Queen, carried in a rich and silk-hung palanquin, like an Oriental jade with bearers. Now it is all noise, with every strange sound and gesture tugging at the audience's sleeve for notice. But despite it – or as Brook said later, 'because of it' – Titania's speech on the 'forgeries of jealousy'[45] triumphs over such punctuation, her cold dissent and fiery anguish mistress of all the tintinnabulation and flying saucers.

Yet none of this uncostumed heat seems to 'come from the farthest steep of India'[44], the orientalisms notwithstanding. Rich and resonant in their discordant passion, the words of it need no Eastern makeweight. For the 'progeny of evils'[45] which afflicts her now appears to reach deep into the silent audience, without benefit of

⁴⁶ *Titania:* The fairy land buys not the child of me.
      His mother was a vot'ress of my order,
      And, in the spicèd Indian air, by night,
      Full often hath she gossiped by my side,
      And sat with me on Neptune's yellow sands . . .
      And for her sake do I rear up her boy,
      And for her sake I will not part with him.
Oberon: How long within this wood intend you stay?
Titania: Perchance till after Theseus' wedding day.
      If you will patiently dance in our round,
      And see our moonlight revels, go with us.
      If not, shun me, and I will spare your haunts.
Oberon: Give me that boy, and I will go with thee.
Titania: Not for thy fairy kingdom. Fairies, away!
      We shall chide downright, if I longer stay.
                              (*Exeunt TITANIA with her train*)
Oberon: Well, go thy way. Thou shalt not from this grove
      Till I torment thee for this injury.
      My gentle Puck, come hither.

                                            (*II.i.122–148*)

⁴⁷ *Demetrius:* Do I entice you? Do I speak you fair?
      Or, rather, do I not in plainest truth
      Tell you, I do not nor I cannot love you?
Helena: And even for that do I love you the more.
      I am your spaniel; and, Demetrius,
      The more you beat me, I will fawn on you.
      Use me but as your spaniel, spurn me, strike me,
      Neglect me, lose me; only give me leave,
      Unworthy as I am, to follow you.
      What worser place can I beg in your love –
      And yet a place of high respect with me –
      Than to be used as you use your dog?

                                            (*II.i.197–210*)

turban or *kimono*. Moreover, for all that Puck lies coiled at her feet like a double of Shiva, twangling a tiny zither, it is of the disorder of the English seasons that she speaks, and in the accents of Roedean or RADA. It is neither 'spicèd' nor 'Indian'[46], in this or any other setting. Now, too, performance plucks up increasing courage, spurred on by what may be increasing attention in the audience. Titania's quarrel with Oberon becomes, once more, both agonized and sensual. 'We shall chide downright, if I longer stay'[46] is a true lover's reproach, petulant and longing, while Oberon now grows into arousal also. His voice and bearing become charged with it, as he summons[46] Puck to torment and bewitch her. But he also seems, suddenly tonight, less fearsome than fearful. He is ill-at-ease, as well as vengeful. Is this tremor stage-fright, or anger? Is this a fear out of the role, or in it? His pallor and staccato manner now perfectly match the moment. Or is the true drama concealed in him, and in the other actors, rather than in the play's hidden impulses?

This new and powerful tension in him is magnifying. But it is as if a feverish struggle to master his own emotion, and not the weeks of search for the lines' inward rhythm, were now taking him deeper into the play and into the crowd's attentions. As the Second Act advances, he seems to loom larger in both than ever. A truly commanding figure, is he a Jacob wrestling privately with his own, or the text's, dark angel? And who dare say, scanning the ranks of the fully-visible and intermittently-stirring audience, what they see and hear in this 'wood near Athens' or in the 'King and Queen of the Fairies'? When Helena pursues Demetrius to ground[47], pinning him beneath her in a coital crouching – as she has never done before – what do the spectators make of this near-copulatory struggle? 'Use me,'[47] she whispers to him, as if completely succumbing to Demetrius. But is this an inspiration on the sexual spur of the moment, or a coquettish and calculated playing to the gallery? Is it Demetrius and his rhythm she so breathlessly feels beneath her, or the hot breath of the audience on her neck, which has suddenly brought her to this passion?

At any rate, it seems that by such means as Helena's the actors are having to fight the audience's reserve, coax it towards its responses, arouse it to animation, and gain its approval. (Is this a live theatre and a dead audience, or vice-versa?) Little of this could be prepared for, or was even mentioned, in rehearsal. Indeed this performance is now as much in the hands of the audience, whether they know it or not, as in the hands of the actors, who certainly do know it. They, in turn, appear

⁴⁸ *ACT TWO. Scene Two. Another part of the wood. Enter TITANIA,*
   with her train.
   Titania: Come, now a roundel and a fairy song . . .
      . . . Sing me now asleep.
      Then to your offices, and let me rest.

   (*Fairies sing*)

   1st Fairy: You spotted snakes with double tongue,
      Thorny hedgehogs be not seen;
      Newts and blindworms, do no wrong,
      Come not near our Fairy Queen.
   Chorus: Philomele, with melody
      Sing in our sweet lullaby;
      Lulla, lulla, lullaby, lulla, lulla, lullaby.

   (*II.ii.1–15*)

⁴⁹
   (*Enter OBERON and squeezes the flower on*
   TITANIA's eyelids)

   Oberon: What thou seest when thou dost wake,
      Do it for thy truelove take;
      Love and languish for his sake.
      Be it ounce, or cat, or bear,
      Pard, or boar with bristled hair,
      In thy eye that shall appear
      When thou wak'st, it is thy dear.
      Wake when some vile thing is near.   (*Exit*)

   (*Enter LYSANDER and HERMIA*)

   Lysander: Fair love, you faint with wand'ring in the wood;
      And to speak troth, I have forgot our way.
      We'll rest us, Hermia, if you think it good,
      And tarry for the comfort of the day.
   Hermia: Be't so, Lysander. Find you out a bed;
      For I upon this bank will rest my head.
   Lysander: One turf shall serve as pillow for us both,
      One heart, one bed, two bosoms, and one troth.

   (*II.ii.27–42*)

to be leaving little or nothing to chance. Gesture is as if redoubled, the voice 'projected', the lily gilded. Moreover, the audience, still uncertain of itself, seems to be showing more interest in oddity than in the familiar, and is most quickly responsive to the 'curious' or the novel. It is wires in the Second Act wood, and trapezes, not love's ardours, which appear to stir and hold attention longest; sleight-of-hand before the subtle; plain magic before the mysterious. Above all, the audience seems impatient for the broadest humour, urging the mechanicals on with its belly-laughter and threatening to make music-hall caricatures of Brook's craftsmen.

Despite all this, as the Second Act approaches its climax with the enchantment of Titania, a sense of possible revelation survives, and begins to flower, deep within the plain-speaking, and plain-dealing, imposed by performance. A 'Chinese' roundelay[48] – bare and exposed in this workaday setting – is its unnerving prelude; absurd in some ears, magical in others. Yet tonight the stillness and apprehension in the audience is its own comment. It is as if the very perversity of the sound has held every attention, and is setting the scene for some magical disclosure. Oberon's entry[49] now appears larger than life, and large enough to frighten. To a piercing off-stage scream, which seems to freeze the audience, he 'squeezes the flower on Titania's eyelids'[49]. It is less the ministration of 'love-in-idleness' than an injection of eye-drops, and less for sleep than for a blinding. Afterwards Brook, who had rejected such a scream at a previous rehearsal, declares that it was 'too ritualistic' and 'too cruel'. It was 'inappropriate' and 'from another play', a *Lear* or *Titus*. He says that he wants, instead, a 'sexual sighing' to accompany the moment of Titania's bewitching. It is a brave decision, with its own integrity of purpose, which casts away tonight's brute but real effect for the sake of another truth, and a different illusion.

Now, though the performance is not yet out of the wood, there is – for the first time in rehearsal – a sense of relief at the entrance of Lysander and Hermia. The swift passage from Oberon's 'boar with bristled hair'[49] to Lysander's 'Fair love, you faint with wand'ring in the wood'[49] is a movement from fear to pleasure. In their true love, writ large for tonight's audience, there is a simple contrast between Hermia's contentment on the arm of Lysander, and Helena's despairing lewdness earlier, astride Demetrius. Yet there is also a volatile and audible restlessness developing in the ranks of spectators, feared by Brook from the outset of rehearsal, as the enchanted lovers become

⁵⁰ *Lysander:* So thou, my surfeit and my heresy,
　　　Of all be hated, but the most of me!
　　　And, all my powers, address your love and might
　　　To honour Helen and to be her knight!　(*Exit*)
Hermia: (*Awaking*) Help me, Lysander, help me! Do thy best
　　　To pluck this crawling serpent from my breast! . . .
　　　Alack, where are you? Speak, an if you hear;
　　　Speak, of all loves! I swoon almost with fear.
　　　No? Then I well perceive you are not nigh.
　　　Either death or you I'll find immediately.

　　　　　　　　　　　　　　　　　　　　　(*Exit*)
　　ACT THREE. Scene One. The Wood. TITANIA lying asleep. Enter
　　QUINCE, SNUG, BOTTOM, FLUTE, SNOUT and
　　STARVELING.
Bottom: Are we all met?

　　　　　　　　　　　　　　(*II.ii.141–156 and III.i.1*)

⁵¹ *Bottom:* There are things in this comedy of Pyramus and Thisby that
　　　will never please. First, Pyramus must draw a sword to kill himself;
　　　which the ladies cannot abide. How answer you that?
Snout: By'r lakin, a parlous fear.
Starveling: I believe we must leave the killing out, when all is done.

　　　　　　　　　　　　　　　　　　　(*III.i.8–14*)

⁵² *Snout:* Will not the ladies be afeared of the lion?
Starveling: I fear it, I promise you.
Bottom: Masters, you ought to consider with yourselves. To bring in
　　　– God shield us! – a lion among ladies, is a most dreadful thing . . .
Snout: Therefore another prologue must tell he is not a lion.

　　　　　　　　　　　　　　　　　　　(*III.i.25–31*)

⁵³ *Bottom:* I have a device to make all well. Write me a prologue, and let
　　　the prologue seem to say, we will do no harm with our swords, and
　　　that Pyramus is not killed indeed; and, for the more better
　　　assurance, tell them that I Pyramus am not Pyramus, but Bottom
　　　the weaver. This will put them out of fear.
Quince: Well, we will have such a prologue, and it shall be writen in
　　　eight and six.
Bottom: No, make it two more; let it be written in eight and eight.

　　　　　　　　　　　　　　　　　　　(*III.i.15–24*)

more deeply entangled in error. Worse, the speeches of Lysander and Hermia which conclude the Second Act[50] seem to shrink (in the hall's growing heat) to a terminal thinness. Their torments have become brittle, and Hermia merely girlish.

The audience can be seen to be divided. Some are giving their attention, agog to the bitter end, while others are glassy-eyed and withdrawing. But with barely a pause to take breath, the mechanicals now burst in upon this stifled recoil from the lovers and all their fancies, for their Third Act rehearsal[50]. They do not steal in; they break and enter, to a wave of welcome. Armed, like circus-clowns, with buckets of eye-wash, they find an audience not so much softened up by sentiment as ready – or impatient – to melt into their arms without further provocation. 'Are we all met?'[50] says Bottom, and the crowd dissolves into laughter for answer, as if helpless. There is goodwill, boredom and connivance in it; and tonight's mirth spreads like wildfire. Even unfunny gesture and words which are not comic provoke it, as if the hilarity were arbitrary or random. 'I believe we must leave the killing out,'[51] Starveling the tailor counsels, in the matter of the plot of *Pyramus and Thisby*. Tonight, this is neither bland, nor sage, nor earnest. It is comic, pure and simple, and met by a gale of laughter which startles the blinking actor. 'Will not the ladies be afeared of the lion?'[52], Snout the tinker asks Starveling a little later. 'I fear it, I promise you,' Starveling replies, to loud and enthusiastic guffaws, when barely a smile greeted the line during weeks of rehearsal. The audience seems almost literally to love it. Indeed, it is as if there were far more love between the audience and the mechanicals, than there was among the four star-crossed lovers. And this love, unlike theirs, is requited.

For there is much more happening now than a mere exchange of actors' jokes and spectators' laughter. The mechanicals are in fact confiding in the audience. Anxiously, and ludicrously, they are entrusting their technical problems – with the Prologue[53], the moonlight and the wall – to the groundlings who surround them. In turn, having gained access to the secret world of the rehearsal, by invitation to *A Midsummer Night's Dream* and by 'chance' to *Pyramus and Thisby*, the spectators are now finding out that it is not so secret after all. The actors in both plays are simply and openly (so it seems) trying their best to mount a successful production. And these characters explaining their dilemmas with such absurd candour before them, are men as well as actors. David Waller is Bottom, but Bottom is also David Waller.

54 *Puck:* What hempen homespuns have we swagg'ring here,
So near the cradle of the Fairy Queen?
What, a play toward! I'll be an auditor;
An actor too perhaps, if I see cause.

(*III.i.68–71*)

55 *Thisby:* Must I speak now?
Quince: Ay, marry, must you. For you must understand he goes but
to see a noise that he heard, and is to come again.
Thisby: Most radiant Pyramus, most lily-white of hue,
Of colour like the red rose on triumphant brier,
Most brisky juvenal, and eke most lovely Jew,
As true as truest horse, that yet would never tire,
I'll meet thee, Pyramus, at Ninny's tomb.
Quince: 'Ninus' tomb', man. Why, you must not speak that yet. That
you answer to Pyramus. You speak all your part at once, cues and
all. Pyramus enter. Your cue is past; it is 'never tire'.
Thisby: O – as true as truest horse, that yet would never tire.
(*Re-enter PUCK, and BOTTOM with an ass's head*)
Pyramus: If I were fair, Thisby, I were only thine.
Quince: O monstrous! O strange! We are haunted.

(*III.i.80–94*)

56 *Bottom:* Why do they run away? This is a knavery of them to make
me afeard . . . I see their knavery. This is to make an ass of me; to
fright me if they could. But I will not stir from this place, do what
they can. I will walk up and down here, and will sing, that they
shall hear I am not afraid. (*Sings*)
The woosel cock so black of hue,
With orange-tawny bill,
The throstle with his note so true,
The wren with little quill –
Titania: (*Awaking*) What angel wakes me from my flow'ry bed? . . .
I pray thee gentle mortal, sing again.

(*III.i.102–125*)

296

Moreover, the innocent company of players is (as if) blind and deaf to the spirits who are about to assail it, while the worldly-wise audience can both see and hear them. The spectators thus become additionally conscious of themselves as an audience, and of their own roles in the drama as knowing accomplices of the action. If not actors themselves, they are no longer passive either. For as the plot of both plays thickens, their presence seems to be both felt and needed. 'What, a play toward!'[54] Puck says, as if on their behalf also, 'I'll be an auditor;/ An actor too perhaps, if I see cause.' And if we as 'auditors' cannot speak, at least we can, and must, show our engagement. We have been button-holed into it, beyond escaping. With their comic vulnerability, the players have solicited and already gained our sympathy for their *Pyramus and Thisby*. But tonight they have begun to engage it on behalf of *A Midsummer Night's Dream* also, and at precisely the time when the spectators' self-assurance and enjoyment are once more growing.

'Must I speak now?'[55] Thisby anxiously inquires of Quince the playwright, for herself and for us, as Pyramus goes off, unwittingly, to be translated. 'Ay, marry, must you. For you must understand,' and so must we, 'he goes but to see a noise that he heard, and is to come again,'[55] Quince answers. But he has gone to the land of Noddy and is already braying – a 'Grotowskian effect', Brook called it later – to the instant and delighted recognition of the audience, who can hear such sounds as Thisby cannot. 'Most radiant Pyramus, most lily-white of hue,'[55] she croons to her absent and neighing lover. Oblivious, unlike us, of what is afoot, Thisby's well-being becomes our problem. An unsuspecting figure, an innocent abroad, the man-in-drag in her and all other such contrivance is forgotten. Pyramus, she tells us, her painted mouth turning from smiling cupid's bow to pursed cat's-arse pucker, is 'as true as truest horse.'[55] 'O,' she repeats – the audience in stitches, the off-stage braying louder – 'as true as truest horse, that yet would never tire.'

But it is man's body and ass's hair-raising head which enter[55], nodding and lipping, putting the mechanicals to headlong flight in horror, and stopping the mouths of the audience as if their blood had frozen. 'Why do they run away?'[56] Bottom bellows, the front rows seeming to shrink back from him as he passes. Yet this is a donkey, or a half-donkey, not a dragon; tender-hearted at bottom, not breathing fire. Moreover we, like children, now want to be consoled, as well as frightened. In fact, it is his fears which reassure us. Alone, save for the

57 *Titania:* Out of this wood do not desire to go.
   Thou shalt remain here, whether thou wilt or no.
   I am a spirit of no common rate.
   The summer still doth tend upon my state:
   And I do love thee. Therefore, go with me.
   I'll give thee fairies to attend on thee,
   And they shall fetch thee jewels from the deep,
   And sing, while thou on pressèd flowers dost sleep:
   And I will purge thy mortal grossness so,
   That thou shalt like an airy spirit go.

   (III.i.138–147)

58 *Titania:* Be kind and courteous to this gentleman;
   Hop in his walks, and gambol in his eyes;
   Feed him with apricocks and dewberries,
   With purple grapes, green figs, and mulberries;
   The honey bags steal from the humblebees,
   And for night tapers crop their waxen thighs,
   And light them at the fiery glowworm's eyes,
   To have my love to bed and to arise;
   And pluck the wings from painted butterflies,
   To fan the moonbeams from his sleeping eyes.
   Nod to him, elves, and do him courtesies.
Peaseblossom: Hail, mortal!
Cobweb: Hail!
Moth: Hail!
Mustardseed: Hail!

   (III.i.150–164)

sleeping Titania and the watching audience, 'This is to make an ass of me,'[56] he tells us bravely, seeking our solace, 'to fright me if they could. But I will not stir from this place, do what they can,' and no more will we. It would take more than a few so-called spirits to shift any of us, Bottom included. 'I will walk up and down here, and will sing,'[56] says Bottom, 'that they shall hear I am not afraid.' And we sing with him, the whole audience, breaths held, together.

Now Titania's waking[56] from her 'flow'ry bed' is into our embraces too, as well as Bottom's. For we have sat, not slept, through his translation and have kept our heads better than any. Indeed we know – though we are not telling – that this ass is no ass, appearances notwithstanding, but Bottom. And Bottom is our familiar, not Titania's. After all, we are mortals and she spirit. Who, then, is the true master of the situation? Is it not the audience? 'I pray thee, gentle mortal, sing again,'[56] she pleads to Bottom (and us), sighing. Her desire seems to weaken her, drawing her down in thought – her thought and our thought together – beneath him. Spirit she may be, but we are discovering that she has a body also, which will soon be well and truly covered. 'I'll give thee fairies to attend on thee,'[57] she tells the silly ass, who is too slow-witted to know, as we know, where all this is heading. 'And they shall fetch thee jewels from the deep,' she promises, 'and sing, while thou on pressèd flowers dost sleep.' But not before – can he be so slow on the uptake? he must be dreaming! – she has purged him of his 'mortal grossness'. 'Thou,' she says in a swoon of rapture, 'shalt like an airy spirit go.'[57] She is pledging herself to him, mind and body; and offering him sexual expiry, in heaven.

It is as if sex were now singing in Titania's voice, and carrying most of the audience into a blazing, not moonlit, world of dreams and raptures. 'Hop in his walks, and gambol in his eyes,'[58] Titania commands her attendants. 'The honey bags steal from the humblebees,' she tells them, 'and for night-tapers crop their waxen thighs.' Loins girded, the actors now bestride the moment. 'And light them at the fiery glowworms' eyes,' Titania orders, her voice thrilling, 'to have my love to bed and to arise,'[58] lust's rhythm rearing its head and beginning to ride towards abandon, with Bottom – resistant – in the saddle. There are fierce cries of 'Hail, mortal!'[58], as bedlam sweeps Titania and Bottom, and (most of) the audience with them, hell for leather to the scene's climax. She is as if collapsing into joy, in a cascade of bells, upon an ass's fist-like organ. The actors crowd the rails of the upper gantry, grinning (with us) in anticipation of Bottom's

⁵⁹ *Titania:* Come, wait upon him; lead him to my bower:
The moon methinks looks with a wat'ry eye;
And when she weeps, weeps every little flower,
Lamenting some enforcèd chastity.
Tie up my lover's tongue, bring him silently.

(Exit TITANIA with BOTTOM and Fairies)
(III.i.182–186)

⁶⁰ *Hermia:* Out, dog! Out, cur! Thou driv'st me past the bounds
Of maiden's patience. Hast thou slain him, then? . . .
And hast thou killed him sleeping? O brave touch!
Could not a worm, an adder, do so much?
An adder did it; for with doubler tongue
Than thine, thou serpent, never adder stung.
Demetrius: You spend your passion on a misprised mood:
I am not guilty of Lysander's blood.

(III.ii.65–76)

⁶¹ *Oberon:* This is thy negligence. Still thou mistak'st,
Or else committ'st thy knaveries wilfully.
Puck: Believe me, king of shadows, I mistook . . .
And so far am I glad it so did sort,
As this their jangling I esteem a sport.
Oberon: Thou see'st these lovers seek a place to fight.
Hie therefore, Robin, overcast the night . . .
Whiles I in this affair do thee employ,
I'll to my queen and beg her Indian boy;
And then I will her charmèd eye release
From monster's view, and all things shall be peace.
Puck: My fairy lord, this must be done with haste.

(III.ii.345–378)

⁶² *Oberon:*   Haste; make no delay.
We may effect this business yet ere day.

(Exit)

Puck: Up and down, up and down,
I will lead them up and down:
I am feared in field and town:
Goblin, lead them up and down.

(III.ii.394–399)

pleasures. For most of the audience, eyes shining, it is an apex of theatrical achievement; for the rest, coarseness and rock-bottom.

'Bring him silently,'[59] Titania whispers. They bring him roaring. But this wildness has its own perils. For against it, the court lovers are pure as driven snow, stage-virgins and bloodless with it. Against Titania's, their passion is a long uphill travail. Worse, their love's labours seem to be lost in a post-coital depression, punctuated out of the blue by audience coughing. Ardour strains at a gnat with ragged movements, under such pressures. 'You spend your passion,' Demetrius irritatedly tells Hermia, 'on a misprised mood;'[60] but so does he, and the others. It is as if the mood-swing from one part of the wood to another has caught everyone off-balance, or as if the anaemia of rehearsal has become pernicious. Tonight, the whole argument of the quartet's crossed love in Act Three, Scene Two, not only seems endless, but pointless also. It is merely a clumsy tangle of false emotion and empty gesture. The actors' rhymed effort, gallantly begun, ends in tatters, their relation with each other and the audience all crossed wires.

Only their departure and replacement by Oberon and Puck[61] bring relief and pleasure. For it is as if we can escape through them from courtly constraint into spiritual freedom, and from the barren civilities of Athens to an underworld of freer emotion. Moreover, what was coiled and convoluted among the mortals will be unravelled by spirits, pointing the way early to the manner of the play's resolution. 'This is thy negligence,'[61] Oberon tells Puck, of the confusions of the lovers. 'Believe me, king of shadows, I mistook,' Puck answers. They promise us to set the world to rights, and undo all mistake and mischief; they will lead us, as well as the actors, to 'plainer ground', if we follow. Tonight, it is as if they are taking the play in hand before it is too late, and redeeming it from error. 'My fairy lord,' Puck tells Oberon, 'this must be done with haste;'[61] . . . 'haste, make no delay,'[62] Oberon echoes him, moments later. Bottom has been led by the snout into Titania's bower, the lovers into a thicket, and the audience from one neck of the wood to another, but 'all things shall be peace'[61], if we trust to the play's directions.

Yet to get there – so performance, and performance alone, tells us – we must all pass through a refining fire: the lovers through fear and sorrow, Bottom through sex, the actor-mechanicals through a first night's terrors, and the audience through a vicarious experience of all of them in succession. We too must be led 'up and down, up and

⁶³ *Helena:* O weary night, O long and tedious night,
   Abate thy hours! . . .
   And sleep, that sometimes shuts up sorrow's eye,
   Steal me awhile from mine own company.   (*Sleeps*)
Puck: Yet but three? Come one more.
   Two of both kinds make up four.
   Here she comes, curst and sad:
   Cupid is a knavish lad,
   Thus to make poor females mad.

                                    (*Enter HERMIA*)

Hermia: Never so weary, never so in woe;
   Bedabbled with the dew and torn with briers,
   I can no further crawl, no further go.

                                    (*III.ii.431–444*)

⁶⁴ *Puck:* That every man should take his own,
   In your waking will be shown.
   Jack shall have Jill;
   Nought shall go ill;
   The man shall have his mare again, and all shall be well.   (*Exit*)
                                    (*III.ii.459–463*)

⁶⁵ *ACT FOUR. Scene One. The wood. LYSANDER, DEMETRIUS,
   HELENA and HERMIA lying asleep. Enter TITANIA,
   BOTTOM and Fairies; and OBERON behind, unseen.*
Titania: Come, sit thee down upon this flow'ry bed,
   While I thy amiable cheeks do coy,
   And stick musk roses in thy sleek smooth head,
   And kiss thy fair large ears, my gentle joy.
Bottom: Where's Peaseblossom?
Peaseblossom: Ready.
Bottom: Scratch my head, Peaseblossom. Where's Mounsieur
   Cobweb?
Cobweb: Ready.
Bottom: Mounsieur Cobweb, good mounsieur, get you your weapons
   in your hand, and kill me a red-hipped humblebee on the top of a
   thistle; and, good mounsieur, bring me the honey bag. Do not fret
   yourself too much in the action, mounsieur; and, good mounsieur,
   have a care the honey bag break not; I would be loath to have you
   overflown with a honey bag, signior.

                                    (*IV.i.1–15*)

down', and it is Puck, striding hugely and looming over actors and audience, who now arrives to lead us[62]. Tonight, the very crux of the play's action is for the first time revealed fully in these moments, when Lysander and Demetrius are led through fear and anger into sleep, and Helena and Hermia through a weary sorrow into a resigned slumber[63]. Buffetted with exhaustion they fall asleep, or fall into sleep, as into a limbo which will purge them. We, for our parts, are aroused to a newly awakened perception of this pilgrims' progress, and are ourselves elevated by its perfection. It is also as if the play's motion in performance, and the weeks of its rehearsal, having led the actors up and down in a yo-yo of 'success' and 'failure', has here and now reached a true assurance of achievement. And, however momentary, it has reclaimed the whole audience. For when Puck tells us – eye to eye in his directness – that, upon the lovers' re-awaking, 'Jack shall have Jill;/ Nought shall go ill;/ The man shall have his mare again, and all shall be well'[64], a chord is struck of a once-more perfect balance, between actor and actor, and actor and audience.

Now, the night seems set fair for new revelation. As the Fourth Act begins[65], the spectators, once more primed to expect it, seem in turn to urge it upon the actors. The lovers lie asleep in a cloud of unknowing before us. We, however, are in full possession of our faculties and of the (as if) moonlit arena. Titania dallies with Bottom[65], she in love with an ass and he with a fairy; he not yet come down to earth, she in a seventh heaven. We are all enchanted together, but we by the play, and the lovers (as if) by the spirits. Bottom may be Titania's 'gentle joy' and she Bottom's, but we are masters of – and, if we choose, may be mastered by – both of them together. Yet these are also moments when their sexual dalliance and our idle fancy seem to course together, with a shared rhythm. 'Where's Peaseblossom?'[65] asks Bottom, as deep in his contentments as we are. 'Scratch my head, Peaseblossom,'[65] he commands her, up to his ears like us in pleasure. He seems the lord of all creation. But the fairies scurrying to his bidding are acting for us as well as for Bottom; while he is not only Bottom and an ass, but also the hired David Waller.

Tonight there is also a new lasciviousness in it, not found before, of sexual jest and sexual laughter. Titania and the audience join in it together, with a wink and a nudge between them, as if each had an elbow in the side of the other. 'Get you your weapons in your hand,'[65] Bottom tells Cobweb; and suddenly the audience is sexually armed to the teeth, too, and laughing loudly. 'Honey bags'[65] overflow with it,

303

⁶⁶ *Bottom:* Methinks I have a great desire to a bottle of hay. Good hay, sweet hay, hath no fellow.
  Titania: I have a venturous fairy that shall seek
    The squirrel's hoard, and fetch thee new nuts.
  Bottom: I had rather have a handful or two of dried peas.

  (*IV.i.29–34*)

⁶⁷ *Oberon:* (*Advancing*) Welcome, good Robin. See'st thou this sweet sight?
    Her dotage now I do begin to pity:
    For, meeting her of late behind the wood . . .
    I then did ask of her her changeling child . . .
    And now I have the boy, I will undo
    This hateful imperfection of her eyes.

  (*IV.i.44–60*)

⁶⁸ *Oberon:* But first I will release the Fairy Queen.
    Be as thou wast wont to be;
    See as thou wast wont to see . . .
    Now, my Titania, wake you, my sweet Queen.
  Titania: My Oberon, what visions have I seen!
    Methought I was enamoured of an ass.
  Oberon: There lies your love.
  Titania: How came these things to pass?
    O, how mine eyes do loathe his visage now!

  (*IV.i.67–76*)

⁶⁹ *Puck:* Fairy King, attend, and mark:
    I do hear the morning lark.
  Oberon: Then, my Queen, in silence sad,
    Trip we after night's shade.

  (*IV.i.90–93*)

⁷⁰ *Theseus:* Go, bid the huntsmen wake them with their horns.
                (*Shout within. They all start up. Wind horns*)
    Good morrow, friends. Saint Valentine is past:
    Begin these wood birds but to couple now?
  Lysander: Pardon, my lord.
  Theseus: I pray you all, stand up.
    I know you two are rival enemies.
    How comes this gentle concord in the world . . ?

  (*IV.i.135–140*)

and tonight Cobweb tickles our fancy as well as Bottom's. 'I have a venturous fairy,'[66] Titania ventures to Bottom, with half a smirking eye on the audience, 'shall . . . fetch thee new nuts.' There is an orgy of delighted laughter; Titania has got Bottom by the balls, and the audience doubled up by the *double entendre*. 'I had rather have a handful or two of dried peas,'[66] says the tired Bottom, weakly, and brings the house's trousers down in a joyful and bawdy uproar. This is not sylvan wit in an Arcadian or Victorian setting, but a riot in a brothel. We could be in a whore-house, by the Avon.

Its sexual charge pulses still when Oberon enters, to find Titania sleeping with Bottom. 'See'st thou this sweet sight?'[67] he asks Puck, and the laughing audience, which has not yet subsided. Indeed, the audience is willing its laughter even against Oberon's pity for his 'sweet Queen' and her 'dotage'. He will 'undo the hateful imperfection of her eyes'[67], but we would prefer it to continue; will release Bottom from the 'fierce vexation' of his dream, but rob us all of our pleasure. 'Be as thou wast wont to be;/ See as thou wast wont to see,'[68] Oberon commands her. And when she wakes, we wake together with Titania – though neither she nor we were really sleeping – from love's (or lust's) night-time enchantments, to the disillusion of the morning after. 'There lies your love,'[68] Oberon tells her bleakly. Now it is as if with her eyes that we see a truly sorry figure. This is no Greek satyr, sleeping off his excesses, but a beach-donkey, knackered. 'O, how mine eyes do loathe his visage now!'[68] Titania exclaims, shocked and remorseful. With 'the morning lark'[69], the truth is dawning. In it there is neither love nor laughter, but an inward and shared silence; a 'sad silence'[69], as Oberon exactly (for the first time) puts it.

Yet now the silence alarmingly persists, and deepens. The trumpets which sound for Theseus' hounds and for Hippolyta's 'sweet thunder', resound in it. Not even the brazen 'winding of horns'[70], which awakens the lovers, stirs the audience. Could it be that this 'gentle concord in the world'[70], as the lovers are now restored to their senses, is anodyne after the alarms and excitements which have preceded? Will the feast, to which Theseus now invites[71] the lovers and the spectators, be too bland for tastes spiced by so many dreams and nightmares? Or is the audience, like Bottom, sleeping off its sadness? There is no means, yet, of telling. Instead, there is the silence of the grave, as love finds its true partners. 'Are you sure that we are awake?'[72] Demetrius asks Hermia. 'It seems to me,' he says, 'that yet we sleep, we dream.'

⁷¹ *Theseus:* These couples shall eternally be knit;
  And, for the morning now is something worn,
  Our purposed hunting shall be set aside.
  Away with us to Athens! Three and three,
  We'll hold a feast in great solemnity.

                                        (*IV.i.178–182*)

⁷² *Demetrius:*   Are you sure
  That we are awake? It seems to me
  That yet we sleep, we dream. Do not you think
  The Duke was here, and bid us follow him?
  Hermia: Yea, and my father . . .
  Demetrius: Why, then, we are awake. Let's follow him,
  And by the way let us recount our dreams.

                                        (*Exeunt*)

  Bottom: (*Awaking*) When my cue comes, call me and I will answer . . .
  I have had a most rare vision. I have had a dream, past the wit of
  man to say what dream it was.

                                        (*IV.i.189–202*)

⁷³ *Flute:* O sweet bully Bottom! Thus hath he lost sixpence a day during
  his life. He could not have scaped sixpence a day. An the Duke had
  not given him sixpence a day for playing Pyramus, I'll be hanged.
  He would have deserved it. Sixpence a day in Pyramus, or nothing.

                                        (*Enter BOTTOM*)

  Bottom: Where are these lads? Where are these hearts?
  Quince: Bottom! O most courageous day! O most happy hour!
  Bottom: Masters, I am to discourse wonders: but ask me not what; for
  if I tell you, I am not true Athenian. I will tell you everything,
  right as it fell out.
  Quince: Let us hear, sweet Bottom.
  Bottom: Not a word of me . . . No more words. Away! Go away!

                                        (*IV.ii.18–43*)

⁷⁴ *Hippolyta:* 'Tis strange, my Theseus, that these lovers speak of.
  Theseus: More strange than true. I never may believe
  These antique fables, nor these fairy toys.
  Lovers and madmen have such seething brains,
  Such shaping fantasies, that apprehend
  More than cool reason ever comprehends.
  The lunatic, the lover and the poet,
  Are of imagination all compact . . .

But this silence is now too solemn for dreaming. It is as if, instead, a deep sense of strangeness − or estrangement − has overtaken the audience. Bottom wakes into it, yawning. There is the merest ripple of anticipation to greet him. The audience, wide-awake, is unmoving; nor is it yawning with him. 'When my cue comes,' he says, taking up where he left off before his transfiguration, 'call me and I will answer.'[72] Alone with one hundred and fifty spectators, there is no reply from his fellows, and no response from the audience either. 'I have had a most rare vision,'[72] Bottom tells us, his conviction paling in the play's morning light and tonight's silence. He is bluff and hearty, as if driven into doggedness by our indifference. Or could he be already looking forward to the earnest workaday world, with barely a glance over his shoulder at the night's transports?

Afterwards, Brook was angry, shaking his head in disbelief. Bottom had 'apologized for his experiences', and 'had pushed aside magic' in insensate favour of a 'quick return to the normal'. The mechanicals might now greet him with our lost ardour, and Flute sing − once more − to 'sweet bully Bottom'[73] and his lost sixpence, but the moment of rehearsal joy and relief at this point had vanished. 'I am to discourse wonders: but ask me not what,'[73] Bottom tells them. 'Let us hear, sweet Bottom,' says Quince, who saw little and heard nothing. But Bottom is not telling. As for us, who saw (and heard) everything, save Bottom's entry into Titania's bower, tonight we are not having anything asked of us at all. For Bottom has turned his back on us ('No more words. Away! Go, away!')[73], as if he were no longer on speaking terms with his audience.

The mood is still unmoved, and unmoving, for Hippolyta's ''Tis strange, my Theseus, that these lovers speak of,'[74], which begins the Fifth Act. It is spoken into as deep an estrangement as ever, and Theseus' reply − 'More strange than true'[74] − is echoed, tonight, by the audience's silence. On the gantry or awaiting entry, if you look closely, you can see the actor's eye lose its focus, or startle to sudden attention. 'I never may believe/ These antique fables, nor these fairy toys,'[74] Theseus says, allowing us to agree or not, according to our fancy. His ducal brow furrowed, he puzzles at the lovers' bewitched story. Are the spectators also inwardly pondering the play's meaning? Could this have been the reason for their long silence since Titania awoke, disenchanted, and laughter faded? Might it be that the actors' words are now catching up with the mood of the spectators? Or is there more unease than speculation in the speech of Theseus, and boredom

One sees more devils than vast hell can hold,
That is the madman. The lover, all as frantic,
Sees Helen's beauty in a brow of Egypt.
The poet's eye, in a fine frenzy rolling,
Doth glance from heaven to earth, from earth to heaven;
And as imagination bodies forth
The forms of things unknown, the poet's pen
Turns them to shapes, and gives to airy nothing
A local habitation and a name.
Such tricks hath strong imagination,
That, if it would but apprehend some joy,
It comprehends some bringer of that joy;
Or in the night, imagining some fear,
How easy is a bush supposed a bear!

(*V.i.1–22*)

75 *Theseus:* Come now, what masques, what dances shall we have . . .
Where is our usual manager of mirth?
What revels are in hand? Is there no play,
To ease the anguish of a torturing hour?
Call Philostrate.
Philostrate: Here, mighty Theseus.
Theseus: Say, what abridgment have you for this evening?
What masque? What music?

(V.i.32–40)

76 *Theseus:* And we will hear it.
Philostrate: No, my noble lord;
It is not for you. I have heard it over,
And it is nothing, nothing in the world;
Unless you can find sport in their intents,
Extremely stretched and conned with cruel pain,
To do you service.
Theseus: I will hear that play;
For never anything can be amiss,
When simpleness and duty tender it.
Go, bring them in: and take your places, ladies.

(*V.i.76–84*)

in this silence? Most of the cast seem to have stopped listening. 'The lunatic, the lover and the poet'[74] pass, all three, for nothing. There is a lolling at the gantry-rail, as weight is shifted from one foot to another; and a glancing 'from heaven to earth, from earth to heaven', undreamed of by the author, or the director.

Afterwards, Brook appeared incensed. It was 'inattention' and 'total ignorance' of what they themselves had 'seen, done and heard' in the action. Quarrelsome, he accused them of a 'lack of capacity to relate to the whole play' in which they were participating. It was 'inconceivable', he told them, that, during a speech such as Theseus', they should 'ignore what he was saying'. Just as the audience had passed over Bottom's clumsy wonder and naive vision, without stirring, so the actors had failed to respond to Shakespeare's soaring account of the powers of the imagination[74]. Later, Brook said to me, with resignation, that they were 'three years away' from such trained 'levels of attention' as would make possible a 'total discovery' of the play's impulses. And only then would the actor be at one with the lunatic, the lover and the poet.

Yet it was Theseus himself who had taken the spectators and the scene in hand. But he had done it in the grand Shakespearian manner, as if born to the acting purple and its regal conventions. This also was not re-creation, but merely a royal bearing; not the impulse of the words, in Brook's sense, but the power of declamation. Nevertheless, without crown or velvet he had swept all before him. 'Come now,'[75] Theseus demanded imperiously of Philostrate, 'what revels are in hand?... What masque? What music?'[75] His voice and gesture were imposing, and beyond all challenge. This perhaps did not meet the verse's inner music, Brook's 'levels of attention', or the demands of ensemble – but might here was right, and with its own imperatives settled the issue. He ordered *Pyramus and Thisby* from the theatrical bill-of-fare with a swift 'We will hear it'[76], against Philostrate's protests; and commanded him to 'Go, bring them in,'[76] as if this were a hanging judge's death-sentence for the quaking actors. Moreover, it had been achieved by manner – or mannerism – alone, not appearance. Tonight, he had neither cloak nor sceptre to enlarge him; only an inward elevation, and the urge to face up to the spectators.

He did not check his lengthening stride even for the unexpected appearance on stage of a large black labrador. It was not Reinhardt's rabbit, mistranslated, but had escaped from *The Two Gentlemen of Verona*. Like any strolling player, Launce's dog Crab was wandering at leisure (to the audience's stifled laughter) across Theseus' line of

77 *Theseus:* Where I have come, great clerks have purposèd
   To greet me with premeditated welcomes;
   Where I have seen them shiver and look pale,
   Make periods in the midst of sentences,
   Throttle their practiced accent in their fears,
   And, in conclusion, dumbly have broke off,
   Not paying me a welcome.

$$(V.i.93-99)$$

78 *Prologue:* If we offend, it is with our good will.
   That you should think, we come not to offend,
   But with good will. To show our simple skill,
   That is the true beginning of our end.
   Consider, then, we come but in despite.
   We do not come, as minding to content you,
   Our true intent is. All for your delight,
   We are not here.

$$(V.i.108-115)$$

79 *Wall:* This loam, this roughcast, and this stone, doth show
   That I am that same wall; the truth is so;
   And this the cranny is, right and sinister,
   Through which the fearful lovers are to whisper.
Theseus: Would you desire lime and hair to speak better?
Demetrius: It is the wittiest partition that ever I heard discourse, my
   lord.

$$(V.i.160-166)$$

80 *Hippolyta:* This is the silliest stuff that ever I heard.
Theseus: The best in this kind are but shadows; and the worst are no
   worse, if imagination amend them.
Hippolyta: It must be your imagination then, and not theirs.
Theseus: If we imagine no worse of them than they of themselves,
   they may pass for excellent men.

$$(V.i.209-214)$$

sight and the middle of the arena, threatening Montezuma's revenge, and come from one play to haunt another. The 'great clerks'[77], in their fears of Theseus, as he was saying when interrupted, might 'make periods in the midst of sentences' – the dog sitting and watching – or 'throttle their practiced accent'[77], but not Theseus. And not for a dog either. His royal disdain, flashing into anger, saw the dog off without a bark or whimper; dog and man, unrehearsed, had between them aroused both the audience and the actor. But if it was a moment as absurd as Quince's Prologue to *Pyramus and Thisby*, which followed[78], it could not disturb this Theseus' invincible *amour propre*. Indeed the mechanicals, as Theseus put the black dog behind him, were now more yokels in his sight than ever: and he recovered his poise in their disorder.

Moreover, the audience now rose again to the seeming familiar. Never was moonshine so warming, as it was on this occasion. Caught like bleating sheep between the frozen court and the laughing spectators, the mechanicals seemed to huddle together for comfort, defending themselves with daftness. Before, there was one ass; now there were many. And with the lash of courtly wit[79], there was blended unwitting mechanical humour on the one hand, and audience laughter on the other: the comic simultaneously at work upon three levels. There was also a rich multiplication of effects in class-division, never plainer than now; as if the audience were more class-conscious than either the actors or the director. This world before us, even to its jests and accents, was two-tiered: the mechanicals, who 'never laboured in their minds till now', penned within one play, and the court within another. Tonight, Hippolyta seemed all weary class-disdain for the plodding proletarian; while Theseus, as if a greater nobility of character dictated it, tempered his witticisms with a more courteous condescension[80]. The audience was divided also. For some, as for Hippolyta, *Pyramus and Thisby* was 'the silliest stuff'[80] they had ever heard, and fit only for laughter. For others it was both risible and tender, with its own compassion.

But it was the struggle to mount and to act their play ('extremely stretched and conned with cruel pain')[76] which united actor-mechanicals and spectators. To Philostrate, it was 'nothing, nothing in the world'.[76] To us, it was a battle against the odds, from lack of a moon to insufficient rehearsal, from poor props to a hostile audience, in which – however divided – we took sides with the actors. And if both audiences were hard to please, we at least were free to keep our own

81 *Hippolyta:* I am aweary of this moon. Would he would change!
   Theseus: It appears, by his small light of discretion, that he is in the
      wane; but yet, in courtesy, in all reason, we must stay the time.
   Lysander: Proceed, Moon.
   Moonshine: All that I have to say is to tell you that the lanthorn is the
      moon; I, the man i' th' moon; this thorn bush, my thorn bush; and
      this dog, my dog.

                                                      (*V.i.245–252*)

82 *Theseus:* No epilogue, I pray you; for your play needs no excuse.
      Never excuse, for when the players are all dead, there need none to
      be blamed. Marry, if he that writ it had played Pyramus and
      hanged himself in Thisby's garter, it would have been a fine
      tragedy: and so it is, truly; and very notably discharged. But come,
      your Bergomask. Let your epilogue alone.

                                                      (*V.i.345–351*)

counsel, and not so aristocratically ill-mannered as to jeer the actors' honest endeavour. 'All that I have to say,' said Moonshine[81], 'is to tell you that the lanthorn is the moon; I, the man i' th' moon; this thorn bush, my thorn bush; and this dog, my dog.' This was only an apology for a moon, a bush, a dog, and even the labrador had vanished. But tonight it was sufficient for us, if not for the courtiers. For with our sympathies, our imaginations had been re-engaged, and we could once more take all such moonshine at face-value. Flawed and frightened, the mechanicals were closer to us than to the courtiers, who had kept us at a distance also. Indeed, we too had been gradually reduced to the ranks by their inattention, row upon row of us, and had been in danger of losing our spectators' commissions. Now, these 'hard-handed men' were more than ever our brothers.

Pyramus and Thisby was indeed 'very tragical mirth'. Through it, ran the path of re-entry into the world of *A Midsummer Night's Dream*: from (feigned) innocence to (feigned) experience, and from Thisby's death to Puck's exit. And if it was Theseus who now damned the grateful mechanicals with the faintest praise, on the court's behalf[82], it was we who applauded both the mechanicals and the courtiers. At the last, the company – all such distinctions dissolving – took hands with the audience. The dream had ended. It was daybreak. Brook himself seemed deeply dissatisfied, as if the actors had failed him. Outside, in the blackened streets of Stratford, it was midnight.

Seventh week, sixth day

For more than three hours there is a *post-mortem*, but, strangely, in the absence of the actors. They were, Brook says, in a 'state of exhaustion' after the performance. Quince had reported to him the 'terrible effort' it had been for them all to 'sustain such intense concentration'. The sense of this 'struggle' – and criticism of the actors – dominates discussion between Brook, the assistant director Bogdanov, the designer, composer and stage-manager. There is random judgment too. A member of the audience, Brook declares, told him that the production had been 'unnerving', and as if the play were being 'reborn' before them. But he appears not to believe it.

Indeed Brook is, or seems, dispirited. (After all, there is reality and illusion off-stage as well as on it.) The actors, for him, had lacked a true impulse, and had lapsed in their attention; had lost rhythm, and

83 *Theseus:* My hounds are bred out of the Spartan kind,
So flewed, so sanded; and their heads are hung
With ears that sweep away the morning dew;
Crook-kneed, and dew-lapped like Thessalian bulls;
Slow in pursuit, but matched in mouth like bells.

(IV.i.116–120)

flagged in their invention. There had been too much movement without poise or purpose, and too much speech without rhyme or reason. Too much of what had been worked for in rehearsal, had been erased in performance, or forgotten; the better not held to, and the worse discovered. 'There is a bad as well as a good improvisation,' Brook wryly commented. Instead of coolness, there had been an idle languor; instead of energy, hard labour. Too many feelings were generalized, and too much action ill-considered.

The role of Oberon was mysteriously empty, because emptily mysterious. Bottom – who makes a sudden peeping appearance during the discussion, and withdraws in haste, apologizing – was inhibited, puritanical and joyless. He had resisted Titania's advances, entered her bower as if to be castrated, and woken, apologizing, to a disaster. Ensemble had given way to the survival of the fittest, and soliloquy had been addressed to the 'fourth wall', instead of to the audience. In fact, it is as if the actors are being condemned at a Star Chamber, and in closed session; the poor harlequinade pitilessly judged *in absentia*, and found wanting. And as discussion continues, stricture is heaped upon stricture. The music, too, was unsound: where not 'messy' and 'unfocused', as it was for Theseus' hounds (who should have been 'matched in mouth like bells'[83]), it was lacking in delicacy and lightness. A guitar embellishment, introduced at this performance to provide a *continuo* of chords and arpeggios, is savaged. The luckless guitarist could 'no longer be a member of our team'. He was, said Brook, 'incapable of listening to the action', 'intimidated' by the task of improvisation, and 'must have nothing further to do with the production'. Ideally, Brook added, truly adept instrumentalists – unlike him – should sit in the centre of the stage, 'as in the Chinese theatre', commenting in sound and 'at will' upon the performance.

Only the very climax of Bottom's elevation, as he was borne away helpless into Titania's embraces, escapes censure. There is laughter in the recollection of its wild clamour, and of Oberon swinging like the clappers over the sacrifice of Bottom. 'There should be real bells ringing,' Brook says; 'let it be a coronation'. The rest is a seeming death-knell for last night's performance, and a day of judgment for the actors. But this *miserere nobis* is too self-indulgent. Brook's openness and ease of manner show it. The true sub-text of this discussion, particularly in Brook, is an unconceded contentment with the production: a felt, but unexpressed, sense that it is set fair for a triumph, its problems notwithstanding.

[84] *Puck:* Gentles, do not reprehend:
If you pardon, we will mend.
And, as I am an honest Puck,
If we have unearnèd luck
Now to scape the serpent's tongue,
We will make amends ere long;
Else the Puck a liar call:
So, good night unto you all.
Give me your hands, if we be friends,
And Robin shall restore amends.   (*Exit*)

(*V.i.418–427*)

These include the incorrigible lovers and their strained ardours; a mannered Theseus with too much style and a mysterious Oberon with too little substance; 'bully Bottom's' dominance over his now somewhat diminished fellows; the tangled music and the too-silent audience. Yet, despite appearances, this is not a council of war but a collective impression of performance: shooting the breeze, as well as the actors. The truth is that the play is loved, but not all its players; the hurdle of a first public outing has been crossed, without unhorsing the riders; while the text's deeper reaches are likely to be sounded only in a full-dress and whole-hearted performance, when the actors' energies are no longer being harboured.

'If you pardon,'[84] Puck had said at the night's end, 'we will mend.' From now on, this 'mending', as Brook must know but does not say, will derive as much from the theatre's technical and physical resources, as from the words' fleeting impulses; as much from open as from hidden devices; from the visual as well as the invisible properties of the drama. Moreover, it is in a heightened sense of theatrical occasion that there may lie the recovered poise of the actors, and the restored momentum of the production.

But what of last night's audience? It had seemed puzzled and uncertain for long periods, reserving its judgment for much of the action, yet loud in its applause when the play ended. Will it become merely the cannon-fodder of a triumph? Will a *succès d'estime* and a sell-out erase all possibility of discrimination between the good, the bad and the indifferent? Or will the audience pay its money, and take its chances? And what price a true judgment, when the *vox populi* is often merely the voice – writ large – of the critic? And how, in any event, arrive at a common impression of shared theatrical experience? Would the actors, or the director, or the audience concur with my own account of last night's performance?

Seventh week, seventh day

This is the first full technical rehearsal in the main theatre. It lasts from noon to midnight. The set, first seen, dazzles the eye. In its fierce clarities, light upon light, voice is resonant and outline clear: you can see face, hands, feet and hair.

It is a small white toy-box, snaked and laddered and with trapezes, set upon a blackened stage without shadows; a boxing-ring with actors

85 *Quince:* Pyramus is a sweet-faced man; a proper man as one shall see in a summer's day; a most lovely, gentlemanlike man: therefore you must needs play Pyramus.

Bottom: Well, I will undertake it. What beard were I best to play it in?

Quince: Why, what you will.

Bottom: I will discharge it in either your straw-colour beard, your orange-tawny beard, your purple-in-grain beard, or your French-crown-colour beard, your perfit yellow.

(*I.ii.75–85*)

86 *Bottom:* I will walk up and down here, and will sing, that they shall hear I am not afraid.   (*Sings*)

The woosel cock so black of hue,
With orange-tawny bill,
The throstle with his note so true,
The wren with little quill –

Titania: (*Awaking*) What angel wakes me from my flow'ry bed?

(*III.i.112–118*)

87 *Thisby:* Asleep, my love?
What, dead, my dove?
O Pyramus, arise!
Speak, speak. Quite dumb?
Dead, dead? A tomb
Must cover thy sweet eyes.
These lily lips,
This cherry nose,
These yellow cowslip cheeks,
Are gone, are gone;
Lovers, make moan;
His eyes were green as leeks.

(*V.i.315–326*)

on the ropes, and all taut wire; the white engine-room of a *Titanic*, with guard-rails to keep the mechanicals on the strait and narrow; a white-tiled gas-chamber, for last words and parting embraces. Its exits and entrances are black holes in white flats, unblinking eyes or dark tunnels. It is a confined space, all restraint and tension; a blazing padded cell in a blackout; an echo–chamber.

Its geometry is a squared circle of right angles, with heightened figures. Close at hand, they are larger than life; but from a distance, gesture is a hierarchy of poses and movement, or a succession of motion-pictures. Against these white flats in such a black setting, the butterfly actors are now fluttering their wings – red, green and purple, yellow, brown and orange – like silken jockeys in the parade-ring, awaiting the starter. They are 'purple-in-grain'[85], 'straw-colour'[85] and 'orange-tawny'[86]; 'green as leeks'[87] and yellow as a cowslip[87].

Does this set contain its own truth, and create its own lines of conduct? Will it sustain, expose, or displace the actors' own impulses? Will its 'coolness', clarity, and poise shield them from the clumsy and mishandled in performance? Or will the setting blind us with its dazzle? (Photographs have appeared in the press this morning, press-releases. They are of the 'US, Marat-Sade team' – director, composer and designer – 'working on its new production'. In these photographs, there are no actors.) Is this sleek and costly structure that of a latter-day Drury Lane panto, with a gantry-entrance to a fairy-grotto, and stainless steel instead of sequins and flounces? Must a set be a set-up? Have yesterday's Principal-Boy-and-Girl become today's Oberon and Titania? And who, or what, are these daring young men on the flying trapezes?

Brook briefly addresses the assembled cast on stage. 'Everything, as you can see,' he begins, 'is sharper than it has been before in rehearsal. Everything stands out.' The actors stand full in the glare, blinking and basking. 'This is a collective problem, a problem for all of us. During today's rehearsal, those not on stage should go into distant parts of the auditorium, to see the effects of the work of others. Use every moment,' he tells them. Light and colour seem at white-heat, radiant. 'Treat the whole theatre as an extension of the acting area. Move from one position in the house to another.' The actors are tumblers; their silks shimmer.

'On the stage, find your footwork,' Brook continues, 'to explore the space and use of the acting area.' They are bright figures in a built landscape, shot-silk and white-face in an engineered setting. 'Don't try

⁸⁸ *ACT ONE. Scene One. The palace of Theseus. Enter THESEUS, HIPPOLYTA, PHILOSTRATE and Attendants.*

Theseus: Now, fair Hippolyta, our nuptial hour
Draws on apace. Four happy days bring in
Another moon; but, O, methinks, how slow
This old moon wanes! She lingers my desires,
Like to a stepdame, or a dowager,
Long withering out a young man's revenue.
Hippolyta: Four days will quickly steep themselves in night,
Four nights will quickly dream away the time;
And then the moon, like to a silver bow
New-bent in heaven, shall behold the night
Of our solemnities.

(I.i.1–11)

⁸⁹ *Egeus:* Thou, thou, Lysander, thou hast given her rhymes,
And interchanged love tokens with my child.
Thou hast by moonlight at her window sung,
With feigning voice, verses of feigning love,
And stol'n the impression of her fantasy
With bracelets of thy hair, rings, gauds, conceits,
Knacks, trifles, nosegays, sweetmeats, messengers
Of strong prevailment in unhardened youth.

(I.i.28–35)

⁹⁰ *Hermia:* O hell! To choose love by another's eyes!
Lysander: Or, if there were a sympathy in choice,
War, death, or sickness did lay siege to it,
Making it momentany as a sound,
Swift as a shadow, short as any dream,
Brief as the lightning in the collied night,
That, in a spleen, unfolds both heaven and earth,
And, ere a man hath power to say 'Behold',
The jaws of darkness do devour it up:
So quick bright things come to confusion.

(I.i.140–149)

to do too many things at once. We need a sensible and cool rehearsal, an exercise in technique, and nothing else.' The actors are waiting. 'Consider that every decision to turn to the right or to the left,' he adds, as the actors break, pent-up energies bounding, 'will be crucial for the strength, clarity and effect of what you are doing.' But this set is no mere backdrop. It is the foreground to action also, is cause and effect together, frame and content, form and substance. There is no empty space here. Its structure is a structure of feeling, as well as of chipboard and metal; its breathing-spaces and confinements themselves act upon the actors. Even in its symmetries there are echoes. Thus to act upon Brook's impulse, whether verbal or pre-verbal, is in practice to act within this set's constraints and limits; and, perhaps, to find stage-directions less in the text than in its setting. Certainly, when words fail the actor, or the audience, there is a sufficient scansion in this framed space to tide over a faltering rhythm, and to buoy up a body. But does it not, in effect, give pride of place to the act rather than the actor, and to the act's director?

Nevertheless, the players are exhilarated in this setting. Surrounded by technicians, there is a new *élan* in their poses and bearing. The brilliant *éclat* of the surroundings seems to be in every plotted stride and measured gesture. These are the last motions of the rehearsal process: a technical 'walk-through', of peacock strutting and silken frustrations, feathers flying. Self-aware, exalted, narrowed and heightened by the set's compressions, the entrance of Theseus and Hippolyta for the play's beginning[88] is of birds-of-paradise, into a cage gilded for a royal marriage. The moon makes no whited sepulchre of this setting. Rather, it is the candlelit glitter of a golden and dramatic triumph, of a haughty sense of self, and of crowned splendour casting a black shadow. This is also a trial of the actors' skills, for the benefit of the stage-technicians, and is carried off almost without error. Simplicity and artifice are struggling together; and with a rustle of silks sufficient to drown the pre-verbal whisper.

There is both truth and fantasy in it: 'rings, gauds and conceits'[89] as well as the 'jaws of darkness'[90] to devour them, the poor 'simplicity of Venus' doves'[91] as well as the 'knacks and trifles'[89] of a theatre of effects and riches. Today's is a slow-motion display of a wealth of talents, and of its resources of truth and illusion. They range from unadorned sleight-of-hand to swinging trapezes, from purring stage-machinery to silent moments of revelation, from sudden impulses of creation to slickness with the smoothest finish. The

321

Hermia: My good Lysander!
    I swear to thee, by Cupid's strongest bow,
    By his best arrow with the golden head,
    By the simplicity of Venus' doves,
    By that which knitteth souls and prospers loves,
    And by that fire which burned the Carthage queen,
    When the false Troyan under sail was seen,
    By all the vows that ever men have broke,
    In number more than ever women spoke,
    In that same place thou hast appointed me,
    Tomorrow truly will I meet with thee.
Lysander: Keep promise, love.

(I.i.168–179)

mechanicals in their working clothes are common house-sparrows in cloth caps, against these fancy birds in their plumage; but they too are high on it, poor craftsmen made rich by the setting. Yet there is also a sharp definition given to their skills in this light's intense focus: we see them neither in outline nor in shadow. Above all, they have been rounded out to a fullness of dimension, by long and hard work in rehearsal. When stage-technicians and actor-mechanicals rub shoulder, they are barely separable in function and gesture from each other; as if workmen all, and working on the same production.

Puck's flying now seems sky-high. His arrival is of a *deus ex machina*, starry-eyed, his hair a halo. In his baggy silks and black pumps, he is a tumbler from a Chinese circus, as if come to balance the play on the tip of his toe or finger, in this treeless wood near 'Athens'. Moments ago, it was a cluttered builders' yard for the mechanicals and technicians; now it is a clearing for Puck and the spirits. As for the entrance of Oberon and Titania, 'ill met by moonlight' – with take and retake for light and sound and make-up – it is of wizards. This is Oz, not Arden; a spectacle, not a vision. It is strident with colour (green, pink, bronze, silver), and clamours for attention. With their huge, straw-like wigs, they have become carnival grotesques: not Harlequin and Columbine but Punch and Judy, with Puck for a Toby.

Minutes turn into hours, as the designers, technicians and wardrobe-assistants busy themselves about the actors. Titania, being dressed to kill, is now as transported by her own appearance, as Bottom is by his ass's nole and agonized braying. Indeed, his translation from earth to heaven is almost outfaced by such a transfiguration. But when she speaks from within a ruck of theatre attendants, the tantalizingly interrupted and repeated fragments of her speeches are as deep and rich in their resonance, as at any time in the rehearsal process. Standing patiently with Oberon, she and he are like contented horses at the blacksmith's, their heads now and again nodding.

At midnight, the play is still being slowly dressed for performance, tricked-out for magic, decorated: to 'discourse wonders' with words, and without them.

Eighth week, first day

The week of public performances, which will culminate in a 'first night', has begun. Tonight, *A Midsummer Night's Dream*, still in the making, has come to the Midland Arts Centre in Birmingham: not lock, stock and barrel, but with little more than the clothes the actors stand up in. They have few props and no costumes; a garden-swing, but no trapezes; a bare theatrical cupboard and a packed auditorium. I sit behind the playing-area, looking out – with the actors – at the expectant audience. Each is looking to the other. Half an hour ago, before the arrival of the first spectators, Brook had spoken briefly to the actors. 'This is your last opportunity,' he told them, 'to explore the words to the fullest degree, using all possibilities, and to make contact with the audience. You are going back to the beginning,' he said, 'relying on the words for effect, and explanation.'

Brook now takes the floor again. Behind him, the troupe of actors waits; sitting beside them, you can see how tired. Last night's technical rehearsal had ended in the small hours. 'This is an experiment,' Brook tells the audience. 'We have left behind the set, and our costumes.' For the night, the 'fat and bean-fed' have become wandering minstrels and strolling players. 'But with whatever is at hand, we will tell you the story we have been studying.' A Birmingham suburb is to be a Persian village. The oral tradition has returned to the roaring city. (Who is Brook kidding?) Is this a theatrical progress, or pure stasis? Are we being presented with a social form, without social content? Who is watching? Does this audience represent the few, the very few, or the many? And is this a step 'towards the poor theatre' of Jerzy Grotowski, or a day-trip from a rich one?

The actors have only an assortment of musical instruments, and seven weeks' rehearsal, behind them. Tonight, there are no silks, and no flounces. It is a masquerade but without disguises. And after three hours of purest make-believe, they received a standing ovation. It was

[1] *Bottom:* Are we all met?
 Quince: Pat, pat; and here's a marvellous convenient place for our
   rehearsal.

(III.i.1)

a feat of invention and repetition, together; of accident and design, without the designer; of art and artifice, memory and reflex, creation and re-creation. The performance passed from vaudeville knockabout deep into nightmare, and from simple truth to complex illusion. In its turn, the audience was moved from fear to laughter, and from raptness in silence to open exhilaration. And the actors, beginning from diffidence and coldness, had in the end achieved a warm and intimate relation with the spectators.

'Here's a marvellous convenient place for our rehearsal,'[1] Quince had said to the mechanicals, with an eye on the audience. And when laughter of deepest complicity greeted him, a compact between actor and spectator – and between play and players, had been forged for the night, beyond breaking. In the First Act, the company had set out from the Palace of Theseus weary in spirit, but had come home with Oberon and Puck dancing and light-hearted, and to a roar of acclamation.

But in the dead silence of the deserted hall, the actors were also silent. Exhausted, they seemed solitary and despairing. ('I felt so close to it all,' I heard a girl say later, outside in the darkness.) They had given their all, to the audience, to the play, to one another. There had been perfect chords – *cui bono?* – struck with voice and gesture, brought to this pitch by hard labour; an orchestra of bodies with Brook as conductor; and a dead-and-gone playwright's word restored to the living. At the night's end, there were these notes too, of a summer beguiled and every solitude deepened, to put away in a bottom drawer.

WITHDRAWN